KU-449-546

Footprint

Cusco & The Inca Trail Handbook

The travel guide

Ben Box, Roger Perkins & Kate Hannay

There is a time for departure even when there's no certain place to go!... Make voyages! Attempt them! - there is nothing else.

Tennessee Williams, *Camino Real*

Cusco & The Inca Trail Handbook

First edition

Published by Footprint Handbooks
6 Riverside Court
Lower Bristol Road
Bath BA2 3DZ. England
T +44 (0)1225 469141
F +44 (0)1225 469461
Email discover@footprintbooks.com
Web www.footprintbooks.com

ISBN 1 903471 07 9
CIP DATA: A catalogue record for this book is available from the British Library

Distributed in the USA by
Publishers Group West

Neither the black and white nor coloured maps are intended to have any political significance.

Credits

Series editors
Patrick Dawson and Rachel Fielding

Editorial
Editor: Alan Murphy
Maps: Sarah Sorensen

Production
Typesetting: Leona Bailey, Jo Morgan and Davina Rungasamy
Maps: Robert Lunn, Claire Benison, Maxine Foster and Leona Bailey
Colour maps: Kevin Feeney

Cover: Camilla Ford

Design
Mytton Williams

Photography
Front cover: Jamie Marshall
Back cover: Robert Harding Picture Library
Inside colour section: South American Pictures, Jamie Marshall

Print
Manufactured in Italy by LEGOPRINT

Every effort has been made to ensure that the facts in this Handbook are accurate. However, travellers should still obtain advice from consulates, airlines etc about current travel and visa requirements before travelling. The authors and publishers cannot accept responsibility for any loss, injury or inconvenience however caused.

Cusco and The Inca Trail

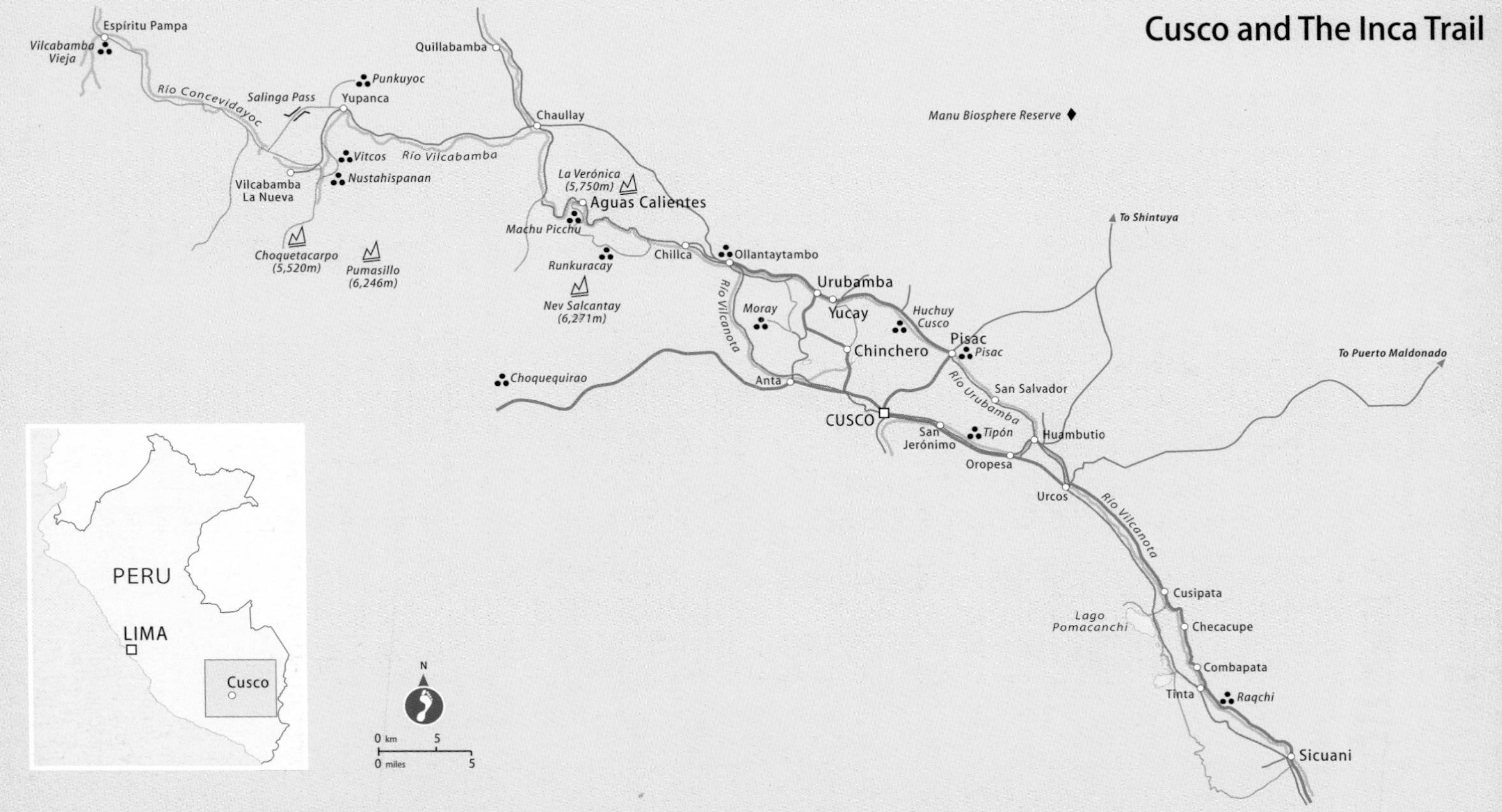

Contents

Facing page: *Enter here...the main door of La Compañía de Jesús, the Jesuit church built on top of the Inca Palace of Serpents in the Plaza de Armas, Cusco. This is one of the most elegant churches in the city.*

A foot in the door

Right: *Spinning a yarn. One of these Quechua women in traditional dress at Pisac is holding the drop spindle, the use of which is second nature, as much a part of her costume as her chumpi (belt) or hat.*
Below: *Cusco's great Plaza de Armas used to be the Incas' Place of Tears, half of their main civic arena. The other half was the Place of Happiness. The Cathedral and La Compañía face the square, while former colonial mansions house travel agents, restaurants and shops.*

Above: *Row upon row of salt pans, in use for hundreds of years, tumble down a ravine near Urubamba. Saline water is fed into the basins to evaporate in the sun.*
Right: *The scarlet macaw, one of the birds most closely associated with the rainforest, is easy to see in either Manu or Tambopata. A highlight is their daily visit to the salt lick to get their minerals.*

Navel of the world

Can you imagine a city laid out in the shape of a puma, a stone to tie the sun to, or a city of fleas? Are you willing to meet the Earth Changer, Our Lord of the Earthquakes and Mother Earth? If so, prepare to follow the pilgrimage to the place which every Inca endeavoured to visit once in a lifetime, Cusco. Navel of the world, Spanish colonial showpiece, gringo capital of South America: the city is all these things.

Built to last

Cusco is, deservedly, the top tourist destination in Peru. It is one of the most fascinating cities in the world, where cultures meet but do not overwhelm the essential nature of the place. The Inca foundations, on which the Spaniards built their churches and mansions, have lasted better than many of the structures imposed upon them. The walls of temples and palaces contain matchless stonemasonry. The colonial buildings, whether or not they use Inca bases, have their own elegance, in dominant churches and opulent mansions. Several are now museums. The best example of the uneasy marriage between Inca and Spanish is the Qoricancha/Santo Domingo complex, the site of the Inca's Temple of the Sun, but there are many other churches and convents to see. Away from the great expanse of the Plaza de Armas and the main commercial street, the Avenida del Sol, many of the streets are cobbled, steep and narrow, linking small squares and winding through old districts. The façades of the houses hide handicraft shops, guesthouses and restaurants.

River deep, mountain high

From the tremendous zig-zag walls of the ceremonial centre of Sacsayhuaman, in the northern outskirts of the city, to the Incas' open-air crop nursery in the three colisseums of Moray or the Inca suspension bridge of Qeswachaca, there are sites of historical interest in every direction, near and far. Just an hour from Cusco is the market town of Pisac, above which is a superb fortress. Follow the Sacred Valley west through towns and villages to Ollantaytambo, a well-preserved Inca town with an unfinished temple, whose stonework is among the finest pre-Columbian architecture in the country. Snaking its course through all this bucolic beauty is the Urubamba river, gliding serenly past fields of cereals and steep terraced hillsides, the Incas' great agricultural legacy to the present-day *campesinos*. Standing guard imperiously over the whole scene are the sacred *apus*, the mountains to which the Incas gave blessing.

Navel-gazing

The Incas dedicated all their efforts to their deities and you can still sense this in what remains of their world. Spanish Catholicism, too, was fervently promoted by the conquerors and many of the churches' decorations reflect its moral lessons. A whole calendar of festivals mixes the Inca and the Christian in days of great piety and celebration. Some, like the famous Inti Raymi, are all Inca; others, like Corpus Christi, are ostensibly Catholic, but below the surface are prehispanic elements which create a depth of feeling which you will find nowhere else. Andean mysticism and shamanism are still adhered to by the local people and those seeking another dimension can be guided in their ways. If all you need, however, is a moment or two to yourself, the list of places where you can find peace for contemplation is endless.

Andes to Amazon

As well as being a fascinating city in its own right, Cusco enjoys the privilege of having many of the country's top attractions virtually on its doorstep. A short bus trip away are beautiful valleys and Andean towns, and an easy train ride will take you to the quintessential South American tourist site, Machu Picchu. You also have access to some of the main features that make Peru one of the eight "mega-diverse" countries on earth, from snow-covered peaks, through a vast array of habitats that drop into river canyons, or descend the eastern slopes of the Andes to the vast lowlands of the Amazon basin.

In the footsteps of the Incas

Machu Picchu is Peru's most visited archaeological site. It was the only major Inca retreat to escape the looting and destruction of the Spaniards and remains the most spectacular site in all the Americas. Getting there now is a lot easier than it was for Hiram Bingham, who discovered it in 1911. The train ride is comfortable, with regular service, but that would just be too easy and you'd miss out on one of South America's great attractions. Quite simply, the best way to approach Machu Picchu is along the Inca Trail. This classic four-day trek along well-preserved Inca paved roads passes through Inca tunnels, down knee-shattering Inca staircases over breathtaking passes and in stretches of beautiful cloud forest. A number of alternatives open up new perspectives and offer shorter and longer variations to the main trail.

A raft of adventure options

Cusco is a city that you can walk out of. In little more than ten minutes you leave the crowds and enter the solitude and limitless horizons of the Cordillera. If you just want to escape for a day, no problem. Alternatively, there are treks that take you from one river valley to another over the highest of passes, following the footsteps of Incas, *conquistadores* and *campesinos*. Where there are trails, now there are mountain bikers and the Cusco region is just opening up to this. Choose between the radical and the (reasonably) relaxing, ride through ruins or from the summits to the Amazon. You can climb as many hills as your muscles can take, or plummet 1,400 metres in two hours. Likewise, Cusco is a paradise for rafting, with gentle half-day trips for beginners to heart-stopping whitewater runs for adrenaline-junkies. Options range from canyons beneath snow peaks to drifting under the forest canopy in the Tambopata Reserve.

Forest of dreams

In Peru's southern jungle are the Manu Biosphere Reserve and the Tambopata-Candamo Reserved Zone/Bahuaja-Sonene National Park. Both are accessible from Cusco, but the Tambopata area is further away. Manu is one of the largest protected areas of rainforest and arguably the most pristine conservation unit in the world. It is over half the size of Switzerland, much of it unexplored. It starts high in the Andes and goes down through elfin, cloud and montane forest into the vast lowland jungle of the Amazon. Here, the romantic image of the jungle found on the glossy pages of National Geographic is alive and well. Tambopata, too, is a brilliant place to see wildlife, including one of the largest macaw salt licks in the world.

Left: *The Sacred Valley of the Urubamba was where the Inca rulers had their country estates. It is not difficult to see why as the grandeur of the scenery matches the divine origins they claimed for themselves.*
Below: *At Sacsayhuaman, a ceremonial centre outside Cusco, the precision with which the massive stones were fitted together never fails to baffle the visitor.*
Next page: *Calle Hatun Rumiyoc contains some of the best surviving Inca stonework. The Spaniards knew they were on to a good thing when they built on top of it. Look for the stone with twelve angles in the wall of the large building in the middle distance (left side of the street).*

Left: *The village of Taray is at the eastern end of the Sacred Valley, where the river changes name from Vilcanota to Urubamba. The level valley floor is ideal for agriculture, as mountainsides shelter patchwork fields.*
Above: *Stripes of every hue emerge from the loom, interspersed with ribbons of ancient motifs. Woven cloth has always been a precious commodity in the Andes .*

Essentials

Essentials

Planning your trip

It is not possible to take an international flight direct to Cusco, other than from Bolivia. You have to fly via Lima and while it may be possible to make a connection to get you to Cusco the same day you land in Peru, as often as not you will have to spend some time in the capital on the coast before flying up to the highlands. Many organized tours build a day or so in Lima as a matter of course. This allows you to get your bearings after your flight and see a bit of the city. A trip to a museum such as the **Museo de la Nación** will help you put the Inca world into context within the rest of Peru's rich past. Lima is a huge place, full of the harsh contradictions of modern, urban Latin America. It is fast, brash and crowded. Rich and very poor live shockingly close to each other. There is no chance that you will get to know Lima if Cusco is the main aim of your trip, so select what you want to see carefully.

Lima to Cusco is the main tourist axis in Peru and there are plenty of flights between the two cities. The flight takes just one hour and all are in the morning, giving people in organized groups and independent travellers an early start. If you prefer to go by road, be aware that it's a full-day's journey. Getting around the country overland can be a difficult task and this is to be expected in a country whose geography is dominated by the Andes, one of the world's major mountain ranges. Great steps have been taken to improve major roads and enlarge the paved network linking the Pacific coast with the Highlands. It is worth taking some time to plan a journey in advance, checking which roads are finished, which have roadworks and which will be affected by the weather. The highland and jungle wet season, from mid-October to late March, can seriously hamper travel. It is important to allow extra time if planning to go overland at this time.

Cusco stands at 3,310 m, so you'll need time to acclimatize to the high altitude. If flying from Lima, don't underestimate the shock to your system of going from sea-level to over 3,000 m in 60 minutes. Two or three hours' rest after arriving makes a great difference. Also avoid smoking, don't eat meat but do eat lots of carbohydrates and drink plenty of clear, non-alcoholic liquid, and remember to walk slowly. A word of advice for those arriving in Cusco by air. It makes a lot of sense to get down to the Urubamba Valley, at 2,800 m, 510 m lower than Cusco itelf, and make the most of your first couple of days. There are a few good hotels in Ollantaytambo, Urubamba, Yucay and Pisac. At this relatively low altitude you will experience no headaches and you can eat and sleep comfortably.

Essentials

Where to go

To see Cusco and the surrounding area properly you'll need 10-14 days. This would allow you to explore the city, enjoy its nightlife, visit the towns and villages of the Urubamba Valley – including Pisac, Ollantaytambo, Urubamba and Chinchero – and, of course, hike the Inca Trail to Machu Picchu (four days). Added to that, you'll need at least 4-5 days for a jungle trip to Manu or Tambopata, plus a few days for mountain biking and whitewater rafting. Three or four weeks, therefore, would allow you to enjoy the region to its full, but the one problem with Cusco is that it is all too easy to find a colonial café with a balcony, toss the guidebook aside, and sit back in the blazing sun to watch the world go by! Whatever you choose to do, have fun.

Useful addresses and websites for checking up on local conditions in advance are listed on page 18. See also Getting around (page 39)

The city's position, up in the heart of the Peruvian Andes, kept it largely isolated until the beginning of the 20th century when the railway arrived. As a result, it may have grown into a sprawling city of almost 300,000 inhabitants, but its centre still has the feel of an unspoilt colonial city.

First you will gaze amazed at the gold altars of churches such as **La Compañía**, then that will fade into insignificance on entering the complex of the **Temple of the Sun**.

Here the Spanish *conquistadores* found so much gold it took them three months to melt it down. It takes only a little imagination to picture the solar garden as it once was: filled with life-sized replicas of men, women and children, insects, plants and flowers – all made from gold. The 700 gold and silver plates that once covered the temple walls here may have gone, but their disappearance has revealed the stunning craftsmanship of the Inca stonemasons whose blocks fit together so perfectly it is impossible to fit even a razorblade into the joints – and that after two major earthquakes.

Out of the city you have to travel only a few hours to discover the wonderful **Sacred Valley**. Take a one-day bus trip if you are on a tight schedule, otherwise see the spectacular Inca ruins, busy indigenous markets and beautiful scenery under your own steam and at your own pace. Some choose to take the bus, others to go off-road on either a mountain bike or motorcycle. If you have the stomach for it, sign up for a condor´s-eye view and paraglide it in tandem with a professional.

For many, Cusco means one thing: **Machu Picchu**, one of only three places in the Americas that has been declared a World Heritage Site for both its natural beauty *and* its history (the other two are Palenque in Mexico and Tikal in Guatemala). The ancient **Inca Trail** there is one of the world's classic trekking routes. After four days of climbing through dizzying 4,000 m-plus mountain passes, the weary hiker emerges at the Sun Gate to look down at last on one of the most awe-inspiring sights in the Americas. And its wonder is not confined to the young and fit. The site is accessible by luxury train and bus, and visitors can even fly most of the way by helicopter.

If you have plenty of time to spare, then trek around – and up! – ice-capped **Ausangate**, the mountain that dominates Cusco´s eastern skyline. The passes here are over 5,000 m. Thrill-seekers can combine a jungle experience with **white-water rafting** the turbulent waters of the Apurímac, the true source of the Amazon. There cannot be many places in the world where you can cast off amid snow-capped mountain scenery or take a trip that later leaves you bumping through caiman-infested jungle. The rivers around Cusco are between a gentle Grade II to a heady Grade V.

And no trip of more than two weeks would be complete without discovering the beauty of the **Manu Biosphere Reserve**, one of the largest conservation areas on Earth. Over one-tenth of all the species of birds in the world live here. Your trip will take you through cloud forest on the eastern slopes of the Andes past the upper tropical zone where Blue-headed and Military Macaws can be found to the untouched forests of the western Amazon.

When to go

Of all the visitors to Peru, 67% go to Cusco and 62% to Machu Picchu. There is no time of year when you will have the place to yourself. Having said that, Peru's high season is from June to September and at that time, Cusco is bursting at the seams. This also happens to be the time of year which enjoys the most stable weather for hiking the Inca Trail or trekking and climbing elsewhere. The days are generally clear and sunny, though nights can be very cold at high altitude. The highlands can be visited at other times of the year, though during the wettest months from November to April some roads become impassable and hiking trails can be very muddy. April and May, at the tail end of the highland rainy season, is a beautiful time to see the Peruvian Andes, but the rain may linger, so be prepared.

On the coast, the summer months are from December to April. If you arrive in Lima between May to October you will find the area covered with what's known locally as *la garúa*, a thick blanket of cloud and mist. As your plane heads towards Cusco in the *garúa* season, you will soon be into clear skies and the mountains below can be seen rising like a new coastline out of the sea of fog.

The best time to visit the jungle is during the dry season, from April to October.

During the wet season, November to April, it is oppressively hot (40° C and above) and while it only rains for a few hours at a time, which is not enough to spoil your trip, it is enough to make some roads virtually impassable.

Tour operators

UK & Ireland

Amerindia, Steeple Cottage, Easton, Winchester, Hants SO21 1EH, England, T01962-779317, F779458, pkellie@yachtors.u-net.com In the USA: 7855 NW 12th Street, Suite 221, Miami, Florida 33126, T(1305)5999008, F5927060, tumbaco@gate.net Standard country tours, as well as customized nature, cultural and adventure tours for groups. ***Austral Tours***, 20 Upper Tachbrook Street, London SW1V 1SH, T020-7233 5384, F7233 5385, www.latinamerica.co.uk

Condor Journeys & Adventures, 1 Valley Rise, Mill Bank, Sowerby Bridge, HX6 3EG, T01422-822068, F825276, www.condorjourneys-adventures.com ***Cox & Kings Travel***, St James Court, 45 Buckingham Gate, London, T020-7873 5001. ***Destination South America***, 51 Castle Street, Cirencester, Gloucestershire, GL7 1QD, T01285-885333, www.destinationsouthamerica.co.uk ***Dragoman***, Camp Green, Debenham, Stowmarket, Suffolk IP14 6LA, T01728-861133, www.dragoman.co.uk Overland camping and/or hotel journeys throughout South and Central America. ***Exodus Travels***, 9 Weir Road, London SW12 0LT, T020-8772 3822, www.exodus.co.uk Experienced in adventure travel, including cultural tours and trekking and biking holidays. ***Explore Worldwide***, 1 Frederick Street, Aldershot, Hants GU11 1LQ, T01252-319448, F760001, www.exploreworldwide.com Highly respected operator with offices in Eire, Australia, New Zealand, USA, Canada, Hong Kong, Belgium, Netherlands, Denmark, Norway, South Africa and Mexico, who run 2 to 5 week tours in more than 90 countries worldwide including Peru.

Essentials

Essentials

Guerba Expeditions, Wessex House, 40 Station Road, Westbury, Wiltshire BA13 3JN, T01373-826611, F858351, info@guerba.demon.co.uk Specializes in adventure holidays, from trekking safaris to wilderness camping. ***Hayes & Jarvis***, 152 King Street, London W6 0QU, T020-8222 7844. Long established operator offering tailor-made itineries as well as packages. ***High Places***, Globe Centre, Penistone Road, Sheffield, S6 3AE, T0114-2757500, F2753870, www.highplaces.co.uk Trekking and mountaineering trips.

Journey Latin America, 12-13 Heathfield Terrace, Chiswick, London, W4 4JE, T020-8747 8315, F8742 1312, and 28-30 Barton Arcade, 51-63 Deansgate, Manchester, M3 2BH, T0161-832 1441, F832 1551, www.journeylatinamerica.co.uk The world's leading tailor-made specialist for Latin America, running escorted tours throughout the region, they also offer a wide range of flight options. ***KE Adventure Travel***, www.keadventure.com Specialist in adventure tours, including three-week cycling trips in and around Cusco. ***Last Frontiers***, Fleet Marston Farm, Aylesbury, Buckinghamshire HP18 0QT, T01296-658650, F658651, www.lastfrontiers.co.uk South American specialists offering tailor-made itineraries as well as discounted air fares and air passes.

Naturetrek, Cheriton Mill, Cheriton, Alresford, Hants, SO24 0NG, T01962-733051, F736426, www.naturetrek.co.uk Birdwatching tours throughout the continent, also botany, natural history tours, treks and cruises. ***Reef and Rainforest Tours Ltd***, 1 The Plains, Totnes, Devon, TQ9 5DR, T01803-866965, F865916, www.reefrainforest.co.uk ***South American Experience***, 47 Causton Street, Pimlico, London, SW1P 4AT, T020-7976 5511, F7976 6908, www.southamericanexperience.com Apart from booking flights and accommodation, also offer tailor-made trips.

Trips Worldwide, 9 Byron Place, Clifton, Bristol, BS8 1JT, T0117-311 4400, www.tripsworldwide.co.uk ***Tucan Travel***, London, T020-8896 1600, london@tucantravel.com Sydney T02-9326 4557, sydney@tucantravel.com Peru,

Useful addresses

Apavit *(Asociación Peruana de Agencias de Viaje y Turismo), Antonio Roca 121, Santa Beatriz, Lima, T332 1720, F433 7610.*

Apotur *(Asociación Peruana de Operadores de Turismo), T445 0382, F446 0422, apotur@amauta.rcp.net.pe*

Agotur *(Asociación de Guías Oficiales de Turismo), Jr Belén 1030, Lima, T424 5113.*

T084-241 1123, cuzco@tucantravel.com Offer adventure tours and overland expeditions. ***Veloso Tours***, 33-34 Warple Way, London W3 0RG, T020-8762 0616, F8762 0716, www.veloso.com

Europe

South American Tours, Hanauer Landstrasse 208-216, D-60314, Germany, T+49-69-405 8970, F+49-69-440432, sat.fre@t-online.de For holidays, business travel, or special packages. Has an office at Avenida Miguel Dasso 230, Suite 401, San Isidro, Lima, T422 7261, F440 8149, satperu@terra.com.pe

North America

Amazonia Expeditions, 10305 Riverbrun Drive, Tampa, FL 33677, T800-262 9669 (toll free), T/F813-907 8475, www.peruandes.com ***Discover Peru Tours***, 7325 West Flagler Street, Miami, Florida 33144, T305-266 5827, F266 2801, T800-826 4845 (toll free), www.discover-chile.com ***eXito***, 1212 Broadway Suite 910, Oakland, CA 94612, T800-655 4053 T510-655 2154 (worldwide), www.exito-travel.com ***GAP Adventures***, 19 Duncan Street, Toronto, Ontario, M5H 3H1, T800-465 5600, (UK) T01373-858956, www.gap.ca ***Inka's Empire Tours***, 156 Fifth Avenue, Suite 1116, New York, NY 10010, T646-638 0035, F638 0037, www.inkas.com ***Kolibri Expeditions***, www.netaccessperu.net/kolibri An agency that specializes in overland birdwatching tours in Peru and throughout South America, contact Gunnar Engblom.

Ladatco Tours, 3006 Aviation Avenue, Suite 4C, Coconut Grove, FL 33133, T305-854 8422, F305-285 0504, T800-327 6162 (toll free), www.ladatco.com Based in Miami, run 'themed' explorer tours based around the Incas, mysticism etc. ***Mila Tours***, 100 South Greenloaf, Gurnee, Illinois 60031, T800-367 7378 (toll free), www.MILAtours.com ***Myths & Mountains***, 976 Tee Court, Incline Village, NV 89451, T800-670 6984, www.mythsandmountains.com ***South American Expeditions***, T/F818 352 8289, T800-884 7474 (toll free), www.southamericaexp.com ***Tambo Tours***, PO Box 60541, Houston, Texas 77205, USA, T1-888-246 7378 (toll free), www.2GOPERU.com Customized trips to the Amazon and archaeological sites of Peru for groups and individuals. Daily departures. ***Wildland Adventures***, 3516 NE 155 Street, Seattle, WA 98155-7412, USA, T206-365 0686, F206-363 6615, T800-345 4453 (toll free), www.wildland.com Specializes in cultural and natural history tours to the Andes and Amazon.

South America *Amazonas Explorer*, see page 57 . In USA, *River Travel Center* (Annie Leroy), PO Box 226, Point Arena, CA 95468, annien@rivers.com Experienced in leading trekking, canoeing, rafting and mountain biking expeditions throughout South America, as well as traditional tourist options (advance booking is advised). *Aracari Travel consulting*, Avenida Pardo 610, no 802, Miraflores, Lima 18, T01-242 6673, F01-242 4856, www.aracari.com Regional tours throughout Peru, 'themed' and activity tours. *Southtrip*, Sarmiento 347, 4th floor, of 19, Buenos Aires, Argentina, T011-4328 7075, www.southtrip.com *InkaNatura Travel*, see page 122.

In Lima: *Cóndor Travel*, Mayor Armando Blondet 249, San Isidro, T442 7305, F442 0935, also has a branch in Cusco, www.condortravel.com.pe *Coltur*, Avenida José Pardo 138, Miraflores, T241 5551, F446 8073, also has an office in Cusco, www.coltur.com.pe Very helpful and well-organized. *Dasatour*, Jirón Francisco Bolognesi 510, Miraflores, T447 7772, F447 0495, also has an office in Cusco, www.dasatariq.com *Explorandes*, Calle San Fernando 320, T445 8683, F242 3496, also has an office in Cusco, www.explorandes.com.pe Offers a wide range of adventure and cultural tours. *KinjyoTravel*, Las Camelias 290, San Isidro, T442 4000, F442 1000, also has an office in Cusco, postmast@kinjyo.com.pe *Lima Tours*, J Belén 1040, Lima centre, T424 5110, F424 6269, and at Avenida Pardo y Aliaga 6908, T222 2525, F 222 5700. Recommended. *Viracocha Turismo*, Avenida Vasco Núñez de Balboa 191, Miraflores, Lima, T445 3986/447 5516, F447 2429. Cultural and mystical tours. Also hiking, rafting, birdwatching for the outdoor types.

Australia *Adventure World*, 73 Walker Street, North Sydney, NSW 2060, T02-9956 7766, F02-9956 7707, www.adventureworld.com.au Offices in Melbourne, Brisbane, Adelaide and Perth. Escorted group tours, locally-escorted tours and packages to Peru and all of Latin America. *Tucan*, see above under UK. *Ya'lla Tours*, 661-665 Glenhuntly Road, Caulfield, Vic 3162, T03-9523 1988, F9523 1934, www.yallatours.com.au Specialists in group tours to Latin America, including Peru.

Finding out more

Peruvian tourism organizations

Outside Peru, tourist information can be obtained from Peruvian Embassies and Consulates

Tourism promotion and information is handled by *PromPerú*, Edificio Mitinci, 13th floor, located at Calle Uno Oeste 50, in Córpac, Lima 27, T01-224 3279, F224 3323, postmaster@promperu.gob.pe www. peru.org.pe They produce promotional material but offer no direct information service to individual tourists. The website does carry plenty of background and other information and they produce a monthly travel news magazine, *Kilca*, available by email: contact the press office, jvicente@promperu.gob.pe Kilca directs enquiries for information to the Service of Tourist Information (SIT), infoperu@promperu.gob.pe There are, however, offices in most towns, either run by the municipality, or independently, which provide tourist information. **The Cámara Nacional de Turismo**, at Alcanfores 1245, Miraflores, Lima, T/F445 2957, www.si.com.pe/CANATUR/epaises.htm

South American Explorers

This non-profit, educational organization functions primarily as an information network for Peru and South America and is and is the most useful organization for travellers in the continent. They have offices in Lima, Cusco, Quito and the USA. Full details are given on pages 223 and 73.

The Latin American Travel Advisor

The ***Latin American Travel Advisor*** is a complete travel information service offering the most up-to-date, detailed and reliable material about 17 South and Central American countries. Comprehensive country profiles, detailed "how to" travel advice, a large selection of excellent maps, and a directory of local services are all available on-line. Public safety, health, weather and natural phenomena, travel costs, economics and politics are highlighted for each country. www.amerispan.com/lata/, LATA@pi.pro.ec Toll free F1-888-2159511.

It is better to seek advice on security before you leave from your own consulate than from travel agencies. Before you travel you can contact: **British Foreign and Commonwealth Office**, Travel Advice Unit, T020-7238 4503, F7238 4545, www,fco.gov.uk **US State Department's Bureau of Consular Affairs**, Overseas Citizens Services, T202-647 4225, F647 3000, http://travel.state.gov/travel_warnings.html Australian Department of Foreign Affairs, T06-6261 3305, www.dfat.gov.au/consular/advice.html

Language

The official language is Spanish. Quechua, the language of the Inca empire, has been given some official status and there is much pride in its use, but despite the fact that it is spoken by millions of people in the Sierra who have little or no knowledge of Spanish, it is not used in schools. Another important indigenous language is Aymara, used in the area around Lake Titicaca. The jungle is home to a plethora of languages but Spanish is spoken in all but the remotest areas. English is not spoken widely, except by those employed in the tourism industry (eg; hotel, tour agency and airline staff). Some basic Spanish for travellers will be found in the Footnotes section.

Language courses are listed in the Essentials of each city and town. ***AmeriSpan***, T800-879 6640 (toll free), www.amerispan.com organizes programmes throughout Latin America from its North American and Guatemalan bases. ***LanguagesAbroad.com***, 317 Adelaide Street West, Suite 900, Toronto, Ontario, Canada, M5V 1P9, T416-925 2112, toll free 1-800-219 9924, F416-925 5990, www.languagesabroad.com, offers Spanish programmes in Peru, as well as every other South American country except Colombia and Paraguay. They also have language immersion courses throughout the world. Similarly ***Cactus***, 9 Foundry St, Brighton, BN1 4AT, T01273-687697, F681412, www.cactuslanguage.com, has courses in Peru and allother countries except Paraguay. For a full list of Spanish schools, see www2.planeta.com/mader/ecotravels/schools/schoolist.html

Disabled travellers

As with most underdeveloped countries, facilities for the disabled traveller are sadly lacking. Wheelchair ramps are a rare luxury and getting a wheelchair into a bathroom or toilet is well nigh impossible, except for some of the more upmarket hotels. The entrance to many cheap hotels is up a narrow flight of stairs. Most archaeological sites, even Machu Picchu, have little or no wheelchair access. Pavements are often in a poor state of disrepair (even fully able people need to look out for uncovered manholes and other unexpected traps). Visually and hearing-impaired travellers are similarly poorly catered for as a rule, but experienced guides can often provide tours with individual attention.

Some travel companies are beginning to specialize in exciting holidays, tailor-made for individuals depending on their level of disability. For those with access to the internet, a Global Access Disabled Travel Network Site is www.geocities.com/Paris/1502 It is dedicated to providing information for 'disabled adventurers' and includes a number of reviews and tips from members of the public. You might want to read ***Nothing Ventured*** edited by Alison Walsh (Harper Collins), which gives personal accounts of worldwide journeys by disabled travellers, plus advice and listings. One company in Cusco which offers tours for disabled people,including rafting, is ***Apumayo*** (details on page 119).

Gay and Lesbian travellers

Movemiento Homosexual-Lesbiana (MHOL), Calle Mariscal Miller 828, Jesús María, T433 5519. English from 1630 on. Great contact about the gay community in Lima. An on-line resource for gay travellers (in Spanish) is www.gayperu.com There are gay-friendly places in Cusco, but the scene is not very active there (perhaps the best place to enquire is the *Café Macondo*). This does not imply, however, that there is hostility towards gay and lesbian travellers. As a major tourist centre which welcomes a huge variety of visitors, Cusco is probably more open than anywhere in Peru.

Student travellers

If you are in full-time education you will be entitled to an International Student Identity Card, which is distributed by student travel offices and travel agencies in 77 countries.

The ISIC gives you special prices on all forms of transport (air, sea, rail etc), and access to a variety of other concessions and services. If you need to find the location of your nearest ISIC office contact: ***The ISIC Association***, Herengracht 479, 1017 BS Amsterdam, Holland, T+31-20-421 2800, F+31-20-421 2810, www.istc.org

Cusco is about the only place in Peru where students can obtain reductions with an international student's card. To be any use in Peru, it must bear the owner's photograph. An ISIC card can be obtained in Lima from ***Intej***, Avenida San Martín 240, Barranco, T477 2864, F477 4105, www.intej.org They can also extend student cards. Certain travel agencies can also arrange for the paperwork to be done to obtain a student card, but all the forms have to go to *Intej*'s office in Lima.

Travelling with children

Visit: www.babygoes2. com

People contemplating overland travel with children should remember that a lot of time can be spent waiting for buses, trains, and especially for aeroplanes. You should take reading material with you as it is difficult, and expensive to find. Travel on trains, while not as fast or at times as comfortable as buses, allows more scope for moving about. Some trains provide tables between seats, so that games can be played.

Food can be a problem if the children are not adaptable. It is easier to take food with you on longer trips than to rely on meal stops where the food may not be to taste. Breastfeeding is best and most convenient for babies, but powdered milk is generally available and so are baby foods in most countries. Papaya, bananas and avocados are all nutritious and can be cleanly prepared. In restaurants, you can normally buy children's helpings, or divide one full-size helping between two children.

On all **long-distance buses** you pay for each seat, and there are no half-fares if the children occupy a seat each. For shorter trips it is cheaper, if less comfortable, to seat small children on your knee. Often there are spare seats which children can occupy after tickets have been collected. In **city and local excursion buses**, small children generally do not pay a fare, but are not entitled to a seat when paying customers are standing. On sightseeing tours you should *always* bargain for a family rate – often children can go free. (In trains, reductions for children are general, but not universal.)

All civil **airlines** charge half price for children under 12. Note that a child travelling free on a long excursion is not always covered by the operator's travel insurance; it is adviseable to pay a small premium to arrange cover. Inform the airline in advance that you're travelling with a baby or toddler and check out the facilities when booking as these vary with each aircraft. Some airlines now have a special seat for under twos; check which aircraft have been fitted with them when booking. Pushchairs can be taken on as hand luggage or stored in the hold. Skycots are available on long-haul flights. Take snacks and toys for in-flight entertainment and remember that swallowing food or drinks during take-off and landing will help prevent ear problems.

In all **hotels**, try to negotiate family rates. If charges are per person, always insist that two children will occupy one bed only, therefore counting as one tariff. If rates are per bed, the same applies. In either case you can almost always get a reduced rate at cheaper hotels. Occasionally when travelling with a child you will be refused a room in a hotel that is 'unsuitable'.

Health More preparation is probably necessary for babies and children than for an adult and perhaps a little more care should be taken when travelling to remote areas where health services are primitive. This is because children can be become more rapidly ill than adults (on the other hand they often recover more quickly). Diarrhoea and vomiting are the most common problems, so take the usual precautions, but more intensively. Upper respiratory infections, such as colds, catarrh and middle ear infections are also common and if your child suffers from these normally take some antibiotics against the possibility. Outer ear infections after swimming are also common and antibiotic eardrops will help. Wet wipes are always useful and sometimes difficult to find in South America, as, in some places are disposable nappies.

Women travellers

Generally women travellers should find visiting Peru an enjoyable experience, and though machismo is alive and well, it is generally harmless and well-intentioned. Try not to over-react, but conversely, don't be too flattered, either.

Those who are unduly bothered by the unwanted attentions of an aspiring suitor could try wearing a fake engagement or wedding ring and carrying a photograph of your 'husband' or 'fiancé' (preferably someone scary looking) and saying that they are close at hand. If politeness fails, do not feel bad about showing offence and departing. When accepting a social invitation, make sure that someone knows the address and the time you left. Ask if you can bring a friend (even if you do not intend to do so).

Travelling with another *gringa* may not exempt you from this attention, but at least should give you moral support, but unless you're actively avoiding foreigners like yourself, don't go too far from the beaten track. There is a very definite 'gringo trail' which you can join, or follow, if seeking company. This can be helpful when looking for safe accommodation, especially if arriving after dark (which is best avoided). Remember that for a single woman a taxi at night can be as dangerous as wandering around on her own. A good rule is always to act with confidence, as though you know where you are going, even if you do not. Someone who looks lost is more likely to attract unwanted attention.

Working in Peru

There are many opportunities for volunteer work in Peru (we give some examples on page 92). The website **www.amerispan.com** which is principally concerned with language learning and teaching, also has a comprehensive list of volunteer opportunities. For information on voluntary work and working abroad, contact Andreas Kornevall, VWIS, PO Box 2759, Lewes, East Sussex, BN7 1WU, UK, T+44-1273-470015, **www.workingabroad.com** Also try: **www.questoverseas.org**; **www.gapyear.com;** www.raleighinternational.org; **www.projecttrust.org.uk**; **www.vacationwork. co.uk** Another site worth trying if you are looking more for a paying job is the **International Career and Employment Center**, **www.internationaljobs.org** If you are seeking more than casual work, then there will be income tax implications which should be researched at a Peruvian consulate before departure. ***Tambofilm Outfitters*** has just set up in Cusco. If you want work as a film extra they may be able to fix you up: T084-237718, tfocus@terra.net.com, or visit **www.filmcusco.com**

Before you travel

Getting in

Visas No Visa is necessary for countries of Western Europe, Asia, North or South America or citizens of Australia, New Zealand or South Africa. Travellers from India do need Visas. Tourist cards are obtained on flights arriving in Peru or at border crossings. The tourist card allows you up to a maximum of 90 days in Peru. The form is in duplicate and you give up the original on arrival and the copy on departure. **NB**: This means you need to keep the copy as you will need to give it to the officials when you leave. A new tourist card is issued on re-entry to Peru but extensions are obtained with your current tourist card so you just take it and your passport to immigration when asking for extensions. If your tourist card is lost or stolen, apply to get a new one at **Inmigraciones**, Avenida España 700 y Avenida Huaraz, Breña, Lima, between 0900 to 1330, Monday to Friday. It shouldn't cost anything to replace your tourist card if you replace it in Lima.

Embassies and consulates

Argentina, *Av del Libertador 1720, 1425 Capital Federal, T54-11-4802, F4802 5887, embperu@arnet.com.ar*
Australia, *40 Brisbane Av Suite 8, Ground Floor, Barton ACT 2600, Canberra, PO Box 106 Red Hill, T61-2-6273 8752, F6273 8754, www.embaperu.org.au Consulate in Sydney.*
Bolivia, *C Fernando Guachalla 300, Sopocachi, La Paz, T591-2-441250, F441240, embbol@caoba.entelnet.bo*
Brazil, *Sector de Embaixadas Sul, Av das Nações Lote 43, Quadra 811, 70428-900 Brasilia DF, T55-61-2429933, F55-61-2449344, embperu@embperu.org.br Consulates in Rio de Janeiro and São Paulo.*
Canada, *130 Albert St, Suite 1901, Ottawa, Ontario, K1P 5G4, T1-613-238 1777, F1-613-232 3062, emperuca@sprint.com Consulates in Montréal and Toronto.*
Chile*, Av Andrés Bello 1751, Providencia, Santiago, T56-2-235 6451, F235 8139, embstgo@entelchile.net*
Finland*, Annankatu 31-33 C, 44, 00100, Helsinki, T358-9-693 3681, F693 3682,*
France, *50 Av Kleber, 75116 Paris, T33-1-5370 4200, F4704 3255, www.amb-perou.fr/*
Germany, *Godesberger Allee 125, 53175 Bonn, T49-228-373045, F49-228-379475, http://members.aol.com/perusipan Consulates in Berlin and Frankfurt.*
Israel*, 37 Revov Ha-Marganit Shikun Vatikim, 52 584 Ramat Gan, Israel, T972-3-613 5591, F751 2286, emperu@netvision.net.il*
Italy, *Via Francesco Siacci N 4, 00197 Roma, T39-06-8069 1510, F8069 1777, amb.peru@agora.stm.it Consulate in Milan.*
Japan, *4-4-27 Higashi Shibuya-ku, Tokyo 150-0011, T81-3-3406 4243, F3409 7589, embperutokio@mb.meweb.ne.jp*
Netherlands*, Nassauplein 4, 2585 EA, The Hague, T31-70-365 3500, embperu@bart.nl*
New Zealand*, Level 8, 40 Mercer St, Cigna House, Wellington, T64-4-499 8087, F499 8057, embassy.peru@xtra.co.nz*
South Africa*, Infotech Building, Suite 201, Arcadia St, 1090 Hatfield, 0083 Pretoria, T27-12- 342 2390, F342 4944, emperu@iafrica.co*
Spain*, C Príncipe de Vergara 36, 5to Derecha, 28001 Madrid, T34-91-431 4242, F577 6861, embaperu@arrakis.es Consulate in Barcelona*
Sweden*, Brunnsgatan 21 B, 111 38 Stockholm, T46-8-440 8740, F205592, www.webmakers/peru*
Switzerland*, Thunstrasse No 36, CH-3005 Berne, T41-31-351 8555, F351 8570, lepruberna02@bluewin.ch Consulates in Geneva and Zurich.*
UK*, 52 Sloane St, London SW1X 9SP, T020-7235 1917, F7235 4463, www.peruembno 1124, Montevidassy-uk.com*
USA*, 1700 Massachusetts Av NW, Washington DC 20036, T1-202-833 9860, F659 8124, www.peruemb.org Consulates in Los Angeles, Miami, New York, Chicago, Houston, Puerto Rico and San Francisco.*

Tourist visas for citizens of countries not listed above cost £9.60 or equivalent, for which you require a valid passport, a departure ticket from Peru, two colour passport photos, one application form and proof of economic solvency. All foreigners should be able to produce on demand some recognizable means of identification, preferably a passport.

You must present your passport when reserving tickets for internal, as well as international, travel. An alternative is to photocopy the important pages of your passport – including the immigration stamp, and have it legalized by a *notario público*, which costs US$1.50. This way you can avoid showing your passport.

Travellers arriving by air are not asked for an onward flight ticket at Lima airport, but it is quite possible that you will not be allowed to board a plane in your home country without showing an onward ticket.

Remember that it is your responsibility to ensure that your passport is stamped in and out when you cross frontiers. The absence of entry and exit stamps can cause serious difficulties: seek out the proper migration offices if the stamping process is not carried out as you cross. Also, do not lose your entry card; replacing one causes a lot of trouble, and possibly expense.

You should always carry your passport in a safe place about your person, or if not leaving the city or town you're in, deposit it in the hotel safe. If staying in Peru for several weeks, it is worthwhile registering at your consulate. Then, if your passport is stolen, the process of replacing it is simplified and speeded up.

Renewals and extensions The extension process in Lima immigration is as follows: go to the third floor and enter the long narrow hall with many 'teller' windows. Go to window number five and present your passport and tourist card. The official will give you a receipt for US$20 (the cost of a one-month extension) which you will pay at the ***Banco de la Nación*** on the same floor. Then go back to the teller room and buy form F007 for S/22 (US$6.35) from window 12. Fill out the form and return to window five. Give the official the paid receipt, the filled-out form, your passport and tourist card. You have now finished your part of the process. Next, you will wait 10-15 minutes for your passport to be stamped and signed. You have just completed a not-so-painful Peruvian bureaucratic process. **NB** Three extensions like this are permitted, although it's unlikely that you will be allowed to buy more than one month at a time. Peruvian law states that a tourist can remain in the country for a maximum of six months, after which time you must leave. Crossing the border out of Peru and returning immediately is acceptable. You will then receive another 90 days and the process begins all over again.

To summarise briefly: you are given 90 days upon entering the country. You can buy 90 more days for US$20 each (not at the same time) for a total of six months (180 days). Once your six months is completed, you must leave Peru (no exceptions). This simply means crossing into a bordering country for the day (depending on where, you can come back immediately) and returning with a fresh 90 days stamped in your passport.

If you let your tourist visa expire you can be subject to a fine of US$20 per day, but this is up to the discretion of the immigration official so it's a good idea to be very courteous. You can extend your visa in Lima, Cusco and Puerto Maldonado (also in Puno, on the shores of Lake Titicaca, and Iquitos on the Amazon), but in the provinces it can take more time than in Lima.

Business visas Visitors who are going to receive money from Peruvian sources must have a business visa: requirements are a valid passport, two colour passport photos, return ticket and a letter from an employer or Chamber of Commerce stating the nature of business, length of stay and guarantee that any Peruvian taxes will be paid. The visa costs US$31. On arrival business visitors must register with the **Dirección General de Contribuciones** for tax purposes.

Student visas To obtain a one-year student visa you must have: proof of adequate funds, affiliation to a Peruvian body, a letter of recommendation from your own and a Peruvian Consul, a letter of moral and economic guarantee from a Peruvian citizen and four photographs (frontal and profile). You must also have a health check certificate which takes four weeks to get and costs US$10. Also, to obtain a student visa, if applying within Peru, you have to leave the country and collect it in La Paz, Arica or Guayaquil from Peruvian immigration (it costs US$20).

Insurance

Always take out travel insurance before you set off and read the small print carefully. Check that the policy covers the activities you intend or may end up doing. Also check exactly what your medical cover includes, ie ambulance, helicopter rescue or emergency flights back home. Also check the payment protocol. You may have to cough up first (literally) before the insurance company reimburses you. It is always best to dig out all the receipts for expensive personal effects like jewellery or cameras. Take photos of these items and note down all serial numbers.

You are advised to shop around. ***STA Travel*** and other reputable student travel organisations offer good value policies. Young travellers from North America can try the International Student Insurance Service (ISIS), which is available through ***STA Travel***, T1-800-7770112, www.sta-travel.com Other recommended travel insurance companies in North America include: ***Travel Guard***, T1-800-8261300, www.noelgroup.com ***Access America***, T1-800- 2848300; ***Travel Insurance Services***, T1-800-9371387; ***Travel Assistance International***, T1-800-8212828; and ***Council Travel***, T1-888-COUNCIL, www.counciltravel.com Older travellers should note that some companies will not cover people over 65 years old, or may charge higher premiums. The best policies for older travellers (UK) are offered by ***Age Concern***, T01883-346964.

Customs

Duty-free allowance When travelling into Peru you can bring 20 packs of cigarettes (400 cigarettes), 50 cigars or 500 g of tobacco, 3 l of alcohol and new articles for personal use of gifts valued at up to US$300. There are certain items that are blacked out and therefore cannot be brought in duty-free: these include computers (but laptops are OK). The value-added tax for items that are not considered duty-free but are still intended for personal use is generally 20%. Personal items necessary for adventure sports such as climbing, kayaking and fishing are duty-free. Most of the customs rules aren't a worry for the average traveller, but anything that looks like it's being brought in for resale could give you trouble.

It is illegal to take items of archaeological interest out of Peru. This means that any precolumbian pottery or Inca artefacts cannot leave Peru. If you are purchasing extremely good replicas make sure the pieces have the artist's name on them or that they have a tag which shows that they are not originals. It is very important to realize that no matter how simple it seems, it is not worth your time to try and take anything illegal out of the country – this includes drugs. The security personnel and customs officials are much smarter than you and are experts at their job. It's best to understand that this is a foolhardy idea and save yourself the horror of 10 years in jail.

Vaccinations

For more information, see page 59

Before you travel make sure the medical insurance you take out is adequate. Have a check up with your doctor, if necessary and arrange your vaccinations well in advance. Try ringing a specialist travel clinic if your own doctor is unfamiliar with health in Latin America. You should be protected against typhoid, polio, tetanus and hepatitis A. A yellow fever vaccination certificate is only required if you are coming from infected areas of the world or, for your own protection, if you are going to be roughing it in the Peruvian jungle. Check malaria prophylaxis for all lowland rural areas to be visited and particularly if you will be on the borders of Bolivia and Brazil. Vaccination against cholera is not necessary, but occasionally immigration officials might ask to see a certificate. For a full and detailed description of necessary vaccinations and all matters relating to health, see Health section on page 58.

What to take

Everybody has their own preferences, but listed here are the most often mentioned. These include: an inflatable **travel pillow** for neck support; hiking boots; waterproof clothing; wax earplugs (vital for noisy hotels); rubber sandals (which can be worn in showers to avoid athlete's foot); a sheet sleeping-bag to avoid sleeping on filthy sheets in cheap hotels; a **clothes line**; a **water bottle**; a universal bath-and basin-**plug** of the flanged type that will fit any waste-pipe; **Swiss Army knife** or card; an **alarm clock** for those early morning departures; **candles** and/or a **torch/**

Cost of living/travelling

In most of Peru, living costs in the provinces are from 20% to 50% below those in Lima, but Cusco is a little more expensive than other, less touristy provincial cities. For a lot of low income Peruvians, many items are simply beyond their reach. In 2001, the approximate budget was US$30-35 per person a day for living comfortably, including transport, or about US$15 a day for low-budget travel. For Hotel prices, see ***Where to stay*** *(page 37) and for restaurant prices, see* ***Food and drink*** *(page 44).*

flashlight; an **adaptor**; **padlocks** (for doors of the cheapest hotels, for tent zip, and for backpacks as a deterrent to thieves); a small **first aid kit**; and a **sun hat**.

A list of useful medicines and health-related items is given in the Health section on page 58. To these might be added some lip salve with sun protection, and pre-moistened wipes (such as 'Wet Ones'). Always carry toilet paper, which is especially important on long bus trips. Contact lens solution is readily available in pharmacies.

Money

Currency

At the beginning of Oct 2001, the exchange rate was US$1 = S/.3.40

The *Nuevo Sol* (New Sol, S/.) is the official currency of Peru. It is divided in 100 *céntimos* (cents) with coins valued at S/.5, S/.2, S/.1 and 50, 20, 10 and 5 *céntimo* pieces, although the latter is being phased out as it is virtually worthless. Notes in circulation are S/.200, S/.100, S/.50, S/.20 and S/.10. Try to break down notes whenever you can as there is a country-wide shortage of change (or so it seems) and it will make life simpler if you get change whenever you can. It is difficult to get change in shops and museums and sometimes impossible from street vendors or cab drivers. Prices of airline tickets, tour agency services, non-backpacker hotels and hostels, among others, are almost always quoted in dollars. You can pay in soles or dollars but it is generally easiest to pay dollars when the price is in dollars, and in soles when the price is in soles. This will save you from losing on exchange rates. In Cusco and Lima dollars are frequently accepted.

NB Almost no one, certainly not banks, will accept dollar bills that are ripped, taped, stapled or torn. Do not accept torn dollars from anyone; simply tell them you would like another bill. Also ask your bank at home to give you only nice, crisp, clean dollars and keep your dollars neat in your money belt or wallet so they don't accidentally tear. Forgeries of dollars and soles are not uncommon. Always check the notes you have received, even at the bank. Hold the bills up to the light, check the watermark and the line down the side of the bill in which the amount of the money is written. There should be tiny flecks of paper in (not on) the money. Check to see that the faces are clear. Also, the paper should not feel smooth like a photocopy but rougher and fibrous. There are also posters in many restaurants, stores and banks explaining exactly what to look for in forged sol notes.

Credit cards

Visa (by far the most widely-accepted card in Peru), ***MasterCard***, ***American Express*** and ***Diners Club*** are all valid. There is often an 8-12% commission for all credit card charges. Often, it is cheaper to use your credit card to get money (dollars or soles) out of an ATM rather than to pay for your purchases. Of course, this depends on your interest rate for cash advances on your credit cards – ask your bank or card provider about this. Another option is to put extra money on your credit cards and use them as a bank card. Most banks are affiliated with Visa/Plus system; those that you will find in Cusco and Lima, and most towns, are ***Banco de Crédito***, ***Banco Wiese Sudameris*** and ***Interbank***. Wiese belongs to the ATM network called *Unicard*, which accepts both Visa/Plus

Plastic facts

***American Express**, Jr Belén 1040, Lima (same building as Lima Tours), T330 4482, open Mon-Fri 0900-1700.*
***Diners Club**, Canaval y Moreyra 535, San Isidro (street also known as Córpac), T221 2050.*

***MasterCard** assistance is handled by **Banco Latino**.*
***Visa** Travel Assistance, T108 and ask the operator for a collect call (por cobrar) to 410-581 9754.*

and MasterCard/Cirrus. Another bank in this network is ***Banco Santander Central Hispano*** (BSCH), but not every branch offers the same services. ***Banco de Crédito***'s ATM is *Telebanco 24 Horas* which accepts Visa and American Express cards. ***Banco Latino*** and ***Banco Wiese*** are affiliated with the Cirrus system. Credit cards are not commonly accepted in smaller towns so go prepared with cash. Make sure you carry the phone numbers that you need in order to report your card lost or stolen. In addition, some travellers have reported problems with their credit cards being 'frozen' by their bank as soon as a charge from a foreign country occurs. To avoid this problem, notify your bank that you will be making charges in Peru.

Exchange

US dollars are the only currency which should be brought from abroad (take some small bills). Other currencies carry high commission fees

There are no restrictions on foreign exchange. Banks are the most discreet places to change travellers' cheques into soles. Some charge commission from 1% to 3%, some don't, and practice seems to vary from branch to branch, month to month. The services of the ***Banco de Crédito*** have been repeatedly recommended. Changing dollars at a bank always gives a lower rate than with *cambistas* (street changers) or *casas de cambio* (exchange houses). Always count your money in the presence of the cashier. For changing into or out of small amounts of dollars cash, the street changers give the best rates, avoiding paperwork and queuing, but you should take care: check your soles before handing over your dollars, check their calculators, etc, and don't change money in crowded areas. In Cusco many of the *cambistas* congregate around the top of Avenida Sol, so be careful.Think about taking a taxi after changing, to avoid being followed. Also, many street changers congregate near an office where the exchange 'wholesaler' operates; these will probably be offering better rates than elsewhere on the street. Soles can be exchanged into dollars at the banks and exchange houses at Lima airport.

American Express will sell travellers' cheques to cardholders only, but will not exchange cheques into cash. Amex will hold mail for cardholders at the Lima branch only. They are also very efficient in replacing stolen cheques, though a police report is needed. Most of the main banks accept American Express travellers' cheques and ***Banco de Crédito*** and ***BSCH*** accept Visa travellers' cheques. ***Citibank*** in Lima and some ***BSCH*** branches handle ***Citicorp*** cheques. Travellers have reported great difficulty in cashing travellers' cheques in the jungle and other remote areas. Always sign travellers' cheques in blue or black ink or ballpen.

Money transfer

To transfer money from one bank to another you must first find out which Peruvian bank works with your bank at home. If in fact one does, you will have to go to that bank in Lima (or wherever you are) and ask them what the process is to make a transfer. Depending on the bank, transfers can be completed immediately or will take up to five working days. Another option is to use ***Western Union***. Their main offices in Lima are: Avenida Petit Thouars 3595, San Isidro, T422 0036, Avenida Larco 826, Miraflores, T241 1220, and Jirón Carabaya 693, Lima centre, T428 7624. Details of the Cusco office is given under the relevant section. ***Moneygram*** also has representation in Lima at Calle Ocharan 260, Miraflores, T447 4044, with offices throughout the capital and the provinces. It exchanges most world currencies and travellers' cheques.

Getting there

Air

From Europe There are direct flights to **Lima** from Amsterdam (***KLM*** via Aruba) and Barcelona and Madrid (***Iberia***). Though there are no direct flights from London, cheap options are available with ***Avianca*** via Bogotá (also the simplest connection from Paris), ***Iberia*** via Madrid and ***KLM*** via Amsterdam. Alternatively, you can fly standby to Miami, then fly the airlines shown below. A little more expensive, but as convenient, are connections via Atlanta with ***Delta***, or Houston with ***Continental***. To avoid paying Peru's 18% tax on international air tickets, take your used outward ticket with you when buying your return passage.

From Israel From Tel Aviv to **Lima** , fly ***El Al*** to New York, then ***Lan Chile*** on to **Lima** three times a week. Otherwise you need to fly from Tel Aviv to London, Paris or Madrid and make onward connections.

From USA & Canada Miami is the main gateway to Peru but Atlanta, Houston, Los Angeles and New York are strong contenders. Direct flights are available from Miami with ***American***, ***Lan Perú*** and ***Copa*** (via Panama City); through New York with American, which also flies from Dallas, ***Continental***, which also flies from Houston, and ***Lan Chile***; from Atlanta with ***Delta***; and from Los Angeles with ***Lacsa***, ***Lan Chile***, ***Lan Perú*** and ***Aeromexico***. Daily connections can be made from almost all major North American cities. From Toronto and Vancouver, the best bet is via Los Angeles.

Discount flight agents

*In the **UK and Ireland**: www.cheapflights.com Cheap flights the world over. **STA Travel**, Priory House, 6 Wrights La, London W8 6TA, T0870-160 6070, www.statravel.co.uk They have other branches in London, Brighton, Bristol, Cambridge, Leeds, Manchester, Newcastle-upon-Tyne, Oxford and on many university campuses. Specialists in low-cost student/youth flights and tours, also good for student IDs and insurance. **Trailfinders**, 194 Kensington High St, London, W8 7RG, T020-7938 3939, also Birmingham T0121-2361234, Bristol T0117-9299000, Manchester T0161-8396969, Newcastle T0191-2612345 and Dublin T01-6777888. **Usit Campus**, 52 Grosvenor Gdens, London SW1 0AG, T020-7730 7285, www.usitcampus.co.uk Student/youth travel specialists with branches also in Belfast (Usit NOW), Birmingham, Edinburgh, Glasgow, Manchester, Newcastle and Oxford. The main Ireland branch is at Aston Quay, O'Connell Bridge, Dublin, T01-6021600.*

*In **North America**: **Air Brokers International**, 323 Geary Street, Suite 411, San Francisco, CA 94102, T01-800-883 3273, www.airbrokers.com Consolidator and specialist on RTW and Circle Pacific tickets. **Council Travel**, 205 E 42 nd Street, New York, NY 10017, T1-888-COUNCIL, www.counciltravel.com Student/budget agency with branches in many US cities. **Discount Airfares Worldwide On-Line**, www.etn.nl/discount.htm A hub of consolidator and discount agent links. **International Travel Network/Airlines of the Web**, www.itn.net/airlines Online air travel information and reservations. **STA Travel**, 5900 Wilshire Blvd, Suite 2110, Los Angeles, CA 90036, T1-800-7770112, www.sta-travel.com Also branches in New York, San Francisco, Boston, Miami, Chicago, Seattle and Washington DC. **Travel CUTS**, 187 College Street, Toronto, ON, M5T 1P7, T1-800-6672887, www.travelcuts.com Specialist in student discount fares, IDs and other travelservices. Branches in other Canadian cities. Other online agents are priceline.com cheaptickets.com travelocity.com and expedia.com www.qixo.com is a good site for comparing prices.*

*In **Australia and New Zealand**: **Flight Centres** 82 Elizabeth Street, Sydney, T13-1600; 205 Queen Street, Auckland, T09-309 6171. Also branches in other towns and cities. **STA Travel** T1300-360960, www.statravelaus.com.au 702 Harris St, Ultimo, Sydney, and 256 Flinders Street, Melbourne. In NZ: 10 High Street, Auckland, T09-366 6673. Also in major towns and university campuses. **Travel.com.au**, 80 Clarence Street, Sydney, T02-9290 1500, www.travel.com.au*

Essentials

From Latin America

There are regular flights, in many cases daily, to Peru from most South American countries: Bogotá, ***Avianca***, ***Aero Continente*** and ***Servivenssa***; Buenos Aires, ***Aerolíneas Argentinas***, ***Taca*** and ***Lan Chile*** (via Santiago de Chile); Caracas, ***Aero Continente***, ***Taca***, ***Servivensa*** and ***Aeropostal***; Guayaquil, ***Tame***, ***Taca*** and ***Aero Continente***; La Paz, ***Lloyd Aéreo Boliviano*** (LAB, also to Cochabamba and Santa Cruz), ***Taca*** (also to Santa Cruz) and ***Aero Continente***; Quito, ***Tame***, ***Taca*** and ***Aero Continente***; ***Varig*** to Rio de Janeiro and São Paulo (also ***Taca***); Santiago de Chile, ***Lan Chile***, ***Lacsa*** and ***Lan Perú***. From Central America: Guatemala, ***Lacsa***; Mexico City, ***Taca*** and ***Aeromexico***; Panama, ***Copa*** and ***Aero Continente***; San José, ***Taca*** and ***Lacsa***. ***Avianca***, ***Lan Chile*** and ***Lacsa/Taca*** generally have the cheapest flights.

From Asia

From Hong Kong, Seoul and Singapore, connections have to be made in Los Angeles. Make connections in Los Angeles or Miami if flying from Tokyo.

From Australia & New Zealand

There are no obvious connecting flights from either Australia or New Zealand to **Lima**. One option would be to go Los Angeles and travel down from there. Alternatively, the round-the-world ticket offered by ***Qantas/British Airways/American Airlines*** includes 12 free stops and goes via Miami. Here you can pick up the American flight to **Lima**.

From South Africa From Johannesburg, make connections in Buenos Aires or New York.

Baggage allowance There is always a weight limit for your baggage. With European carriers, this is generally two bags per person of checked luggage weighing up to 20 kg for regular class and 30 kg for first class. American carriers generally allow two bags totalling up to 64 kg per person regardless of ticket class. The American airlines are usually a bit more expensive but if you are travelling with a 40 kg bag of climbing gear, it may be worth looking into. Occasionally tickets on US carriers offer one piece of checked baggage at 32 kg and a second at 20 kg for a total of 52 kg. People should check this when purchasing their tickets. At busy times of the year it can be very difficult and expensive to bring items such as bikes and surf boards along. The going rate from the US varies between US$50-100, regardless of whether the oversize item is your second or third checked piece of luggage. Many airlines will let you pay a penalty for overweight baggage – often this is US$5 per kg – but this usually depends on how full the flight is. Check first before you assume you can bring extra luggage. Internal carriers have a weight limit of 20 kg per person so keep this in mind if you plan to take any internal flights.

Prices & discounts

If you foresee returning home at a busy time (eg Christmas or Easter), a booking is advisable on any type of open-return ticket

Lima is generally the cheapest destination in South America for flights from the US. From Atlanta fares range from US$550 in low season to US$750 in high season (end-June to September and December). From Los Angeles low season fares are roughly similar, but high season fares start at US$670 in July, but are over US$1,000 at Christmas-time. Miami is cheaper all round, with low season fares at about US$440 and high season fares starting at US$500 in July, rising to US$680 in December. From the UK, high season prices are also much higher than low season (US$1,100-1,30, compared with US$650-850), but here again, Lima tends to be a good value destination outside busy times. From Sydney, Australia, expect to pay in the region of US$1,200 at any time of year (December is the most expensive). **NB** All fares are the cheapest available for a return ticket at the time of going to press. (For internal flight prices see page 39.)

Most airlines offer discounted fares on scheduled flights to South America, including Peru, through agencies who specialize in this type of fare. For a list of these agencies see page 13.) The very busy seasons are 7 December-15 January and 10 July-10 September. If you intend travelling during those times, book as far ahead as possible. Between February-May and September-November special offers may be available. Do not assume that student tickets are the cheapest.

Airline Websites

Aerolíneas Argentinas, *www.aerolineas.com.ar*
Aeromexico, *www.aeromexico.com*
Air France, *www.airfrance.com*
American Airlines, *www.aa.com*
Avianca, *www.avianca.com.co*
British Airways, *www.britishairways.com*
Continental, *www.continental.com*
Copa, *www.copaair.com*
Delta, *www.delta-air.com*
El Al, *www.elal.co.il*
Iberia, *www.iberia.com*
KLM, *www.klm.com*
LAB, *www.labairlines.com*
Lacsa, *www.grupotaca.com*
Lan Chile, *www.lanchile.com*
Lufthansa, *www.lufthansa-peru.com*
Qantas, *www.qantas.com*
Servivensa, *www.avensa.com.ve*
Taca, *www.grupotaca.com*
Tame, *www.tame.com.ec*
Varig, *www.varig.com.br*

Road

International buses

There are bus services from all the major capitals to Lima. If coming from Bolivia, there are direct buses to Puno, Cusco, Arequipa and Lima from La Paz. On rare occasions, customs officials at international borders may ask for a forwarding ticket out of the country. This means you'll have to buy the cheapest bus ticket out of Peru before they let you in. Note that these tickets are not transferable or refundable.

Touching down

Airport information

For details on Cusco airport, see page 72

Lima will be your point of entry into Peru. The city's **Jorge Chávez Airport** is located deep in the district of Callao. Passengers arriving from international flights will find the *aduana* (customs) process to be relatively painless and efficient (a push-button, red light/green light system operates for customs baggage checks). Once outside and past the gate separating arriving passengers from the general public, you're subject to the inevitable mob of taxi drivers all vying to offer you their services. Fares depend on where you pick up the taxi and how good you are at bargaining.

Transport into Lima

Taxis No taxis use meters, so make sure you fix the price before getting in and insist on being taken to the hotel of your choice, not the driver's. It's always best to have exact change in *soles* to avoid having to break a large bill along the way.

An official taxi from the tourist desk inside International Arrivals is certainly your safest option, but also the most expensive: US$15 to the city centre (US$20 at night), US$20 to Miraflores. Once you're out of the airport building and in the parking lot, the price decreases greatly US$4-6 to the centre of town and US$6-8 to San Isidro/Miraflores. These fares are quoted in soles.

NB All vehicles can enter the airport for 15 minutes at no charge. After that, it's about US$1 every 30 minutes. Taxis that have been waiting for more than the allotted free time will try to make the passenger pay the toll upon leaving the airport. Always establish who will pay before getting in.

Buses There is a service called Airport Express, every 20 minutes to Miraflores from the national exit. These comfortable micro buses cost US$5.50 per person, but they only operate during the day. Local buses (US$0.35) and colectivos run between the airport perimeter and the city centre and suburbs. Their routes are given on the front window: 'Tacna' for the centre, 'Miraflores' for Miraflores, and 'Brasil' for South

Touching down

Tourist Protection Bureau (Indecopi) *24-hr hotline for travellers' complaints, T/F01-224 7888, or, outside Lima, toll free on 0800-42579 (not from pay phones), tour@indecopi.gob.pe At Jorge Chávez airport, Lima, T01-574 8000, T/F01-575 1434; in Cusco T/F084-252974, or, at the airport, T084-237364. This is run by the Tourist Bureau of Complaints and will help with complaints regarding customs, airlines, travel agencies, accommodation, restaurants, public authorities or if you have lost, or had stolen, documents. There is an office in every town as well as kiosks and information stands in airports and public buildings. They are very effective.*

Tourist Police *Jr Moore 268, Magdalena at the 38th block of Av Brasil, Lima, T4601060, open daily 24 hrs. You should come here if you have had property stolen. They are friendly, helpful and speak English and some German.*

Official time *5 hrs behind GMT.*

IDD code *51.*

Business hours *Shops: 0900 or 1000-1230 and 1500 or 1600-2000. In the main cities, supermarkets do not close for lunch and Lima has some that are open 24 hrs. Some are closed on Saturday and most are closed on Sunday. Most banks around the country are open 0930 to 1200 and 1500 to 1800. Banks in Lima generally do not take a siesta so are open throughout the lunch hours. Many banks in Lima and Cusco have Saturday morning hours from 0930 to 1230. Offices: 0830-1230, 1500-1800 all year round. Some have continuous hours 0900-1700 and most close on Saturday. Government Offices: Monday-Friday 0830-1130, January to March. The rest of year Monday-Friday 0900-1230, 1500-1700, but this changes frequently.*

Voltage *220 volts AC, 60 cycles throughout the country.*

Weights & measures *The metric system of weights and measures is compulsory.*

American Explorers. Outside the pedestrian exit are the bus, colectivo and taxi stops, but there is more choice for buses at the roundabout by the car entrance. At busy times (which is anytime other than very late at night or early morning) luggage may not be allowed on buses.

Car hire All hire companies have offices at the airport. The larger international chains, ***Budget***, ***Dollar***, ***Hertz***, are usually cheaper and have better-maintained vehicles than local firms. The airport in Lima is the best, most cost-effective place to arrange car hire. (For addresses in Lima, see page 238.)

Airport facilities

The larger, more expensive hotels in Miraflores and San Isidro have their own buses at the airport, and charge for transfer. For details of hotels near the airport, see page222

There are ATMs between the national and international foyers accepting Visa, MasterCard and the Plus and Cirrus systems. There are three ***Casas de Cambio*** (money changing desks) in the airport, operated by Banco Santander Central Hispano: in the national foyer opposite desk 19, in the international foyer opposite desks 13 and 32. They are open 24 hours and change all types of travellers' cheque (they claim) and most major currencies. There are also exchange facilities for cash and travellers' cheques in the international arrivals hall. ***Banco de Crédito*** stands, in the national foyer opposite desk 25 and in the international foyer opposite desks 1 and 11 only collect the international or domestic airport tax that must be paid in order to get through the gate. There is another such (unmarked) desk in the international foyer by desk 20. **NB** The operators of the tax collection desks change frequently.

Although public telephones are everywhere in and around the airport, there is also a ***Telefónica del Peru*** office in the international foyer opposite desk 20, open 0700-2300 seven days a week. Fax service is available. There are two post offices, one in the national foyer opposite desk 26, the other at the far end of the international foyer.

There is a 24-hour pharmacy, on the second level to the left of the escalator near international departures, which offers everything from normal medication to yellow fever shots. Also opposite the departure gate is a First Aid post (not open in the early morning). The left luggage lock-up, located near international arrivals, offers safe 24-hour storage and retrieval for about US$3 per bag per day.

Information desks can be found in the national foyer opposite 9 and in the international foyer opposite 35 and at the departure gate. There is also a helpful desk in the international arrivals hall. It can make hotel and transport reservations. The *Zeta* books kiosk near international departures offers one of the best selections of English language guidebooks in the country. On the second level there are various cafés and restaurants, some accepting major credit cards. Food tends to be pricey and not very good.

Airport departure information

It is recommended to arrive at the airport 2 ½ hours before international flights and 1 ½ hours before domestic flights. You will be early in the queue, but this is a small price to pay to avoid possible hassle. Moreover, check-in for international flights technically closes one hour before departure, 30 minutes for domestic flights, after which you may not be permitted to board. Cars entering the parking lot are subject to a document check of the driver, only. Security has become much more relaxed in the past couple of years and spot luggage and passport checks are very rare.

Airport departure tax

There is a US$25 departure tax for international flights which is never included in the price of your ticket. It may be paid in dollars or soles. For national flights (at all airports in Peru), the airport tax is 12 soles (US$3.45), payable only in soles. Tickets purchased in Peru will also have the 18% state tax, but this will be included in the price of the ticket. **NB** It is very important to reconfirm your flights when flying internally in Peru or leaving the country. This is generally done 48-72 hours in advance and can be done by phoning or visiting the airline office directly or, sometimes, by going to a travel agent for which you may have to pay a service charge. If you do not reconfirm your internal or international flight, you may not get on the plane. See also Customs, page 25.

Customs and local laws

Clothing

In general, clothing is less formal in the tropical lowlands, where men and women do wear shorts. In the highlands, people are more conservative, though wearing shorts is acceptable on hiking trails. Men should not be seen bare-chested in populated areas.

Courtesy

Politeness – even a little ceremoniousness – is much appreciated in Peruvian society. Men shake hands when introducing themselves to other men. Women or men meeting women usually greet each other with one kiss on the cheek. When introduced, Peruvians will probably expect to greet visitors in the same way. Always say "Buenos días" (until midday) or "Buenas tardes" and wait for a reply before proceeding further.

Always remember that the traveller from abroad has enjoyed greater advantages in life than most Latin American minor officials, and should be friendly and courteous at all times. Never be impatient and do not criticize situations in public (the officials may know more English than you think and they can certainly interpret gestures and facial expressions). In some situations, however, politeness can be a liability. Most Latin Americans are disorderly queuers. In commercial transactions (buying a meal, goods in a shop, etc) politeness should be accompanied by firmness, and always ask the price first. Politeness should also be extended to street traders. Saying "No, gracias" with a smile is better than an arrogant dismissal.

In Peru it is common for locals to throw their garbage, paper, wrappers and bottles into the street. Sometimes when asking a local where the rubbish bin is, they will indicate to you that it is the street. This does NOT give travellers the right to apply the "when in Rome" theory. There are rubbish bins in public areas in many centres and tourists should use them. If there isn't one around, put the garbage in your pocket. You will always find trash bins in bathrooms.

Time-keeping Peruvians, as with most Latin Americans, have a fairly 'relaxed' attitude towards time. They will think nothing of arriving an hour or so late on social occasions. If you expect to meet someone more or less at an exact time, you can tell them that you want to meet "en punto", or better still, meet in a bar or somewhere you don't mind waiting.

Tipping In most of the better restaurants a 10% service charge is included in the bill, but you can give an extra 5% as a tip if the service is good. The most basic restaurants do not include a tip in the bill, and tips are not expected. Taxi drivers are not tipped – bargain the price down, then pay extra for good service if you get it. Tip cloakroom attendants and hairdressers (very high class only), US$0.50-$1; railway or airport porters, US$0.50; car wash boys, US$0.30; car 'watch' boys, US$0.20. If going on a trek or tour it is customary to tip the guide, as well as the cook and porters.

Responsible tourism

Travel to the furthest corners of the globe is now commonplace and the mass movement of people for leisure and business is a major source of foreign exchange and economic development in many parts of South America. In some regions (eg Machu Picchu) it is probably the most significant economic activity.

The benefits of international travel are self-evident for both hosts and travellers – employment, increased understanding of different cultures, business and leisure opportunities. At the same time there is clearly a downside to the industry. Where visitor pressure is high and/or poorly regulated, adverse impacts to society and the natural environment may be apparent. Paradoxically, this is as true in undeveloped and pristine areas (where culture and the natural environment are less 'prepared' for even small numbers of visitors) as in major resort destinations.

The travel industry is growing rapidly and increasingly the impacts of this supposedly 'smokeless' industry are becoming apparent. These impacts can seem remote and unrelated to an individual trip or holiday (eg air travel is clearly implicated in global warming and damage to the ozone layer, resort location and construction can destroy natural habitats and restrict traditional rights and activities), but individual choice and awareness can make a difference in many instances (see box) and collectively, travellers are having a significant effect in shaping a more responsible and sustainable industry.

In an attempt to promote awareness of and credibility for responsible tourism, organizations such as ***Green Globe*** (www.greenglobe.org T+44-1202-312001) and the ***Centre for Environmentally Responsible Tourism*** (CERT, www.c-e-r-t.org) now offer advice on destinations and sites that have achieved certain commitments to conservation and sustainable development. Generally these are larger mainstream destinations and resorts but they are still a useful guide and increasingly aim to provide information on smaller operations.

Of course travel can have beneficial impacts and this is something to which every traveller can contribute – many National Parks are part funded by receipts from visitors. Similarly, travellers can promote patronage and protection of important archaeological sites and heritage through their interest and contributions via entrance and performance fees. They can also support small-scale enterprises by staying in locally run hotels and hostels, eating in local restaurants and by purchasing local goods, supplies and arts and crafts.

There has been a phenomenal growth in tourism that promotes and supports the conservation of natural environments and is also fair and equitable to local communities. This 'ecotourism' segment is probably the fastest growing sector of the travel industry and provides a vast and growing range of destinations and activities. While the authenticity of

How big is your footprint?

- *Where possible choose a destination, tour operator or hotel with a proven ethical and environmental commitment – if in doubt ask*
- *Spend money on locally produced (rather than imported) goods and services and use common sense when bargaining – your few dollars saved may be a week's salary to others*
- *Use water and electricity carefully – travellers may receive preferential supply while the needs of local communities are overlooked*
- *Learn about local etiquette and culture – consider local norms and behaviour and dress appropriately for local cultures and situations*
- *Protect wildlife and other natural resources – don't buy souvenirs or goods made from wildlife unless they are clearly sustainably produced and are not protected under CITES legislation (CITES controls trade in endangered species)*
- *Always ask before taking photographs or videos of people.*
- *Consider staying in local accommodation rather than foreign owned hotels – the economic benefits for host communities are far greater – and there are far greater opportunities to learn about local culture.*
- *The heart-breaking sight of children begging for money, shining shoes and selling sweets and postcards often at midnight in Cusco town centre leaves many visitors guilt-ridden if they refuse, or doubtful they have really helped if they do give money. The best advice is not to give children money; in some cases this goes on glue sniffing or to an alcoholic parent.*
- *It is better to give children food. Not sweets, which rot their teeth, but fruit (many are badly malnourished) or a sandwich. They will also appreciate something to keep them warm such as a pair of gloves or a scarf.*
- *Otherwise make a donation to a local charitable organization such as* ***Los Niños*** *which is actively helping reverse the plight of hundreds of similar children.*

some ecotourism operators' claims need to be interpreted with care, there is clearly both a huge demand for this type of activity and also significant opportunities to support worthwhile conservation and social development initiatives. If you are concerned about the application of the principles of ecotourism, in Peru as elsewhere, you need to make an informed choice by finding out in advance how establishments such as jungle lodges cope with waste and effluent disposal, whether they create the equivalent of 'monkey islands' by obtaining animals in the wild and putting them in the lodge's property, what their policy is towards employing and training local staff, and so on.

Organizations such as ***Conservation International*** (T001-202-912 1000/1-800-406 2306, www.ecotour.org), the ***International Ecotourism Society*** (T001-802-651 9818, www.ecotourism.org), ***Planeta*** (www.planeta.com) and ***Tourism Concern*** (T+44-020-7753 3330, www.tourismconcern.org.uk with a very useful links page) have begun to develop and/or promote ecotourism projects and destinations and their web sites are an excellent source of information and details for sites and initiatives throughout South America. Additionally, organizations such as, ***Earthwatch*** (T+44-1865-318838, www.earthwatch.org) and ***Discovery Initiatives*** (T+44-1285-643333, www.discoveryinitiatives.com) offer opportunities to participate directly in scientific research and development projects throughout the region.

Safety

In Cusco more police patrol the streets, trains and stations than in the past, which has led to an improvement in security, but you still need to be vigilant. Look after your belongings, leaving valuables in safe keeping with hotel management, not in hotel rooms. Places in which to take care are: when changing money on the streets; in the railway and bus stations; the bus from the airport; the Santa Ana market; the San Cristóbal area and at out-of-the-way ruins. Also take special care during Inti Raymi. Avoid walking around alone at night on narrow streets, between the stations and the centre, or in the market areas. Stolen cameras often turn up in the local market and can be bought back cheaply. If you can prove that the camera is yours, contact the police.

On no account walk back to your hotel after dark from a bar, nightclub or restaurant; strangle muggings and rape are on the increase. For the sake of your own safety pay the US$1 taxi fare, but not just any taxi. Ask the club's doorman to get a taxi for you.

The tourist police in Lima are excellent and you should report any incidents to them (see page 32). Dealings with the tourist police in Cusco have produced mixed reviews; you should double check that all reports written by the police in Cusco actually state your complaint. There have been some mix-ups, and insurance companies seldom honour claims for 'lost' baggage. In the event of a vehicle accident in which anyone is injured, all drivers involved are automatically detained until blame has been established, and this does not usually take less than two weeks.

Advice & suggestions

You can check in at South American Explorers, for latest travel updates. Also recommended is The Latin American Travel Advisor published by Latin American Travel Consultants (see page 19)

Be especially careful arriving at or leaving from bus and train stations. Stations are obvious places to catch people (tourists or not) with a lot of important belongings. Do not set your bag down without putting your foot on it, even just to double check your tickets or look at your watch; it will grow legs and walk away. Take taxis to stations, when carrying luggage, before 0800 and after dark (look on it as an insurance policy). Avoid staying in hotels too near to bus companies, as drivers who stay overnight are sometimes in league with thieves. Also avoid restaurants near bus terminals if you have all your luggage with you, it is hard to keep an eye on all your gear when eating. Try to find a travel companion if alone, as this will reduce the strain of watching your belongings all the time.

Keep all documents secure and hide your main cash supply in different places or under your clothes. Keep cameras in bags, take spare spectacles (eyeglasses) and don't wear wrist-watches (even cheap ones have been ripped off arms!) or jewellery. If you wear a shoulder-bag in a market, carry it in front of you. Backpacks are vulnerable to slashers: a good idea is to cover the pack with a plastic sack, which will also keep out rain and dust. It's best to use a pack which is lockable at its base. Make photocopies of important documents and give them to your family, embassy and travelling companion, this will speed up replacement if documents are lost or stolen and will still allow you to have some ID while getting replacements. If you have an email account, before you leave home send yourself a message containing all your important details and addresses which you can access in an emergency. If someone tries to extract a bribe from you, insist on a receipt.

Ignore mustard smearers and paint or shampoo sprayers, and don't bend over to pick up money or other items in the street. These are all ruses intended to distract your attention and make you easy for an accomplice to steal from. Be aware that there are some police scams and that you are required to carry some identification even if it is just a photocopy of your passports. But be wary of 'plainclothes policemen'. Insist on seeing identification and don't get in a cab with any police officer, real or not. Tell them instead that you will walk to the nearest police station. Before handing anything over, ask why they need to see it and make sure you understand the reason. Note, however, that incidents such as these are very infrequent. The ***South American Explorers*** in Lima has not recorded a case of a police ruse since 1997 when they were commonplace. Never offer a bribe unless you are fully conversant with local customs. If an official suggests that a bribe must be paid before you can proceed on your way, be patient (assuming you have the time) and he may relent.

Drugs

Soft and hard drugs are part of the scene in Cusco and easy to score, but be aware that anyone found carrying even the smallest amount is automatically assumed to be a drug trafficker. The use or purchase of drugs is punishable by up to 15 years' imprisonment and the number of foreigners in Peruvian prisons on drug charges is still increasing. If arrested on any charge the wait for trial in prison can take up to a year and is particularly unpleasant. Be wary of anyone approaching you in a club and asking where they can score – the chances are they'll be a plain-clothes cop. Also, we we have received reports of drug-planting, or mere accusation of drug-trafficking by the PNP on foreigners in Lima, with US$1,000 demanded for release. If you are asked by the narcotics police to go to the toilets to have your bags searched, insist on taking a witness.

Where to stay

Cusco is full of excellent value hotels throughout the price ranges and finding a hotel room to suit your budget should not present any problems. The exception to this is during the Christmas and Easter holiday periods, Carnival, in June and Independence celebrations at the end of July, when all hotels seem to be crowded. It's advisable to book in advance at these times and during school holidays and local festivals (see Holidays and festivals, page 49).

Accommodation, as with everything else, is more expensive in Lima, where good budget hotels are few and far between and, therefore, tend to be busy. Remote jungle towns such as Puerto Maldonado tend to be more expensive than the norm. And if you want a room with air conditioning expect to pay around 30% extra.

All hotels and restaurants in the upper price brackets charge 18% state tax and 10% service on top of prices (neither is included in prices given in the accommodation listings, unless specified). The more expensive hotels also charge in dollars according to the parallel rate of exchange at midnight. Most lower grade hotels only charge the 18% IGV but some may include a service charge.

By law all places that offer accommodation now have a plaque outside bearing the letters **H** (Hotel), **Hs** (Hostal), **HR** (Hotel Residencial) or **P** (Pensión) according to type. A hotel has 51 rooms or more, a hostal 50 or fewer, but the categories do not describe quality or facilities. Generally speaking, though, a *pensión* or *hospedaje* will be cheaper than a hotel or *hostal*. Most mid-range hotels have their own restaurants serving lunch and dinner, as well as breakfast. Few budget places have this facility, though many now serve breakfast. Many hotels have safe parking for motor cycles. Most places are friendly and helpful, irrespective of the price, particularly smaller *pensiones* and *hospedajes*, which are often family-run and will treat you as another member of the family. Cheaper places don't always supply soap, towels and toilet paper. In colder (higher) regions they may not supply enough blankets, so take your own or a sleeping bag.

Advice & suggestions

If travelling alone, it's usually cheaper to share with others in a room with three or four beds. If breakfast is included in the price, it will almost invariably mean continental breakfast. During the low season, when many places may be half empty, it's often possible to bargain the room rate down. Reception areas in hotels may be misleading, so it is a good idea to see the room before booking. Many hoteliers try to offload their least desirable rooms first. If you're shown a dark box without any furniture, ask if there's another room with a window or a desk for writing letters. The difference is often surprising. **NB** The electric showers used in many hotels (basic up to mid-range) are a health and safety nightmare. Avoid touching any part of the shower while it is producing hot water and always get out before you switch it off.

When booking a hotel from an airport, or station by phone, always talk to the hotel

Hotel prices and facilities

__LL__ (over US$151) to __AL__ (US$66-99) Hotels in these categories are usually only found in Cusco, Lima and the main tourist centres. They should offer pool, sauna, gym, jacuzzi, all business facilities (including email), several restaurants, bars and often a casino. Most will provide a safe box in each room.
__A__ (US$46-65) and __B__ (US$31-45) The better value hotels in these categories provide more than the standard facilities and a fair degree of comfort. Most will include breakfast and many offer 'extras' such as cable TV, minibar, and tea and coffee making facilities. They may also provide tourist information and their own transport. Service is generally better and most accept credit cards. At the top end of the range, some may have a swimming pool, sauna and jacuzzi.
__C__ (US$21-30) and __D__ (US$16-20) Hotels in these categories range from very comfortable to functional, but there are some real bargains to be had. At these prices you should expect your own bathroom, constant hot water, a towel, soap and toilet paper, TV, a restaurant, communal sitting area and a reasonably sized, comfortable room with air conditioning (in tropical regions).
__E__ (US$11-15) and __F__ (US$7-10) Usually in these ranges you can expect some degree of comfort and cleanliness, a private bathroom with hot water (certainly in __E__, less common in __F__) and perhaps continental breakfast thrown in. Again, the best value hotels will be listed in the travelling text. Many of those catering for foreign tourists in the more popular regions offer excellent value for money and many have their own restaurant and offer services such as laundry, safe deposit box, money exchange and luggage store
__G__ (up to US$6) A room in this price range usually consists of little more than a bed and four walls, with barely enough room to swing the proverbial cat. If you're lucky you may have a window, a table and chair, and even your own bathroom, though this tends to be the exception rather than the rule.
Prices given in the accommodation listings are for two people sharing a double room with bathroom (shower and toilet) in high season. Where possible, prices are also given per person, as some hotels charge almost as much for a single room.

yourself; do not let anyone do it for you (except an accredited hotel booking service). You will be told the hotel of your choice is full and be directed to a more expensive one.

Toilets Except in the most upmarket hotels and restaurants, most Peruvian toilets are barely adequate at best. The further you go from main population and tourist centres, the poorer the facilities, so you may require a strong stomach and the ability to hold your breath for a long time. Many hotels, restaurants and bars have inadequate water supplies. Almost without exception used toilet paper or feminine hygiene products should not be flushed down the pan, but placed in the receptacle provided. This applies even in quite expensive hotels. Failing to observe this custom will block the pan or drain, which can be a considerable health risk. If you are concerned about the hygiene of the facility, put paper on the seat.

Youth hostels The only International Youth Hostel (***Asociación Peruana de Albergues Turísticos Juveniles***) in Lima is on Avenida Casimiro Ulloa 328, Miraflores, Lima, T446-5488, F444-8187. It has information about Youth Hostels all around the world. For information about International Student Identity Cards (ISIC) and lists of discounts available to cardholders contact ***Intej***, see page 21.

Camping This presents no problems in Peru. There can, however, be problems with robbery when camping close to a small village. Avoid such a location, or ask permission to camp in a backyard or *chacra* (farmland). Most Peruvians are used to campers. Be casual about it, do not unpack all your gear, leave it inside your tent (especially at night) and never leave a tent unattended.

Camping gas in little blue bottles is available. Those with stoves designed for lead-free gasoline should use *ron de quemar*, available from hardware shops (*ferreterías*). White gas is called *bencina*, also available from hardware stores. If you use a stove system that requires canisters make sure you dispose of the empty canisters properly. Keep in mind as well that you are responsible for the trash that your group, guide or muledriver may drop and it is up to you to say something and pick up the rubbish.

Getting around

Air

If you're on a tight schedule, then by far the best option is to fly **Lima- Cusco**, and **Cusco-Puerto Maldonado** if you're planning a trip to Tambopata. Flights to Boca Manu for Manu are normally arranged through a tour operator. There are regular daily flights to **Lima**, 55 minutes, with ***Aero Continente**, **Tans**, **Taca**, **Lan Perú*** and ***Aviandina***. Fares range from US$69 one way, through US$79, US$89 to US$139. Few seats at US$69 are available on each flight; US$79 and US$89 are the most secure bet for getting a seat. Flights are heavily booked on this route in the school holidays (May, July, October and December-March) and national holidays. To **Puerto Maldonado**, for the souteastern jungle, flights take 30 minutes and go daily with ***Tans*** and Monday, Thursday, Saturday and Sunday with ***Aero Continente***. Fares are US$59-99. The most popular ticket is the US$69.

Low promotional tariffs are renewed monthly; often it is best to wait to purchase internal flights until your arrival. There are no deals for round trip tickets

Following the earthquake which hit southren Peru in mid-2001, flights on the route to/from Lima from/to Juliaca, by Lake Titicaca, have been subject to cancellation. Passengers have been transported from Julicaca to Cusco and flown to Lima from there. If you wish to move on from Cusco to Bolivia, there are flights on Tuesday, Thursday and Saturday to/from **La Paz** (55 mins) and **Cochabamba** with ***Lloyd Aéreo Boliviano*** (LAB). The fare from Cusco to La Paz is US$100, including all taxes except the US$10 international departure tax. Be at the airport 2½ hours before departure. The fare from La Paz is US$106, including taxes.

Advice & information

On the Cusco-Lima route there is a high possibility of cancelled flights during the wet season; tourists are sometimes stranded for several days. It is possible for planes to leave early if the weather is bad. Always give yourself an extra day between national and international flights to allow for any schedule changes. Flights are often overbooked so it is **very important** to reconfirm your tickets within 72 hours of your

Sit on right side of the aircraft for the best view of the mountains when flying Cusco-Lima; it is worth checking in early to get these seats

Domestic airlines

Addresses of head offices in Lima. Cusco office addresses are given on page 126.
Aero Continente, Av José Pardo 651, Miraflores, T242 4242. Flights to most major destinations in Peru.
***Tans**, Jr Belén 1015, Lima Centre, Av Arequipa 5200, Miraflores, T241 8510. Flights to most major destinations in Peru*

***Taca Perú**, Av Comandante Espinar 331, Miraflores, T213 7000, www.grupotaca.com Flights between Lima and Cusco and Lima and Iquitos.*
***LanPerú**, C Paz Soldán 225, San Isidro, T213 8200, www.lanperu.com*

flight and in the high season make sure you arrive at the airport two hours before departure to avoid problems. By law, the clerk can start to sell reserved seats to stand-by travellers 30 minutes before the flight. To save time and hassle, travel with carry-on luggage only (48cm x 24cm x 37cm). This will guarantee that your luggage arrives at the airport when you do.

Internal flight prices are given in US dollars but can be paid in soles and the price should include the 18% state tax. Tickets are not interchangeable between companies but sometimes exceptions will be made in the case of cancellations. Do check with companies for special offers. If the price sounds too good to be true double check your ticket to make sure you are not being sold a ticket for Peruvian nationals; these tickets are often half price but you need to show Peruvian ID to get on the plane. Prices for tickets should be the same whether sold by the airline or an agent.

Road

Peru is no different from other Latin American countries in that travelling by road at night or in bad weather should be treated with great care. It is also true that there are many more unpaved than paved roads, so overland travel is not really an option if you only have a few weeks' holiday. In the Cusco area a number of roads in the Sacred Valley are paved, but in the main, mountain roads are of dirt, some good, some very bad. Each year they are affected by heavy rain and mud slides, especially those on the eastern slopes of the mountains. Repairs can be delayed because of a shortage of funds. This makes for slow travel and frequent breakdowns. Note that some of these roads can be dangerous or impassable in the rainy season. Check beforehand with locals (not with bus companies, who only want to sell tickets) as accidents are common at these times.

Bus

It is best to try to arrive at your destination during the day; it is safer and easier to find accommodation

Services south of Lima and inland to Cusco are improving as the road gets better. There are *ejecutivo* service buses (different companies use different titles for their top class or executive services, eg ***Imperial, Ideal, Royal***). Many bus companies have direct (*ejecutivo*) service and regular (local) service and the difference between the two is often great. There are several bus lines that run between Lima and the towns on the route to Cusco.

With the better companies or *ejecutivo* service you will get a receipt for your luggage, it will be locked under the bus and you shouldn't have to worry about it at stops because the storage is not usually opened. Tickets for *ejecutivo* service buses, however, can cost up to double those of the local service buses. For mountain routes, take a fleece and sleeping bag as the temperature at night can drop quite low. Night buses along the coast and into main highland areas are generally fine. Once you get off the beaten track, the quality of buses and roads deteriorates and you may want to stick to the day buses. Attacks on buses are extremely sporadic and not limited to any particular area.

If your bus breaks down and you have to get on another bus, you will probably have to pay for the ticket, but keep your old ticket as some bus companies will give refunds. The back seats tend to be the most bumpy and the exhaust pipe is almost always on the left hand side of the bus. **NB** Prices of tickets are raised 60-100% during Semana Santa (Easter), Fiestas Patrias (Independence Day – July 28 and 29) and Navidad (Christmas). Prices will usually go up a few days before the holiday and possibly remain higher a few days after. Tickets also sell out during these times so if travelling then, buy your ticket as soon as you know what day you want to travel.

Car hire

The minimum age for renting a car is 25. If renting a car, your home driving licence will be accepted for up to six months. Car hire companies are given in the text. They do tend to be very expensive, reflecting the high costs and accident rates. Hotels and tourist agencies will tell you where to find cheaper rates, but you will need to check that you have such basics as spare wheel, toolkit and functioning lights etc.

Check exactly what the hirer's insurance policy covers. In many cases it will only protect you against minor bumps and scrapes, not major accidents, nor 'natural' damage (eg flooding). Ask if extra cover is available. Also find out, if using a credit card, whether the card automatically includes insurance. Beware of being billed for scratches which were on the vehicle before you hired it.

Combìs, colectivos & trucks

Combis operate between most small towns in the Andes on 1-3-hour journeys. This makes it possible, in many cases, just to turn up and travel within an hour or two. On rougher roads, combis are minibuses, while on better roads there are also slightly more expensive and much faster car colectivos. Both operate in the Sacred Valley area. Colectivos are shared taxis which, usually charge twice the bus fare and leave only when full. Most firms have offices. If you book one day in advance, they will pick you up at your hotel or in the main plaza. Trucks are not always much cheaper than buses. They charge 75% of the bus fare, but are wholly unpredictable. They are not recommended for long trips, and comfort depends on the load.

Cycling

Unless you are planning a journey almost exclusively on paved roads a mountain bike is strongly recommended. The good quality ones are incredibly tough and rugged, with low gear ratios for difficult terrain, wide tyres with plenty of tread for good road-holding, cantilever brakes, and a low centre of gravity for improved stability. A chrome-alloy frame is a desirable choice over aluminium as it can be welded if necessary. Once an aluminium frame breaks, it's broke. *Richard's New Bicycle Book* (Pan, £12.99) makes useful reading for even the most mechanically minded. ***South American Explorers*** have valuable cycling information that is continuously updated. The Expedition Advisory Centre, administered by the ***Royal Geographical Society***, 1, Kensington Gore, London SW7 2AR has published a useful monograph entitled *Bicycle Expeditions*, by Paul Vickers. Published in March 1990, it can be downloaded from the RGS's website. A useful website is *Bike South America*, www.e-ddws.com/bsa/ Also recommended is *Cyclo Accueil Cyclo*, 3 rue Limouzin, 42160 Andrezieux, cacoadou@netcourier.com An organization of long-haul tourers who open their homes for free to passing cyclists.

Hitchhiking

Hitchhiking is not easy, owing to the lack of private vehicles, and requires a lot of patience. It can also be a risky way of getting from A to B, but with common sense, it can be an acceptable way of travelling for free (or very little money) and a way to meet a range of interesting people. For obvious reasons, a lone female should not hitch by herself. Besides, you are more likely to get a lift if you are with a partner, be they male or female. The best combination is a male and female together. Three or more and you'll be in for a long wait. Your appearance is also important. Someone with matted hair and a large tattoo on their forehead will not have much success. Remember that you are asking considerable trust of someone.

NB Drivers usually ask for money but don't always expect to get it. In mountain and jungle areas you usually have to pay drivers of lorries, vans and even private cars; ask the driver first how much he is going to charge, and then recheck with the locals.

Motorcycling

The motorcycle should be off-road capable. A road bike can go most places an off-road bike can go at the cost of greater effort.Most hotels will allow you to bring the bike inside (see accommodation listings in the travelling text for details). Look for hotels that have a courtyard or more secure parking and never leave luggage on the bike overnight or whilst unattended.

Taxis

Taxi prices are fixed and cost around US$0.60-0.85 in the urban areas. Fares are not fixed in Lima although some drivers work for companies that do have standard fares. Ask locals what the price should be and **always** set the price beforehand. Taxis at airports are often a bit more expensive, but ask locals what the price should be as taxi drivers may try to charge you three times the correct price. Many taxi drivers work for commission from hotels and will try to convince you to go to that hotel. Feel free to choose your own hotel and go there. If you walk away from the Arrivals gate a bit, the fares should go down to a price that is reasonable.

Train

Peru's national rail service was privatized in 1999. The lines in the Cusco area are all administered by ***PerúRail SA***. Service has improved, but prices have also risen substantially. ***PerúRail's*** services are Cusco-Machu Picchu and **Cusco-Juliaca-Puno**, with the extension from Puna and Juliaca to Arequipa. For information, T084 (Cusco) 221931/221992, reservas@perurail.com, www.perurail.com

Keeping in touch

Communications

Internet

For more Cusco details, see page 127

The internet craze has definitely hit Peru. You can find internet access everywhere. Cusco and Lima have internet cafés on almost every corner; many of them have net-phone. Internet cafés in smaller places are listed in the travelling text. Internet cafés are incredibly cheap to use, often less than US$1 per hour. The downside of this popularity is that cafés frequently have no free terminals, so you have to queue, unless you pick your time carefully. When they first open in the morning is often a good time.

In addition, the system is often overloaded, so getting access to your server can take a long time. Internet access is more expensive in hotel business centres and in out of the way places. Since 2000, ***Terra*** has taken over most internet providers. Its only real rival is Red Científica Peruana, ***rcp***.

Post

The name of the postal system is Serpost

Parcels Sending parcels and mail can be done at any post office but Correo Central on the Plaza de Armas in Lima is the best place. The office is open Monday to Friday from 0800 to 1800. Stamps, envelopes and cloth sacks (to send bigger parcels in) can all be bought there. It costs US$1 to mail a letter anywhere in the Americas and US$1.20 to the rest of the world. You can also mail letters 'expreso' for about US$0.55 extra to the Americas, US$0.90 to the rest of the world, and they will arrive a little more quickly. Don't put tape on envelopes or packages, wait until you get to the post office and use the glue they have. It is very expensive to mail large packages out of Peru so it is best not to plan to send things home from here. For emergency or important documents, DHL and Federal Express are also options in Lima (check in city of Lima section for addresses). For Cusco post office see page 127.

Essentials

Receiving mail To receive mail, letters can be sent to Poste Restante/General Delivery (*lista de correos*), your embassy, or, for cardholders, American Express offices. Members of the ***South American Explorers*** can have post and packages sent to them at either of the Peruvian offices. Remember that there is no W in Spanish; look under V, or ask. For the smallest risk of misunderstanding, use title, initial and surname only. If having items sent to you by courier (eg DHL), do not use poste restante, but an address such as a hotel: a signature is required on receipt. Try not to have articles sent by post to Peru – taxes can be 200% of the value.

Telephone

Telephone dialling codes will be found on the inside front cover

The breaking of ***Telefónica del Perú***'s monopoly in 1998 has seen prices for national and international calls plummet. There is still no service provider other than ***Telefónica***, or ***Telser*** in Cusco, which offers service that is of direct use for the traveller, but competition has helped all the same. The average cost for a three-minute call to North America or Western Europe is now about US$6-7. Collect calls are possible to almost anywhere by ringing the international operator (108). You can also reach a variety of countries' operators direct if you wish to charge a call to your home calling card. 108 has the 0-800 numbers for the international direct options and they speak English. Your home telephone company can give you the number to call as well. You can also receive calls at many ***Telefónica*** offices, the cost is usually around US$1 for 10 minutes. Net Phones are becoming increasingly popular, especially in Lima. Costs and service varies but can be as cheap as US$5 per hour to the USA. Calls to everywhere else are usually at least 50% more. Faxes cost about US$1.50 per page to North America, US$2 to most of Western Europe and US$2.50 to Israel. The cost to receive is about US$1 per page. For ***Telefónica*** office in Cusco, see page 127.

Media

Newspapers

There are several national daily papers. The most informative are *El Comercio* and *La República*. *El Comercio* is good for international news and has a near monopoly on classified ads. It also has a good weekly tourism section. *La República* takes a more liberal-left approach and contains the *Crónica Judicial*. Its weekly tourism section, *Andares*, is recommended. Among the others are *Expreso* and *Ojo*. *Síntesis* and *Gestión* are business dailies. Very popular are the sensationalist papers, written in raunchy slang and featuring acres of bare female flesh on their pages. There are a number of sites which provide regular news updates:

El Comercio www.elcomercio.com.pe/

Expreso www.expreso.com.pe
Gestión www.gestion.com.pe/
La República www.larepublica.com.pe
Síntesis www.sintesis.com.pe
Perú Home Page/Red Científica Peruana www.rcp.net.pe
Perú al Día news service, www.perualdia.com, or through www.rcp.net.pe
The following also have access to the daily news: www.terra.com.pe www.peru.com www.hys.com.pe
For access to all the newspapers' websites, www.peruonline.com

Magazines The most widely read magazine is the weekly news magazine *Caretas*, which gives a very considered angle on current affairs and is often critical of government policy, www.caretas.com.pe *Rumbos*, a glossy magazine, is published every two months in Cusco for US$5.70. Articles, in English and Spanish, feature cultural events, people and places of Peru and the region. To subscribe log on to www.rumbos.delperu.com Monthlies include *Business*, *Proceso Económico*, *Debate* and *Idede*. There is a weekly economic and political magazine in English, the *Andean Report*, with useful information and articles.

Radio Radio is far more important in imparting news to Peruvians than newspapers, partly due to the fact that limited plane routes make it difficult to get papers to much of the population on the same day. There are countless local and community radio stations which cover even the most far-flung places. The most popular stations are Radioprogramas del Perú, which features round-the-clock news, and Cadena Peruana de Noticias.

A shortwave (world band) radio offers a practical means to brush up on the language, keep abreast of current events, sample popular culture and absorb some of the richly varied regional music. International broadcasters such as the ***BBC World Service***, the ***Voice of America***, Boston (Mass)-based ***Monitor Radio International*** (operated by *Christian Science Monitor*) and the Quito-based Evangelical station, ***HCJB***, keep the traveller informed in both English and Spanish. Details of local stations is listed in *World TV and Radio Handbook* (WTRH), PO Box 9027, 1006 AA Amsterdam, The Netherlands, £19.99. Both of these, free wavelength guides and selected radio sets are available from the BBC World Service Bookshop, Bush House Arcade, Bush House, Strand, London WC2B 4PH, UK, T020-7557 2576.

Food and drink

Peruvian cuisine
For a glossary of food and drink terms, see Footnotes

Not surprisingly for a country with such a diversity of geography and climates, Peru boasts the continent's most extensive and varied menu. In fact, Peru is rivalled in Latin America only by Mexico in the variety of its cuisine. One of the least expected pleasures of a trip to Peru is the wonderful food on offer, and those who are willing to forego the normal traveller's fare of pizza and fried chicken are in for a tasty treat.

Not surprisingly, the best **coastal dishes** are those with seafood bases, with the most popular being the jewel in the culinary crown, *ceviche*. This delicious dish of white fish marinated in lemon juice, onion and hot peppers can be found in neighbouring countries, but Peruvian is best. Traditionally, *ceviche* is served with corn-on-the-cob, *cancha* (toasted corn), yucca and sweet potatoes. Another mouth-watering fish dish is *escabeche* – fish with onions, hot green pepper, red peppers, prawns (*langostinos*), cumin, hard-boiled eggs, olives, and sprinkled with cheese. For fish on its own, don't miss the excellent *corvina*, or white sea bass. You should also try *chupe de camarones*, which is a shrimp stew made with varying and somewhat surprising ingredients. Other fish dishes include *parihuela*, a popular bouillabaisse which includes *yuyo de mar*, a tangy seaweed, and *aguadito*, a thick rice and fish soup said to have rejuvenating powers.

The staples of **highland cooking**, corn and potatoes, date back to Inca times and are found in a remarkable variety of shapes, sizes and colours. Two good potato dishes are *Causa* and *carapulca*. *Causa* is made with yellow potatoes, lemons, pepper, hard-boiled eggs, olives, lettuce, sweet cooked corn, sweet cooked potato, fresh cheese, and served with onion sauce. Another potato dish is *papa a la huancaina*, which is topped with a spicy sauce made with milk and cheese. The most commonly eaten corn dishes are *choclo con queso*, corn on the cob with cheese, and *tamales*, boiled corn dumplings filled with meat and wrapped in banana leaf.

Meat dishes are many and varied. *Ollucos con charqui* is a kind of potato with dried meat, *sancochado* is a meat and all kinds of vegetables stewed together and seasoned with ground garlic and *lomo a la huancaína* is beef with egg and cheese sauce. A dish almost guaranteed to appear on every restaurant menu is *lomo saltado*, a kind of stir-fried beef with onions, vinegar, ginger, chilli, tomatoes and fried potatoes, served with rice. *Rocoto relleno* is spicy bell pepper stuffed with beef and vegetables, *palta rellena* is avocado filled with chicken salad, *Estofado de carne* is a stew which often contains wine and *carne en adobo* is a cut and seasoned steak. Others include *fritos*, fried pork, usually eaten in the morning, *chicharrones*, deep fried chunks of pork ribs and chicken, and *lechón*, suckling pig. And not forgetting that popular childhood pet, *cuy* (guinea pig), which is considered a real delicacy.

Very filling and good value are the many soups on offer, such as *yacu-chupe*, a green soup which has a basis of potato, with cheese, garlic, coriander leaves, parsley, peppers, eggs, onions, and mint, and *sopa a la criolla* containing thin noodles, beef heart, bits of egg and vegetables and pleasantly spiced. And not to be outdone in the fish department, *trucha* (trout) is delicious, particularly from Lake Titicaca.

The main ingredient in much **jungle cuisine** is fish, especially the succulent, dolphin-sized *paiche*, which comes with the delicious *palmito*, or palm-hearts, and the ever-present yucca and fried bananas. Other popular dishes include *sopa de motelo* (turtle soup), *sajino* (roast wild boar) and *lagarto* (caiman). *Juanes* are a jungle version of *tamales*, stuffed with chicken and rice.

The Peruvian sweet tooth is evident in the huge number of **desserts** and confections from which to choose. These include: *cocada al horno* – coconut, with yolk of egg, sesame seed, wine and butter; *picarones* – frittered cassava flour and eggs fried in fat and served with honey; *mazamorra morada* – purple maize, sweet potato starch, lemons, various dried fruits, sticks of ground cinnamon and cloves and perfumed pepper; *manjar blanco* – milk, sugar and eggs; *maná* – an almond paste with eggs, vanilla and milk; *alfajores* – shortbread biscuit with *manjar blanco*, pineapple, peanuts, etc; *pastelillos* – yuccas with sweet potato, sugar and anise fried in fat and powdered with sugar and served hot; and *zango de pasas*, made with maize, syrup, raisins and sugar. *Turrón*, the Lima nougat, is worth trying. *Tejas* are sugar candies wrapped in wax paper; the pecan-flavoured ones are tastiest.

The various Peruvian **fruits** are wonderful. They include bananas, the citrus fruits, pineapples, dates, avocados (*paltas*), eggfruit (*lúcuma*), the custard apple (*chirimoya*) which can be as big as your head, quince, *papaya*, mango, guava, the passion-fruit (*maracuyá*) and the soursop (*guanábana*). These should be tried as juices or ice cream – an unforgettable experience.

Eating out

For a full list of restaurants, see under Eating for each town

Lunch is the main meal, and apart from the most exclusive places, most restaurants have a set lunch menu, called *menú* or *menú económico*. The set menu has the advantage of being ready and is served almost immediately and it is usually **cheap**; as little as US$1.75-3.50 for a three course meal. But don't leave it too late – most Peruvians eat lunch around 1230-1300. There are many Chinese restaurants (*chifas*) which serve

Eating categories

Prices for individual restaurant meals given in the travelling text refer to the price of a two-course meal for one person, excluding tips or drinks, or, where stated, the price of a main course only.

Expensive *US$12 and over*
Mid-range *US$5-12*
Cheap *US$1-5*

good food at reasonable prices. For really economically-minded people the *Comedores populares* found in the markets of most cities offer a standard three course meal for as little as US$1 (see **Health**, page 60).

For those who wish to eschew such good value, the menu is called *la carta*. An *à la carte* lunch or dinner costs US$5-8, but can go up to an **expensive** US$80 in a first-class Lima restaurant, with drinks and wine included. Middle and high-class restaurants add 11% tax and 17% service to the bill (sometimes 18% and 13% respectively). This is not shown on the price list or menu, so check in advance. Lower class restaurants charge only 5% tax, while cheap, local restaurants charge no taxes. Dinner in restaurants is normally about 1900 onwards, but choice may be more limited than lunchtime.

The situation for **vegetarians** is improving, but slowly. In Cusco you should have no problem finding a vegetarian restaurant (or a restaurant that has vegetarian options), and the same applies to Lima. Elsewhere, choice is limited and you may find that, as a non-meat eater, you are not understood. Vegetarians and people with allergies should be able to list (in Spanish) all the foods they cannot eat. By saying "no como carne" (I don't eat meat), people may assume that you eat chicken and eggs. If you do eat eggs, make sure they are cooked thoroughly. Restaurant staff will often bend over backwards to get you exactly what you want but you need to request it.

Drink Peru's most famous drink is *pisco*, a grape brandy made in the Ica valley, used in the wonderful pisco sour, a deceptively potent cocktail which also includes egg whites and lime juice. Other favourites are *chilcano*, a longer refreshing drink made with *guinda*, a local cherry brandy, and *algarrobina*, a sweet cocktail made with the syrup from the bark of the carob tree, egg whites, milk, pisco and cinnamon.

Peruvian wine is acidic and not very good. The best of a poor lot are the Ica wines Tacama and Ocucaje, and both come in red, white and rosé, sweet and dry varieties. Tacama blancs de blancs and brut champagne have been recommended, also Gran Tinto Reserva Especial. Viña Santo Tomás, from Chincha, is reasonable and cheap, but Casapalca is not for the discerning palate.

Peruvian beer is very good, but is becoming pretty much the same the country over now that many individual brewers have been swallowed up by the multinational Backus and Johnson. This has happened to the *Cusqueña*, *Arequipeña*, *Callao* and *Trujillo* brands. Peruvians who had their favourites are lamenting this change. In Lima, the *Cristal* and *Pilsener* are both pretty good and served everywhere. Those who fancy a change from the ubiquitous pilsner type beers should look out for the sweetish 'maltina' brown ale. A good dark beer is Trujillo Malta.

Chicha de jora is a strong but refreshing maize beer, usually homemade and not easy to come by, and *chicha morada* is a soft drink made with purple maize. Coffee in Peru is usually execrable. It is brought to the table in a small jug accompanied by a mug of hot water to which you add the coffee essence. If you want coffee with milk, a mug of milk is brought. Those who crave a decent cup of coffee will find recommended places listed in the café section of each town. There are many different kinds of herb tea: the commonest are *manzanilla* (camomile) and *hierbaluisa* (lemon grass).

Bars as we understand them in Europe or North America are not prevalent in Peru. Other than in the poorer working class districts, most people seem to do their drinking in restaurants, *peñas*, discos or at *fiestas*. In saying that, there are some very good bars/pubs in Cusco.

A limp excuse

Did you know there is a potato that has the opposite effect of Viagra? It´s a tuber named año *and Cusqueño women have been known to use it to take revenge on cheating husbands. If a man is unfaithful, his wife will boil his trousers in a vat containing the potato – enough to stop him rising to any occasion!*

Stories like these are part of the fun of discovering Cusco´s markets. Wandering round one is a great experience, packed with new sights, smells and the bright colours of unknown fruit and veg.At San Jerónimo you'll find huacatay *– a mint grown at high altitude and used in the preparation of guinea pig – bulls´ testicles, which are boiled, sliced and used in salads, huge sacks of dirt-cheap garlic, massive 20-25 kg pumpkins,* pepiño *(which has a creamy-coloured skin and is very refreshing), as well as strawberries from the coast, basil, coriander, green chilli peppers and spinach.*

There is caihua, *from the cucumber family, which grows only in sub-tropical valleys and which can be stuffed or chopped for stir-fry or salad. Then there is a dried black potato which smells of bad feet when it is cooked, but is favoured by locals nevertheless; they grind it up and add it to food.*

Then there are potatoes frozen overnight as hard as rocks to bring out their flavour; these are mixed with salt and eaten with cheese. These, together with olives, oranges and tomatoes piled high in large mounds, are weighed out by indigenous women who proudly show off their region of origin by the different hats they wear.

*Most westerners will shirk at ever sampling some of these foodstuffs – especially when a lamb´s head, complete with lipless, grinning teeth bobs to the surface of the favourite soup here (*caldo de cabeza*) for which locals pay a premuim if it includes brain and tongue.*

However, the sight of so much variety, of brown guinea pigs scurrying around cages, of bright yellow bananas balanced chest-high and of heady herbs sold by the sackful, is one worth seeking out. Just don´t try the tuber named año*! Aurelio Aguirre of Andes Nature Tours will tailor-make market tours around Cusco* *(see page 115).*

Shopping

Almost everyone who visits Cusco will end up buying a souvenir of some sort from the vast array of arts and crafts (*artesanía*) on offer. The best, and cheapest, place to shop for souvenirs, and pretty much anything else, is in the street markets which can be found absolutely everywhere.

Bartering

Bartering is an accepted method of determining prices in Peru. This can be an exciting and new approach to shopping that many people have little experience with. There is no way to know how much to offer, but as a general rule, places that have more tourists tend to have slightly higher prices. Often you can get a greater discount when buying quantity. With the fun of bartering also comes the responsibility of it. It is not necessary to get the lowest price possible. Ask around and you will get an idea of what the price should be – this applies to everything from weavings to the price of a taxi. Keep in mind, these people are making a living not playing a game and often one sol means a lot more to them than it does to you. You want the *fair* price not the lowest one.

What to buy

Good buys are: silver and gold handicrafts; Indian hand-spun and hand-woven textiles; manufactured textiles in Indian designs; llama and alpaca wool products such as ponchos, rugs, hats, blankets, slippers, coats and sweaters; *arpilleras* (appliqué pictures of

Peruvian life), which are made with great skill and originality by women in the shanty towns; and fine leather products which are mostly hand made. Another good buy is clothing made from high quality Pima cotton, which is grown in Peru.

The *mate burilado*, or engraved gourd found in every tourist shop, is cheap and one of the most genuine expressions of folk art in Peru. Alpaca clothing, such as sweaters, hats and gloves, is cheaper in the Sierra, the best value being found in Puno. Nevertheless, Cusco is one of the main weaving centres and a good place to shop for textiles, as well as excellent woodcarvings (see the **Shopping** section on page 112). **NB** Geniune alpaca is odourless wet or dry, wet llama 'stinks'. For a more detailed look at Peruvian arts and crafts, see under Arts and crafts on page 258).

Photography Pre-paid Kodak slide film cannot be developed in Peru and is also very hard to find. Kodachrome is almost impossible to buy. Some travellers (but not all) have advised against mailing exposed films home. Either take them with you, or have them developed, but not printed, once you have checked the laboratory's quality. Note that postal authorities may use less sensitive equipment for X-ray screening than the airports do. Developing black and white film is a problem. Often it is shoddily machine-processed and the negatives are ruined. Ask the store if you can see an example of their laboratory's work and if they hand-develop. Exposed film can be protected in humid areas by putting it in a balloon and tying a knot. Similarly keeping your camera in a plastic bag may reduce the effects of humidity.

Entertainment and nightlife

In Cusco

Look out for the vast range of flyers which give you free entry plus a complimentary drink

One of Cusco's main attractions – aside from Inca ruins, colonial architecture, great trekking, wonderful scenery and wild adventure sports – is its nightlife. This is party central, where hedonism takes on a whole new meaning. There is a staggering selection of bars to suit every taste and disposition, all crammed into a few streets on and around the main Plaza de Armas, and all within vomitting distance of each other. You can large it up in the frenzied atmosphere of the ***Cross Keys***, get blissed out in the laid-back ambience of ***Los Perros***, or go all Oirish in ***Paddy Flaherty's***. The choice, as they say, is yours. After the bars close the nightclubs kick into action with a vengeance. The old faves such as ***Mama Africa*** and ***Ukuku's*** have been joined by a rash of new pretenders, some with decent sound systems and DJs spinning the latest happening tunes. But it's not all brain-numbing techno and thumping drum and bass. There are also places where you can wiggle your hips to the sensuous sounds of salsa and merengue. And if even that brings you out in a cold sweat, there are *peñas* offering relatively sedate folklore floorshows.

Be warned that Cusco's nightlife is so prolific you may be so off your face every night and not even have the energy to do the Inca Trail. More seriously, take it easy on the booze when first arriving. Having altitude sickness and a hangover is no joke. Also, be aware of the potential dangers of trying to score drugs in nightclubs (see page 37).

In Lima

The chances are you won't have much time in Lima and will want to move on to Cusco as soon as possible. But if you do have a free night before flying on you should check out the nightlife in Barranco, a pleasant, bohemian seaside suburb of Lima. It's only a short taxi ride from Miraflores and at weekends is positively throbbing with young *Limeños* out for a good time. It's also a great place for romantic early evening drink while you watch the sun slip into the Pacific Ocean. There are lots of trendy bars and nightclubs in Miraflores.

Holidays and festivals

Festivals

A full list of local festivals is listed under each town

Every bit as important as knowing where to go and what the weather will be like, is Peru's festival calendar. At any given time of the year there'll be a festival somewhere in the country, at which time even the sleepiest little town or village is transformed into a raucous mixture of drinking, dancing and water throwing (or worse). Not all festivals end up as choreographed drunken riots, however. Some are solemn and ornate holy processions. But they all draw people from miles around. So it helps a great deal to know about these festivals and when they take place.

Two of the major festival dates are *Carnaval*, which is held over the weekend before **Ash Wednesday**, and *Semana Santa* (Holy Week), which ends on **Easter Sunday**. Carnival is celebrated in most of the Andes and **Semana Santa** throughout most of Peru. Accommodation and transport is heavily booked at these times and prices rise.

Another important festival is *Fiesta de la Cruz*, held on the first of **May** in much of the central and southern highlands and on the coast. In Cusco, the entire month of **June** is one huge *fiesta*, culminating in *Inti Raymi*, on **24 June**, one of Peru's prime tourist attractions. Accommodation can be very hard to find at this time in Cusco.

The two main festivals in Lima are *Santa Rosa de Lima*, on **30 August**, and *Señor de los Milagros*, held on several dates throughout **October**. Another national festival is *Todos los Santos* (All Saints) on **1 November**, and on **8 December** is *Festividad de la Inmaculada Concepción*.

For a description of some of the main festivals and their historic roots, see under **Culture**, on page 262. For more dates, check the websites of PromPerú and ***South American Explorers*** (see page 18). Also check out www.whatsonwhen.com

National holidays

Aside from the festivals listed above, the main holidays are: **1 January**, New Year; **6 January**, *Bajada de Reyes*; **1 May**, Labour Day; **28-29 July**, Independence (Fiestas Patrias); **7 October**, Battle of Angamos; **24-25 December**, *Navidad*.

NB Most businesses such as banks, airline offices and tourist agencies close for the official holidays while supermarkets and street markets may be open. This depends a lot on where you are so ask around before the holiday. Sometimes holidays that fall during mid-week will be moved to the following Monday. Find out what the local customs and events are. Often there are parades, processions, special types of food or certain traditions (like yellow underwear at New Year's) that characterize the event. The high season for foreign tourism in Peru is June to September while national tourism peaks on certain holidays, Navidad, Semana Santa and Fiestas Patrias. Prices rise and accommodation and bus tickets are harder to come by. If you know when you will be travelling buy your ticket in advance.

Sport and special interest travel

Birdwatching

Peru is the number one country in the world for birds. Its varied geography and topography, and its wildernesses of so many different life zones have endowed Peru with the greatest biodiversity and variety of birds on earth. 18.5% of all the bird species in the world and 45% of all neotropical birds occur in Peru. This is why Peru is best destination for birds on the continent dubbed 'the bird continent' by professional birders.

A birding trip to Peru is possible during any month of the year, as birds breed all year round. There is, however, a definite peak in breeding activity – and consequently birdsong – just before the rains come in October, and this makes it rather easier to locate many birds between September and Christmas.

Rainwear is recommended for the mountains, especially during the rainy season between December and April. But in the tropical lowlands an umbrella is the way to go. Lightweight hiking boots are probably the best general footwear, but wellingtons (rubber boots) are preferred by many neotropical birders for the lowland rainforests.

Apart from the usual binoculars, a telescope is helpful in many areas, whilst a tape recorder and shotgun microphone can be very useful for calling out skulking forest birds, although experience in using this type of equipment is recommended, particularly to limit disturbance to the birds.

The birds If your experience of Neotropical birding is limited, the potential number of species which may be seen on a three or four week trip can be daunting. A four-week trip can produce over 750 species, and some of the identifications can be tricky! You may want to take an experienced bird guide with you who can introduce you to, for example, the mysteries of foliage-gleaner and woodcreeper identification, or you may want to 'do it yourself' and identify the birds on your own. There is no single field-guide or book that covers all the birds of Peru, and some species are not illustrated anywhere. However, taking a combination of a few books will ensure that 99 of your sightings can be identified (see page 66).

The key sites The **Tambopata-Candamo Reserved Zone** (page 214) and the **Manu Biosphere Reserve** (page 205) are two of the premier birding sites in Peru. Full details will be found in the text.

Also worth considering are **Machu Picchu and Abra Málaga**: Machu Picchu may be a nightmare for lovers of peace and solitude, but the surrounding bamboo stands provide excellent opportunities for seeing the Inca wren. A walk along the railway track near Puente Ruinas station can produce species which are difficult to see elsewhere. This is *the* place in Peru to see white-capped dipper and torrent duck. From Ollantaytambo (see page 148), it is only two hours' drive to one of the most accessible polylepsis woodlands in the Andes, whilst the humid temperate forest of Abra Málaga is only 45 minutes further on. In the polylepsis some very rare birds can be located without too much difficulty, including royal cinclodes and white-browed tit-spinetail (the latter being one of the 10 most endangered birds on earth). The humid temperate forest is laden with moss and bromeliads, and mixed species flocks of multi-coloured tanagers and other birds are common. A great three-week combination is about 16 days in Manu, then 2-3 days in the highlands at Abra Málaga. You can extend this by including one or more of the other highly recommended spots outside the scope of this guidebook. More information on the birds of Peru is given on page 266.

Climbing and trekking

While Peru has some of the best **climbing** in the world, Cusco is not developed for the sport. Near the city are the **Cordilleras Vilcabamba and Vilcanota** (see page 194) have the enticing peaks of **Salkantay** (6,271 m) and **Ausangate** (6,398 m).

Peru has some outstanding **trekking** circuits around the Nevados, its snow-capped mountains. Among the best known is the **Ausangate circuit**. The other type of trekking for which Peru is justifiably renowned is walking among ruins, and, above all, for the **Inca Trail** (see page 167). However, there are many other walks of this type in a country rich in archaeological heritage. Beyond Machu Picchu, for example, there are magnificent, if strenuous treks, to **Vilcabamba** (see page 175) and **Choquequirao**.

Most walking is on clear trails well trodden by campesinos who populate most parts of the Peruvian Andes. If you camp on their land, ask permission first and, of course, do not leave any litter. Tents, sleeping bags, mats and stoves can easily be hired in Cusco but check carefully for quality.

Conditions for trekking and climbing May to September is the dry season in the Cordillera. October, November and April can be fine, particularly for trekking. Most bad weather comes from the east and temperatures plummet around twilight. The optimum months for extreme ice climbing are from late May to mid July. In early May there is a risk of avalanche from sheered neve ice layers. It is best to climb early in the day as the snow becomes slushy later on.

After July successive hot sunny days will have melted some of the main support (compacted ice) particularly on north facing slopes. On the other hand, high altitude rock climbs are less troubled by ice after July. On south facing slopes the ice and snow never consolidates quite as well.

Contact addresses and websites *APTAE (Asociación Peruana de Turismo de Aventura y Ecoturismo)*, www.andeantravelweb.com/peru/aptae.html
Asociación de Deprtes de Aventura, Caminos Perú www.caminosperu.org
Asociación de Deportes de Montaña, Aire Puro http://argos/pucp.edu.pe/~airepuro/index3.html
Aventurismo Perú www.aventurismoperu.com
Club Andino Peruano Av La Mar 725, Pueblo Libre, Casilla Postal 18-1357, Lima 18, club_andino@geocities.com
El Excursionismo en el Perú www.geocities.com/TheTropics/Shores/8717
Liga de Lima www.geocities.com/Yosemite/4166
Montañistas 4.0 www.geocities.com/Yosemite/7363
PeruAdventura clubs.yahoo.com/clubs/peruadventura

Cultural tourism

This covers more esoteric pursuits such as archaeology and mystical tourism. Several of the tour operators listed on page 13 offer customized packages for special interest groups. Local operators offering these more specialized tours are listed in the travelling text under the relevant location. Cultural tourism is a rapidly growing niche market. Under the umbrella heading *Al-Tur*, ***PromPerú*** has several interesting community-based tourism projects as a joint venture with the European Union. A list is available from ***PromPeru***'s website: www.peru.org.pe and go to Especiales, Promoperú Unión Europea.

Federico Kaufmann-Doig is a great source of information on Peruvian archaeology, for serious students and archaeologists. He has worked on various sites in Peru and is currently engaged on a three-year project in the Kuelap area. He is the director of the Instituto de Arqueología Amazónica, T449 0243, or (home) T449 9103. His book, *Historia del Perú: un nuevo perspectivo*, in two volumes (*Pre-Inca*, and *El Incario*) is available at better bookshops. The **Instituto Nacional de Cultura**, in the Museo de la Nación (see page 228), should be contacted by archaeologists for permits and information. The Museo Nacional de Antropología y Arquelogía in Pueblo Libre (see page 228) is the main centre for archaeological investigation and the Museo de la Nación holds exhibitions.

For more information, visit www.peruonline.net and go to the Cultura and Turismo sections, which give lots of information and links, including Turismo místico/religioso and Turismo histórico. Also try ***Arqueología del Perú*** (www.arqueologia.com.ar/peru/index.html). For specialized shamanic healing tours, contact ***K'uichy Light International***, Avenida Sol 814, oficina 219, Cusco, T/F084-221166, kuichy@amauta.edu.pe

Kayaking

Peru offers outstanding whitewater kayaking for all standards of paddlers form novice to expert. Many first descents remain unattempted due to logistical difficulties, though they are slowly being ticked off by a dedicated crew of local and internationally-renowned kayakers. For the holiday paddler, you are probably best joining up with a raft company who will gladly carry all your gear (plus any non-paddling companions) and provide you with superb food while you enjoy the river from an unladen kayak. There is a surprising selection of latest model kayaks available in Peru for hire from approximately US$10-20 a day.

For complete novices, some companies offer two-three day kayak courses on the Urubamba and Apurímac that can be booked locally. For expedition paddlers, bringing your own canoe is the best option though it is getting increasingly more expensive to fly with your boats around Peru. A knowledge of Spanish is virtually indispensable.

Mountain biking

With its amazing diversity of trails, tracks and rough roads, Peru is surely one of the last great mountain bike destinations yet to be fully discovered. Whether you are interested in a two-day downhill blast from the Andes to the Amazon Jungle or an extended off-road journey, then Peru has some of the world's best biking opportunities. The problem is finding the routes as trail maps are virtually non-existent and the few main roads (especially the Pan-American highway) are often congested with traffic and far from fun to travel along. Recently, however, a few specialist agencies run by dedicated mountain bikers have begun to explore the intricate web of paths, trails, single tracks and dirt roads that criss-cross the Andes, putting together exciting routes to suit everyone from the weekend warrior to the long-distance touring cyclist, the extreme downhiller to the casual day tripper.

Here are a few mouth-watering statistics to tempt: 80 km dirt road downhills, 40 km single tracks from 4,200 m to 2,800 m in under two hours, 550 km Trans Andean Challenges and as much hill climbing as you could ever wish for! And all just a matter of hours away from the main tourist towns of Peru.

If you are considering a dedicated cycling holiday, then you are best advised to bring your bike from home. It's pretty easy, just get a bike box from your local shop, deflate the tyres, take the pedals off and turn the handlebars. It is worth checking first that your airline is happy to take your bike. Some are, some will want to charge. Make sure your bike is in good condition before you depart as spares and repairs are hard to come by, especially the more complicated your bike (eg XT V-brake blocks are virtually impossible to find and rear suspension/disc brakes parts are totally unavailable). A tip from a Peruvian Mountain bike guide: bring plenty of inner tubes, brake blocks, chain lube and a quick release seat. Leave all panniers at home and rely on the support vehicle whenever you get tired, as there will be plenty more riding later.

If you are hiring a bike, be it for one-day or longer, basically you get what you pay for. For as little as US$5-10 a day you can get a cheap imitation of a mountain bike that will be fine on a paved road, but will almost certainly not stand up to the rigours of off-roading. For US$20 –25 you should be able to find something half-decent with front shocks, v-brakes, helmet and gloves. Bear in mind, there are not many high-quality, well maintained bikes available in Peru so you should check any hire bike thoroughly before riding it.

Where to ride Cusco is one of the main areas for biking. From a half-day downhill exploring the nearby ruins to the ultimate 550-km Andes to Amazon challenge, Cusco offers a multitude of varying rides to suit all abilities. Here is just a selection of the rides available. All ideally require a guide, as it's very easy to get lost in the Andes.

1 Cusco Ruins tour: Cheat by taking a taxi to Puca Pucara and enjoying a tarmac descent (if un-guided) via Tambo Machay, Kenko and Sacsayhuaman. Don't forget your ruins entrance tickets. Alternatively, with a guide, explore some of Cusco's less visited ruins on the mass of old Inca Trails and tracks open only for those in the know!

2 Chinchero - Moray – Maras - Las Salinas - Urubamba: Probably the best one-day trip in Peru, best done with a guide as it is easy to get lost. Largely downhill on a mix of dirt road and single track, this trip takes you to the interesting circular ruins of Moray and into the spectacular salt pans of Maras on an awesome mule track (watch out for mules!).

3 Huchuy Quosqo: For experts only, this unbelievable trip is best described as "trekking with your bike"! Various routes, again hard to find, followed by what must be one of the hairiest single tracks in the world along the top of and down into the Sacred Valley of the Incas. Totally radical!

4 Lares Valley: This offers some incredible down and uphill options on 2-3 day circuits including a relaxing soak in the beautiful Lares Hotsprings.

5 Abra de Málaga: From 4,200 m, an 80-km descent to the jungle, or alternatively a radical Inca Trail back to Ollantaytambo – both brilliant rides.

6 Tres Cruces to Manu: From Pisac to Manu is a 250 km, beautiful, dirt road ride offering big climbs and an even bigger (two-day) descent. A side trip to Tres Cruces to see the sunrise is a must if time permits. Be warned, the road to Manu only operates downhill every other day so be sure to check you've got it right or else beware of irate truck drivers not giving way on a very narrow road!

7 Cusco-Puerto Maldonado: Possibly the greatest "Trans-Andean Challenge" on a bike, 550 km of hard work from 3,200 m up to 4,700 m, then down to 130 m on one of the roughest roads out (with the odd full-on single track thrown in for good measure). Be prepared to get wet as there are a lot of river crossings, sometimes up to waist deep! Either a nine-day epic, or cheat on the hills and enjoy some of the biggest downhills out (3-4 days).

8 Cusco-Puno on Lake Titicaca (or vice-versa): Now almost totally paved, this is a strictly road ride, quite pretty but nothing spectacular (once you've seen a bit of Altiplano you've seen the Altiplano!).

9 Extreme Mule Biking: Not quite taking off yet, but in its planning stages, this radical sport (that will never be in the Olympics) involves trekking with your bike on a mule to the top of some really high passes and descending to inaccessible places on outrageous single tracks you probably wouldn't dream of doing at home! Experts only.

Choosing the right tour When signing up for a mountain bike trip, bear in mind you are in the Andes, so if you are worried about your fitness and the altitude, make sure you get a predominantly downhill trip. Check there is a support vehicle available throughout the entire trip, not just dropping you off and meeting you at the end. Check the guide is carrying a first aid kit, at very least a puncture repair kit (preferably a comprehensive tool kit) and is knowledgeable about bike mechanics. Bikes regularly go wrong, punctures are frequent and people do fall off, so it is essential your guide/company provides this minimum cover. On longer trips ask for detailed trip dossiers, describing the ups and downs and total distances of the routes, check how much is just dirt road (suitable for just about any one of reasonable fitness) and how much is single–track (often demanding considerable experience and fitness). Also it is good to know what support will be provided in the way of experienced bike guides, trained bike mechanics on hand, radio communications, spare bikes provided, cooking and dining facilities, toilet facilities etc.

Agencies in Cusco: In Cusco, there are various agencies around the Plaza de Armas offering 1-7 day bike hire with and without guides (see page 119). It is important to check out the bikes before hiring, as some are woefully badly maintained. If possible, talk to your guide to find out his knowledge of English/ bikes/ routes/ first aid etc.

Oveseas agencies: Several companies now offer specialist multi-day biking holidays to Peru for experienced bikers, as well as shorter multi-activity adventures that offer 2-3 days biking as part of a raft-hike-bike package. In the UK and USA, a very professional company called ***KE Adventure Travel*** offers a 20-day "off-road extravaganza" combining the best of Peru's single tracks, hill climbs and hotsprings with a chance to visit Machu Picchu. They also offer a multi-activity trip combining rafting, canoeing, mountain biking in the Sacred Valley of the Incas followed by trekking the Inca Trail to Machu Picchu.

Also from the UK, ***Discover Adventure*** offers a shorter "Best of Peru", 16-day mountain bike adventure around the Sacred Valley of the Incas. Once a year, Trailbreak Adventures organizes the "Trans-Andean Challenge", a full-on mountain bike ride from Cusco to Puerto Maldonado, which is possibly one the toughest rides anywhere in the World (see above). This ride is for those looking for a real challenge (it is certainly not a holiday!) High altitude climbs, monster descents, boulder strewn roads, outrageous single tracks, waist deep river crossings, mud, mud and more mud, followed by the most glorious 12 km of tarmac in the world!

Amazonas Explorer and ***Journey Latin America*** also offer a three-day mountain bike extension to their Apurímac rafting and Inca Trail trekking the trip. Largely downhill, bikes, gloves and suspension mountain bikes are provided for this moderately strenuous trip that includes a mix of dirt road and single track options to suit all riding styles, plus a night in the Lares hotsprings. *Amazonas Explorer* are also the pioneers of "Mule-Biking". Contact them via their website for details of their exploratory biking adventures, only for the serious off-roader.

KE Adventure Travel, 32 Lake Road, Keswick, Cumbria, CA12 5DQ, UK, T017687-73966, www.keadventure.com Members of ABTA, AITO and ATOL licensed. In USA, ***KE Adventure Travel***, 1131 Grand Avenue, Glenwood Springs, CO 81601, T1-800-497 9675 (toll free), www.keadventure.com ***Discover Adventure***, 5 Netherhampton Cottage, Netherhampton, Salisbury, Wiltshire, SP2 8PX, UK, T01722-741123, www.discoveradventure.com ***Journey Latin America*** (see **Tour operators**, page 16). ***Trailbreak Adventures***, 241 Whitley Wood Road, Reading, Berkshire, RG2 8LD, UK, T0118-986 0652, www.trailbreak.co.uk ***Amazonas Explorer*** (see **Rafting**, page 57).

Parapenting and hang-gliding

'Vuelo Libre' is just taking off in Peru. The area with the greatest potential is the Sacred Valley of Cusco which has excellent launch sites, thermals and reasonable landing sites. 45 km from Cusco is Cerro Sacro (3,797 m) on the Pampa de Chincheros with 550 m clearance at take-off. It is the launch site for cross-country flights over the Sacred Valley, Sacsayhuaman and Cusco. Particularly good for parapenting is the Mirador de Urubamba, 38 km from Cusco, at 3,650 m, with 800 m clearance and views over Pisac.

The season in the Sierra is May to October, with the best months being August and September. Some flights in Peru have exceeded 6,500 m.,

Rafting

Peru is rapidly becoming one of the world's premier destinations for whitewater rafting. Several of their rivers are rated in the world's top 10 and a rafting trip, be it for one or 10 days, is now high on any adventurer's "must-do" list of activities while travelling in Peru. It is not just the adrenaline rush of big rapids that attract, it is the whole experience of accessing areas beyond the reach of motor vehicles, whether tackling sheer-sided, mile-deep canyons, travelling silently through pristine rainforest, or canoeing across the stark Altiplano, high in the Andes.

Rafting in Peru is undoubtedly excellent. The country has the world's deepest canyon (the Cotahuasi in Southern Peru), the source of the world's greatest river (the Apurímac is the true source of the Amazon), rivers that flow through the world's most biologically diverse region (the Amazon basin) with the world's highest bird count as well as the world's largest macaw lick (the Río Tambopata and Río Madre de Dios) and the world's highest concentration of condors (the Río Colca). Unfortunately for avid rafters, not all of the above fall within the scope of this book; Footprint's *Peru Handbook* can supply the rest of the details.

But before you leap in the first raft that floats by, a word of warning and a bit of advice will help you ensure that your rafting 'trip of a lifetime' really is as safe, as environmentally friendly and as fun as you want it to be.

Basically, the very remoteness and amazing locations that make Peruvian whitewater rivers so attractive mean that dealing with an emergency (should it occur) can be difficult, if nigh on impossible. As the sport of rafting has increased in popularity over the last few years, so too have the number of accidents (including fatalities), yet the rafting industry remains virtually unchecked. How then, do you ensure your safety on what are undoubtedly some of the best whitewater runs anywhere in South America if not the whole world?

If you are keen on your rafting and are looking to join a rafting expedition of some length, then it is definitely worth signing up in advance before you set foot in Peru. Some of the rivers mentioned below will have fewer than two or three scheduled departures a year and the companies that offer them only accept bookings well in advance as they are logistically extremely difficult to organize. If it is just a day trip, or possibly an overnighter, then you can just turn up a few days in advance and chances are there will be space on a trip departing shortly.

Choosing an operator

It is hoped that by 2002 the Peruvian government will have put in place new regulations governing rafting operators and their river guides. If this does come into legislation, it will mean a major shake up for the companies. The new regulations demand that Class IV+ guides hold the internationally recognized qualifications of Swift Water Rescue Technician and hold current first aid certificates. All rafting equipment will be checked regularly to ensure it meets basic safety standards, eg life jackets that actually float etc. At present there are just two or three guides who meet these qualifications (and Paul Cripps, author of this section, is one of them). Moreover, equipment standards in some of the companies are woefully low so how exactly the new legislation will work will be interesting. Cripps' personal feeling is that, as with the Inca Trail regulations, it will make little or no difference.

Safety At present (and probably in the foreseeable future), as with many of Peru's adventure options, it simply boils down to 'You get what you pay for' and, at the end of the day, it's your life. Rafting is an inherently dangerous sport and doing it in Peru with the wrong operator can quite seriously be endangering your life. If price is all that matters bear in mind the following comments: the cheaper the price, the less you get, be it with safety cover, experience of guides, quality of equipment, quantity of food, emergency back up and environmental awareness.

Often on trips you will be required to sign a disclaimer and show proof that your travel insurance will cover you for whitewater rafting. If you are unsure about it, and are planning to go rafting, it is worth checking with your insurance company before you leave, as some policies have an additional charge. When signing up you should ask about the experience of the guides or even, if possible, meet them. At present there is no exam or qualification required to become a river guide, but certain things are essential of your guide. Firstly find out his command of English (or whatever language – there are a few German speaking guides available), essential if you are going to understand his commands. Find out his experience. How many times has he done this particular stretch of river? Many Peruvian guides have worked overseas in the off-season, from Chile to Costa Rica, Europe and New Zealand. The more international experience your guide has, the more aware he will be of international safety practices. All guides should have some experience in rescue techniques. While most guides own a rescue knife, some pulleys and a few slings, do they really know how to extract a raft safely from a rock, or a swimmer from dangerous location? All guides must have knowledge of First Aid. Ask when they last took a course and what level they are at.

Above all it is your safety on the river that is important. Some companies are now offering safety kayaks as standard as well as safety catarafts on certain rivers. This is definitely a step in the right direction but one that is open to misuse. Sometimes safety kayakers have little or no experience of what they are required to do and are merely along for the ride, sometimes they are asked to shoot video (rendering the safety cover useless). A safety cataraft is a powerful tool in the right hands, but weigh it down with equipment and it is of little use. All companies should carry at the very least a 'wrap kit' consisting of static ropes, carabiners, slings and pulleys should a raft unfortunately get stuck. But more importantly, do the guides know how to use it?

Equipment Good equipment is essential for your safe enjoyment of your trip. If possible ask to see some of the gear provided. Basic essentials include self-bailing rafts for all but the calmest of rivers. Check how old your raft is and where it was made. Paddles should be of plastic and metal construction (locally made wooden ones have been known to snap regularly and give nasty blisters). Helmets should always be provided and fit correctly (again, home-made fibreglass copies are an accident waiting to happen). Life jackets must be of a lifeguard-recognized quality and be replaced regularly as they have a tendency to lose their flotation. Locally made jackets look the business, but in fact are very poor floaters. Does your company provide wetsuits (some of the rivers are surprisingly cold), or, at the very least, quality Splash jackets, as the wind can cause you to chill rapidly? On the longer trips, dry bags are provided – what state are these in? How old are they? Do they leak? There is nothing worse than a soggy sleeping bag at the end of a day's rafting. Are tents provided? And most importantly (for the jungle) do the zips on the mosquito net work and is it rain proof? Do the company provide mosquito netting dining tents? Tables? Chairs? These apparent excesses are very nice when camping for some time at the bottom of a sandfly infested canyon!

Back onto First Aid: ask to see the First Aid kit and find out what is in there and, most importantly, do they know how to use it? When was it last checked? Updated? Pretty basic stuff, but if someone used all the lomotil you could come unstuck.

Food and hygiene After a tough day on the river, the last thing you want to do is get sick from the food. Good, wholesome food is relatively cheap in Peru and can make all the difference on a long trip. Once again, you pay for what you get. Ask if there's a vegetarian option. On the food preparation, simple precautions will help you stay healthy but seem to be ignored by many companies. Are all vegetables soaked in iodine before serving? Do the cooks wash their hands and is there soap available for the clients? Are the plates, pots and cutlery washed in iodine or simply swilled in the river? (Stop and think how many villages up stream use that river as their main sewage outlet.) All simple ways to avoid getting sick.

Toilet routine Sadly, on the Apurímac, on certain beaches, a completely uncaring attitude by many of the companies has left a string of pink toilet paper and quantities of human excrement. Certain companies are now providing septic toilets and/or removing all excrement. This is the way forward and will, it is hoped, become legislation soon. At the very least your company should provide a lighter for burning the paper and a trowel to go dig a hole. Simple rules to follow are always shit below the high-water mark so at least in the rainy season it will wash clean, always bury it good and deep and watch out when burning the paper so as not to start a fire.

Rubbish and general environmental awareness If your company does not, make it your responsibility to encourage other members of the group to keep the campsites clean. One nationality is infamous for their lack of care. Some campsites are becoming rubbish tips. Surely all waste brought in can just as easily be taken out, save perhaps the organic waste that should be disposed of in a suitably inconspicuous way. When camping, is a campfire really necessary? On some rivers, due to rafting companies, the drift wood supplies are critically low, forcing even the locals to cut down trees. This is an environmental disaster waiting to happen. Is it really necessary for companies to cook using wood when gas or kerosene is so readily available?

So if all this doom and gloom has not put you off, you are now equipped to go out there and find the company that offers what you are looking for at a price you think is reasonable. Bear in mind a day's rafting in the USA can cost between US$75-120 for a basic one-day. In Peru you might get the same for just US$25 but ask yourself "What am I getting for so little". After all, rafts and equipment cost the same, in fact more, in Peru. As we said before, it's your life.

Amazonas Explorer SA can be contacted in Peru at PO Box 722, Cusco, Peru, T/F+51-84-227137, M+51-84-653366, info@amazonas-explorer.com, www.amazonas-explorer.com In the UK, Riverside, Black Tar, Llangwm, Haverfordwest, Pembs, Wales, SA 62 4JD, T/F01437-891743.

Rivers

The Cusco region is probably the 'rafting capital' of Peru, with more whitewater runs on offer than anywhere else in Peru.

The Urubamba is perhaps the most popular day run in the whole country.

Huambutio – Pisac (all year availability, Grade II): a scenic half-day float with a few rapids to get the adrenaline flowing right through the heart of the Sacred Valley of the Incas. Fits in perfectly with a day trip to Pisac Market. A sedate introduction to rafting for all ages.

Ollantaytambo – Chilca (all year availability, Grade III+): a fun half-day introduction to the exciting sport of whitewater rafting with a few challenging rapids and beautiful scenery near the Inca 'fortress' of Ollantaytambo. This trip also fits in perfectly with the start of the Inca Trail. Try to go early in the morning as a strong wind picks up in the late morning.

Huaran Canyon (all year, Grade III-IV +): a short section of fun whitewater that is occasionally rafted and used as site of the Peruvian National Whitewater Championships for kayaking and rafting.

Santa María to Quillabamba (May – December, Grade III-IV): a rarely-rafted two-day, high jungle trip. A long way to go for some fairly good whitewater but mediocre jungle.

Chuquicahuana (December-April, Grade IV-V): a technically demanding one-day trip for genuine adrenaline junkies, only available in the rainy season.

Kiteni-Pongo Manaiqui – the bit made famous by Michael Palin: an interesting jungle gorge, but logistically hard to reach and technically pretty average except in the rainy season.

The Río Apurímac is technically the true source of the Amazon. It cuts a 2,000-m deep gorge through incredible desert scenery and offers probably some of the finest whitewater rafting sections on the planet.

Puente Hualpachaca – Puente Cunyac (May-November, Grade IV-V): three (better in four) days of non-stop whitewater adventure through an awesome gorge just five hours drive from Cusco. Probably the most popular multi-day trip, this is one definitely to book with the experts as there have been fatalities on this stretch. Owing to the amount of people rafting this river, some of the campsites are getting overused and dirty, but the whitewater is superb with rapids with names like *U-first*, *Tooth ache* and *Last laugh* – an adventure worth doing.

Canoeing the Source: high up in the Andes at the very start of the mighty Amazon river is a beautiful section that is brilliant for trying the fun new sport of "Duckies", or inflatable kayaking. Three days of awesome scenery, Inca ruins and much more. Contact *Amazonas Explorer* for more information.

The Abyss: below Puente Cunyac is a section of rarely-run whitewater. This extreme expedition involves days of carrying rafts around treacherous rapids – a total expedition that seldom gets done.

Choquequirao: another rarely-run section, this 10-day adventure involves a walk in with mules, a chance to visit the amazing ruins of Choquequirao and raft huge rapids in an imposing sheer-sided canyon all the way to the jungle basin. Definitely only for the experts.

The Tambopata offers wilderness, wildlife and whitewater (June-October, Grade III-IV). Although not strictly in the Cusco region, most expeditions either start or end in Cusco. The Tambopata is probably the ultimate jungle adventure for those looking to get away from the standard organized jungle package. Starting with a drive from the shores of Lake Titicaca to virtually the end of the road, the Tambopata travels through the very heart of the Tambopata-Candamo national reserve, which boasts over 1,200 species of butterfly, 800 species of birdlife and many rare mammals including, jaguar, giant otter, tapir, capybara and tayra. Four days of increasingly fun whitewater followed by two days of gently meandering through virgin tropical rainforest where silent rafts make perfect wildlife watching platforms. Finally a visit to the world's largest macaw clay lick and a short flight out from Puerto Maldonado, this once again rarely-rafted river was the subject of a BBC documentary in 1998. Definitely book in advance with the experts as this is a total expedition through one of the remotest places in all South America.

Health

For anyone travelling overseas health is a key consideration. With the following advice and sensible precautions the visitor to Peru should remain as healthy as at home. Most visitors return home having experienced no problems at all apart from some travellers' diarrhoea.

There are English (or other foreign language) speaking doctors in Cusco and Lima who have particular experience in dealing with locally-occurring diseases, but don't expect good facilities away from the major centres. Your Embassy representative will often be able to give you the name of local reputable doctors and most of the better hotels have a doctor on standby. If you do fall ill and cannot find a recommended doctor, try the Outpatient Department of a hospital – private hospitals are usually less crowded and offer a more acceptable standard of care to foreigners.

Before travelling take out medical insurance. Make sure it covers all eventualities especially evacuation to your home country by a medically equipped plane, if necessary. You should have a dental check up, obtain a spare glasses prescription, a spare oral contraceptive prescription (or enough pills to last) and, if you suffer from a chronic illness (such as diabetes, high blood pressure, ear or sinus troubles, cardio-pulmonary disease or nervous disorder) arrange for a check up with your doctor, who can at the same time provide you with a letter explaining the details of your disability in English and if possible Spanish. Check the current practice in countries you are visiting for malaria prophylaxis (prevention). If you are on regular medication, make sure you have enough to cover the period of your travel.

There is very little control on the sale of drugs and medicines in Peru. You can buy any and every drug in pharmacies without a prescription. Be wary of this because pharmacists can be poorly trained and might sell you drugs that are unsuitable, dangerous or old. Many drugs and medicines are manufactured under licence from American or European companies, so the trade names may be familiar to you. This means you do not have to carry a whole chest of medicines with you, but remember that the shelf life of some items, especially vaccines and antibiotics, is markedly reduced in hot conditions.

Buy your supplies at the better outlets where there are refrigerators, even though they are more expensive and check the expiry date of all preparations you buy. Immigration officials occasionally confiscate scheduled drugs (Lomotil is an example) if they are not accompanied by a doctor's prescription.

Vaccinations

Smallpox vaccination is no longer required anywhere in the world. Neither is cholera vaccination recognized as necessary for international travel by the World Health Organization – it is not very effective either. Nevertheless, some immigration officials are demanding proof of vaccination against cholera following the outbreak of the disease which originated in Peru in 1990-91 and subsequently affected most surrounding countries. Although very unlikely to affect visitors, the cholera epidemic continues making its greatest impact in poor areas where water supplies are polluted and food hygiene practices are insanitary.

Vaccination against the following diseases are recommended:

Yellow Fever This is a live vaccination not to be given to children under nine months of age or persons allergic to eggs. Immunity lasts for 10 years, an International Certificate of Yellow Fever Vaccination will be given and should be kept because it is sometimes asked for. Yellow fever is very rare in Peru, but the vaccination is practically without side effects and almost totally protective.

Typhoid A disease spread by the insanitary preparation of food. A number of new vaccines against this condition are now available; the older TAB and monovalent typhoid vaccines are being phased out. The newer, eg Typhim Vi, cause less side effects, but are more expensive. For those who do not like injections, there are now oral vaccines.

Poliomyelitis Despite its decline in the world this remains a serious disease if caught and is easy to protect against. There are live oral vaccines and in some countries injected vaccines. Whichever one you choose it is a good idea to have booster every 10 years if visiting developing countries regularly.

Tetanus One dose should be given with a booster at six weeks and another at six months and 10 yearly boosters thereafter are recommended. Children should already be properly protected against diphtheria, poliomyelitis and pertussis (whooping cough), measles and HIB all of which can be more serious infections in Peru than at home. Measles, mumps and rubella vaccine is also given to children throughout the world, but those teenage girls who have not had rubella (german measles) should be tested and vaccinated. Hepatitis B vaccination for babies is now routine in some countries. Consult your doctor for advice on tuberculosis inoculation: the disease is still widespread in Peru.

Infectious Hepatitis Is less of a problem for travellers than it used to be because of the development of two extremely effective vaccines against the A and B form of the disease. It remains common, however, in Peru. A combined hepatitis A & B vaccine is now available – one jab covers both diseases.

Other vaccinations Might be considered in the case of epidemics eg meningitis. There is an effective vaccination against rabies which should be considered by all travellers, especially those going through remote areas or if there is a particular occupational risk, eg for zoologists, veterinarians, research students working in remote or jungle regions.

Further information Further information on health risks abroad, vaccinations etc will be available from a local travel clinic and your local doctor. If you wish to take specific drugs with you such as antibiotics these are best prescribed by your own doctor. Beware, however, that not all doctors can be experts on the health problems of remote countries. More detailed or more up-to-date information than local doctors can provide are available from various sources.

In the UK there are hospital departments specializing in tropical diseases in London, Liverpool, Birmingham and Glasgow and the Malaria Reference Laboratory at the London School of Hygiene and Tropical Medicine provides advice about malaria, T09065-508908 (US$1.50 per minute). British Airways Travel Clinics can also be contacted: www.british-airways.com/travelga/fyi/health/health.shtml In the USA the local Public Health Services can give such information and information is available centrally from the Centres for Disease Control (CDC), 1600 Clifton Road, Atlanta, GA30333, T404-639 3534, www.cdc.gov In Canada contact IAMAT (International Association for Medical Assistance to Travelers), 40 Regal Road, Guelph, Ontario N1K 1B5, T519-836 0102, with offices in Toronto, New York, Christchurch NZ, and Switzerland, www.sentex.net/~iamat/

There are in addition computerized databases which can be accessed for destination-specific, up-to-the-minute information. In the UK there is MASTA (Medical Advisory Service to Travellers Abroad), Keppel St, London WC1E 7HT, T0906-822 4100, www.masta.org And Travax, in Glasgow, www.fitfortravel.scot.nhs.uk Other information on medical problems overseas can be obtained from the book by Dr Richard Dawood (Editor) – *Travellers' Health, How to Stay Healthy Abroad* (Oxford University Press 1992 £7.99). We strongly recommend this revised and updated edition, especially to the intrepid traveller heading for the more out of the way places. General advice is also available in the UK in Health Information for Overseas Travel (Department of Health), available from HMSO and International Travel and Health (WHO – www.who.ch/). Handbooks on First Aid are produced by the British and American Red Cross and by St John's Ambulance (UK).

Staying healthy

Intestinal upsets The commonest affliction of visitors to Peru is probably traveller's diarrhoea. Diarrhoea and vomiting is due, most of the time, to food poisoning, usually passed on by the insanitary habits of food handlers. As a general rule the cleaner your surroundings and the smarter the restaurant, the less likely you are to suffer.

Foods to avoid Uncooked, undercooked, partially cooked or reheated meat, fish, eggs, raw vegetables and salads, especially when they have been left out exposed to flies. Stick to fresh food that has been cooked from raw just before eating and make sure you peel fruit yourself. Avoid raw food, undercooked food (including eggs) and reheated food. Food that is cooked in front of you and offered hot all through is generally safe. Wash and dry your hands before eating – disposable wet-wipe tissues are useful for this. Shellfish are always a risk eaten raw (as in *ceviche*) and at certain times of the year some fish and shellfish concentrate toxins from their environment and cause various kinds of food poisoning. The local authorities notify the public not to eat these foods. Do not ignore the warning.

Tap water in Peru is unsafe to drink. Filtered or bottled water is usually available and safe, although you must make sure that somebody is not filling bottles from the tap and hammering on a new crown cap. Ice for drinks should be made from boiled water, but rarely is so stand your glass on the ice cubes, rather than putting them in the drink. The better hotels have water purifying systems. Stream water, if you are in the countryside, is often contaminated by communities living surprisingly high in the mountains.

Travellers' diarrhoea

This is usually caused by eating food which has been contaminated by germs through hands or flies, or wather contaminated by human faeces. Some infections come directly from animals and are caught from eating undercooked eggs or meat. Sea water or river water is more likely to be contaminated by sewage and so swimming in such dilute effluent can also be a cause.

Infection with various organisms can give rise to travellers' diarrhoea. They may be viruses, bacteria, eg Escherichia coli (probably the most common cause worldwide), protozoal (such as amoebas and giardia), salmonella and cholera. Other infections common in undercooked meat are cysticercosis, trichinella and tape worms. The diarrhoea may come on suddenly or rather slowly. It may or may not be accompanied by vomiting or by severe abdominal pain and the passage of blood or mucus when it is called dysentery.

How do you know which type you have caught and how to treat it? If you can time the onset of the diarrhoea to the minute ('acute') then it is probably due to a virus or a bacterium and/or the onset of dysentery. The treatment in addition to rehydration is Ciprofloxacin 500 mg every 12 hours; the drug is now widely available and there are many similar ones. One day's treatment with Ciprofloxacin is as good as five.

If the diarrhoea comes on slowly or intermittently ('sub-acute') then it is more likely to be protozoal, ie caused by an amoeba or giardia. Antibiotics such a Ciprofloxacin will have little effect. These cases are best treated by a doctor as is any outbreak of diarrhoea continuing for more than three days. Sometimes blood is passed in ameobic dysentery and for this you should certainly seek medical help. If this is not available then the best treatment is probably Tinidazole (Fasigyn) one tablet four times a day for three days. If there are severe stomach cramps, the following drugs may help but are not very useful in the management of acute diarrhoea: Loperamide (Imodium) and Diphenoxylate with Atropine (Lomotil) They should not be given to children.

Any kind of diarrhoea, whether or not accompanied by vomiting, responds well to the replacement of water and salts, taken as frequent small sips, of some kind of rehydration solution. There are proprietary preparations consisting of sachets of powder which you dissolve in boiled water or you can make your own by adding half a teaspoonful of salt (3.5 g) and four tablespoonsful of sugar (40 g) to a litre of boiled water. If you have had attacks of diarrhoea it is worth having a stool specimen tested when you return home, in case you have picked up amoebas.

Paradoxically **constipation** is also common, probably induced by dietary change, inadequate fluid intake in hot places and long bus journeys. Simple laxatives are useful in the short-term and bulky foods such as maize, beans and plenty of fruit and vegetables are also useful.

Altitude sickness

Travelling to high altitudes can cause medical problems, all of which can be prevented if care is taken. On reaching heights above about 3,000 m, heart pounding and shortness of breath, especially on exertion are a normal response to the lack of oxygen in the air. A condition called acute mountain sickness (*Soroche*) can also affect visitors. It is more likely to affect those who ascend rapidly, eg by plane and those who over-exert themselves (teenagers for example). Soroche takes a few hours or days to come on and presents with a bad headache, extreme tiredness, sometimes dizziness, loss of appetite and frequently nausea and vomiting.

Insomnia is common and is often associated with a suffocating feeling when lying in bed. Keen observers may note their breathing tends to wax and wane at night and their face tends to be puffy in the mornings – this is all part of the syndrome. Altitude sickness will also affect bad teeth (eg poorly done root canal work).

The treatment of acute mountain sickness is simple – rest, painkillers, (preferably not aspirin based) for the headache and anti sickness pills for vomiting. Oxygen is actually not much help, except at very high altitude. Various local panaceas – Coramina glucosada, Effortil, Micoren are popular and mate de coca (an infusion of coca leaves widely available and perfectly legal) will alleviate some of the symptoms.

To **prevent** the condition: on arrival at places over 3,000 m have a few hours rest in a chair and avoid alcohol, cigarettes and heavy food. If the symptoms are severe and prolonged, it is best to descend to a lower altitude and to reascend slowly or in stages. If this is impossible because of shortage of time or if you are going so high that acute mountain sickness is very likely, then the drug Acetazolamide (Diamox) can be used as a preventative and continued during the ascent. There is good evidence of the value of this drug in the prevention of soroche, but some people do experience peculiar side effects. It is also worth noting that it is a diuretic.The usual dose is 500 mg of the slow release preparation each night, starting the night before ascending above 3,000 m.

A more unusual condition can affect mountaineers who ascend rapidly to high altitude – **acute pulmonary oedema**. Residents at altitude sometimes experience this when returning to the mountains from time spent at the coast. This condition is often preceded by acute mountain sickness and comes on quite rapidly with severe breathlessness, noisy breathing, coughing, blueness of the lips and frothing at the mouth. Anybody who develops this must be brought down as soon as possible, given oxygen and taken to hospital.

Insects

These are mostly more of a nuisance than a serious hazard and if you try, you can prevent yourself entirely from being bitten. Some, such as mosquitos are, of course, carriers of potentially serious diseases, so it is sensible to avoid being bitten as much as possible.

Sleep off the ground and use a mosquito net or some kind of insecticide. Preparations containing Pyrethrum or synthetic pyrethroids are safe. They are available as aerosols or pumps and the best way to use these is to spray the room thoroughly in all areas (follow the instructions rather than the insects) and then shut the door for a while, re-entering when the smell has dispersed. Mosquito coils release insecticide as they burn slowly. They are widely available and useful out of doors. Tablets of insecticide which are placed on a heated mat plugged into a wall socket are probably the most effective. They fill the room with insecticidal fumes in the same way as aerosols or coils.

You can also use insect repellents, most of which are effective against a wide range of pests. The most common and effective is diethyl metatoluamide (DEET). DEET liquid is best for arms and face (care around eyes and with spectacles – DEET dissolves plastic). Aerosol spray is good for clothes and ankles and liquid DEET can be dissolved in water and used to impregnate cotton clothes and mosquito nets. Some repellents now contain DEET and Permethrin, insecticide. Impregnated wrist and ankle bands can also be useful.

If you are bitten or stung, itching may be relieved by cool baths, antihistamine tablets (care with alcohol or driving) or mild corticosteroid creams, eg. hydrocortisone (but take great care: never use if there's any hint of infection). Careful scratching of all your bites once a day can be surprisingly effective. Calamine lotion and cream have limited effectiveness and antihistamine creams are not recommended – they can cause allergies themselves.

Ticks attach themselves usually to the lower parts of the body often after walking in areas where cattle have grazed. They take a while to attach themselves strongly, but swell up as they start to suck blood. The important thing is to remove them gently, so that they do not leave their head parts in your skin because this can cause a nasty allergic reaction some days later. Do not use petrol, vaseline, lighted cigarettes etc to remove the tick, but, with a pair of tweezers remove the beast gently by gripping it at the attached (head) end and rock it out in very much the same way that a tooth is extracted.

Certain tropical flies which lay their eggs under the skin of sheep and cattle also occasionally do the same thing to humans with the unpleasant result that a maggot grows under the skin and pops up as a boil or pimple. The best way to remove these is to cover the boil with oil, vaseline or nail varnish so as to stop the maggot breathing, then to squeeze it out gently the next day. Various other tropical diseases can be caught in jungle areas, usually transmitted by biting insects. Wearing long trousers and a long sleeved shirt in infected areas protects against these flies. DEET is also effective.

Sunburn

The burning power of the tropical sun, especially at high altitude, is phenomenal. Always wear a wide brimmed hat and use some form of suncream lotion on untanned skin. Normal temperate zone suntan lotions (protection factor up to seven) are not much good; you need to use the types designed specifically for the tropics or for mountaineers or skiers with protection factors up to 15 or above. These are often not available in Peru. Glare from the sun can cause conjunctivitis, so wear sunglasses especially on tropical beaches, where high protection factor sunscreen should also be used.

AIDS

AIDS (*SIDA*) is increasing but is not wholly confined to the well known high risk sections of the population, ie homosexual men, intravenous drug abusers and children of infected mothers. Heterosexual transmission is now the dominant mode and so the main risk to travellers is from casual sex. The same precautions should be taken as with any sexually transmitted disease.

The HIV virus that causes AIDS can be passed by unsterilized needles which have been previously used to inject an HIV positive patient, but the risk of this is negligible. It would, however, be sensible to check that needles have been properly sterilized or disposable needles have been used. If you wish to take your own disposable needles, be prepared to explain what they are for. The risk of receiving a blood transfusion with blood infected with HIV is greater than from dirty needles because of the amount of fluid exchanged. Supplies of blood for transfusion should now be screened for HIV in all reputable hospitals, so again the risk is very small indeed.

Malaria

In Peru malaria is theoretically confined to jungle zones, but is now on the increase again. Mosquitos do not thrive above 2,500 m, so you are safe at altitude. There are different varieties of malaria, some resistant to the normal drugs. Make local enquiries if you intend to visit possibly infected zones and use a prophylactic regime.

Start taking the tablets a few days before exposure and continue to take them for six weeks after leaving the malarial zone. Remember to give the drugs to babies and children also. Opinion varies on the precise drugs and dosage to be used for protection. All the drugs may have some side effects and it is important to balance the risk of catching the disease against the albeit rare side effects.

The increasing complexity of the subject is such that as the malarial parasite becomes immune to the new generation of drugs it has made concentration on the physical prevention from being bitten by mosquitos more important. This involves the use of long sleeved shirts or blouses and long trousers, repellants and nets. Clothes are now available impregnated with the insecticide Permethrin or Deltamethrin or it is possible to impregnate the clothes yourself. Wide meshed nets impregnated with Permethrin are also available, are lighter to carry and less claustrophobic to sleep in.

Prophylaxis and treatment If your itinerary takes you into a malarial area, seek expert advice before you go on a suitable prophylactic regime. This is especially true for pregnant women who are particularly prone to catch malaria. You can still catch the disease even when sticking to a proper regime, although it is unlikely. If you do develop symptoms (high fever, shivering, headache, sometimes diarrhoea), seek medical advice immediately. If this is not possible and there is a great likelihood of vivax malaria, the treatment is: Chloroquine, a single dose of four tablets (600 mg) followed by two tablets (300 mg) in six hours and 300 mg each day following. Remember to take your antimalarial tablets for six weeks after leaving the malarial area.

If it is likely to be falciparum malaria, take local advice. If falciparum type malaria is definitely diagnosed, it is wise to get to a good hospital as treatment can be complex and the illness very serious.

Dengue fever This is increasing worldwide including in South American countries. It can be completely prevented by avoiding mosquito bites in the same way as malaria. However, the mosquitoes that transmit dengue are generally day-biters so are not so easy to avoid as the night-biters that transmit malaria. No vaccine is available. Dengue is an unpleasant and painful disease. Symptoms are a high temperature and body pains and a red rash, but at least visitors are spared the more serious forms which are more of a problem for local people who have been exposed to the disease more than once. There is no specific treatment for dengue – just pain killers, plenty to drink and rest.

Rabies Remember that rabies is endemic throughout Latin America, so avoid dogs that are behaving strangely and cover your toes at night from the vampire bats, which also carry the disease. If you are bitten by a domestic or wild animal, do not leave things to chance: scrub the wound with soap and water and/or disinfectant, try to have the animal captured (within limits) or at least determine its ownership, where possible, and seek medical assistance at once. The course of treatment depends on whether you have already been satisfactorily vaccinated against rabies. If you have (this is worthwhile if you are spending lengths of time in developing countries) then some further doses of vaccine are all that is required. Human diploid vaccine is the best, but expensive: other, older kinds of vaccine, such as that derived from duck embryos may be the only types available. These are effective, much cheaper and interchangeable generally with the human derived types. If not already vaccinated then anti rabies serum (immunoglobulin) may be required in addition. It is important to finish the course of treatment whether the animal survives or not.

Further reading and useful websites

History & culture For the whole period of the Conquest John Hemming's *The Conquest of the Incas* is invaluable; he himself refers us to Ann Kendall's *Everyday Life of the Incas*, Batsford, London, 1978. Also *Oro y tragedia de los Incas* by Manuel Portal Cabellos, excellent on the division of the empire, civil war, the conquest and *huaqueros*. Other recommended books on Peru's history and culture are: *The Ancient Civilizations of Peru*, J Alden Mason, (1991); *The Prehispanic Cultures of Peru*, Justo Cáceres Macedo (1988); *The Incas and their Ancestors: The Archaeology of Peru*, Michael E Mosely; *Peruvian Prehistory. An overview of pre-Inca and Inca Society*, edited by Richard W Keatinge (1988); *Chachapoyas; The Cloud People*, Morgan Davis (1988); *Warriors of the Clouds: A Lost Civilization in the Upper* Amazon, Keith Muscutt; *Pyramids of Túcume*, Thor Heyerdahl, Daniel H Sandweiss & Alfredo Narváez (Thames & Hudson, 1995); *The City of Kings: A guide to Lima*, Carolyn Walton (1987); *Lima monumental*, Margarita Cubillas Soriano (1993). A very readable account of the last decade of the 20th century is *The Fujimori File. Peru and its President 1990-2000*, by Sally Bowen (2000; it ends at the election of that year so the final momentous events of Fujimori's term happened after publication).

Literature

A detailed account of Peruvian literature and its finest writers is given in the **Literature** section on page 262. The following novels are also recommended: *The Bridge of San Luis Rey*, Thornton Wilder (Penguin books, 1941); *At Play in the Fields of the Lord*, Peter Matthiessen (1965); *The Vision of Elena Silves*, Nicholas Shakespeare (1989). Three good travel books are: *Cut Stones and Crossroads: a Journey in Peru*, Ronald Wright (Viking, 1984); *Inca-Kola*, Matthew Parris (1990); and *Eight Feet in the Andes*, Dervla Murphy (1994).

General travel & advice

A very useful book, highly recommended, aimed specifically at the budget traveller is *The Tropical Traveller*, by John Hatt (Penguin Books, 3rd edition, 1993). Ask for the free and helpful *Peru Guide* published in English by Lima Editora (T444 0815, info@limaeditora.com), available at travel agencies or other tourist organizations.

Maps

It is a good idea to get as many as possible in your home country before leaving, especially if travelling by land. A recommended series of general maps is that published by ***International Travel Map Productions*** (ITM), 345 West Broadway, Vancouver BC, V5Y 1P8, Canada, T604-879 3621, F604-879 4521, compiled with historical notes, by the late Kevin Healey. Relevant to this Handbook are South America North West (1:4M) and Amazon Basin (1:4M). Another map series that has been mentioned is that of New World Edition, Bertelsmann, Neumarkter Strasse 18, 81673 München, Germany, *Südamerika Nord, Südamerika Sud* (both 1:4M).

Good maps of the Lima area and the whole country are available from street sellers in the centre of Lima, or in better bookshops (published by ***Lima 2000,*** Av Arequipa 2625, Lima 14, T440 3486, F440 3480, US$10, or US$14 in booklet form). Other maps can be bought from street vendors on Colmena and in the Plaza San Martín, Lima. 'Westermanns Monatshefte; folio Ecuador, Peru, Bolivien has excellent maps of Peru, especially the archaeological sites. A cheaper, less accurate, and less discreet map is published by ***Cartográfica Nacional*** for US$3-4. The ***Instituto Geográfico Nacional***, Avenida Aramburú 1190, Surquillo, T475 9960, F465 3085, Lima, sells a selection of good, accurate country and regional maps. The office is open Monday-Friday 0830-1730. They have topographical maps of the whole country, mostly at 1:100,000, political and physical maps of all departments and satellite and aerial photographs. They also have a new series of tourist maps for trekking, including of the Cusco area, at 1:250,000. **Ingemmet** (Instituto Geológico Minero Y Metalúrgico), Avenida Canadá 1470, San Borja, T225 3128. Open Monday-Friday 0800-1300, 1400-1600. Sells a huge selection of geographic maps ranging from US$12 to US$112. Also satellite, aeromagnetic, geochemical and departmental mining maps. Enquire about new digital products. Aerial photographs are available at **Servicio Aerofotográfico Nacional**, Las Palmas Airforce Base, open Mon-Fri 0800-1400. Photos from mid-1950's aerial survey available, but they are expensive. Expect a waiting period as short as one day or as long as two weeks. ***South American Explorers*** stock an excellent collection of country, regional and topographical maps. Maps of the city of Cusco, the Inca Trail and the Urubamba Valley are available at tour companies.

Cusco & the Sacred Valley

There are lots of information booklets on Machu Picchu and the other ruins at the bookshops. *New World News* published every other week has lots of useful information and useful addresses and phone numbers, editor Stephen Light, T/F270302, newworldnews_int@hotmail.com The best book on Cusco, the Sacred Valley, Inca Trail, Machu Picchu and other ruins is *Exploring Cusco* (5th edition 1999), by Peter Frost, which is available in Cusco bookshops. Also recommended for general information on

Cusco is *Cusco Peru Tourist Guide*, published by Lima 2000. *The Sacred Center*, by Johan Reinhard, explains Machu Picchu in archaeological terms. *Apus and Incas*, by Charles Brod, describes cultural walks in and around Cusco, and treks in the Cordilleras Vilcabamba, Vilcanota and Urubamba, plus the Manu National Park (2nd edition, ***Inca Expeditions***, 2323 SE 46th Avenue, Portland, OR 97215, USA, US$10.95 plus US$1.50 postage, or from bookshops in North America, Europe and Peru). Tony Morrison's *Qosqo. The Navel of the World* (Special Book Services, Lima, 1997), contains 100 colour photographs of Cusco and its surroundings together with background history of the city from Inca times to the present. The most recent is Max Milligan's *Realm of the Incas* (Harper Collins), 250 pages, foreward by John Hemming.

Climbing, trekking & cycling

Touching the Void, Joe Simpson, is a nail-biting account of Simpson's almost fatal accident in the Cordillera Huayhuasah. For an account of the Andean Inca road, see Christopher Portway, *Journey Along the Andes* (Impact Books, London, 1993). National Geographic has published *Along the Inca Road. A Woman's Journey into an Ancient Empire*, by Karin Muller (2000). Ricardo Espinosa, who has walked the length of the Camino Real de los Incas, from Quito to La Paz, including some of the Inca routes from the coast to the Sierra, has not yet published his account of the walk. He has, however, walked the length of Peru's coast, described in *El Perú a toda Costa* (Editur, 1997). The same company has published *Por los Caminos del Perú en Bicicleta*, by Omar Zarzar. For more information, www.caminanteperu.com For information on ***Bradt Publications'*** Backpacking Guide Series, other titles and imported maps and guides, contact 19 High Street, Chalfont St Peter, Bucks SL9 9QE, UK, T01753 893444, F01753 892333, www.bradt-travelguides.com Relevant to this Handbook is *Backpacking and Trekking in Peru and Bolivia*, by Hilary Bradt (7th edition).

Rafting

A recommended read is Joe Kane's *Running the Amazon* (The Bodley Head, 1989); as is *Rafting the Amazon*, François Ordendaal. There are a number of magazine articles on rafting in Peru: Kurt Casey, 'Cotahuasi Canyon – an Ultimate Peruvian Adventure', in *American Whitewater* (July/August, 1995); in the same edition is 'Paddling the Inca Trail' by John Foss, an account of runs on the Ríos Colca, Apurímac and Urubamba; by the same author are: 'Diarios de Cotahuasi', in *Caretas* magazine, 6 July 1995; and 'Rio Cotahuasi: the World's Deepest Canyon – Really!' in *South American Explorer*, Spring 1996 edition.

Wildlife & environment

See also the Southern Amazon section for more titles covering birds, tropical environments and related topics

Peter Frost et al (Edited by Jim Bartle), *Machu Picchu Historical Sanctuary*, with superb text and photos on all aspects of the Inca Trail and the endangered ecosystem of the sanctuary. Gino Cassinelli, *Trees and Bushes from the Sacred Valley of the Incas*, published by Rumbos (see page 44). Recommended for bird watchers are: Barry Walker, *The Birds of Machu Picchu*, details more than 400 species of birds in the Machu Picchu Sanctuary, illustrated in full colour, published by Programa Machu Picchu 2001. *Birds of the High Andes* (1990) by Nils Krabbe and Jon Fjeldsa, which covers all Peruvian birds that occur above 3,000 m – a large proportion of the birds likely to be seen in the Andes; *An Annotated checklist of Peruvian Birds* by Ted Parker, Susan Parker and Manuel Plenge (1982), is slightly outdated but still useful, it lists all Peruvian birds by habitat type; *The Birds of the Department of Lima* by Maria Koepcke (1983), is useful for the coast.

Cuisine

Elisabeth Lambert Ortiz, *The Flavour of Latin America* Recipes and Stories (Latin America Bureau, 1998) contains various Peruvian recipes in English. A comprehensive series in Spanish is produced by the Escuela Profesional de Turismo y Hotelería, Universidad San Martín de Porres (www.usmp.edu.pe) 1. *Amazonia*, 2. *Centro del Perú*, 3. *Lima*, 4. *Sur del Perú*, 5. *Norte del Perú* (all 1999, 2000). The series contains many other cookery titles.

Useful websites

www.cuzcoguide.com The Insider's Guide to Cusco (in English).
www.cbc.org.pe Centro Bartolomé de las Casas.
www.municusco.gob.pe Municipality of Cusco (in Spanish only).
www.machupicchu.com Machu Picchu .
www.machupicchu.org Also accessed via **geog.gmu.edu/ gess/classes/students/studgeog411/miked/library.html** More than just Machu Picchu, a library of all things related to the Inca region and Peru.
www.ex.ac.uk/~Rdavies/inca/links.html Has masses of links and other information on the Inca Trail.
http://freespace.virgin.net/andy.carling/incatrail.html A site which intends to publish inforamtion on conserving the Inca Trail; still awaiting clarification. It is part of the Mountain Path Repair International site.

General sites on Peru

www.magicperu.com
www.rcp.net.pe/rcp/rcp-peru.shtml Perú, Imagen y Turismo.
www.rcp.net.pe/home/rcp-peru.shtml Red Científica Peruana travel page.
www.terra.com.pe/turismo/index1.shtml Terra travel page.
www.peru.com/turismo Peru.Com's travel page.
www.perutraveller.cjb.net and **www.peruonline.com** General Peru information.
www.perugobierno.gob.pe/ Peruvian government portal.
www.saexplorers.org South American Explorers.
www.traficoperu.com Tráfico on-line travel agent with lots of useful information.
www.andeantravelweb.com/peru Andean adventure travel, advice, links and

more. **www.posadas.com.pe/inkajournal** Tourism magazine of the Sonesta Posadas del Inca chain.

www.perurail.com reservas@perurail.com Peru Rail.

www.conam.gob.pe Consejo Nacional del Ambiente/National Environmental Commission.

Folklore & culture

www.best.com/~gibbons Cultures of the Andes.

www.best.com/~gibbons Quechua.

www.perucultural.org.pe The site of the Instituto Nacional de Cultura (INC). For information on cultural activities, museums and Peruvian precolumbian textiles.

Gastronomy

www.geocities.com/TheTropics/4100/ Cevichería Virtual.

www.rcp.net.pe/cocina/index.htm Cocina Internacional con Sabor Peruano.

General

www.adonde.com (good, with a news feature) and **www.perulinks.com/** Search facilities

www.oanda.com Currency converter and for all your financial needs.

www.cdc.gov Center for Disease Control, health advice, from Atlanta, GA.

Cusco

Cusco

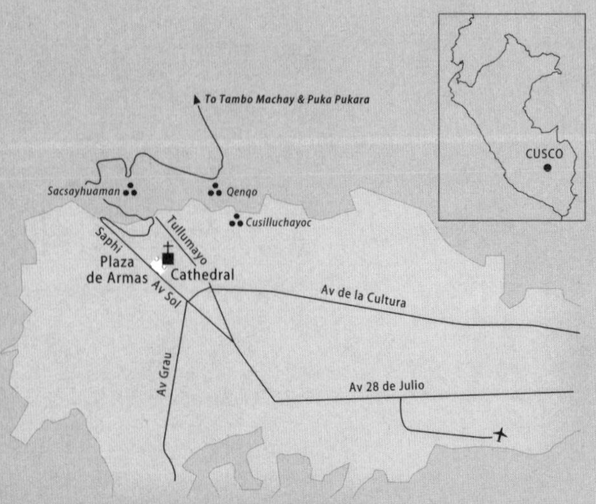

To Tambo Machay & Puka Pukara
Sacsayhuaman
Qenqo
Cusilluchayoc
Tullumayo
Saphi
Plaza de Armas
Cathedral
Av Sol
Av de la Cultura
Av Grau
Av 28 de Julio
CUSCO

Cusco stands at the head of the Sacred Valley of the Incas and is the jumping off point for the Inca Trail and famous Inca city of Machu Picchu. Not surprising, then, that this is the prime destination for the vast majority of Peru's visitors. In fact, the ancient Inca capital is now the 'gringo' capital of the entire continent. And it's easy to see why. There are Inca ruins aplenty, as well as fabulous colonial architecture, stunning scenery, great trekking, river rafting and mountain biking, beautiful textiles and other traditional handicrafts – all within easy reach of the nearest cappuccino or comfy hotel room.

The history books describe the Incas' mythical beginnings, their rapid rise to power, their achievements and their equally rapid defeat by the Spaniards, who converted the pulse of the Inca empire into a jewel of their own. Yet Cusco today is not some dead monument. Its history breathes through the stones and the Quechua people bring the city to life with the combination of prehispanic and Christian beliefs.

Things to do in Cusco

- See the remarkable carved pulpit in San Blas church and get your fill of traditional crafts in the surrounding streets.
- See the museum of Cusqueño school painting in Santa Catalina with its explanations of how European themes were adapted by local artists.
- Even if you are not staying there, visit the hotels which have been converted from colonial palaces. The *Monasterio, Libertador* and *Los Marqueses* are the best examples.
- Take a look at the Ina stonework, especially the Stone of 12 Angles on Calle Hatun Rumiyoc, and imagine how the city once was.
- For shopping the choice is endless, from piles of weavings to the most singular modern designs. Don't forget the markets to see the everyday items, especially San Jerónimo for weird and wonderful fruit and veg.
- Take a tour by car, horse, or on foot, to Sacsayhuaman, Qenqo, Puka Pukara and Tambo Machay, the Inca sites outside the city on the way to Pisac.

Ins and outs

Getting there

By air

Colour map 2, grid B3

For flight details see page 39

Most travellers arriving from Lima will do so by air. The airport is at Quispiquilla, near the new bus terminal, 1.6 km southeast of the centre. Airport information T222611/222601. A taxi to and from the airport costs US$2-3 (US$3.50 by radio taxi). Colectivos cost US$0.20 from Plaza San Francisco or from outside the airport car park to the centre. You can book a hotel at the airport through a travel agency, but this is not really necessary. Many representatives of hotels and travel agencies operate at the airport, with transport to the hotel with which they are associated. Take your time to choose your hotel, at the price you can afford. There is a post office, phone booths, restaurant and cafeteria at the airport. Also a Tourist Protection Bureau desk, which can be very helpful if your flight has not been reconfirmed (not an uncommon problem). Do not forget to pay the airport tax at the appropriate desk before departure.

By road

For bus information, see page 125

All long distance buses arrive and leave from the new bus terminal near the Pachacútec statue in Ttio district. Transport to your hotel is not a problem as representatives are often on hand.

Train

For information on trains to Juliaca and Puno see page 126; to Machu Picchu see page 160

There are 2 stations in Cusco. To **Juliaca and Puno**, trains leave from the Estación Wanchac on C Pachacútec, T221931. The office here offers direct information and ticket sales for all PerúRail services. Look out for special promotional offers. When arriving in Cusco, a tourist bus meets the train to take visitors to hotels whose touts offer rooms on the train. **Machu Picchu** trains leave from Estación San Pedro, T 2221313, opposite the Santa Ana market.

Getting around

Take heed of the warnings given on page 35

The centre of Cusco is small and is easily explored on foot. Bear in mind, however, that at this altitude walking up some of the city's steep cobbled streets may leave you out of breath, so you'll need to take your time. It is even possible to walk up to Sacsayhuaman, but a better idea is to take a Combi to Tambo Machay and walk back downhill to town via Qenqo and Sacsayhuaman.

Taxis in Cusco are cheap and recommended when arriving by air, train or bus. They have fixed prices: in the centre US$0.60 (a little more after dark); to the suburbs US$0.85 (touts at the airport and train station will always ask much higher fares). In town it is safest to take taxis which are registered; these have a sign with the company's name on the roof, not just a sticker in the window. Taxis on call are reliable but more expensive, in the centre US$1.25 (Ocarina T247080, Aló Cusco T222222). Taxi trips to Sacsayhuaman cost US$10; to the ruins of Tambo Machay US$15-20 (3-4 people); a whole-day trip costs US$40-70. For US$50 a taxi can be hired for a whole day (ideally Sun) to take you to Chinchero, Maras, Urubamba, Ollantaytambo, Calca, Lamay, Coya, Pisac, Tambo Machay, Qenqo and Sacsayhuaman.

If you wish to explore this area on your own, Road Map (*Hoja de ruta*) No 10 is an excellent guide. You can get it from the ***Automóvil Club del Perú***, Av Sol 457, next to Banco Santander, 3rd floor. They have other maps. Motorists beware; many streets end in flights of steps not marked as such. There are very few good maps of Cusco available.

Information

Tourist offices Official tourist information is at Portal Mantas 117-A, next to La Merced church, T263176, open 0800-2000. There is also a tourist information desk at the airport. ***Ministry of Tourism***, Av de la Cultura 734, 3rd floor, T223701/223761. Open Mon-Fri 0800-1300. The University is also a good source of information, especially on archaeological sites. They sell good videos of Cusco and surroundings. See Visitors Ticket box on next page for OFEC offices and INC office for Machu Picchu.

Tourist information *South American Explorers*, Av Sol 930, T/F223102, saec@amauta.rcp.net.pe Open 0930-1700, Sun 0930-1300 from 1 Oct-30 Apr, Mon-Fri 0930-1700, Sat 0930-1300; also in Lima (see page 223), an excellent resource and haven for the traveller.

Asociación de Conservación para la Selva Sur (ACSS), Ricaldo Palma J-1, Santa Mónica (same office as *Peru Verde*), T243408, F226392, acss@telser.com.pe For information and free video shows about Manu National Park and Tambopata-Candamo Reserve. They are friendly and helpful and also have information on programmes and research in the jungle area of Madre de Dios, as well as being distributors of the expensive (US$75), but beautiful book on the Manu National Park by Kim MacQuarrie and André Bartschi.

The **Tourist Police** are on C Saphi, block 1, T221961. If you need a *denuncia* (a report for insurance purposes), which is available from the Banco de la Nación, they will type it out. Always go to the police when robbed, even though it will cost you a bit of time. The Tourist Protection Bureau (Indecopi) has been set up to protect the consumer rights of all tourists and will help with any problems or complaints. They can be very effective in dealing with tour agencies, hotels or restaurants. They are at Portal Carrizos, Plaza de Armas. T252974, T01-224 7888 (Lima), or toll free T0800-42579 (24-hr hotline, not available from payphones).

Background

The ancient Inca capital is said to have been founded around 1100 AD. According to the central Inca creation myth, the Sun sent his son, Manco Capac and the Moon her daughter, Mama Ocllo, to spread culture and enlightenment throughout the dark, barbaric lands. The Sun pitied the people of this savage region because they could not cultivate the land, clothe themselves, make houses, nor had they any religion. Manco and Mama Ocllo

Visitors' tickets

*A combined entry ticket to most of the sites of main historical-cultural interest in and around the city, called **Boleto Turístico Unificado** (BTU), costs US$12 (expected to rise to US$20) and is valid for 5-10 days. It permits entrance to the Cathedral, San Blas, Santa Catalina Convent and Art Museum, Qorikancha or Temple of the Sun Museum (but not Santo Domingo/Qoricancha itself), Museo de Arte Religioso del Arzobispado, Museo Histórico Regional (Casa Inca Garcilazo de la Vega) and Museo Palacio Municipal de Arte Contemporáneo, plus the archaeological sites of Sacsayhuaman, Qenqo, Puka Pukara, Tambo Machay, Pisac, Ollantaytambo, Chinchero, Tipón and Piquillacta.*

The BTU can be bought at the OFEC office (Casa Garcilazo), Plaza Regocijo, esquina Calle Garcilazo, Monday-Friday 0745-1800, Saturday 0830-1300, or at any of the sites included in the ticket. There is a 50% discount for students with a green ISIC card, which is only available at the OFEC office (Casa Garcilazo) upon presentation of the student card. Take your ISIC card when visiting the sites, as some may ask to see it.

Note that all sites are very crowded on Sunday, when many churches are closed to visitors, and the 'official' visiting times are unreliable. Photography is not allowed in the Cathedral, churches, and museums. On the back of the BTU is a map of the centre of Cusco with the main sites of interest clearly marked. It also includes a map of the tourist routes from Cusco to the Sacred Valley following the Río Urubamba towards Machu Picchu, as well as the southeastern area of Cusco on the road to Puno. The ticket includes days and hours of visiting.

Entrance tickets for Santo Domingo/Qoricancha, the Inka Museum (former Archaeological Museum), El Palacio del Almirante, and La Merced are sold separately. Machu Picchu ruins and Inca trail entrance tickets are sold at the Instituto Nacional de Cultura (INC), San Bernardo s/n entre Mantas y Almagro, Monday-Friday 0900-1300, 1600-1800, Saturday 0900-1100.

emerged from the icy depths of Lake Titicaca and began their journey in search of the place where they would found their kingdom. They were ordered to head north from the Lake until a golden staff they carried could be plunged into the ground for its entire length. The soil of the altiplano was so thin that they had to travel as far as the valley of Cusco where, on the mountain of Huanacauri, the staff fully disappeared and the soil was found to be suitably fertile. This was the sign they were looking for. They named this place Cusco – meaning 'navel of the earth'. The local inhabitants, on seeing Manco Capac and Mama Ocllo with their fine clothes and jewellery (including the adornments in their long, pierced ears, which became a symbol of the Incas) immediately worshipped them and followed their instructions, the men being taught by Manco Capac, the women by Mama Ocllo. (See also **Children of the Sun**, page 242, and **The inn of origin**, page 150.)

Thus was the significance of Cusco and the sacred Urubamba Valley established for many centuries to come. As Peter Frost states in his *Exploring Cusco*: "Cusco was more than just a capital city to the Incas and the millions of subjects in their realm. It was a Holy City, a place of pilgrimage with as much importance to the Quechuas as Mecca has to the Moslems. Every ranking citizen of the empire tried to visit Cusco once in his lifetime; to have done so increased his stature wherever he might travel."

Today, the city's beauty cannot be overstated. It is a fascinating mix of Inca and colonial Spanish architecture: colonial churches, monasteries and convents and extensive Pre-Columbian ruins are interspersed with countless hotels, bars and restaurants that have sprung up to cater for the hundreds of thousands of tourists who flock here to savour its unique atmosphere. Almost every central street has remains of Inca walls, arches and doorways. Many streets are lined with perfect Inca stonework, now serving as the foundations for more modern dwellings. This stonework is tapered upwards (battered); every wall has a perfect line of inclination towards the centre, from bottom to top. The stones have each edge and corner rounded. The curved stonework of the Temple of the Sun, for example, is probably unequalled in the world.

Cusco has developed into a major, commercial centre of 275,000 inhabitants, most of whom are Quechua. The city council has designated the Quechua, Qosqo, as the official spelling. Despite its growth, however, the city is still laid out much as it was in Inca times. The Incas conceived their capital in the shape of a puma and this can be seen from above, with the river Tullumayo forming the spine, Sacsayhuaman the head and the main city centre the body. The best place for an overall view of the Cusco valley is from the puma's head – the top of the hill of Sacsayhuaman.

Sights

As most of the sights do not have any information or signs in English, a good guide can really improve your visit. Either arrange this before you set out or grab one of those hanging around the sight entrances. The latter is much easier to do in the low season as good guides are often booked up with tour agencies at busy times of year. A tip is expected at the end of the tour; this gives you the chance to reward a good guide and get rid of a bad one!

Since there are so many sights to see in Cusco city, not even the most ardent tourist would be able to visit them all. For those on a tight time limit, or for those who want a whistle-stop tour, a list of must-sees would comprise: the combination of Inca and colonial architecture at Qoricancha; the huge Inca ceremonial centre of Sacsayhuaman; the paintings of the Last Supper and the 1650 earthquake in the Cathedral; the main altar of La Compañía de Jesús; the pulpit of San Blas; the high choir at San Franciso; the monstrance at La Merced; the view from San Cristóbal. If you have the energy catch a taxi up to the White Christ and watch the sunset as you look out upon one of the most fascinating cities in the world. If you visit one museum make it the Museo Inka; it has the most comprehensive collection.

Plaza de Armas

The heart of the city in Inca days was *Huacaypata* (the place of tears) and *Cusipata* (the place of happiness), divided by a channel of the Saphi river. Today, Huacaypata is the Plaza de Armas and Cusipata is Plaza Regocijo. This was the great civic square of the Incas, flanked by their palaces, and was a place of solemn parades and great assemblies. Each territory conquered by the Incas had some of its soil taken to Cusco to be mingled symbolically with the soil of the Huacaypata, as a token of its incorporation into the empire.

As well as the many great ceremonies, the Plaza has also seen its share of executions, among them Túpac Amaru, the last Inca, the rebel conquistador Diego de Almagro the Younger, and Túpac Amaru II, the 18th century indigenous leader.

Around the present-day Plaza de Armas are colonial arcades and four churches. In the mid-1990s the mayor insisted that all the native trees be pulled down as they interrupted views of the surrounding buildings. The trees were replaced with the flowerbeds you see today. You may be forgiven for thinking the graceful, imposing church on the southeast side of the plaza is the Cathedral. However, this is La Compañía de Jesús. When the Jesuits started building, the other Catholics asked the Pope to intervene complaining it was too ornate and over-shadowed the presence of the Cathedral. The Pope failed to act in time and La Compañía de Jesús was completed in all its present-day splendour.

Cathedral The early 17th century baroque Cathedral (on the northeast side of the square) forms part of a three-church complex: the Cathedral itself, Iglesia **Jesús y María** (1733) on the left as you look at it and **El Triunfo** (1533) on the right. There are two entrances; the Cathedral doors are used during Mass but the tourist entrance is on the left-hand side through Iglesia Jesús y María. This may change when restoration work is completed.

Two interesting legends surround the western tower of the Cathedral. According to the first, a captured Inca prince is bricked up in the tower. His only means of escape is for the tower to fall, at which point he will reclaim his people and land. Believers' hopes were raised when the tower was severely damaged in the 1950 earthquake, but it failed to fall before restoration started, incarcerating the prince until this very day.

The same tower holds the largest bell in the city, weighing 5,980 kg. After two failed attempts at casting the bell, *María Angola*, an Afro-Peruvian woman, is said to have thrown a quantity of gold into the smelting pot on the

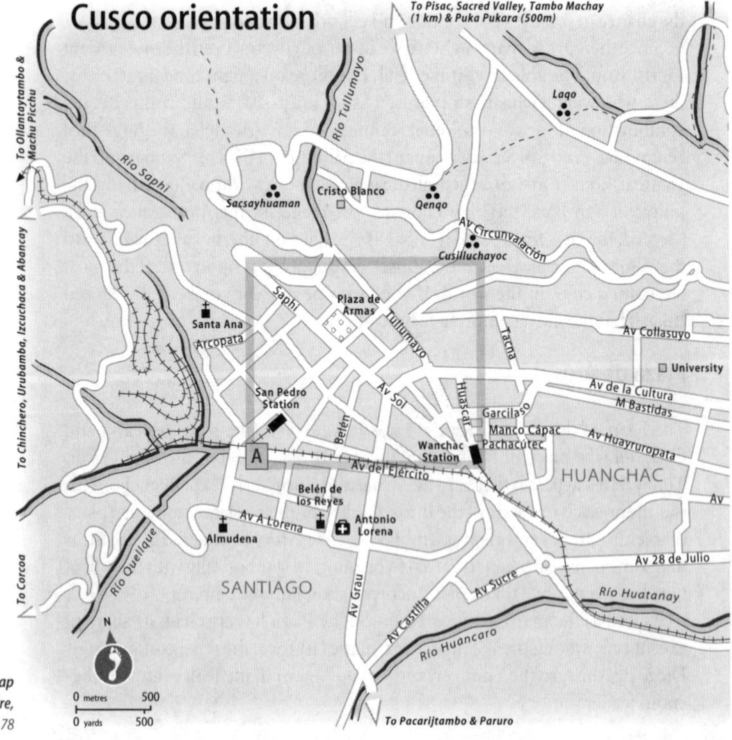

Related map
A Cusco centre,
page 78

third, successful attempt. The bell was then named after her. During the 1950 earthquake *María Angola* was damaged and her hoarse voice is now only heard on special occasions. The Cathedral itself was built on the site of the Palace of Inca Wiracocha (*Kiswarcancha*). Stones from Sacsayhuaman were used in its construction after the architect, Juan Miguel de Veramendi, ordered the destruction of the Inca fortress. Although Spanish designers and architects supervised its construction, it took nearly 100 years of Quechuan blood, sweat and tears to build. The ground plan is in the shape of a Latin cross with the transept leading into the two side-churches.

Built on the site of *Suntur Huasi* (the Roundhouse), **El Triunfo** was the first Christian church in Cusco. The name El Triunfo (The Triumph) came from the Spanish victory over an indigenous rebellion in 1536. It was here that the Spaniards congregated, hiding from Manco Inca who had besieged the city, almost taking it from the invaders. Here the Spaniards claim to have witnessed two miracles in their hour of need. First, they were visited by the Virgin of the Descent, who helped put out the flames devouring the thatched roofs, then came the equestrian saint, James the Greater, who helped kill many indigenous Indians. The two divinities are said to have led to the Spanish victory; not only was it the triumph of the Spaniards over the Incas, but also of the Catholic faith over the Indians' religion.

The gleaming, newly-renovated gilded main altar of the **Iglesia Jesús y María** draws the eyes to the end of the church. However, take the time to look up at the colourful murals which have been partially restored. The two gaudy, mirror-encrusted altars towards the front of the church are also hard to miss.

At the time this book went to press the Cathedral was under restoration and many of the statues, paintings and ornaments may have moved. As far as possible we have tried to describe things where they should be once the work is completed

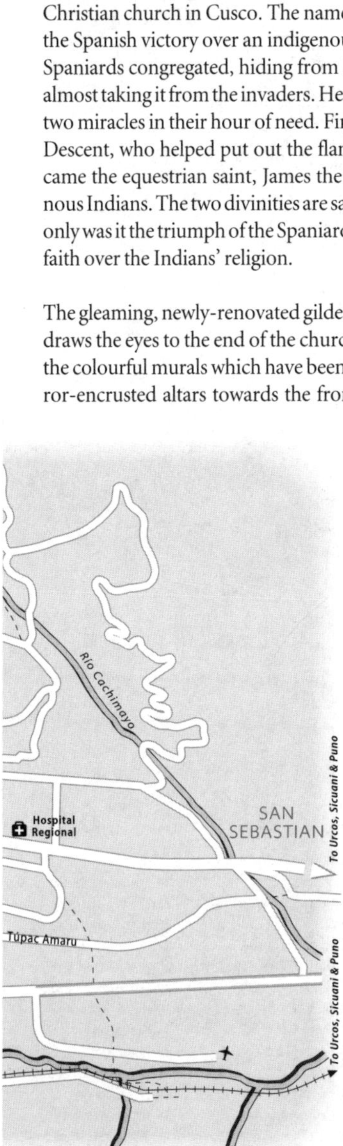

Walking through into the Cathedral's transept, the oldest surviving painting in Cusco can be seen. It depicts the 1650 earthquake. It also shows how within only one century the Spaniards had already divided the main plaza in two. El Señor de los Temblores (The Lord of the Earthquakes) can be seen being paraded around the Plaza de Armas while fire rages through the colonial buildings with their typical red-tiled roofs. Much of modern-day Cusco was built after this event. The choir stalls, by a 17th-century Spanish priest, are a magnificent example of colonial baroque art (80 saints and virgins are exquisitely represented), as is the elaborate pulpit. On the left is the solid-silver high altar; the original altar *retablo* behind it is a masterpiece of native wood carving by the famous Quechuan **Juan Tomás Tuyro Túpaq.** In the far right-hand end of the Cathedral is an interesting local painting of the Last Supper. But this is the Last Supper with a difference, for Jesus is about to tuck into a plate of *cuy*, washed down with a glass of *chicha* (as opposed to the standard Cusco fare of pizza and chicken wings washed down with a bottle of *Cusqueño*). In the sacristy there is a good selection of artwork including portraits of all the bishops and archbishops of Cusco, including Vicente de Valverde, the Dominican friar who accompanied Pizarro and who was instrumental in the

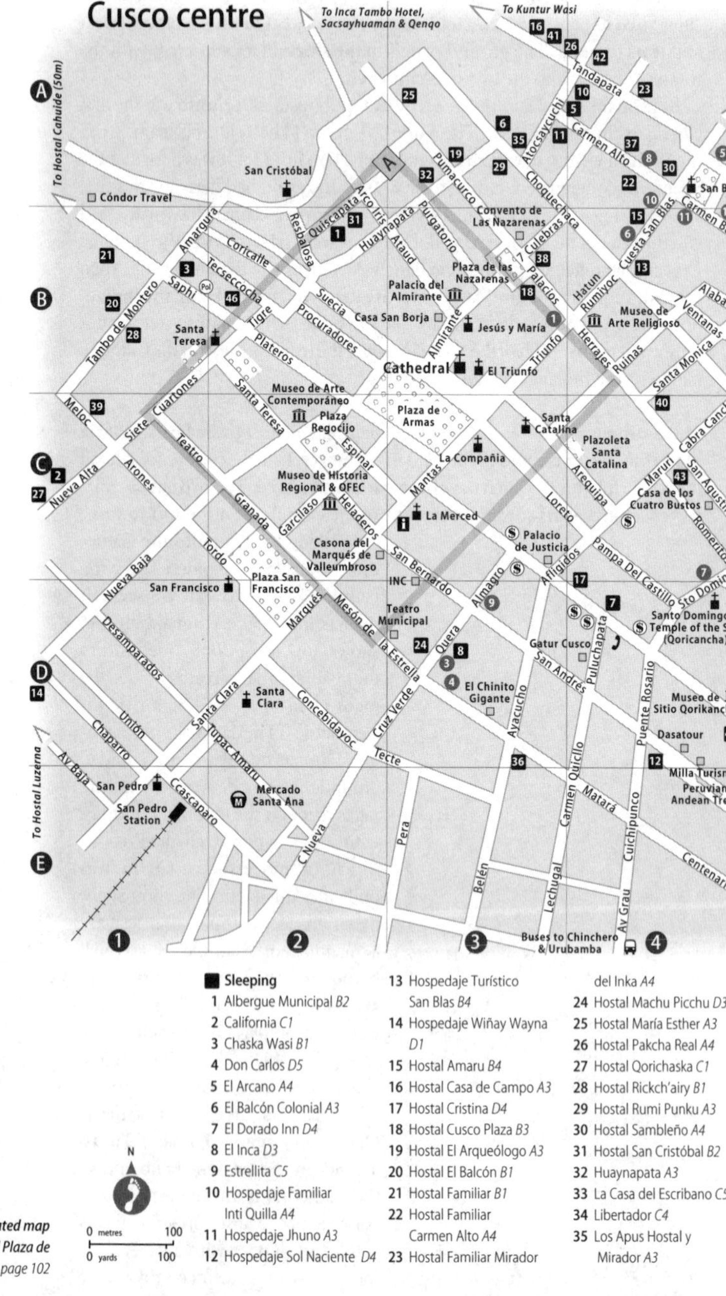

Sleeping

1 Albergue Municipal *B2*
2 California *C1*
3 Chaska Wasi *B1*
4 Don Carlos *D5*
5 El Arcano *A4*
6 El Balcón Colonial *A3*
7 El Dorado Inn *D4*
8 El Inca *D3*
9 Estrellita *C5*
10 Hospedaje Familiar Inti Quilla *A4*
11 Hospedaje Jhuno *A3*
12 Hospedaje Sol Naciente *D4*
13 Hospedaje Turístico San Blas *B4*
14 Hospedaje Wiñay Wayna *D1*
15 Hostal Amaru *B4*
16 Hostal Casa de Campo *A3*
17 Hostal Cristina *D4*
18 Hostal Cusco Plaza *B3*
19 Hostal El Arqueólogo *A3*
20 Hostal El Balcón *B1*
21 Hostal Familiar *B1*
22 Hostal Familiar Carmen Alto *A4*
23 Hostal Familiar Mirador del Inka *A4*
24 Hostal Machu Picchu *D3*
25 Hostal María Esther *A3*
26 Hostal Pakcha Real *A4*
27 Hostal Qorichaska *C1*
28 Hostal Rickch'airy *B1*
29 Hostal Rumi Punku *A3*
30 Hostal Sambleño *A4*
31 Hostal San Cristóbal *B2*
32 Huaynapata *A3*
33 La Casa del Escribano *C5*
34 Libertador *C4*
35 Los Apus Hostal y Mirador *A3*

Related map
A Around Plaza de Armas, page 102

death of Atahualpa. He was bishop of Cusco until 1541, the year he died. The painting of the crucified Christ is strange because his body is rather effeminate. This is also noted in other paintings of Christ from the Cuzqueño school. This may be due to the artists using female models, or simply how the Quechuan artists perceived Him.

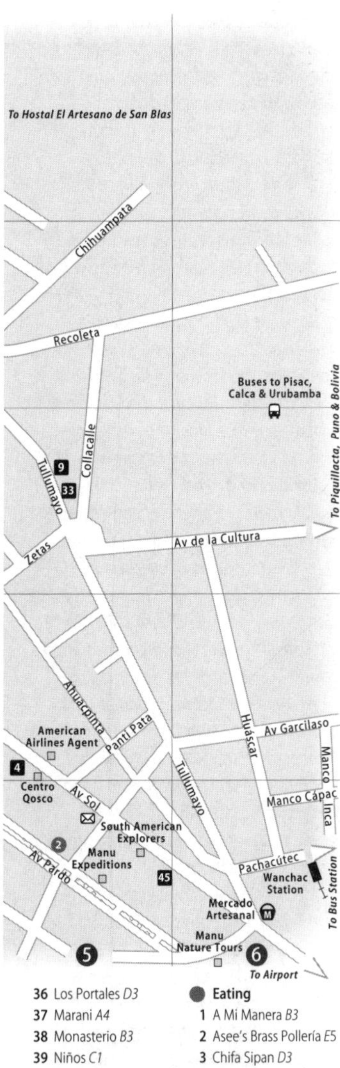

36 Los Portales *D3*
37 Marani *A4*
38 Monasterio *B3*
39 Niños *C1*
40 Novotel *C4*
41 Pensión Alemana *A3*
42 Posada del Sol *A4*
43 San Augustín Internacional *C4*
44 San Augustín Plaza *D4*
45 Savoy Internacional *E5*
46 Suecia II *B2*

Eating
1 A Mi Manera *B3*
2 Asee's Brass Pollería *E5*
3 Chifa Sipan *D3*
4 El Trujillano *D3*
5 Green's *A4*
6 Heidi Granja *B4*
7 Inkanato *C4*
8 La Bodega *A4*
9 Los Toldos *D3*
10 Macondo *A4*
11 Pacha-Papa *B4*
12 Witches Garden *A4*

Many of the Cathedral's treasures are hidden in a safe behind one of the carved doors. Much venerated is the crucifix of *El Señor de los Temblores* (The Lord of Earthquakes), the object of many pilgrimages and viewed all over Peru as a guardian against earthquakes. You may be forgiven for thinking he has a Quechuan complexion but this is actually due to many years' exposure to candle smoke! This is the most richly-adorned Christ in the Cathedral with His gold crown and His hands and feet pierced by solid gold, jewel-encrusted nails. The original wooden altar was destroyed by fire and dedicated locals are slowly covering the new plaster one with silver. (At the time of writing the statue was positioned in front of the main altar of El Triunfo for safe keeping).

The chapel of **St James the Greater** contains a statue of the saint on horseback. The painting depicts the saint killing the indigenous Indians as he appeared in the miracle. Entering El Triunfo there is a stark contrast between the dark, heavy atmosphere of the Cathedral and the light, simple structure of this serene church. The fine granite altar is a welcome relief from the usual gilding. Here the statue of the Virgin of the Descent resides and, above her, is a wooden cross known as the Cross of Conquest, said to be the first Christian cross on Inca land brought from Spain by Vicente de Valverde.

Going down into the catacomb (not open on Sundays), originally used to keep the bodies of important people, you will find a coffer containing half the ashes of the Cuzqueño chronicler Garcilaso Inca de la Vega, born of a Spanish father and Inca princess mother. The ashes were sent back from Spain only in 1978. The

Treasure hunt

Legend has it that deep below the foundations of Qorickancha (the complex of the Temple of the Sun) are riches of the lost Inca empire – and archeologists are in hot pursuit.

Qorikcancha was supposed to be linked by secret passageways to another religious complex overlooking Cusco, that of Sacqsaywhuaman. It is here the treasures may be buried.

Stories tell of an Inca prince named Carlos Inca, grandson of Cristóbal Paullu Inca and direct descendant of the powerful Huayna Cápac, who fuelled speculation of riches beyond avarice in the 17th century when he told his fiancée that he was phenomenally rich, despite the state of poverty to which the conquistadors had reduced him.

After the marriage, assailed by much nagging, he finally blindfolded the woman and led her through alleys and cellars before stopping and revealing to her "the most valuable treasure that could be imagined", she later told.

"Thousands of golden objects that temptingly shined in the light of the lantern. There were statues of the Incas, all of them of gold and the size of a 12-year-old child. There were also cups, glasses, plates and whatever tableware and cutlery that could be imagined, also of gold. And thus comprising a wealth as had never been seen before."

When he forced the blindfold back on her face and led her out again, she was furious and told the authorities everything, it being a crime to hide treasures that belonged to the King of Spain. Carlos Inca´s arrest was ordered and he fled to the mountains of Vilcabamba.

A similar story was told in 1814 when Mateo Garcíia Pumakahua, another descendant of the Incas, was preparing to revolt against the Spanish. He took Colonel Domingo Luis Astete to part of the Inca treasure to convince him there was enough economic funds to carry out a revolution.

Astete was led, again blindfolded, this time through the Plaza de Armas, along a stream, possibly the Choquechaca, then down a secret path underground. Astete saw awesome riches: enormous puma cubs with emerald eyes, gold and silver bricks. While he was there he clearly heard the clock of the cathedral chime.

Other tales speak of gold formed into trees with leaves and fruits, with birds perched on their branches, as well as the golden chair of Atahualpa, the great warrior Inca emperor.

Bohic Ruz Explorer, an international exploration society, is now working at Qorickancha and Sacqsaywhuaman to unearth the truth behind the legend. It is a painstaking process for the professional archeologists that will take many years.

Using radar they believe the tunnel does exist, 7 m down somewhere between the first and second pillars of Santo Domingo, the church the Spaniards built in place of the Temple of the Sun ripped down in the 15th century. Sadly it will take at least three years for all the data to be properly assessed before digging can begin.

The tunnel at Sacqsaywhuaman is no easier to find. The Army blew up its entrance in the early 1950s in a somewhat radical measure to prevent people from entering and becoming lost in the labyrinth below. It is now a mess of fragile earthworks with water filtering down inside.

Meanwhile, the archeologists are working in the crypts of Santo Domingo, one of which had been lost since the 16th century until they rediscovered it with radar.

And what will happen to the gold they find? It will be placed for all to see in the museums of Cusco.

For more information, see www.bohic-ruz.org/web%20bohic/menu/menu.html

paintings of the parables which used to hang on the central columns have been moved to the Museum of Religious Art.

■ *The Cathedral is open until 1000 for genuine worshippers – Quechua mass is held 0500-0600. Those of a more secular inclination can visit*

1000-1130 Mon, Tue, Wed, Fri and Sat or Mon. Sun 1400-1730. Entrance with the BTU tourist ticket.

La Compañía de Jesús

On the southeast side of the plaza is the beautiful church of La Compañía de Jesús, built on the site of the Palace of the Serpents (*Amarucancha*, residence of the Inca Huayna Cápac) in the late 17th century. First it was given to Pizarro after the Spanish conquest, then it was bought by a family who eventually donated it to the Jesuits after their arrival in 1571. The church was destroyed in the earthquake of 1650. The present-day building took 17 years to construct and was inaugurated in 1668. When the Jesuits were expelled from Peru most of the valuables were taken to Spain. The altarpiece is a dazzling work of art. Resplendent in its gold leaf, it stands 21 m high and 12 m wide. It is carved in the baroque style, but the indigenous artists felt that this was too simple to please the gods and added their own intricacies in an attempt to reach perfection. Gold leaf abounds in the many altarpieces and on the carved pulpit. The painting on the left-hand side of the door as you enter is historically interesting. It depicts the marriage of Beatriz Qoya, niece of Túpac Amaru, to Martín García de Loyola, the nephew of one of Túpac's captors. Thus de Loyola joins the line of succession for the Inca king's inheritance. The cloister is also noteworthy, though it has been closed since 1990 for restoration.

Túpac Amaru was imprisoned next door, in San Ignacio chapel (now an artisans´ market), before being taken to the centre of the plaza where he was executed in front of his family. His head was planted on a stick and placed on a hill by the main pass to the city. ■ *Free.*

Cusco

Northeast of the Plaza de Armas

Museo Inka

The **Palacio del Almirante**, just north of the Plaza de Armas on Calle Ataud, is one of Cusco's most impressive colonial houses. Note the pillar on the balcony over the door, showing a bearded man from inside and a naked woman from the outside. During the high season local Quechuan weavers can be seen working in the courtyard. The weavings are for sale, expensive but of very good quality. It houses the interesting Museo Inka, run by the Universidad San Antonio de Abad, which exhibits the development of culture in the region from pre-Inca, through Inca times to the present day. The museum has a good combination of textiles, ceramics, metalwork, jewellery, architecture, technology, photographs and 3D displays. They have an excellent collection of miniature turquoise figures and other objects made as offerings to the gods. The display of deliberately deformed skulls with trepanning is fascinating, as is the full-size tomb complete with mummies stuck in urns! The section on coca leaves gives a good insight into the sacred Inca leaf. Old photographs of Machu Picchu are good to see after a visit for 'then and now' comparisons. The painting of the garrotting of Inca Atahualpa, watched over by Vicente de Valverde, is gory but informative. There are no explanations in English so a guide is a good investment. ■ *Mon-Fri 0800-1700, Sat 0900-1600. US$1.40.*

Opposite, in a small square on Cuesta del Almirante, is the colonial house of **San Borja**, which was a Jesuit school for the children of upper-class mestizos.

Museo de Arte Religioso

The **Palacio Arzobispal** stands on Hatun Rumiyoc y Herrajes, two blocks northeast of Plaza de Armas. It was built on the site of the palace occupied in 1400 by the Inca Roca and was formerly the home of the Marqueses de Buena Vista. It contains the Museo de Arte Religioso which has a fine collection of colonial paintings, furniture and mirrors. The Spanish tiles are said to be 100 years old and each carved wooden door has a different design. The collection includes the paintings by the indigenous master, **Diego Quispe Tito**, of a 17th century Corpus Christi procession that used to hang in the church of Santa Ana. They now hang in the two rooms at the back of the second smaller courtyard .

The first picture on the right-hand side in the first room is an example of a travelling picture. The canvas can be rolled up inside the cylindrical wooden box which becomes part of the picture when it is hanging. The stained-glass windows in the chapel were made in Italy. The one on the left-hand side depicts the Lord of the Earthquakes. The priest´s vestments belonged to Vicente de Valverde; the black was used for funerals, white for weddings and red for ceremonial masses. There are many paintings of the Virgin of the Milk, in which the Virgin Mary is breastfeeding Jesus, a sight not seen in Western religious paintings. The throne in the old dining-room is 300 years old and was taken up to Sacsayhuaman for the Pope to sit on when he visited in 1986. Vistors can also see a bed that Simón Bolívar slept in. ■ *Mon-Sat, 0830-1130, 1500-1730. Entrance with BTU tourist ticket.*

Convento de las Nazarenas

Male visitors only will be able to see the place at the back of the main courtyard where monks were imprisoned for transgressions – because today it´s the men´s toilets! An inscription can be seen in which one monk tells how he was locked up for a day for ringing a bell 10 mins late

The Convento de las Nazarenas, on Plaza de las Nazarenas, is now an annex of *El Monasterio* hotel. You can see the Inca-colonial doorway with a mermaid motif, but ask permission to view the lovely 18th century frescos inside. *El Monasterio* itself is well worth a visit – ask at reception if it´s OK to have a wander (see page 91). Built in 1595 on the site of an Inca palace, it was originally the Seminary of **San Antonio Abad** (a Peruvian National Historical Landmark). One of its most remarkable features is the Baroque chapel, constructed after the 1650 earthquake. Look at the altar: to the right is a painting that slides to one side allowing access to a stairway down which the statues of saints on high can be liberated for use in the Corpus Christi procession of June. Attempts have been made to restore paintings outside in the cloister but, as can be seen in an alcove, the paint keeps peeling away and much is painted white. If you are not disturbing mealtimes, check out the dining room. This is where the monks used to sing. The masks on the walls represent the Spaniards when they arrived in Cusco – the eyes are red with greed and the skin yellow from all the gold they took. Moving back, to the second cloister, turn left at the restored painting in the alcove to see a small courtyard which used to be a farm; guests claim to have seen ghosts here. One last curiosity is Samson´s Martyrdom, an 18th century painting in the Mestizo style, next to room 422. Look at the tray on the floor – those are Samson´s eyes. Gruesome!

Also on Plaza Nazarenas is **Casa Cabrera**, which is now a gallery and used by *Banco Continental.*

San Blas

There are also many hostales and eating places on the steep, narrow streets, which are good for a day-time wander (take care after dark). Much of the area is unsuitable for cars

The smaller and less well-known church of San Blas, on Carmen Bajo, is a simple rectangular adobe building whose walls were reinforced with stone after the 1650 and 1950 earthquakes. It comes as some surprise then to learn that it houses one of the most famous pieces of wood carving found in the Americas, a beautiful *mestizo* pulpit carved from a single cedar trunk. Eight heretics are carved at the basin of the pulpit. See if you can spot Henry VIII and Queen Elizabeth I among them. Above are carved the four Evangelists and, crowning the pulpit, supported by five archangels, is the statue of Saint Paul of Tarsus, although some believe it to be Jesus Christ. The skull is supposed to be that of the sculptor. There are many stories surrounding the artist. Some say he was an indigenous leper who dedicated his life to the carving after he was cleansed of the disease. The church was built and used by indigenous inhabitants and the Cusco baroque altarpiece was designed to compete with any in Cusco. ■ *Mon-Sun 1800-1130, 1400-1730, closed Thu mornings.*

The San Blas district, called Tococache in Inca times, has been put on the tourist map by the large number of shops and galleries which sell local carvings, ceramics and paintings. (See page 112).

Southeast of the Plaza de Armas

Santa Catalina

The magnificent Santa Catalina church, convent and museum are on Arequipa at Santa Catalina Angosta. Santa Catalina was the founder of the female part of the Dominican Order, which also founded the beautiful convent in Arequipa of the same name. The Cusco convent is ironically built upon the foundations of the Acllahuasi, or the House of the Chosen Women, the most important Inca building overlooking the main plaza. The Quechuan women were chosen for their nobility, virtue and beauty to be prepared for ceremonial and domestic duties – some were chosen to bear the Inca king's children. No man was allowed to set eyes on the Chosen Women and if he were to have any relationship with one, he, his family and livestock were all killed.

Today the convent is a closed order where the nuns have no contact with the outside world. There is a room at the back of the church where the nuns can participate in Sunday mass. It is separated from the church by a heavy metal grill so although they cannot be seen their voices can still be heard. In this room there is the only signed painting in the museum. He was, of course, a Spanish artist as local artists were either forbidden or unable to sign theirs. The church has an ornate, gilded altarpiece and a beautifully-carved pulpit. The altarpieces are all carved by different craftsmen and the paintings are anonymous.

The museum has a wonderful collection of Cuzqueño school paintings spanning the decades of Spanish rule – a good guide can point out how the style changes from the heavy European influence to the more indigenous style. One obvious difference can be seen in the paintings in the corridor of the Lord of the Earthquakes. Early paintings show Christ wearing a white loin cloth typical of European paintings, but in others he is seen wearing a very light, almost transparent skirt. The beautifully coloured murals in the Scriptures Room show the difference between the devoted lives of the religious order in the upper section and the frivolity of the courtiers' life. The floral designs covering the lower section and the archways are the indigenous artists' way of paying tribute to *Pachamama*, Mother Earth. This can also be seen in the upstairs room, which has many paintings of the Virgin. The dresses are all triangular, the shape of mountains which were seen as gods by the indigenous people. Another addition can be seen in the painting of the Virgin of Bethlehem. The baby Jesus is held at an awkward angle because He has been swaddled tightly from neck to feet in the manner of indigenous babies. The gold patterns are applied to these paintings by the use of a stamp. This is carried out by a separate artist once the painting has dried. The most fascinating article in this museum is the trunk which unfolds to reveal a religious tableau used by travelling preachers to take the word of the Lord to remote villages. Many of the works of art, bureaux and ornaments were given to the Order by the families of joining novices. ■ *Daily 0900-1730, except Fri 0900-1500. There are guided tours by English-speaking students; a tip is expected. Church open 0700-0800 daily.*

Also worth a visit is the palace called **Casa de los Cuatro Bustos**, whose colonial doorway is at San Agustín 400. This palace is now the Golden Tulip's *Hotel Libertador*. The general public can enter the Hotel from Plazoleta Santo Domingo, opposite the Temple of the Sun/Qoricancha.

Qoricancha at Santo Domingo

This is one of the most fascinating sights in Cusco. Behind the walls of the Catholic church are remains of what was once the centre of the vast Inca society. The Golden Palace and Temple of the Sun was a complex filled with such fabulous treasures of gold and silver it took the Spanish three months to melt it all down. You will be able to see what was the Solar Garden – where life-sized gold sculptures of men, women, children, animals, insects and flowers were placed in homage to the Sun God – and marvel at near-complete temples boasting the best Inca stonework in Cusco. On the walls were more than 700 gold sheets weighing about 2 kg each. These the conquistadores sent back intact to prove to the King of Spain how rich was their discovery.

The first Inca, Manco Cápac, is said to have built the temple when he left Lake Titicaca and founded Cusco with Mama Ocllo. However, it was the ninth Inca, Pachacútec, who transformed it. When the Spaniards arrived, the complex was awarded to Juan Pizarro, the younger brother of Francisco. He in turn willed it to the Dominicans who ripped much of it down to build their church.

The temple complex

Walk first into the courtyard then turn around to face the door you just passed through. Behind and to the left of the paintings (representing the life of Santo Domingo Guzmán) is Santo Domingo. This was where the *Sun Temple* stood, a massive structure 80 m wide, 20 m deep and 7 m in height. Only the curved wall of the western end still exists and will be seen (complete with a large crack from the 1950 earthquake), when you later walk left through to the lookout over the Solar Garden. The Temple of the Sun was completely covered with gold plates and there would have been a large solar disc in the shape of a round face with rays and flames. One story, with no historic basis to it, is that conquistador Mancio Sierra de Leguizamo was given this in the division of spoils, but he lost it one night playing dice. Whether a conquistador lost it, or the Incas spirited it away, the solar disc has not been found.

Still in the baroque cloister, close by and facing the way you came in, turn left and cross to the remains of the *Temple of the Moon*, identifiable by a series of niches. The moon, or Mamakilla, was the Sun's wife. The walls were covered in silver plates and the dark horizontal stripe in the niches shows where they were attached. Have a look at the stonework. This is a fantastic example of polished joints so perfectly made it is impossible to slip even a playing card in between. In fact, all the walls of the temples around this courtyard are fine examples of Inca stonemasonry.

Further round the courtyard, heading anti-clockwise, is a double door-jamb doorway. Beyond this is the so-called *Temple of Venus and the Stars*. Stars were special deities used to predict weather, wealth and crops. There's a window around which, on the inside, can be seen holes out of which the Spaniards prised precious stones. The roofs of all these temples would have been thatched, but on the ceiling here was a beautiful representation of the Milky Way. The 25 niches would have held idols and offerings to the cult of the stars and the walls around them were plated in silver (notice again the dark stripes). In the *Temple of Lightning* on the other side of the courtyard is a stone. Stand on this and you will appreciate how good the Incas were as stonemasons: all three windows are

Getting stoned

Just wandering around the streets of Cusco gives you a sense of the incredible craftsmanship of the Inca stonemasons. Some of the best examples can be seen in the ***Callejón Loreto****, running southeast past La Compañía de Jesús from the main plaza. The walls of the Acllahuasi (House of the Chosen Women) are on one side, and of the Amarucancha on the other. There are also Inca remains in* ***Calle San Agustín****, to the east of the plaza. The famous stone of 12 angles is in* ***Calle Hatun Rumiyoc*** *halfway along its second block, on the right-hand side going away from the plaza. The finest stonework is in the celebrated curved wall beneath the west end of* ***Santo Domingo.*** *This was rebuilt after the 1950 earthquake, at which time a niche that once contained a shrine was found at the inner top of the wall. Excavations have revealed Inca baths below here, and more Inca retaining walls. Another superb stretch of late-Inca stonework is in* ***Calle Ahuacpinta*** *outside Qoricancha, to the east or left as you enter. True Inca stonework is wider at the base than at the top and features ever-smaller stones as the walls rise. Doorways and niches are trapezoidal. The Incas clearly learnt that the combination of these four techniques helped their structures to withstand earthquakes. This explains why, in two huge earthquakes (1650 and 1950), Inca walls stayed standing while colonial buildings tumbled down. The walls of El Libertador hotel, near Santo Domingo, show an Inca stonemason following a Spanish architect – the walls are vertical and the doorways square. However, the stones are still beautifully cut and pieced together.*

in perfect alignment. The lightning was the sun's servant while the rainbow, subject of the next and last temple, was also important because it came from the sun. A rainbow was painted onto the gold plates which coated the walls.

The gold thread used in the vestments of Catholic priests (on display in the sacristy you pass on your way to the Solar Garden) pales into insignificance when one considers the vast quantities of gold housed in this most special of Inca temple complexes. Yet, to the Incas, gold and silver had little monetary value, and was prized only for its religious significance. As you gaze over the grass lawn to the Avenida Sol, this may help you believe that there truly was once a garden here filled with flowers, insects, animals and people, all fashioned in gold and silver. What a sight that must have been!

■ *Mon-Sat 0800-1700, Sun 1400-1600 (except holidays). US$1.15 (not on the BTU Visitor Ticket). There are guides outside who charge around US$2-3.*

Museo de Sitio Qorikancha

The former Museo Arqueológico is now housed in an underground site on Avenida Sol, in the gardens below Santo Domingo. It contains a limited collection of precolumbian artefacts, a few Spanish paintings of imitation Inca royalty dating from the 18th century, photos of the excavation of Qoricancha, and some miniature offerings to the gods. It's a good idea to visit Santo Domingo before the museum, in order to understand better the scant information given.

■ *Mon-Fri 0800-1730, Sat 0900-1700. Entrance by the BTU Visitor Ticket, or US$2. The staff will give a guided tour in Spanish, but please give a tip.*

Southwest of the Plaza de Armas

La Merced

La Merced (on Márquez) was originally built in 1534 by the religious Order of Mercedarians (founded in 1223 by the French Saint Peter Nolasco), whose main aim was to redeem the natives. The church was razed in the 1650 earthquake and rebuilt by indigenous stonemasons in the late-17th century. The high altar is neoclassical with six gilded columns. There are a further 12 altars. Inside the church are buried Gonzalo Pizarro, half-brother of Francisco, and the two Almagros, father and son. Their tombs were discovered in 1946.

Attached is a very fine monastery. The first cloister is the most beautiful with its two floors, archways and pillars. The pictures on the first floor depict the Saints of the Order, but unfortunately those of the second floor have been removed for restoration. The small museum can also be found here. This houses the Order's valuables including the priceless monstrance (a vessel used to hold the consecrated host). It is 1.2 m high, weighs over 22 kg and is decorated with thousands of precious stones. Note the two huge pearls used for the body of a mermaid. There are many other precious religious objects including a small Christ carved in ivory, crowns and incense burners. The painting of the Holy Family is ascribed to Rubens. The superb choir stalls, reached from the upper floor of the cloister, can be seen by men only, but you must persuade a Mercedarian friar to let you see them. ■ *The monastery and museum are open 1430-1700. The church is open 0830-1200, 1530-1730, except Sun. US$1.85.*

The **Casona del Marqués de Valleumbroso,** on San Bernardo y Márquez, three blocks southwest of the Plaza de Armas, was gutted by fire in 1973 and is being restored.

Around Plaza Regocijo

Museo de Historia Regional, in the Casa Garcilaso, Jirón Garcilaso y Heladeros, tries to show the evolution of the Cuzqueño school of painting. It also contains Inca agricultural implements, a mummy from Nasca complete with 1 m-long hair, colonial furniture and paintings, a small photographic exhibition of the 1950 earthquake and mementos of more recent times. Upstairs there is an exhibition room which holds temporary exhibits from photography to recently excavated finds. The museum is disjointed and even the Spanish explanations are minimal. ■ *Open 0730-1700. Entrance with BTU tourist ticket. A guide is recommended; they are usually available at the ticket office and many of them speak English.*

If you are walking up Garcilaso, drop into **Hostal Los Marqueses** on the right. This has one of the most unusual colonial courtyards. Attractive brick arches single this out from other patios in Cusco as do the sculpted faces of the previous noble owners which stare out from above them. This house is sadly run down but that is also part of its charm. A hotel chain may be taking it over with promises of renovation (see **Sleeping** section).

Museo de Arte Contemporáneo is in the Casa de Gobierno, on Plaza Regocijo. Even though entrance is free with the tourist ticket it is only worth popping into if you are in the area and it is raining. The museum holds very few pieces and none of them has the artists' names, let alone any explanations.

Around Plaza San Francisco

San Francisco church, on Plaza San Francisco, three blocks southwest of the Plaza de Armas, is an austere church reflecting many indigenous influences, but it has a wonderful monastery, cloister and choir. Although at the time of writing the monastery was not officially open to the public, it is possible to visit. Approach the door to the left of the church, shake it, look puzzled and the administrator will appear as if by magic. Agree on a price before you enter and stick to it. If he starts asking for money to take photographs and then a further tip at the end because of his good service ask him for a *boleta de venta* for the money you paid up front.

Getting in a flap

Some love it, some hate it – but travel a couple of kilometres down the Av de la Cultura (the route to Paucartambo) and you won´t miss it! Standing on a column in the middle of the road six storeys high is a massive condor, the Inca god called upon to protect the kingdom from the conquistadors. This modern-day marvel (or monstrosity, depending on your point of view) was built from the aluminium of a plane donated by the Army. The artist (who died young) also created the monument of Pachacútec, the greatest Inca ruler ever, which visitors see on arrival at Cusco airport.

The condor´s construction (which stands in sight of the poor barrios of San Sebastián) cost US$1.5 mn and three people´s lives in two accidents. The day of its inauguration, the massive bird caused a flap among the dignatories below as an earth tremor started up and the wings began to move up and down!The beak is said to be gold, a sorry sight to the poor below who have no way of preying upon its treasure – the tower can be scaled only by locked stairs within.

The cloister is the oldest in the city, built in the Renaissance style, but with diverse influences. The ground floor has several crypts containing human bones. Some have been used to write phrases to remind the visitor of his or her mortality! The fabulous high choir contains 92 detailed carvings of martyrs and saints. The rotating lectern inlaid with ivory skulls (the Franciscan monks' symbol) was used to hold large books. Over the years the wooden ledge has been worn away by the continuous turning of pages. On one of the stairways the largest painting (12 m high, 9 m wide) in South America can be seen. It records the 12 branches of the Franciscan Order – 683 people are present! Make sure you look up at the colourful, painted ceiling, restored after the 1950 earthquake. Few tourists during restoration means this cloister can be visited in the peace and tranquillity for which it was meant. ■ *Church open 0600-0800, 1800-2000.*

Around Santa Ana market

Heading towards Santa Ana market and San Pedro station from Plaza San Francisco, you pass Santa Clara arch and the nuns' church of **Santa Clara.** It is singular in South America for its decoration, which covers the whole of the interior. Its altars are set with thousands of mirrors. ■ *Only open 0600-0700.*

San Pedro, in front of the Santa Ana market, was built in 1688. Its two towers were made from stones brought from an Inca ruin. The most interesting aspect of this church is the walk to it through the Santa Clara arch early in the morning. If you have only seen the Plaza de Armas and surrounding area a walk here will show you another side of Cusco life. The street stallholders will be setting up and the Santa Ana market is worth a visit. ■ *Mon-Sat 1000-1200, 1400-1700.*

Other sights south of the centre

Belén de los Reyes, in the southern outskirts of the city, was built by an *indígena* in the 17th century. It has a striking main altar, with silver embellishments at the centre and gold-washed *retablos* at the sides. ■ *Daily 1000-1200, 1500-1700, except Thu and Sun.*

Between the centre and the airport on Alameda Pachacútec, the continuation of Avenida Sol, 20 minutes' walk from the Plaza de Armas, there is a statue of the **Inca Pachacútec** placed on top of a lookout tower, from which there are excellent views of Cusco. Inside are small galleries and a coffee shop (temporarily closed). ■ *Open 1000-2000. Entrance free.*

The festival of Inti Raymi

The sun was the principal object of Inca worship and at their winter solstice, in June, the Incas honoured the solar deity with a great celebration known as Inti Raymi, the sun festival. The Spanish suppressed the Inca religion, and the last royal Inti Raymi was celebrated in 1535.

However, in 1944 a group of Cusco intellectuals, inspired by the contemporary 'indigenist' movement, revived the old ceremony in the form of a pageant, putting it together from chronicles and historical documents. The event caught the public imagination, and it has been celebrated every year since then on 24 Jun, now a Cusco public holiday. Hundreds of local men and women play the parts of Inca priests, nobles, chosen women, soldiers (played by the local army garrison), runners, and the like. The coveted part of the Inca emperor Pachacuti is won by audition, and the event is organized by the municipal authorities.

It begins around 1000 at the Qoricancha – the former sun temple of Cusco – and winds its way up the main avenue into the Plaza de Armas, accompanied by songs, ringing declarations and the occasional drink of chicha. At the main plaza, Cusco's presiding mayor is whisked back to Inca times, to receive Pachacuti's blessing and a stern lecture on good government. Climbing through Plaza Nazarenas and up Pumacurcu, the procession reaches the ruins of Sacsayhuamán at about 1400, where scores of thousands of people are gathered on the ancient stones.

Before Pachacuti arrives the Sinchi *(Pachauti's chief general) ushers in contingents from the four* Suyus *(regions) of the Inca empire. Much of the ceremony is based around alternating action between these four groups of players. A* Chaski *(messenger) enters to announce the imminent arrival of the Inca and his* Coya *(queen). Men sweep the ground before him, and women scatter flowers. The Inka takes the stage alone, and has a dialogue with the sun. Then he receives reports from the governors of the four* Suyus*. This is followed by a drink of the sacred chicha, the re-lighting of the sacred fire of the empire, the sacrifice (faked) of a llama, and the reading of auguries in its entrails. Finally the ritual eating of* sankhu *(corn paste mixed with the victim's blood) ends the ceremonies. The Inca gives a last message to his assembled children, and departs. The music and dancing continues until nightfall.*

Northwest of the Plaza de Armas

Above Cusco, on the road up to Sacsayhuamán, is **San Cristóbal**, built to his patron saint by Cristóbal Paullu Inca. The church's atrium has been restored and there is a sidewalk access to the Sacsayhuamán Archaeological Park. North of San Cristóbal, you can see the 11 doorway-sized niches of the great Inca wall of the Palacio de Colcampata, which was the residence of Manco Inca before he rebelled against the Spanish and fled to Vilcabamba. Above San Cristóbal church, to the left, is a private colonial mansion (Quinta Colcampata), once the home of the infamous explorer and murderer, Lope de Aguirre. It has also been home to many other important personages including Simón Bolívar and Hiram Bingham during the years of his excavation of Machu Picchu in 1915-16. It has been restored but is not open to the public.

Cristo Blanco, arms outstretched and brilliantly illuminated at night, stands over the town and is clearly visible if you look north from the Plaza de Armas. He was given to the city as a mark of gratitude by Palestinian refugees in 1944. A quick glance in the local telephone directory reveals there is still a large Arab population in Cusco.

Sacsayhuaman

The site is about a 30-min walk from the town centre. Walk up Pumacurco from Plaza de las Nazarenas

There are some magnificent Inca walls in the ruined ceremonial centre of Sacsayhuaman, on a hill in the northern outskirts. The Incaic stones are hugely impressive. The massive rocks weighing up to 130 tons are fitted together with absolute perfection. Three walls run parallel for over 360 m and there are 21 bastions.

Sacsayhuaman was thought for centuries to be a fortress, but the layout and architecture suggest a great sanctuary and temple to the Sun, which rises exactly opposite the place previously believed to be the Inca's throne – which was probably an altar, carved out of the solid rock. Broad steps lead to the altar from either side. Zig-zags in the boulders round the 'throne' are apparently '*chicha* grooves', channels down which maize beer flowed during festivals. Up the hill is an ancient quarry, the Rodadero, which is now used by children as a rock slide. Near it are many seats cut perfectly into the smooth rock.

For a detailed description, and map, of walks around Sacsayhuaman, see page 129

The hieratic, rather than the military, hypothesis was supported by the discovery in 1982 of the graves of priests, who would have been unlikely to be buried in a fortress. The precise functions of the site, however, will probably continue to be a matter of dispute as very few clues remain, due to its steady destruction. The site survived the first years of the conquest. Pizarro's troops had entered Cusco unopposed in 1533 and lived safely at Sacsayhuaman, until the rebellion of Manco Inca, in 1536, caught them off guard. The bitter struggle which ensued became the decisive military action of the conquest, for Manco's failure to hold Sacsayhuaman cost him the war, and the empire. The destruction of the hilltop site began after the defeat of Manco's rebellion. The outer walls still stand, but the complex of towers and buildings was razed to the ground. From then, until the 1930s, Sacsayhuaman served as a kind of unofficial quarry of pre-cut stone for the inhabitants of Cusco.

■ *Daily 0700-1730. You can get in earlier if you wish and definitely try to get there before midday when the tour groups arrive. Free student guides are available, but you should give them a tip.*

Other sites near Cusco

It is safest to visit the ruins in a group, especially if you wish to see them under a full moon. Take as few belongings as possible, and hide your camera in a bag

Along the road from Sacsayhuaman to Pisac, past a radio station, at 3,600 m, is the temple and amphitheatre of **Qenqo**.These are not exactly ruins, but rather one of the finest examples of Inca stone carving *in situ*, especially inside the large hollowed-out stone that houses an altar. The rock is criss-crossed by zig-zag channels that give the place its name and which served to course *chicha*, or perhaps sacrificial blood, for purposes of divination. The open space many refer to as the 'plaza' or 'amphitheatre' was used for ceremonies. The 19 trapezoidal niches, which are partially destroyed, held idols and mummies.

On the same road is **Cusilluchayoc** (K'usilluyuq; see also page 129), a series of caves and Inca tunnels in a hillside. Take a torch/flashlight to find your way around. There are remains of aqueducts and a well-made fountain which may have been used in ceremonies or as a drinking hole for travellers.

The Inca fortress of **Puka Pukara** (Red Fort), was actually more likely to have been a *tambo*, a kind of post-house where travellers were lodged and goods and animals housed temporarily. It is worth seeing for the views alone.

A few hundred metres up the road is the spring shrine of **Tambo Machay**, still in excellent condition. There are many opinions as to what this place was used for. Some say it was a resting place for the Incas and others that it was used by Inca Yupanqui as a hunting place – the surrounding lands, even today, hide many wild animals including deer and foxes. As this Inca was a living god, Son of the Sun, his palace would also have been a sacred place. There are three ceremonial water fountains built on different levels. As water was considered a powerful deity it is possible that the site was a centre of a water cult. Water still flows by a hidden channel out of the masonry wall, straight into a little rock pool traditionally known as the Inca's bath.

Taking a guide to the sites mentioned above is a good idea and you should visit in the morning for the best photographs. Carry your multi-site ticket, there are roving ticket inspectors. You can visit the sites on foot. It's a pleasant walk through the countryside requiring half a day or more, though remember to take water and sun protection, and watch out for dogs. An alternative is to take the Pisac bus up to Tambo Machay (which costs US$0.35) and walk back. Another excellent way to see the ruins is on horseback, arranged at travel agencies (US$16 per person for five hours). An organized tour (with guide) will go to all the sites for US$6 per person, not including entrance fees. A taxi will charge US$15-20 for three to four people. Some of these ruins are included in the many City Tours available.

Essentials

Sleeping

■ *on maps, see pages 78 and 102*

Prices given are for double rooms with bathroom in the high season of Jun-Aug and include 28% tax and service, unless stated. When there are fewer tourists hotels may drop their prices by as much as half. Always ask for discounts; the prices shown at reception are usually negotiable. Also, hotel prices, especially in the mid to upper categories, are often lower when booked through tour agencies. You should book more expensive hotels well in advance through a good travel agency, particularly for the week or so around Inti Raymi, when prices are much higher.

On the Puno-Cusco train there are many unlicensed hotel agents for medium-priced hotels, but they are often misleading about details; their local nickname is *jalagringos* (gringo pullers), or *piratas*. Rooms offered at Cusco station are usually cheaper than those offered on the train. Taxis and tourist minibuses meet the train and take you to the hotel of your choice for US$0.50, but be insistent.

It is cold in Cusco, and many hotels do not have heating. It is worth asking for an *estufa*, a space heater, which some places will provide for an extra charge. When staying in the big, popular hotels, allow yourself plenty of time to check out if you have a plane or train to catch: front desks can be very busy. All the hotels listed below offer free luggage storage unless otherwise stated. Assume hotels have 24-hr hot water in pre-heated tanks unless otherwise stated. Cusco´s low-power electric showers often do a poor job of heating the very cold water and their safety is sometimes questionable.

LL *Libertador*, in the Casa de los Cuatro Bustos at Plazoleta Santo Domingo 259 (see page 85), T231961, F233152, www.libertador.com.pe Buffet breakfast is US$15 extra. This splendid 5-star, award-winning hotel is built on Inca ruins (the walls can be seen in the restaurant and bar) and is set around courtyards. It has 254 well-appointed rooms; the attention to detail is so great there are even Nazca Lines drawn in the sand of the ashtrays! Enjoy Andean music and dance over dinner in the excellent *Inti Raymi* restaurant. Recommended.

LL *Monasterio*, Palacios 136, T241777, F237111, www.monasterio.orient-express.com This 5-star, beautifully-restored Seminary of San Antonio Abad is central and quite simply the best hotel in town for historical interest; it is worth a visit even if you cannot afford the price tag (see page 82). Soft Gregorian chants follow you as you wander through the Baroque chapel, tranquil courtyards and charming cloisters, admiring the excellent collection of religious paintings. There are 106 spacious rooms with all facilities, including cable TV, as well as 16 suites and a US$521 presidential suite. Staff, who all speak English, are very helpful and attentive. The price includes a great buffet breakfast (US$12 to non-residents) which will fill you up for the rest of the day. The restaurant, where the monks used to sing, serves lunch and dinner à la carte. The chapel is used as a conference centre and there is email for guests (US$3 per hr) open 0930-1300, 1730-2130. Recommended.

LL ***Novotel***, San Agustín 239, T228282, F228855, corphotelera@terra.com.pe 4-star, US$25 cheaper – US$160 as opposed to US$185 – in modern section; price includes buffet breakfast. This is probably the best hotel converted from a colonial house in Cusco. Opened in June 2000, it was originally built as a home for conquistador Miguel Sánchez Ponce who accompanied Pizarro in the taking of Cajamarca. It was remodeled after the 1650 earthquake by General Pardo de Figueroa who built the lovely stone archways and commissioned paintings of the saints of his devotion on the grand stairway. Today the beautiful courtyard, roofed in glass, has sofas, coffee tables and pot plants around the central stone fountain. The modern 5-storey rear extension has 83 excellent spacious, airy and bright rooms. All have sofas, cable TV, central heating and bathtubs. Those above the second floor have views over Cusco's red-tiled rooftops. The 16 in the colonial section are not much different but have high, beamed-ceilings and huge, 2 m-wide beds. There are two restaurants and a French chef.

L ***Don Carlos***, Av Sol 602, T226207 (Lima T224 0263, F224 8581), www.tci.net.pe/doncarlos The price includes buffet breakfast. This 50-bedroom, modern hotel is clean and bright and has a friendly front desk but lacks character. All rooms have cable TV, a safe, fridge and heating as well as 24-hr room service. Some also have facilities for the

Cusco

Good Samaritans

"Shoeshine? Shoeshine?" Everyone who visits Cusco will experience the sad sight of children as young as five struggling to shine shoes, sell sweets or postcards.

Grubby, crouched in the gutter on a homemade box, knees poking through what´s left of their jeans, these urchins have been banned from the Plaza de Armas, but persevere to survive by pestering every tourist in sight in the streets nearby. Their plight is extraordinary. Often the offspring of alcoholic parents, many of them sleep huddled together in shacks you wouldn´t allow a pig to inhabit.

But equally amazing is the story of a pair of Dutch backpackers who have set out to change the children´s lives forever and the tale behind two other foreigners who are working to help Cusco´s downtrodden and who need your help.

Titus Bovenberg, now 43, and his girlfriend Jolanda, 36, came as tourists to Cusco in 1996. Five years later they are still here – with a family of 12 adopted boys and a programme by the name of ***Los Niños*** *that feeds and helps educate and clothe a further 126. The 126 are the worst cases sent from three local schools. Many arrive with TB, bronchitis, pneumonia and numerous skin diseases. Some have been fainting through malnutrition; all are too small for their age. Doctors and dentists first attend to the children then Los Niños give the youngsters healthy food, ensure they clean their teeth and shower 10 or 15 of them every day at their centre.*

This is all funded by an excellent hostel named Niños Hotel and a set of apartments (see page 97). Staying here is a way of directly helping the street children (no volunteers are taken).

The couple, who now have a baby girl of their own as sister to their 12 adopted sons, have plans to open another food hall, a sports centre as well as arrange for the adoption of a further 12 children with another couple.

Titus says: "We want to give these children not only food but hope that they can escape this; we must teach

disabled. Not the best value in this price range. **L *Picoaga***, Santa Teresa 344 (two blocks from the Plaza de Armas), T227691, F221246, www.computextos.com.pe/picoaga Price includes buffet breakfast. Originally the home of the Marqués de Picoaga, this beautiful colonial building has large original bedrooms set around a shady courtyard and a modern section, with a/c, at the back. All have cable TV, minibar and safe. There are conference facilities and the staff are very pleasant. Pricey but recommended.

L *San Agustín Internacional*, San Agustín y Maruri 390, T221169, F221174, www.hotelsanagustin.com.pe Price includes continental breakfast. There is a rustic Mexican feel to the lobby with its fireplace and water feature, while Andean music is piped to the communal areas. There are 74 heated bedrooms and the staff will organize tours. **L *Savoy Internacional***, Av Sol 954, T224322, F221100 (Lima T/F446 7965), www.cusco.net/savoyhotel Price includes American breakfast. This is one of the earliest modern hotels in the city and some of the features such as TV sets (cable) and minibars are dated. However, bedrooms are spacious, with heating and some have good views, as does the Sky Room. There is also a bar, coffee shop, and the staff speak many languages. For a large hotel, this has a warm, friendly feel.

L *Sonesta Posada del Inca*, Portal Espinar 142, one block from the central plaza, T222 4777 ((Lima), F01-422 4345, www.sonesta.com Price includes buffet breakfast but internet is a whopping US$6 an hr – use one of the cafés on the plaza instead. All 53 warmly decorated rooms in this modern hotel have heating and cable TV. There are no-smoking bedrooms on the first floor, but for best views of the Plaza, over rooftops, reserve nos 316, 318, 320 or 321 on the third floor. The restaurant serves Andean food and there is an open fire in the lobby. The all English-speaking staff provide an excellent service. Recommended.

them they are human beings."

Meanwhile, in San Blas, another Dutch couple are battling for the underdogs through the ***Hope Foundation****. In 10 years Walter Meekes and his wife Tineke have built 20 schools in poor mountain villages and barrios around Cusco.*

They have a program to teach teachers and, in town, there is a 30-bed burns unit at the hospital that would have been just a dream were it not for their efforts.

Again, work is funded by an excellent hostel (Marani, see page 96) at which Walter will gladly tell you about his work. He does need volunteers.

A British woman aged just 23 is spearheading Cusco´s third amazing project.

Suzy Ugaz, formerly from Brighton, has set up ***Kiya Survivors****, which is educating 20 children with special needs aged 4-16 at a day centre being built in Urubamba. There is no other provision for these children locally.*

She says: "One of the kids is 16 and has Downs Syndrome. She had been out of her family house only once in all her life. Within two days of coming to us she was like a new person, smiling and wanting to write."

The centre is run by a Peruvian special needs teacher named Mario, one of the best in the country. By September 2001 they plan to have four teachers and three classrooms.

Suzy spends her time fundraising and organising gap-year students to help the project. Volunteers are asked to raise US$2,900, half of which goes straight to the centre and the rest on the volunteer´s air fares, a four-day Inca Trail, a two-week Spanish course in Peru, training for special needs and accommodation (in Cusco).

To help Los Niños or the Hope Foundation, simply book a room at their hostels. For Kiya Survivors, log on to their website: www.kiyasurvivors.co.uk, or call call 625405 in Cusco.

AL ***Don Carlos IncaTambo Hacienda Hotel***, at Km 2, close to Sacsayhuaman, above the town, reservations: T01(Lima)-224 0263, F01-224 8581; hotel direct: T221918, F222045, www.tci.net.pe/doncarlos Price, 25% cheaper if booked through *Luzma Tours* (see page 117), includes buffet breakfast and transport from the airport. Built on the site of Pizarro's original house, this 23-bedroom rustic-style hacienda is very peaceful, but this may not be enough to lure you out of town. The patio is a pleasant suntrap, but the garden is rough and, despite its height above the city, the views are not spectacular. Rooms have heaters and Peruvian-only TV. Horse riding can be arranged in the 60 ha of hotel grounds or around the nearby ruins. **AL** ***El Dorado Inn***, Av Sol 395, T231135, F240993, doratour@telser.com.pe Price includes buffet breakfast. Modern meets colonial in this sophisticated 3-star hotel. Visitors to Barcelona will be reminded of Gaudi as they gaze up at the elevator shaft which dominates the central lobby with its white adobe exterior and wild sci-fi eye sockets for windows. The 85 bedrooms, renewed in 2000, are individually decorated in colonial style. In particular, ask to see room 304. A good restaurant (*Sky Room*), serves lunch and dinner for US$10. The trendy cafeteria is open to the public.

AL ***Los Apus Hostal y Mirador***, Atocsaycuchi 515 y Choquechaca, San Blas, T264243, F264211, www.losapushostal.com Price includes buffet breakfast and airport pick-up; laundry costs US$1 per kg. Character and mod-cons combine in this Swiss-owned hostal. It is all varnished wood, very clean and smart with beamed bedrooms fitted with cable TV and real radiators! Tall travellers will love the 2.3m-long beds, but views are limited, even from the breakfast lookout on the top floor.

AL ***Royal Inka I***, Plaza Regocijo 299, T231067/222284, F234221, royalin@terra.com.pe Price includes buffet breakfast. The 29 bedrooms, with cable TV and heating, are set in a colonial house around an enclosed shady central patio. Those to the front have balconies overlooking the plaza. The building is decorated with heavy colonial furnishings and has a tranquil atmosphere. There is a bar and the restaurant has a set menu, some days including roast leg of lamb! Recommended. **AL** ***Royal Inka II***, close by, on Santa Teresa. More modern and expensive but the price includes buffet breakfast, saunas and Jacuzzi. Massages are an extra US$25. The old colonial façade hides a modern building, the rooms of which open out onto a huge atrium dominated by an incongruous, three-storey high mural. All rooms have cable TV, heating and are identical, except for 218 and three others which are much larger for the same price. These hotels run a free bus for guests to Pisac at 1000 daily, returning at 1800. **AL** ***San Agustín Plaza***, Av Sol 594, T238121, F237375, website as above. Price includes buffet breakfast. Decorated in a Spanish style with a central fireplace in the lobby, this hotel has 26 bedrooms which are very well decorated, clean and airy. Street front rooms have views of Qoricancha. The staff are exceptionally helpful.

A ***Emperador Plaza***, Santa Catalina Ancha 377, T227412, F263581, emperadr@terra.com.pe Price includes buffet breakfast. A modern, light, airy hotel with friendly and helpful English-speaking staff. They will even order food for you from the Irish pub over the road! Rooms have cable TV, hairdryer, gas-heated showers and electric radiators. **A** ***Hostal Carlos V***, Tecseccocha 490, T/F223091. Price includes continental breakfast; heating is US$2.30 a night extra, TV costs more too. Take time to explore the 30 rooms and you should be able to find one with character and reasonable décor in the refurbished first floor section. However, many bathrooms are shabby. At its listed price this would be poor value for money, but the owners are definitely open to negotiation. Worth a look. **A** ***Hostal Cusco Plaza***, Plaza Nazarenas 181 (opposite *El Monasterio*) T246161, F263842. Price includes continental breakfast. Situated on a lovely small plaza in the town centre, there are 33 clean rooms all with cable TV. Room 303 has the best view. The management was due to open a second hotel at Saphi 486 in August 2001.

A ***Hostal El Balcón***, Tambo de Montero 222, T236738, F225352, balcon1@terra.com.pe Price includes breakfast and you can pay with Visa, AmEx, Diners and Visa electrón. This lovingly restored 1630 colonial house has 16 large rooms, all with views. Ask for a TV if you want – there is no extra charge. As well as a restaurant there is a kitchen for guests to use, a laundry service. Homely atmosphere. Recommended. **A** ***Hostal Garcilaso***, Garcilaso 233, T233031, F222401, hotelgarcilaso@hotmail.com Price includes continental breakfast, heater and cable TV. Services include oxygen, laundry and excursions can be organized. This is a 30-bedroom modernised colonial house. It has a comfortable lobby with a large open fireplace and cable TV. The spacious carpeted rooms are somewhat lacking in style and character. There is a bar, cafeteria and dining room. Staff are helpful. ***Garcilaso II*** at No 285, T233501/227951, at the same price, is also good.

A ***Hostal Plaza de Armas***, Plaza de Armas, corner of Mantas, T222351, F247130, PO Box 502, hostal_plaza@terra.com.pe Price includes breakfast, from 0500. This is a clean, modern hotel with 38 rooms, each with cable TV, mineral water and heaters. However, in spite of its excellent position, only the lacklustre restaurant has views over the plaza. **A** ***Pensión Alemana***, Tandapata 260, San Blas, T/F226861, pensioalemana@terra.com Price includes American breakfast; laundry is US$1.10/kilo and heating extra. Car parking available. This Swiss-owned pension has clean, modern European décor with a comfy lounge area in which to watch cable TV or listen to music. There is a lovely garden with patio furniture. Recommended.

B ***Hostal Cahuide***, Saphi 845, T222771, F222361. Price (discount for longer stays) includes American breakfast but you need to ask for the free TV in your room (cable is only available in sitting rooms). Heating is US$1.40 per night, laundry costs US$.90 per kg. This is a modern 45-room hotel with 70s furniture, plain white walls and comfortable beds. Helpful, good value breakfasts. **B** ***Hostal Casa de Campo***, Tandapata 296-B (at the end of the street), T244404, F241422, info@hotelcasadecampo.com (or contact via *La Tertulia* café). Price (10% discount for SAE members and Footprint Handbook owners) includes continental breakfast and free airport/rail/bus transfer with reservations. Guests get a work-out thrown in for free in the shape of many steep steps up to the multi-level hotel! Consequently the 20 bedrooms have fabulous views over Cusco.. There is a safe deposit box, laundry service, meals on request and a sun terrace. Dutch and English are spoken; take a taxi there after dark.

B ***Hostal Corihuasi***, C Suecia 561, T/F232233, www.corihuasi.com Price (can pay by Visa or AmEx) includes continental breakfast and airport pick-up. Electric heaters cost an extra US$1.50 per night; services include a free book exchange. A tough climb up from the northernmost corner of the Plaza de Armas, this tranquil 18-bedroom guest house is popular with tour groups. It is friendly and has some good views (the best is from room 1) as well as cable TV in the breakfast room. Recommended. **B** ***Hostal Cristina***, Av Sol 341, T227233, F227251, hcristina@terra.com.pe Price includes continental breakfast. This is more of a hotel than a hostal with good, comfortable rooms which all have cable TV and were redecorated in July 2001. Rebuilt after the 1950 earthquake, this well-positioned, friendly place nevertheless retains colonial features. Good value.

B-C ***Hostal El Arqueólogo***, Pumacurco 408 (entrance may still be via Ladrillos 425), T232569, F235126, reservation@hotelarquelogo.com Price includes buffet breakfast. Services include oxygen, a library and hot drinks. A colonial building on Inca foundations, this has rustic but stylish décor. There is a lovely sunny garden with comfy chairs and a small restaurant that serves interesting Peruvian food and fondue. French and English spoken. Recommended. **B** ***Hostal Qosqo***, Portal Mantas 115, near the Plaza de Armas, T252513, bargain hard for prices. Price includes continental breakfast, a heater and cable TV. The state of décor and quality of mattresses varies from room to room but most stay here for its proximity to the plaza. Clean, friendly and helpful.

B ***La Casa del Escribano*** (formerly *La Casa de Mariscal*), Av Tullumayo 465, T233472. This is a well-maintained colonial building housing a college for mature students. They rent out 20 bedrooms which are very modern and sparsely decorated but they do have desks. It is about a 15-min walk from the centre. **B** ***Los Marqueses***, Garcilaso 256, T232512, F227028, marqueseshotel@hotmail.com Price includes breakfast, heaters extra. The showers are electric. A splendid colonial house from the 17th century with perhaps the most interesting courtyard in Cusco. The place is littered with antiques and the breakfast room even has its own altarpiece rescued from a church! The bedrooms will not be to everyone´s taste – all are in need of loving renovation – but you won´t regret coming to have a look. The building is a photographer´s dream and you won´t have a more memorable stay than this. A chain is putting in a bid to rent it so get there before they do. Rooms are in a better state at the back but far less interesting.Recommended. **B** ***Los Portales***, Matará 322, T/F223500, portales01@ terra.com.pe Price includes continental breakfast and airport pickup; heaters are extra. Services include safe deposit box, laundry (US$3/kg), oxygen and a money exchange. TV is local channels only and check-out time is an unfriendly 0900! A modern hotel with modern facilities, the whole place is painted in magnolia, relieved by wall paintings of local scenes. Very friendly and helpful, children welcome. Recommended.

B ***Pensión Loreto***, Pasaje Loreto 115, Plaza de Armas (it shares the same entrance as *Norton's Rat* pub), T226352, hostalloreto@telser.com.pe Price includes continental breakfast and a heater which you will need as the original Inca walls make the rooms cold. Again, the best feature of this hostal is its location, although the rooms are spacious and they will serve you breakfast in bed if you are finding it too cold to get up.

They have a laundry service and will help organize any travel services including guides and taxis. A bit pricey but where else can you fall out of a pub into your hostal?

C ***Hostal Amaru***, Cuesta San Blas 541, T/F225933, www.cusco.net/amaru Price (US$16 without bathroom) includes breakfast and airport/train/bus pick-up. Services include oxygen, kitchen for use in the evenings only, laundry and free book exchange. Rooms are grouped around a pretty colonial courtyard, covered in geraniums in Jul. They have TVs with national channels only (cable in sitting area), good beds and carved wardrobes. This has pleasant places to relax and some Inca walls. Rooms in the first courtyard are best. Recommended. **C** ***Hostal Horeb***, San Juan de Dios 260, T236775. Price includes a simple breakfast.There are 7 large rooms but most have no outside windows and some of the beds are hard. Couples would do better in one of the upstairs rooms at *Frankenstein*'s in the same building. **C** ***Hostal Imperial Palace***, Tecseccocha 490-B, T223324, celazo@hotmail.com **D** without bathroom, price includes continental breakfast and heaters. Rooms are large and have comfortable beds but are in need of redecoration. There is a café, bar and restaurant. Very friendly.

C ***Hostal Incawasi***, Portal de Panes 147, Plaza de Armas, T223992, incawasi@telser.com.pe The communal area and rooms are rather dark and they don't have outside windows, let alone views of the plaza, but with a location like this you won't be spending much time indoors. Perhaps for this reason there is no cable TV. The beds are good and the staff helpful. You can get good bargains for longer stays. **C** ***Hostal María Esther***, Pumacurco 516, T/F224382. Price includes continental breakfast and heating available for US$2 extra (US$14.30 without bathroom).This very friendly, helpful establishment has a lovely garden in which to relax and a variety of rooms. There is also a lounge with sofas and car parking. Recommended. **C** ***Hostal Pakcha Real***, Tandapata 300, San Blas, T237484, pakcharealhostal@hotmail.com Price includes breakfast, the use of the kitchen (there is no fridge) and free airport/train/bus pick-up; heaters are an extra US$1.50. This is a family-run hostal where you can expect all the comforts of home including a large lounge with a fireplace and cable TV. There is a laundry service and they own the shop next door. The rooms are spotless although sparsely decorated and the front two rooms have great views. Taxis can drop you at the door. A friendly, relaxed place.

C ***Hostal Q'Awarina***, at the top of Suecia 575, T228130. Price includes continental breakfast, heating is US$2 extra per night. No laundry service. Rooms are OK, ask for those with a view – they cost the same. There is a lovely living room with views across the city and the breakfast area upstairs is even better. Group rates available, good value. **C** ***Hostal Rumi Punku*** Choquechaca 339, T221102, F242741, www.rumipunku.com Said to be built on a former Inca temple, this has a genuine Inca doorway that leads to a sunny, tranquil courtyard. All 17 rooms (22 by end of 2001, along with a lighter breakfast room) are large, clean and comfortable. Contintental breakfast is included in the price and laundry costs US$0.90/kg. Highly recommended.

C ***Huaynapata***, Huaynapata 369, T228034. Price includes breakfast; heaters are optional. There is a laundry service and a safe but, while there is a patio on the roof, views are limited. This is a modern-style hostal which is a bit shabby in parts, but the bedrooms are OK and the beds are comfortable. To ring the bell you have to put your arm through the bars in the door! **C** ***El Inca***, Quera 251, T/F 221110, oscaralianza@yahoo.com Price (can pay by Visa or MasterCard) includes breakfast; services include laundry (US$1.40/kg). Some of the rooms here need redecorating and one smells damp but if you choose carefully and avoid those on the first floor (there is a noisy disco in the basement) this can be a bargain find for a centrally-located hotel.

C ***Marani***, Carmen Alto 194, San Blas, T/F249462, marani@terra.com.pe Breakfasts available. Services include beginnings of a book exchange and information on Andean life and culture. Walter Meekes and his wife Tineke opened this spotless hostal in Aug 2000. The rooms are large with beamed ceilings and have heaps of character, set around a courtyard. There is a breakfast room to the same standards. Some of the rooms are decorated with gifts of gratitude from communities the couple have helped through their association, the Hope Foundation (www.stichtinghope.org). In 10 years the Dutch couple have built 20 schools in poor mountain villages and barrios, established a program to teach teachers and set up a 30-bed burns unit in Cusco general hospital. Good value, a great cause and highly recommended.

C ***Niños Hotel***, C Meloc 442, T/F231424, www.targetfound.nl.ninos Price (US$24 without bathroom) does not include the excellent breakfast (fruit salad, home-made wholemeal bread, locally-produced jam and tea or coffee) which costs just US$1.70. Services include the cafeteria, laundry service (US$1.15/kg) and book exchange. Dutch, English, German and French are all spoken. Spotless, beautiful rooms funding a fantastic charity make this our most highly recommended hotel in this price category. Dutch couple Titus and Jolande Bovenberg have converted this 18th century colonial house into a stylish, comfortable place, typified by painted-wood floors and fresh lilies everywhere. All bedrooms lead onto a well-renovated courtyard. Those downstairs are named after the 12 streetchildren Titus and Jolande have adopted and care for at the back of the hotel, while upstairs rooms bear the names of various benefactors. Nearby are some equally well-appointed apartments (US$20) which share a kitchen, bathroom, but are cold. These help fund a restaurant in the same complex where the Niños foundation everyday feeds, cares for and helps educate 126 more streetchildren.

C ***Posada del Sol***, Atocsaycuchi 296, T/F246394. Includes American breakfast, heater and airport pick-up. Cheerfully decorated with rustic charm, the hotel also has a sun terrace with great views of Cusco and fantastic showers. Guests may use the kitchen and laundry costs only US$0.50/kg. Food is available. The hostal is up some steps and cannot be reached by taxi. Recommended.

Cusco

D ***El Arcano***, Carmen Alto 288, T/F232703. The old *Hostal Cristales* and *El Arcano* are now run by one person and share the same name. Breakfast and laundry are available in both, cheaper rooms with shared bath. On the one side there is a lovely little communal area with comfortable seating covered by a colourful glass roof and on the other there is a small breakfast area with cable TV and a book exchange. The owners are very friendly as is their large German Shepherd dog. They will help arrange trips and own two lodges; one in the jungle and another in cloudforest. Highly recommended. **D** ***Hospedaje Turístico San Blas***, Cuesta San Blas 526, T225781. The price includes continental breakfast and there is cable TV in the comfortable, covered courtyard. Heaters are extra. The bedrooms are very well decorated and the place has a lot of charm for a basic hostal.

D ***Hostal Familiar***, Saphi 661, T239353. **E** without bathroom, luggage deposit costs US$2.85 a day for a big pack. For 25 years the owners have run this popular 32-bedroom hostal, which is based in a pleasing colonial house with benches around a central courtyard, 3 blocks from the central plaza. Most beds are comfy and there is now hot water all day from tanks. Recommended. **D** ***Hostal Familiar Mirador del Inka***, Tandapata 160, off Plaza San Blas, T261384. At the moment breakfast is not available but they are in the process of building a cafeteria. You can use the dilapidated kitchen and there is a laundry service. This hostal looks very stylish with its Inca foundations and white colonial walls but the interior courtyard is only good for a game of footie. The bedrooms with private bathrooms can be musty although they are spacious and some have great views. The owner's son Edwin runs trekking trips and has an agency on site.

D ***Hostal Kuntur Wasi***, Tandapata 352-A, San Blas, T227570. **E** without bathroom, services include a safe, use of the kitchen (for US$0.60 a day) and laundry (US$0.85/kg). There are great views from the terrace where you can breakfast. Owned by a very welcoming, helpful, family. The showers are electric. A very pleasant place to stay. **D** ***Hostal Machu Picchu***, Quera 282, T231111. **E** without bathroom; there is a public phone, a safe but no TVs; laundry costs US$0.85/kg. This is a central, pleasant place to stay if you can afford the better rooms. Those with a bathroom in this very clean colonial house are of a high standard but those "sin baño" are dark inside. Floors are stylishly tiled and there are plenty of places to relax in the flower-filled garden and escape the busy road outside.

D ***Hostal Royal Frankenstein***, San Juan de Dios 260 (next to *Horeb*), 2 blocks from the Plaza de Armas, T236999, ludwigroth@hotmail.com One thing is for sure, you will never forget this place. Greeted by a grinning skull whose eyesockets light up as you enter, things just become more peculiar. Passing through the fully-equipped kitchen (just US$0.30 a day), you can sit next to a (caged) tarantula while watching cable TV in the living room or gaze at Franken Fish. Rooms, fortunately, follow this theme in name only, thus you can stay in Mary Shelley or the Laboratorio. Nearly all 10 have excellent mattresses but few have outside windows. Downstairs, with one exception, they also run straight off the living room, which has an open fire. However, Ludwig, the mildly eccentric German owner, has two excellent matrimonials/family rooms on the open-air top floor which are excellent and come with heaters. There is also a safe and laundry facilities. Recommended.

E ***El Artesano de San Blas***, Suytuccato 790, T/F263968. Price includes use of kitchen. Rooms in this colonial house are large, if a little dark, very clean and decorated to a high standard; many bathrooms are brand new. The staff are also very friendly. Recommended. **E** ***Hospedaje Jhuno***, Carmen Alto 281, San Blas, T233579. Breakfast is not included but guests can use the tiny kitchenette. This is a small family-run hospedaje with 8 clean, decorated rooms and a family lounge with a stereo. **E** ***Hospedaje Killipata***, just off Tambo de Montero, T 236668. Very clean, family-run lodging with good showers and 24-hr hot water. Recommended.

E ***Hostal Cáceres***, Plateros 368, T232616, 1 block from the Plaza de Armas. **F** without bathroom, services include use of the kitchen for US$0.30 a day, a free book exchange and laundry (US$1/kg). This is not the prettiest colonial budget hostal but it is well-positioned with large, if basic rooms. Not all the foam mattresses are comfortable so be sure to check. The owners are very friendly, helpful and will let you park your motorcycle in the patio. **E** ***Hostal Casa Grande***, Santa Catalina Ancha 353, T264156. Price includes continental breakfast. Other facilities include a laundry service (US$1/kg), free parking, towels, cable TV in the 2 communal areas; heaters are extra. There is a kitchen but it is rather run-down. This colonial family-run hostal is set around a cluttered courtyard and has charm for a basic backpackers' haunt. With its great location and the relaxed atmosphere you can forgive them the foam matresses. Rooms over the road seem to be in a better state of decor. Most rooms are multiples but there are some with double beds.

E ***Munay Wasi***, Huaynapata 253, not far from Plaza de Armas, T223661. The price includes free hot drinks and clothes-washing facilities. There are plans to put in cable TV. Bargain for a bed in this quiet, run-down colonial house. The 7 bedooms are basic and very clean and most matresses are sprung. The 2 front rooms have views of the Plaza de Armas. The owner is friendly and helpful. **E** ***Posada del Viajero***, Santa Catalina Ancha 366, down lane next to *Rosie O'Grady's*. Select your room carefully and you could find a real bargain at this centrally-located hostal. Some are drab with dodgy mattresses piled three high but the student owners are making real efforts and others have newly-tiled bathrooms and comfy beds. By Sep 2001 a new kitchen should also be ready for daily use for a small fee.

E ***Hostal Qorichaska***, Nueva Alta 458, T228974, F227094. Price includes a continental breakfast, use of the well-equipped kitchen and safe. Laundry is US$0.85/kg.

Rooms in this colonial house are clean, sunny although watch out for the odd sagging mattress in the new section. Ask for the older rooms which are bigger and have traditional balconies overlooking the paved courtyard. Friendly, recommended. **E-F** ***Hostal Resbalosa***, Resbalosa 494, T224839. **F** without a bathroom, full breakfast is US$1.45 extra; laundry costs US$0.85/kg. For superb views of the Plaza de Armas from a sun-drenched terrace look no further. Owner Georgina is very hospitable but her best rooms are those with a view (US$1.45 extra). Others may be pokey and suffer from foam mattresses. The electric showers are reportedly cool, but most guests love this place.

E ***Hostal Sambleño***, Carmen Alto 114, T221452. Heating extra, breakfast is available and there is a laundry service. A lovely jumble of staircases overlooks a central courtyard in this San Blas cheapie which has some rooms of varying quality. Beds are comfortable but the showers are electric. Recommended. **E** ***Hostal Santa María***, Santa Catalina Angosta 156, near Plaza de Armas, down a passageway. With its excellent location you can't expect any creature comforts with this price tag. Rooms are bare, dark but clean and the beds are fine. **E** ***Suecia II***, Tecseccocha 465 (no bell – knock!), T239757 (it is wise to book ahead). **F** without bathroom, breakfast US$1.40. You´ll find Suecia II opposite *Los Perros* lounge bar close to Gringo Alley. Rooms are set around a glass-covered colonial courtyard and consequently are warm. Beds have foam mattresses but these are thick and guests can sit at tables on verandahs overlooking the patio. Drawbacks: no seats on the toilets, water not always hot or bathrooms clean, can be noisy and the luggage store is closed at night, otherwise OK.

E ***Hostal Tahuantinsuyo***, Jr Tupac Yupanqui 204, Urb Tahuantinsuyo (15-min walk from the Plaza de Armas), T/F261410. Rooms are cheaper without bathroom, price includes breakfast, also drinks and snacks available. The atmosphere is warm, friendly and very helpful. There is a laundry service and clothes washing facilities, secure parking for bikes and motorbikes, English, French and Italian spoken. Tours can be arranged. Recommended. **E** ***Hostal Tikawasi***, Tandapata 491, San Blas, T/F231609, tikawasi@latinmail.com Price includes breakfast; no private bathrooms. A family-run hostal with a nice garden overlooking the city, very quiet and pleasant.

F ***California***, Nueva Alta 444, T/F242997. Services include free use of the somewhat grubby kitchen (which has no fridge), and there is a TV (no cable) in the living area downstairs. Some bedrooms are beamed, but the mattresses are ropey and the showers are electric. There´s a good area to sit and eat or just chat and a second courtyard at the back where you can relax in the sun – but neither are too pretty. A step up from basic in a hostal of character. Very friendly and hospitable. **F** ***Chaska Wasi***, Amargura 130 (there is no sign), T622831. For US$3 extra you´ll be given cable TV in your room and American breakfast. Guests can also use the basic kitchen (there is no fridge) and there´s a laundry service for US$1.40/kg. This family house, formerly known as La Cabaña, has character and 10 well-presented rooms. Sadly the beds are hard but showers are good and downstairs there is a clay oven in the living area to warm the guests´ hearts. Drawback: there are no double beds, otherwise this is excellent value for 1 block away from the central plaza. **F** per person ***El Balcón Colonial***, Choquechaca 350, T238129. Continental breakfast is included. Use of the kitchen costs US$1.50 per day and laundry costs US$1/kg. There is accommodation for 16 people in 6 rooms of this family house. Rooms are basic with foam mattresses but the hospitality of the owner is exceptional.

F per person ***Hospedaje Inka***, Suytuccato 848, San Blas, T231995. Taxis leave you at Plaza San Blas, walk steeply uphill for 5-10 mins, or phone the hostal. Price includes bath and breakfast. There are wonderful views, the rooms are spacious and owner Américo is very helpful, with lots of information. **F** ***Hospedaje Sol Naciente***, Av Pardo 510, T228602. This is a very basic but clean and comfortable hostal approximately 10 mins away from the centre. One bedroom has private bath. There is a small fee for storing luggage and laundry can be arranged. **F** ***Hospedaje Wiñay Wayna***, Vitoque 628 (at the top of Nueva Baja) T246794, miriamojeda@yahoo.com Price includes continental breakfast, no rooms have bath. Heating is available (US$1.40 a night), there is a safe and guests can use the kitchen. Laundry service costs US$0.70/kg. This hostal is fantastic value, perhaps reflecting its position away from Plaza, near the market. All but one room is bright and airy, comfortable and pleasant, as is the cafeteria. Rugs on the floor typify this family's effort to make this colonial house a very pleasant place to stay for the money. Highly recommended.

F ***Hostal Familiar Carmen Alto***, Carmen Alto 197, first on the right down steps (there is no sign), 3 blocks from central plaza. Budget hostal owners could take a leaf out of owner Carmen's books: she has succeeded in giving basic rooms great character with traditional wall hangings and, in one case, by constructing a room around a huge live tree! This tranquil hostal is very much family run and guests can use the kitchen and washing machine. All rooms have shared bath and the showers are electric. Recommended. **F** ***Hostal Residencial Santa Rosa de Lima***, Ahuacpinta 676, T262698. Run by nuns, accommodation is not available during holy festivals (eg Christmas, Easter). Price includes breakfast. This clean, friendly place has hot water, kitchen and laundry facilities, luggage store and is safe. **F** ***Hostal Rickch'airy***, Tambo de Montero 219, T236606. All rooms are without bath, except for one which costs US$20.This highly popular backpackers' haunt has views from the garden where travellers swop Machu Picchu tales while waiting for their tents to dry. There is full breakfast available (US$2) and owner Leo has tourist information and will collect guests from the station. In Jan 2002 he will open 14 more rooms, all with private bathrooms for US$20. Recommended.

F ***Tumi 1***, Siete Cuartones 245, 2 blocks from Plaza de Armas, T24413. Price includes use of the kitchen and laundry area. There is a free book exchange and laundry service costs US$0.85. This lovely colonial house has 16 bedrooms (none with bath) around a sunny, paved courtyard. All are clean, traditional and huge with bare wooden floors and walls in need of a lick of paint. The toilets all lack a toilet seat and it seems tight to charge poor backpackers US$1.40 if they have more than one shower (some are electric) a day. However, this is a very friendly, popular place and good value, especially if you bargain for longer stays.

G ***Estrellita***, Av Tullumayo 445, parte Alta, T234134. Price includes breakfast and free tea and coffee all day. There is a TV, video and old stereo system in the tiny communal sitting area and a very basic kitchen, which is just for guests. 11 rooms are multiples with shared bathrooms and there are 2 with private bathrooms. It is basic but the wooden floors, good mattresses and clean decor make this excellent value. It is about a 15-min walk from the centre. When you arrive ring the bell several times and wait; you will be given your own keys when you register. Cars and bikes can be parked safely. Recommended. **G** ***Hospedaje Familiar Inti Quilla***, Atocsaycuchi 281, T252659. Breakfast is not included and there are no facilities for either providing or making food. There are 6 colourfully-decorated bedrooms around a pleasant little courtyard. It is situated on a quiet pedestrian street which means taxis cannot drop you off at the door. Good value.

G ***Hostal Luzerna***, Av Baja 205, near San Pedro train station (take a taxi at night), T232762/ 237591/227768. Price includes breakfast. A nice family runs this hostal which has hot water, good beds and is clean. It is safe to leave luggage. Recommended. **G** ***Hostal Pumacurco***, Pumacurco 336, Interior 329, T243347 (3 mins from the Plaza de Armas). This is in the newly-restored part of a very old colonial house. Everywhere is clean and secure and there are some large rooms as well as washing facilities. Owner Betty is very friendly and helpful. **G** per person ***Hostal San Cristóbal***, Quiscapata 242, near San Cristóbal. Beds are saggy in this all-dormitory hostal, next door to the 50%

more expensive youth hostel. Guests can use a basic kitchen which has no fridge and wash their clothes. Showers are good. The owner is friendly and reliable – if full Sra Ema de Paredes will let you spread a sleeping bag on the floor. Recommended.

Family lodgings There is a network of local families offering tourist accommodation in 3 categories: *Inti* (room with private bath), *Quilla* (room with shared bathroom), and *Chaska* (rooms with use of family's bathroom). Guests are also invited to participate in family events. Contact: Small Business Association of Family Lodgings, C San Augustin 415, T244036, F233912.

Youth hostels F ***Albergue Municipal***, Quiscapata 240, near San Cristóbal, T252506. There are private rooms with double beds as well as dormitories (US$4.30 per person) in this very clean, helpful 56-bed youth hostel. No rooms have bath. It has the added bonus of great views as well as a cafeteria and place to wash clothes (laundry service US$0.85/kg). Showers are electric and, unusually for a youth hostel, there is no kitchen but this is great value. **F** ***El Procurador del Cusco***, Coricalle 440, Prolongación Procuradores (at the end of Procuradores), T243559, hostal-procurador-cusco@hotmail.com **G** without bathroom; price includes use of the basic kitchen (no fridge) and laundry area. The rooms are basic and the beds somewhat hard but upstairs is better. There is a place to relax and gaze over the city and the people are very friendly and helpful. This is good value for money. Recommended.

Eating

Expensive

• *on map, see* *pages 78 and 102*

El Monasterio, Palacios 136, T241777. Even ilf you are not staying here, it is worth visiting for its food as well as its architecture. The dining room is where the monks used to sing. Main course, including poached salmon and grilled Peruvian seabass medallions will set you back around US$13/14. ***El Truco***, Plaza Regocijo 261. Excellent local and international dishes, used a lot by tour groups, buffet lunch 1200-1500, nightly folk music at 2045, next door is ***Taberna del Truco***, which is open 0900-0100.

Inka Grill, Portal de Panes 115, Plaza de Armas, T262992, open 0900-2300 (Sun 1800-2300). According to many the best food in town, specializing in Novo Andino cuisine (the use of native ingredients and 'rescued' recipes), also homemade pastas, live music, breakfast service from 0800 with excellent coffee and homemade pastries 'to go'. Try the French onion soup, *lomos*, risottos and gnocchi. Owner Rafael changes the menu at least once a year. A good place to spoil yourself, recommended. ***Kintaro***, Heladeros 149. Excellent home-style food, set menu (1200-1500) particularly good value at US$2.85. Run by Japanese, the chicken teriyaki on rice is mouth-watering as is the sashimi of trout and avocado on sushi rice (watch out for the hot paste masquerading at the side of the plate as avocado!). Inca rolls and raw spinach in sesame is good, as is the tofu and saki. Low fat food is also said to be good for high altitude. Open 1200-2200, closed Sun.

La Retama, Portal de Panes 123, 2nd floor. Excellent new-age Andean food and service. Recommend the mouth-watering trout sashimi as a starter followed by steak. There is also a balcony, an enthusiastic music and dance group andart exhibitions.***Mesón de los Espaderos***, Espaderos y Plaza de Armas, 2nd floor with balcony overlooking the plaza. Good *parrilladas* and other typical local dishes. ***Mesón de los Portales***, Portal de Panes 163, Plaza de Armas, international and Peruvian cuisine. ***Novotel***, San Agustín 239, T228282, is in another historic building. The French chef creates dishes such as king prawns in puff pastry with leek in a mango sauce for US$10.

Pachacútec Grill and Bar, Portal de Panes 105, Plaza de Armas. International cuisine, including seafood and Italian specialities, also features folk music shows nightly. Excellent value quality *menú* for just US$2. ***Paititi***, Portal Carrizos 270, Plaza de Armas.

Around Plaza de Armas

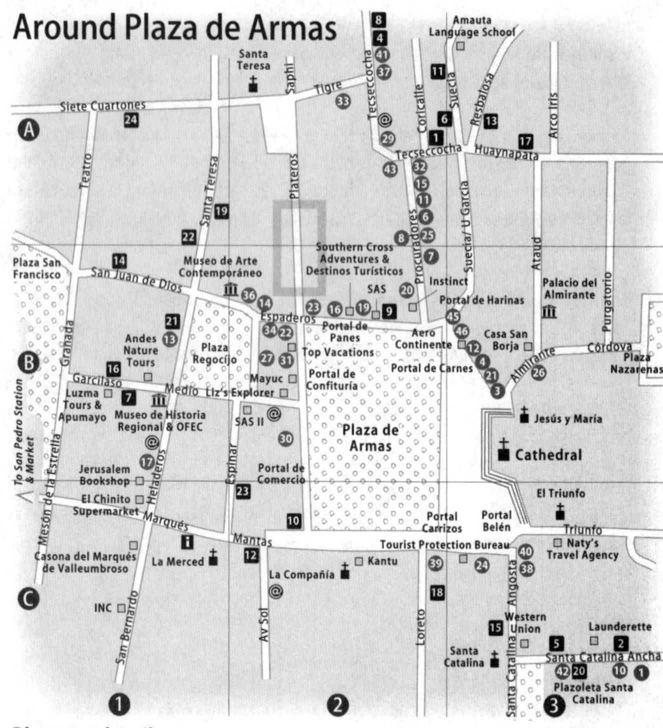

Plateros detail

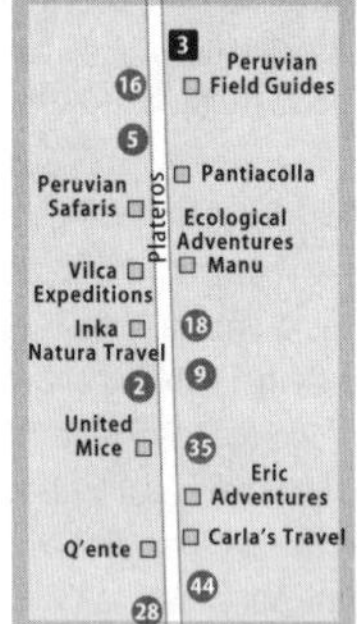

Sleeping

1 El Procurador del Cusco *A2*
2 Emperador Plaza *C3*
3 Hostal Cáceres *Plateros detail*
4 Hostal Carlos V *A2*
5 Hostal Casa Grande *C3*
6 Hostal Corihuasi *A3*
7 Hostal Garcilaso *B1*
8 Hostal Imperial Palace *A2*
9 Hostal Incawasi *B2*
10 Hostal Plaza de Armas *C2*
11 Hostal Q'Awarina *A2*
12 Hostal Qosqo *C2*
13 Hostal Resbalosa *A3*
14 Hostal Royal Frankenstein & Hostal Horeb *B1*
15 Hostal Santa María *C3*
16 Los Marqueses *B1*
17 Munay Wasi *A3*
18 Pensión Loreto *C2*
19 Picoaga *A1*
20 Posada del Viajero *C3*
21 Royal Inka I *B1*
22 Royal Inka II *A1*
23 Sonesta Posada del Inca *C2*
24 Tumi I *A1*

Eating

1 Al Grano *C3*
2 Ama Lur *Plateros detail*
3 Ayllu *B3*
4 Café Bagdad *B3*
5 Café Halliy *Plateros detail*
6 Chez Maggy Clave de Do *A2*
7 Chez Maggy El Corsario *B2*
8 Chez Maggy La Antigua *A2*
9 Chez Maggy Millenium *Plateros detail*
10 Due Mondi *C3*
11 El Cuate *A2*
12 El Patio & Explorandes *B3*
13 El Truco & Taberna del Truco *B1*
14 Govinda & Café Varayoc *B2*
15 Green's Juice Bar *A2*
16 Inka Grill *B2*
17 Kintaro *B1*
18 Kusikuy *Plateros detail*
19 La Retama *B2*
20 La Tertulia *B2*
21 La Yunta *B3*
22 Mesón de los Espaderos *B2*
23 Pachacútec Grill & Bar *B2*
24 Paititi *C3*
25 Paloma Imbil *A2*
26 People *B3*
27 Pizzería Marengo *B2*
28 Pucará *Plateros detail*
29 Tizziano Trattoria *A2*
30 Trotamundos *B2*
31 Tunupa & Cross Keys Pub *B2*
32 Ukuku's *A2*
33 Victor Victoria *A2*

Bars & clubs

34 Bre@k Latin Disco *B2*
35 Eko *Plateros detail*
36 Kamikaze *B2*
37 Los Perros *A2*
38 Mama Africa Pub *C3*
39 Norton Rat's Tavern *C2*
40 Paddy Flaherty's *C3*
41 Peliclub *A2*
42 Rosie O'Grady's *C3*
43 Sunset Video Café *A2*
44 Ukuku's *Plateros detail*
45 Uptown *B3*
46 Xcess *B3*

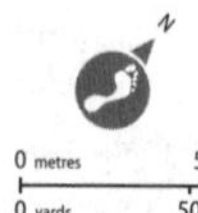

Live music and good atmosphere in a setting with Inca masonry. Excellent pizzas but the service is variable, depending on how busy they are. ***Parrilla Andina,***, Maruri. Good value meat-fest. Mixed grill will feed two for around US$15. Features beef, chicken, alpaca and pork. Restaurant is part of the former palace of the Inca Túpac Yupanqui.

Tunupa, Portal Confiturías 233, 2nd floor, Plaza de Armas (same entrance as *Cross Keys*). One of the finest restaurants on the Plaza, its large restaurant (accommodates 120-140) is often used by tour groups. Also has the longest (glassed-in) balcony but this is narrow and best for couples only. Owner Antonio studied for 10 years in Switzerland and designs the menu himself, changing it every 6 months. Food is international, traditional and Novo Andino; try *piqueos del pescador* as a starter (US$7.40 for two) and alpaca mignons or steak (US$10.30) to follow. Wine list, as everywhere in Cusco, is limited. Also a good buffet for US$15 including a pisco sour and a hot drink. From 2000-2015 there is an excellent group playing 16th/17th century-style Cusqueñan music of their own composition accompanied by dancers. Recommended.

Mid-range

Al Grano, Santa Catalina Ancha 398, T228032. Lunchtime menu US$2.15 is a good option if you are fed up with other menus. Evening serves five authentic Asian dishesfor US$4.50, menu changes daily. Not a typical English curry but good and without doubt the best coffee in town, vegetarian choices, open 1000-2100, closed on Sun. Recommended. ***A Mi Manera***, corner of Triunfo and Palacio. Great tasting food and good value if you ask for a set menu (not often advertised). ***El Patio***, Portal de Carnes 236, Plaza de Armas, left of the cathedral (closed 1530-1830). In a colonial courtyard, this has a short menu (great for the indecisive!) with great pasta, Mediterranean dishes and salads as well as agood value lunch. Great for a quick meal; get there early, the sun disappears around 1300/1330 Recommended. ***Greens***, Tandapata 700, behind the church on Plazoleta San Blas, T243820, greens_cusco@hotmail.com Great modern international, rich-tasting food in a trendy but warm and relaxed setting with sofas to kick back in while sipping wine and reading English magazines. Famous for huge lunch- and dinnertime-Sun roasts (US$10, booking essential) as well as English breakfasts (0700-1500) and curries. Vegetarian options. Desserts and toasted sandwiches only 1500-1830, choose a video to watch; restaurant re-opens 1830, closes 2300. Two-for-one cockatils 1830-1900. Games, book exchange and library. Deservedly popular.

Inkanato, Plazoleta Santo Domingo 279, interior 2A, T222926. Staff dressed in Inca and Amazonian outfits should not scare you off this interesting restaurant. Kitsch it may be but you can watch the staff preparing the food in the open plan kitchen that stretches into the dining area. ***Los Toldos***, Almagro 171 and San Andrés 219. If you´re feeling peckish, on a budget and fancy being served by waiters in a bow tie you could do worse than try their great chicken *brocheta*. Comes with fries, trip to salad bar and is enough for 2 at just US$2.30. Also *trattoria* with homemade pasta and pizza, delivery T229829. ***Los Tomines,*** Triunfo 384. Excellent 4-course set meal for US$5-6. Recommended.

Macondo, Cuesta San Blas 571, T229415, macondo@ telser.com.pe Bit pricier than others in this range but fantastic. Walking into *Macondo* is like walking into an artistic creation. Owner Andrés has dreamed up a casual, cosy, arty and comfortable restaurant where sofas of iron bedsteads covered in dozens of cushions mix with chairs, tables and candles. Walls are decorated with local art, which changes every 15 days and his mum cooks in the kitchen of this colonial house that belonged to his grandmother. Popular, gay-friendly and a steep 3-block walk from the central plaza, *Macondo* has 13 dishes of local ingredients with an artistic twist – eg vinaigrette of passion fruit with Amazonian salad. It is also renowned for its tasty alpaca mignon à la Parisienne (US$7). Sweets US$4.30 each – the Marquis au Chocolate is great. Daiquiris (US$3.70) are delicious. Happy hour 1500-1800. The tree house upstairs is great if you are 5ft tall, otherwise take a seat fast! Visa attracts 10% surcharge. Recommended.

Food for thought

Hungry for exceptional food at prices that would struggle to buy you a burger and fries at home? Then look no further than Cusco.

Start the day at Amaru *in Plateros (325, 2nd floor), a stone's throw from the Plaza de Armas, for one of the best value breakfasts in town. If it's a nice morning, grab a table on the colonial balcony from where you can watch the world go by. All the breakfasts come with limitless supplies of tea or coffee, excellent bread, juice and eggs (if these last two are included in your meal). Thus a real feast can be had for as little as US$1.15, but we recommend you 'splash out' on the* buffet simple *(US$2.40), or English breakfast (US$2.85).*

If you stay at Amaru long enough you can leave straight for lunch! Walk down the stairs and try their sister restaurant's (Ama Lur's) great menú (just US$1.70). If this is full, Ccross the road to the corner of the Plaza de Armas and drop into posh Pachacútec Grill and Bar *for a quality set lunch which will set you back only US$2. Then head back and walk up Plateros to* Kusikuy *(Plateros 348) to place your order for one of the best set menus around (just US$1.70). At the same time you could put in your order there for cuy (guinea pig – US$10) later that evening – it's reportedly the best in town and even better if you give the chef at least an hour´s notice.*

Most will, of course, want to dine somewhere different so save this for another day and take yourself off to Green's *in the lovely area of San Blas. There, sink into a sofa and indulge in a pre-dinner drink of pisco sour. If it's Sunday and you've had the foresight to book it's now time for the huge Sunday roast (US$10), otherwise tuck into one of* Green's *very tasty curries.*

Moving up in price bracket (but still amazing value), breakfast with the better-off locals at El Ayllu *where the blue-jacketed waiters (always seemingly on the run) will bring you Americano for US$3.40 and a big cup of mocha for just US$1.14. From 1300 drop into* Los Perros *wine and couch bar in Tecsecocha at the top of Gringo Alley for their famous Thai-style wantons with three different fillings.*

In the evening try Macondo's *on the way up to San Blas for amazing alpaca, delicious daiquiris and the type of decor you'll be writing home about.*

Those with money to burn should not ignore the recommendations above. However, think about breakfasting at El Monasterio *where a fabulous US$12 buffet is so huge it will remove any desire for lunch later in the day! You will probably want to dine in one of the good restaurants on the Plaza de Armas, such as* Tunupa's, *which has the longest balcony on the square, or the* Inka Grill. *Expect excellent service.*

Pacha-Papa, Plazoleta San Blas 120, opposite church of San Blas, T241318. A beautiful patio restaurant in a wonderful old colonial house. Very good typical Peruvian dishes with a European influence – owner Lucho has cooked abroad and has his own style. Excellent alpaca steaks, also try the trout in caper sauce. At night diners can sit in their own, private colonial dining room. Friendly, Andean harp music. Recommended. ***Planeta Sur***, on Plazoleta San Blas. Tiny with a so-so menu but the only place on the plazoleta where you can eat outside in the sunshine (the authorities are trying to stop this on the grounds that it upsets the traditional feel).

Pizzería Americana, Plateros 369. Perhaps the best pizzas in town in the most basic environment! Cheap beer too and a good set meal for US$1.50. Don´t expect candles. Recommended. ***Pizzería Marengo,*** Plaza Regocijo 246, T252627. Excellent pizzas for US$ per person. Ask for a table in the back room next to the cosy clay oven and watch your food being prepared. Also does deliveries. ***Pucará,*** Plateros 309. Peruvian and international food. Japanese owner does very good US$3.50 set lunch and excllent *ají de gallina* (garlic chicken) and cream of potato soup. Open 1230-2200, closed on Sun, pleasant atmosphere.

Tizziano Trattoria, Tecseccocha 418. Good Italian food, homemade pasta, excellent value *menú* served Tue-Sat 1200-1500 and daily 1800-2300, also serves vegetarian dishes. ***Varayoc,*** Almagro 136. Good *brochetas* and fast foods, see also *Café Varayoc*. ***Keros***, on the corner of Procuradores and Plaza de Armas, 2nd floor. Lunchtime menu for US$4.30 includes pisco sour, three courses and a tea. ***Witches Garden***, in Carmen Bajo (just off the Plazoleta). A great little place for huge hot chicken salad, the rest of the menu follows this theme of a break from the typical Cusco dishes. Decor is very modern and the good house wine just US$1.70 a glass. Lighting could be more subtle but ambience will improve with more custom.

Cheap

Procuradores, or 'Gringo Alley' as the locals call it, is good for a value feed and takes the hungry backpacker from Mexico to Italy, to Spain and Turkey with its menus. None is dreadful, many are very good indeed, especially for the price; do not be too worried if a tout drags you into one (demand your free pisco sour) before you´ve reached the restaurant you have chosen from the list below:

Cusco

Chez Maggy, have 4 branches: ***La Antigua*** (the original) at Procuradores 365 and, on the same street, ***El Corsario*** No 344 and ***Clave de Do*** No 374 (open at 0700 for buffet breakfast), plus ***Millenium***, Plateros 348 (opens 0700, buffet breakfast). All have good atmosphere, are popular with pizzas freshly baked in wood-burning oven, pastas, Mexican food and soups. As they share the kitchens, it´s fun to sit in one restaurant and watch the waiters hurrying in from another where your food has been prepared. Hotel delivery: T234861. ***El Mexicanito***, Procuradores 392. Menus from US$2-3, good food. ***El Cuate***, Procuradores 386. Mexican food, great value, big portions and simple salads. Recommended.

La Barceloneta, Procuradores 347. Spanish, Italian and Peruvian dishes, good value lunches. Has Spanish music on Thu. ***Paloma Imbil***, Procuradores 362, has doner kebabs. The *rollo mixto* is US$2.15 and comes in delicious home-baked bread. ***Ukuku´s Restaurant***, at the very top of the alley, has menus for US$2 which includes a trip to the salad bar.

Plateros, parallel with Gringo Alley but further southwest, also has good value food. Try ***Ama Lur***, at number 327. This is the restaurant below *Amalu* where you go for breakfast. Clean, cheap, very good menú for US$2 as well as tasty evening meals. ***El Nevado***, Plateros 345. Good set meals, also good soups and fish. ***Kusikuy***, Plateros 348B, T262870. Some say this serves the best cuy (guinea pig, US$10.90) in town and the owners say if you give them an hour´s warning they will produce their absolute best. Set lunch is unbeatable value at only US$2. Open 0800-2300 Mon-Sat. Good service, highly recommended. ***Los Candiles***, Plateros 323. Good set lunch for US$2.50.

Chifa Sipan, Quera 251 (better than their other branch for tourists in Plateros). Owner Carlos may not sound Chinese but he is and joins in the cooking at this excellent restaurant. There is no great ambience but it´s busy at lunchtimes with locals which speaks volumes. Skip to the back of the menu for their better deals and try *chancho* (pork) *con tamarindo* (US$2.60) or wanton soup and *pollo tipakay* (US$2.85). ***La Bodega***, Carmen Alto, San Blas. Snug Dutch and Peruvian-owned café/restaurant of just 7 tables. You'll love it. Sip creamy hot chocolate by candlelight in the afternoons and read one of the English magazines. *House of the Rising Sun* sums up choice in music. Pisco sour US$1.70, *pollo al vino* US$3.70. *Tallarines con pollo* are delicious! Dishes come with side trip to salad bar. ***People***, Cuesta del Almirante (up the hill to left of cathedral). Like the Tardis, this tiny restaurant opens up at the back to offer sofas and three more tables to supplement the two up front. Four-course menus with a drink are US$2.85. ***Víctor Victoria***, Tigre 130. Israeli and local dishes, highly recommended for breakfast, good value. ***Yaku Mama Grill***, Portal del Comercio, 2nd floor, balcony restaurant over the plaza, has pricey Israeli breakfast (US$3.20). House wine very good.

Nice burgers (US$1.70), shame about the chips! Internet too. ***La Yunta***, Portal de Carnes, Plaza de Armas. Good salads, pancakes and juices, also vegetarian, popular with tourists, same owners as *Instinct Travel Agency*.

Between 1200 and 1400 on Puente Rosario, just off Av Sol, pick up a piece of deep-fried potato or deep-fried, battered yucca from one of the street stalls for just US$0.15

To eat really cheaply, and if your stomach is acclimatized to South American food, make your main meal lunch and escape the Plaza de Armas. Head for the market 5 blocks southwest at Túpac Amaru and eat at one of the many stalls. Food will cost no more than US$0.70 and 3 fruit juices are just US$0.45! Otherwise, look for the set *menus*, usually served between 1200-1500, although they are no good for vegetarians. We recommend: ***Asee's Brass Pollería***, at Av Pardo 789D. It has friendly staff and a good 3-course meal with a drink for just US$0.85. The floor is concrete but clean and the food is better than most cheapies.

Local restaurants *El Trujillano*, Matará 261 (mind your head), is the place where people with restaurants go. It has plastic table clothes but great for *ceviche* of fish, squid, seafood (US$2.60-5.70). *Ají de gallina* (US$3.14) is good. A starter version (US$1.70) off the all-Spanish menu is enough for a light lunch. Wash it all down with a glass of *chicha morada*. ***Las Machitas***, Progreso, also serves *ceviche* and is possibly the safest place to try it. Cold and impersonal, it still serves up some of the best food in Cusco. Try also ***Puerto Atico*** on Av Infancia for *ceviches* until 1700.

Vegetarian ***Auliya***, C Garcilaso 265, on 2nd floor. Beautifully-renovated colonial house, excellent vegetarian food, also stocks a wide range of dried food for trekking. ***Frutos***, C Triunfo 393, 2nd floor, tienda 202. Open Mon-Sat 0630-2200, Thu 0900-1500, excellent value set lunch. ***Govinda***, Espaderos 128, just off the Plaza de Armas. This is not up to the standard of other Govindas around Latin America. The cheap set menu has limp salad, unpleasant soup and tasteless basic lentils and rice. The decor is poor and the toilet dreadful. Try instead ***La Naturaleza***, Procuradores 351. Cheap. ***Paccha***, Portal de Panes 167. Good for breakfast, it also has a bookstore, posters for sale, English and French spoken.

Cafés ***Amaru,*** Plateros 325, 2nd floor. Limitless coffee, tea, (great) bread and juices served, even on 'non-buffet' breakfasts (US$1.15 for simple). Colonial balcony. Recommended. ***Antojitos***, Marqués 284, 3 blocks from Plaza de Armas, T246334. Good tea and cakes, friendly, cheap (ignore the decor, though). ***Ayllu***, to the left of the cathedral, at Portal de Carnes 208, is probably one of the oldest cafés in Cusco and a great place to go. Fantastic breakfasts (have the special fruit salad, US$2.30), sandwiches, coffee and classical music as well as wonderful apple pastries. Try *leche asada*. Very much a local venue – menu refreshingly all-Spanish. Service superb, handled by blue-jacketed waiters permamently on the run.

Next door upstairs is ***Café Bagdad***. It has a nice balcony with good views of the plaza, it does a cheap set lunch, good atmosphere, happy hour 1930-2130, German owner Florian Thurman speaks good English, but the service is variable. ***Café Halliy***, Plateros 363. Popular meeting place, especially for breakfast, good for comments on guides, has good snacks and 'copa Halliy' – fruit, muesli, yoghurt, honey and chocolate cake, also good vegetarian *menú* and set lunch. ***Café Illary***, Procuradores 358. Open for breakfast at 0600, good. ***Café Manu*** , Av Pardo 1046. Good coffee and good food too in a jungle decor. If the sun's over the yard-arm it would be a sin to miss one of their liqueur coffees. ***Café Varayoc***, Espaderos 142, T232404. Swiss restaurant with a pleasing atmosphere. Cheese fondue US$10, *wiener schnitzel* (US$5.14) and *goulash* (US$4.30).

Green's Juice Bar, at the top of Procuradores, is new, tiny and funky. A great place to sit amid candles and leopard-skin(!)-covered stools. Choose from many fruits including strawberry, mango and pear – drinks are huge and US$1.15. There's a book-lending service and exchange as well as English magazines. ***Heidi Granja***, Cuesta San

Blas 525, near the bottom, T233759. German owner Carlos serves up yoghurt, granolla, ricotta cheese and honey and other great breakfast options. Evening meals are US$2.15 for soup and a main course. Recommended.

La Tertulia, Procuradores 50, 2nd floor. Run by Johanna and Alfredo, who also run the *Amauta* Language School downstairs, the breakfast buffet, served 0630-1300, includes muesli, bread, yoghurt, eggs, juice and coffee, eat as much as you like for around US$3, superb value, vegetarian buffet served daily 1800-2200, set dinner and salad bar for US$3.50, also fondue and gourmet meals, book exchange, newspapers, classical music, open till 2300. Off the beaten track, at Meloc 442, Dutch-run ***Niños Hotel*** has good breakfast in a lovely sunny colonial courtyard. Just US$1.70 for fruit salad, home-made bread, locally-made jam and large mugs of tea or coffee. This has the added bonus of supporting one of Cusco´s most worthwhile charities for street children (see page 97).

Trotamundos, Portal Comercio 177, 2nd floor. This is one of the most pleasant cafés in the Plaza if a bit pricey (hot chocolate US$1.40). Has a balcony overlooking the plaza and a warm atmosphere, especially at night with its open fire. Good coffees and cakes, safe salads, *brochetas*, sandwiches and pancakes as well as 4 machines on the internet. Open Mon-Sat 0800-2400. ***Yaku Mama***, Procuradores 397. Good for breakfast, unlimited fruit and coffee, good value.

Panaderías & ice cream parlours

Panadería El Buen Pastor, Cuesta San Blas 579. Very good bread and pastries, the proceeds from which go to a charity for orphans and street children. Serves up *empanadas* and endless hot drinks. Very popular with backpackers. Recommended. Another good *panadería* is in the basement of the *Cusco Hotel*, C Espinar, opposite *Posada del Inca*. ***Picarones***, Ruinas and Tullumayo, is good for doughnuts. It is very small, very local and very typical for classic Peruvian sweet stuff. ***Le Croissant***, Plaza San Francisco 134. French run, excellent pastries, good coffee. ***La Dulcería***, Heladeros 167. Good for cakes, sandwiches, snacks and tea. ***Due Mondi***, Santa Catalina Ancha (near *Rosie O'Grady's*). Open 1000-2100. At just US$0.30 per delicious Italian scoop, this is an absolute must. There's even *chicha* flavour!

Entertainment and nightlife

Bars

On the Plaza de Armas *Cross Keys Pub*, Plaza de Armas, Portal Confiturías 233 (upstairs). Open 1100-0130, run by Barry Walker of *Manu Expeditions*, a Mancunian and ornithologist, darts, cable sports, pool, bar meals, happy hours 1800-1900 and 2130-2200, plus daily half price specials Sun-Wed, great pisco sours, very popular, loud and raucous, great atmosphere. ***Norton Rat's Tavern***, Loreto 115, 2nd floor, is on the Plaza but has a side entrance off a road to the left of La Compañía (same entrance as *Hostal Loreto*), T246204, nortonrats@yahoo.com Pleasant pub with a pool table, dart board, cable TV and lots of pictures of motorbikes! Owner Jeffrey Powers loves the machines and can provide information for bikers. He has opened a juice bar inside the pub serving Amazonian specials – some even said to be aphrodisiacs. Happy hour 1900-2100 every night with other, daily, specials such as Whisky Wednesday. ***Paddy Flaherty's***, C Triunfo 124 on the corner of the plaza is an Irish theme pub, serving cans of Guinness (although the supply to Cusco seems sadly sporadic and they cost US$3.40 a go). This is a great pub, deservedly popular and a good place to be for the Corpus Christi procession with its views over the Plaza de Armas. It's open 1300-0100.

On Plateros, try ***Amaru Quechua Café Pub*** (No 325, 2nd floor), T246976. Bar with pizzería, also serves breakfast for US$2.50, games, happy hour 1030-1130, 2000-2200. Above Gringo Alley (Procuradores), in Tecseccocha is ***Los Perros Bar***, No 436. Completely different vibe and a great place to chill out on comfy couches listening to excellent music. Owner Tammy is very friendly and welcoming and occasionally locks

Happy Hour Trail

It is possible to spend your nights hopping from one happy hour to another in Cusco. Here are some suggestions:

Macondo's	*1500-1800*
Green's	*1830-1900*
Cross Keys	*1800-1900*
Norton's Rat	*1900-2100*
Amaru	*2000-2200*
Cross Keys	*2130-2200*
Paddy Flaherty's	*2200-2230*
Rosie O'Grady's	*2300-2330*

Time for a kebab? Head up Gringo Alley to Paloma Imbil on the right. Delicious!

If you are still standing it is time to hit the clubs. Their happy hours tend to change from day to day but you should have details on all the flyers you have picked up on your trail. As these usually provide you with a free drink you won't care too much when happy hour is. Enjoy, but do make sure you keep US$1 back for your taxi home!

the doors if there´s a good party atmosphere going. She regularly returns to her native Australia to research new menus; the Thai-style wantons (US$2) are famous in Cusco, but also give her sautéed chicken salad (US$3.40) with avocado a go. In addition, try the thick curried soups and good coffee. There´s a book exchange, English and other magazines and board games. Opens 1100 for coffee and pastries; kitchen opens at 1300. Jazz/blues/funk live every Monday from 2200 (free entry).

Rosie O'Grady's, at Santa Catalina Ancha 360, T247935, has good music, tasty food. English and Russian(!) are both spoken. It´s open 1100 till late (food served till midnight, happy hours 1300-1400, 1800-1900, 2300-2330). ***La Jarra***, Av Infancia 409, Wanchac, Cusco. You´ll need a short taxi ride to reach this *chichería* – it´s just off our map, past Wanchac station – but if you want to try chicha, the local alcoholic drink fermented from blue maize, it´s worth the effort. Owners explain how the drink is made on the premises. Try it with fruits of the region and typical Cusqueñan food.

Nightclubs Before your evening meal don´t turn down flyers being handed out around the Plaza de Armas. You should work out from these over dinner your free drink circuit – for each coupon not only gives you free entry, it is worth a *cuba libre*. On the back of this tour you will be able to check out which club is the ´in´ place to be that week – they are constantly changing. If you fancy learning a few Latin dance steps before hitting the local nightlife many of the clubs offer free lessons. Ask at the door for details or look out for flyers.

Bre@k Latin Disco, Espaderos 123, is very much a Peruvian hangout with plenty of salsa and merengue. There is a drinking area overlooking the dance floor where you can watch the young locals make salsa look easy. During the high season of 2001, ***Eko*** (Plateros 334, 2nd floor) was the place to be. A large open room with DJ at the front and bar at the back. The music tends to be more dance-oriented than the others, no *YMCA* or *Boney M* here. Sometimes they have a Latin night or a techno night – look out for the adverts. There is a tiny place to sit above the dance floor, but you need to get there early to grab it. A separate chill-out room opens at midnight with couches and candles. Some nights it is open to everyone but on others it is used for private parties. Opens 2100 till the early hours, free drink on presentation of Eko card obtainable at entrance, happy hours 2100-2300.

Kamikaze, Plaza Regocijo 274, T233865. *Peña* at 2200, good old traditional rock music, candle-lit cavern atmosphere, entry US$2.50 but usually you don't have to pay.Templo, Espaderos 135, 2nd floor, is new so check it out. The owner spent a small fortune on importing the sound system from the US. It was set up as a techno, trance, garage club but, owing to demand, it has now become much like all the other clubs playing a range of music including Latin sounds. Entrance is free all night and happy hour is 2130-1130 and covers all drinks except beer. ***Mama Africa Pub***, Portal Belén 115, 2nd floor. Decorated in a jungle theme there is a dance floor to the far left with a large video screen, although people dance anywhere they can. The music is middle of the road, from local music through '70s classics to the latest releases. There is something for everyone. Free entry with a pass which you can get on the plaza.

Ukuku's, Plateros 316. US$1.35 entry or free with a pass. This is somewhat different to the other clubs as every night there is a live local band that might play anything from rock to salsa. The DJ then plays a mixture of local and international music but the emphasis is on local. It has a good mix of locals and tourists. Happy hour 0730-0930. ***Uptown***, Suecia 302 on the corner of the plaza. Good music including drum and bass and great atmosphere. It is very popular with locals and backpackers, happy hours 2100-2200 and 2300-2330. There have been several reports of drinks being spiked. Don't leave drinks hanging around and don't accept drinks from strangers. If you get bored with a track playing here, dash next door to ***Xcess***, which is supposedly the cheapest for drink. It´s packed with sofas, locals and backpackers but the music is pretty much the same as *Uptown*´s.

Cusco

Video Bars

When you´ve seen enough ruins, colonial architecture or are simply in need of a rest, there are plenty of video bars in which to relax. Below are some of the best places, but new ones are opening all the time. For the real silver screen, check out ***Peliclub***, left of *Los Perros* at Tesecocha 458 (T246442). They screen 14 films a month repeated at different times, 3 times a day; afternoon, early evening and at 2100. Closed on Mon. Look for their tear-off fliers around the central pubs. US$1.70. ***Sunset Video Café*** inside *Hostal Royal Qosqo*, turn left at the top of Gringo Alley, shows 3 films a day: 1600, 1900, 2130. It has good sound and you can order popcorn and other snacks while you watch. US$0.60. ***Mama Africa***, to the right of the Cathedral, has 2 showings a day at 1545 and 1800. Films are free if you buy a drink. ***Ukuku´s***, on Plateros, also has 2 showings at 1600 and 1800. Films are free with any purchase. ***Green´s*** restaurant behind Plazoleta San Blas allows customers to choose a video between 1500 and 1800. It works on a first-come first-served basis, so get there early if you want to choose what you watch.

Folklore

There's a regular nightly folklore show at ***Centro Qosqo de Arte Nativo***, Av Sol 604, T227901. The show runs from 1900 to 2030, entrance fee US$3.50. ***Teatro Inti Raymi***, Saphi 605, nightly at 1845, US$4.50 entry and well worth it. There's a peña at ***Inka's Restaurant Peña***, Portal de Panes 105, Plaza de Armas. Good menú at lunchtime for US$3. ***Teatro Municipal***, C Mesón de la Estrella 149 (T227321 for information 0900-1300 and 1500-1900). This is a venue for plays, dancing and shows, mostly on Thu-Sun. Ask for their programmes. They also run classes in music and dancing from Jan to Mar which are great value.

Festivals

On **20 Jan** is a procession of saints in the *San Sebastián* district of Cusco. **Carnival** in Cusco is a messy affair with flour, water, cacti, bad fruit and animal manure thrown about in the streets. Be prepared. **Easter Monday** sees the procession of *El Señor de los Temblores* (Lord of the Earthquakes), starting at 1600 outside the Cathedral. A large crucifix is paraded through the streets, returning to the Plaza de Armas around 2000 to bless the tens of thousands of people who have assembled there.

On **2-3 May** the *Vigil of the Cross*, which takes place at all mountaintops with crosses on them, is a boisterous affair. In **Jun** is ***Corpus Christi***, on the Thu after Trinity Sunday, when all the statues of the Virgin and of saints from Cusco's churches are

Corpus Christi in Cusco

Corpus Christi is an annual festival celebrated on the Thursday after Trinity Sunday (generally in early June) by Roman Catholics everywhere. In Cusco Corpus is an exuberant and colourful pageant, where profound faith and prayer share predominance with abundant eating and copious drinking.

All the Saints and Virgins are paraded through the city to the Plaza de Armas and, after being blessed, they are carried into the great Cathedral to be placed in prearranged order, in two rows facing each other. The images are kept in the Cathedral until the octava (the eighth day after their internment), when they are all escorted in procession back to their respective parishes and churches.

During these days and nights in each others' company, the Saints and Virgins , so the stories go, decide among themselves the future of the people for the forthcoming year. It is also said that they gamble at dice with each other. Five hundred years ago, at the very same time of year and in this precise location, the mummified remains of the Incas were paraded in similar fashion and then laid in state. They consulted the sun, the moon, the lightning and the rains to learn what fate these elements were to bring in the course of the following year.

The Saints are the first to be paraded. The traditional race between San Jerónimo and San Sebastián is a joyous event. San Cristóbal, carved from a single tree trunk, is a heroic, elaborately painted figure, who leans upon a great staff. His powerful muscles and thick sinews forever shoulder the body of the infant Jesus as they ford a river. It is the heaviest statue of all and popular legend tells that underneath it lies a huaca, or sacred rock.

Santiago the warrior saint enters astride his white horse, brandishing a sword. Trampled under the hooves of his steed lies a vanquished demon in the likeness of a Moorish soldier. Santiago, once the brother of Jesus, is now the patron saint of Cusco. His name was the battle cry of the Spanish soldiers, but Santiago soon became the representation of Illapa, the Andean deity of thunder and lightning.

Next come the Virgins, dressed in pomp, some of them accompanied by archangels and cherubs. For the Andean people, the Virgins are the equivalent of the Mother Earth, Pachamama. The Virgin of Belén is always first and is escorted by San José, who then stands at a side of the entrance of the Cathedral, waiting for all the Virgins to be carried inside. Santa Bárbara, the pregnant virgin is the last of the line.

Corpus is perhaps the city's greatest event. All the streets and the huge expanse of the Plaza de Armas are thronged with enormous crowds. The revered images, each several hundred years old and from a distinct parish of the city, command a host of fervent followers from whom is drawn a retinue of attendants, including a band of musicians and troupe of dancers. Most important and conspicuous are the bearers, whose strenuous efforts are relieved at preordained resting points, known as the descanso. The bier carrying the image is placed on top of a scaffold and the bearers and followers are all given a round of chicha, and/or beer., while the band plays on and Ave Marias are prayed one after the other, like a mantra. The respite over, one final toast is made to the statue, also to Pachamama and to the surrounding mountain summits, Los Apus. In many cases this is accompanied by fresh coca leaves and lime. Then the parade resumes its journey.As the processions converge upon the centre, they merge together into a larger procession, which becomes engulfed by the multitudes in the Plaza de Armas. The images as they are carried along seem to become swaying vessels navigating a sea of humanity, riding its waves, tossing and rolling in the swells and tides.

It's no fun at the snow festival

Qoyllur Rit'i is not a festival for the unitiated or the faint-hearted. It can be very confusing for those who don't understand the significance of this ancient ritual. To get there involves a two hour walk up from the nearest road at Mawayani, beyond Ocongate, then it's a further exhausting climb up to the glacier. It's a good idea to take a tent, food and plenty of warm clothing. Many trucks leave Cusco, from Limacpampa, in the days prior to the full moon in mid-June; prices from US$2 upwards. This is a very rough and dusty overnight journey lasting 14 hrs, requiring warm clothing and coca leaves to fend off cold and exhaustion. Several agencies offer tours (see also page 194). Peter Frost writes:

"The pilgrimage clearly has its origins in Inca or pre-Inca times, although the historical record dates it only from a miraculous apparition of Christ on the mountain, around 1780. It is a complex and chaotic spectacle, attended by hundreds of dance groups, and dominated by the character of the ukuku, the bear dancer, whose night vigil on the surrounding glaciers is the festival's best-known feature. Under the best of circumstances the journey there is lengthy, gruelling and dusty, the altitude (4,600 m at the sanctuary) is extremely taxing, the place is brutally cold, very crowded, unbelievably noisy around the clock (sleep is impossible), and the sanitary conditions are indescribable."

paraded through the streets to the Cathedral. This is a colourful event. The Plaza de Armas is surrounded by tables with women selling *cuy* and a mixed grill called *chiriuchu* (*cuy*, chicken, *tortillas*, fish eggs, water-weeds, maize, cheese and sausage) and lots of Cusqueña beer. In **early Jun**, 2 weeks before Inti Raymi (see below) is the highly recommended *Cusqueño beer festival*, held near the rail station, which boasts a great variety of Latin American music. The whole event is well-organized and great fun. Also in **Jun** is *Qoyllur Rit'i*, the Snow Star festival, held at a 4,700-m glacier north of Ocongate (Ausangate), 150 km southeast of Cusco. It has its final day 58 days after Easter Sunday.

On **24 Jun** *Inti Raymi*, the Inca festival of the winter solstice (see page 89), where locals outnumber tourists, is enacted at the fortress of Sacsayhuamán. The spectacle starts at 1000 at the Qoricancha (crowds line the streets and jostle for space to watch), then proceeds to the Plaza de Armas. From there performers and spectators go to Sacsayhuaman for the main event, which starts at 1300. It lasts 2½ hrs, and is in Quechua. Locals make a great day of it, watching the ritual from the hillsides and cooking potatoes in pits in the ground. Tickets for the stands can be bought in advance from the *Emufec* office, Santa Catalina Ancha 325 (opposite the Complejo Policial) and cost US$35. Standing places on the ruins are free but get there at about 1030 as even reserved seats fill up quickly, and defend your space. Travel agents can arrange the whole day for you, with meeting points, transport, reserved seats and packed lunch. Those who try to persuade you to buy a ticket for the right to film or take photos are being dishonest. On the night before Inti Raymi, the Plaza de Armas is crowded with processions and food stalls. Try to arrive in Cusco 15 days before Inti Raymi. The atmosphere in the town during the build up is fantastic and something is always going on (festivals, parades etc).

On the last Sun in **Aug** is the *Huarachicoy festival* at Sacsayhuaman, a spectacular reenactment of the Inca manhood rite, performed in dazzling costumes by boys of a local school. On **8 Sep**, the *Day of the Virgin*, is a colourful procession of masked dancers from the church of Almudena, at the southwest edge of Cusco, near Belén, to the Plaza de San Francisco. There is also a fair at Almudena, and a bull fight on the following day. **8 Dec** is *Cusco day*, when churches and museums close at 1200. And, on **24**

Dec, when all good little travellers should be tucked up in bed, is *Santuranticuy*, 'the buying of saints'. This is a huge celebration of Christmas shopping, with a big crafts market in the Plaza de Armas, which is very noisy until the early hours of the 25th.

Shopping

Arts & crafts

Cusco has some of the best craft shopping in all Peru

In the Plaza San Blas and the surrounding area, authentic Cusco crafts still survive and wood workers can be seen in almost any street. A market is held on Sat. Leading artisans who welcome visitors include ***Hilario Mendivil***, Plazoleta San Blas 634, who makes biblical figures from plaster, wheatflour and potatoes and ***Edilberta Mérida***, Carmen Alto 133, who makes earthenware figures showing the physical and mental anguish of the Indian peasant. ***Víctor Vivero Holgado***, at Tandapata 172, is a painter of pious subjects, while ***Antonio Olave Palomino***, Siete Angelitos 752, makes reproductions of Pre-Columbian ceramics and colonial sculptures. ***Maximiliano Palomino de la Sierra***, Triunfo 393, produces festive dolls and wood carvings, and ***Santiago Rojas***, near San Blas, statuettes. Note that much of the wood used for picture frames etc is *cedro*, a rare timber not extracted by sustainable means.

Cusco is the weaving centre of Peru and excellent textiles can be found at good value; but watch out for sharp practices when buying gold and silver objects and jewellery

Museo Inca Art Gallery is good for contemporary art, run by Amílcar Salomón Zorrilla, it's at Huancaro M-B – L8, T231232 (PO Box 690), telephone between 0900 and 2100. Visit ***Nemesio Villasante***, Av 24 de Junio 415, T222915, for Paucartambo masks. There's a market on the corner of San Andrés and Quera, which is good for local handicrafts. ***Mercado Artesanal***, Av Sol, block 4, is also good for cheap crafts. ***Coordinadora Sur Andina de Artesanía***, C del Medio 130, off Plaza de Armas, has a good assortment of crafts and is a non-profit organization. ***Feria Artesanal Tesores del Inka***, Plateros 334, open daily 0900-2300.

In its drive to ´clean up´ Cusco, the authorites have moved the colourful **artisans´ stalls** from the pavements of Plaza Regocijo to the main market at the bottom of Av Sol. There are, however, small markets of 10 or so permament stalls dotted around the city which offer goods made from alpaca as well as modern materials. For example, in Plateros, below *Eko* nightclub, the first stall in the doorway will tailor-make reversible fleeces in two colours for US$10.

Upmarket shops include ***Miski***, in the same courtyard as *El Patio* restaurant, Portal de Carnes, Plaza de Armas, which sells good, less touristic pottery, hammocks and handmade jewellery, while ***Werner & Ana***, at the top of C Garcilaso, has designer clothes in leather, alpaca and cotton. ***Pedazo de Arte***, Plateros 334B. A tasteful collection of Andean handicrafts, many designed by Japanese owner Miki Suzuki. ***La Mamita***, Portal de Carnes 244, Plaza de Armas, sells the ceramics of Pablo Seminario (see under Urubamba), plus cotton, basketry, jewellery, etc. A visit is highly recommended for those who do not have time to go to their studio in Urubamba (see page 144). ***Maky Artesanías***, Carmen Alto 101, T653643. A great place to buy individually-designed ceramics. Ask for discounts if buying several pieces. ***La Pérez***, Urb Mateo Pumacahua 598, Huanchac, T232186/222137, is a big cooperative with a good selection. They will arrange a free pick-up from your hotel.

The private Miori-Bernasconi Collection of Andean art may be viewed by appointment, T271215, T652975 (mob), Pallay-Andean Textile website www.geocities.com/SoHo/Atrium/7785/ Quechua and Aymara pieces, 18th, 19th century, antique coins, wooden keros and other objects.

Alpaca clothing and fabrics: ***Alpaca III***, Plaza Regocijo 202, ***Alpaca 3***, Ruinas 472, and ***Cuzmar II***, Portal Mantas 118T (English spoken). ***Away***, Procuradores 361, T229465. Sells handmade shoes, traditional blankets and leather goods, prices from US$15-40 for a pair, allow two days delivery for your own design. ***Josefina Olivera***, Portal Comercio 169, Plaza de Armas. She sells old ponchos and antique mantas, without the usual haggling. Her prices are high, but it is worth it to save pieces being cut up to make other items, open daily 1100-2100.

Traditional musical instruments: *Ima Sumac*, Triunfo 338, T244722. ***Taki Museo de Música de los Andes***, Hatunrumiyoq 487-5. Shop and workshop selling and displaying musical instruments, knowledgeable owner, who is an ethnomusicologist. Recommended for anyone interested in Andean music.

Jewellery: *Joyerías Peruanas*, C del Medio 130, gold, silver and other items in precolumbian, Inca and contemporary designs. ***Joyería H Ormachea***, Plateros 372, T237061. Handmade gold and silver. ***Spondylus***, Cuesta San Blas 505, T246964. A tiny shop with a good selection of silver jewellery and fashion tops with Inca and pre-Inca designs.

Bookshops

Los Andes, Portal Comercio 125, Plaza de Armas. ***Jerusalem***, Heladeros 143, T235408, English books, guidebooks, music, postcards, book exchange. ***Centro de Estudios Regionales Andinos Bartolomé de las Casas***, Heladeros 129A, good books on Peruvian history, archaeology, etc, Mon-Sat 1100-1400, 1600-1900. ***Special Book Services***, Av Sol 781-A, Wanchaq, T248106. Sells Footprint Handbooks.

Camping equipment

There are several places around the plaza area which rent out equipment but check it carefully as it is common for parts to be missing

An example of prices per day: tent US$3-5, sleeping bag US$2 (down), US$1.50 (synthetic), stove US$1. A deposit of US$100 is asked, plus credit card, passport or plane ticket. ***Explorandes***, at Portal de Carnes 236 (left of the cathedral, next to *El Patio* restaurant) hires out Eureka tents and WhisperLite stoves (both US$4/night), as well as ThermaRest sleeping mats (US$2/night). ***Soqllaq'asa Camping Service***, owned by English-speaking Sra Luzmila Bellota Miranda, at Plateros 365 no 2F, T252560, is recommended for equipment hire, from down sleeping bags (US$2/day) to gas stoves (US$1/day) and ThermaRest mats (US$1/day); pots, pans, plates, cups and cutlery are all provided free by the friendly staff. They also buy and sell camping gear and make alpaca jackets, open Mon-Sat 0900-1300, 1600-2030, Sun 1800-2030. Wherever you hire equipment, check the stoves carefully. White gas (*bencina*) costs US$1.50 per litre and can be bought at hardware stores, but check the purity. Stove spirit (*alcohól para quemar*) is available at pharmacies. Blue gas canisters, costing US$5, can be found at some hardware stores and at shops which rent gear. You can also rent equipment through travel agencies.

Markets

To buy back your stolen camera, visit the Santiago area of Cusco on Sat morning

There are a number of options. ***San Jerónimo***, just out of town (see page 182) is the new location of the wholesale Sat morning fruit and vegetable market, but food just as good, not much more expensive and washed can be bought at the markets in town: ***Huanchac*** on Av Garcilaso (not to be confused with C Garcilaso), or ***Santa Ana***, opposite Estación San Pedro, which sells a variety of goods. The best value is at closing time or in the rain. Take care after dark. Sacks to cover rucksacks are available in the market for US$0.75. Both Huanchac and Santa Ana open every day from 0700.

Just down from Santiago church (an unsafe area at night because of drunks high on the 96%, chemically-produced alcohol on sale there) is a sprawling affair of stall upon stall laid out on the pavements. Everything from stolen car jacks to useless junk is for sale – well, would you have use for the arm of a doll or a broken-off piece of computer motherboard? It´s a fascinating sight – just be sensible and leave the other camera at home.

The second less legitimate market – but equally well-tolerated by Cusqueño authorities – is ***El Molino***, for contraband goods, brought in from abroad without duty or tax being paid. Everything from computers to hi-fis, personal stereos to trekking boots, cheap camera film to wine can be bought here, under the Puente Grau (take a taxi for US$0.60). It is clean and safe (but take the usual commonsense precautions about valuables) and is open daily 0600-2030.

On Sat mornings you may see small plazas around the city given over to furniture markets where beds and wardrobes are sold at a fraction of the store price. Plaza Túpac Amaru doubles this up with a flower market, which gets going proper around 1000.

Supermarkets If the wonderful value of market shopping is not for you – maybe the sight of so many cows´ and sheep´s heads is too much – the best supermarket to be found is ***El Chinito***, either at Heladeros 109, down from Plaza Regocijo, or its big brother, ***El Chinito Gigante***, at Matará 271. ***Gato's Market***, Portal Belén 115. ***Shop Market***, Plateros 352, open daily 1000-0300. ***El Pepino***, Plaza San Francisco, Mon-Sat 0900-2000, closed lunchtime. Sells a wide variety of imported goods, delicatessen, stocks multi-packs of food (eg chocolate bars) much cheaper than other shops, a good bargain for trekking supplies.

Tour operators

The agencies listed below are divided into their respective categories and listed alphabetically

There are a million and one tour operators in Cusco, most of whom are packed into the Plaza de Armas. The sheer number and variety of tours on offer is bewildering and prices for the same tour can vary dramatically. Do not deal with guides who claim to be employed by agencies listed below without verifying their credentials. You should only deal directly with the agencies and seek advice from visitors returning from trips for the latest information. Read trip reports in the South America Explorers´ clubhouse on Av Sol (you must join first – it's excellent value). Beware also of tours which stop for long lunches at expensive hotels.

Ask questions such as: what is the itinerary? How many meals a day are there? What will the food be? Does the guide speak English (some have no more than a memorised spiel and every ruin is a "sacred special place")? In general also beware agencies quoting prices in dollars then converting to soles at an unfavourable rate when paying. Check what the cancellation fee will be – one reader fell ill the day before trekking the Inca Trail, found a replacement but still had to pay US$20 after a big fight. Students will normally receive a discount on production of an ISIC card.

Inca Trail & general tours

It is now impossible to trek the Inca Trail independently following regulations brought in at the beginning of 2001; *see page 167*

To choose a tour group, start first with the price. If the cost is under US$140, then you should be concerned. Bear in mind that the company has to pay US$25 for your train fare, US$50 to get you into Machu Picchu as well as supply food and equipment. If they´re cutting costs this means that something has to give and usually this is the salary of the guides and porters. Only poor guides accept poor wages and you may be surprised to learn that porters can be paid as little as US$4.20 a day. This may make tipping at the end of the trek an uncomfortable experience. However, you won´t always get what you pay for. Agencies often pool their clients together to create commercially-viable groups and trekkers sometimes find, en route, they paid hundreds of dollars more than others.

Ask the tour agencies some general questions and, if you´re lucky, get them to put their answers in writing. Then, if you have a complaint, you can take it to *Indecopi* (see page 73) on your return and seek compensation. As well as the questions listed on the previous page, also ask if there's a toilet and dining tent (if this concerns you); if they carry a first aid kit which must (under the new regulations) include an oxygen bottle; do they carry radios; and, most of all, does the price include the return train ticket? Trekkers have been caught out unable to pay for their fare home – there is nowhere to obtain money in Aguas Calientes. Check also if the train takes you back all the way. The budget tour companies buy the cheapest ticket back to Ollantaytambo and from there put you on a bus. This does, in fact, shave an hour off the 4½-hr return journey, but many are expected to stump up the US$2.85 bus fare. This should be part of the deal. Ask to see the equipment if possible (it has been known for tent pegs to be missing!), otherwise ask what tents they supply (some leak). How good is the sleeping mat and sleeping bag (you need a down bag – "pluma"), if these are supplied?

Agencies vary in quality from week to week, season to season, but we can give the hassled reader some more concrete advice. The expensive agencies are all dependable. In the mid-range price bracket, *United Mice* consistently receives good reports for the Inca Trail. *SAS* is also excellent with only the odd bum report. At the budget end of the market, agencies band clients together to form groups so you do not always know who will actually be running the trip. This makes it difficult to recommend one above the other. However, *Liz´s Explorer* and *Top Vacations* have both received generally good reports.

Many of these agencies have their main offices away from the centre, but have a local contact, cellular phone or hotel contact downtown

Andean Life, Plateros 341, T224227, www.andeanlife.com Offer a number of variations on the Inca Trail, as well as Salkantay and Ausangate, day trips in and around Cusco and jungle trips. ***Andes Nature Tours***, Garcilaso 210, Casa del Abuelo, oficina 217, T245961, F233797, ant@terra.com.pe Owner Aurelio speaks excellent English and has 25 years' experience in Cusco and will tailor treks "anywhere". Specialises in natural history and trekking, botany and birdwatching. Machu Picchu 4-day/3-night US$321 (cheaper if part of a group). Planning an adventure trip to Machu Picchu for 2002 to include studies of coca plantations and production. ***APU Expediciones***, Av Sol 344, oficina 10, PO Box 24, T272442, F243453, (mob 652975), www.geocities.com/ TheTropics/Cabana/4037 Office open 0900-1300, 1500-2000. Deals mostly through internet. Cultural, adventure, educational/academic programmes, nature tours and jungle packages to Manu and Tambopata, bilingual personnel, very knowledgeable. Andean textiles a speciality. Mariella Bernasconi Cillóniz has 18 years experience and can plan individually-customized trips, as well as traditional and alternative routes to Machu Picchu.

Carla's Travel, Plateros 320, T/F253018, carlastravel@telser.com.pe Inca Trail 4-day/3-night US$150 – excludes sleeping bag and bus from Machu Picchu to Aguas Calientes. Group size 12-16 people. Will also arrange treks to Ausangate but only with a minimum of 7 people US$100 – excludes sleeping bag. They will book all other tours. ***Cóndor Travel***, C Saphi 848-A, T225961/248282, www.condortravel.com.pe (for flights diviajes@condortravel.com.pe) A high-quality, exclusive agency that will organise trips throughout Peru and the rest of the world. They have a specialized section for adventure travel and are representatives for American Airlines, Servivensa, Avensa, Continental and most other international airlineswith ticket sales, connections, etc (contact for flights Ms Eliana Manga).

Dasatour, Pardo 589, T223341, F225220, www.dasatariq.com Run from a small office, offers traditional tours. Half-day city tour US$20, up to 30 people; Sacred Valley US$25, lunch included; 1-day Machu Picchu US$125, includes 1st class train ticket, entry fees and lunch. Also runs day trips to Maras salt mines, Moray agricultural system and Chinchero for US$150 in car with guide. ***Destinos Turísticos***, Portal de Panes 123, oficina 101-102, Plaza de Armas, T/F228168, www.destinosturisticosperu.com The owner speaks Spanish, English, Dutch, Portuguese and specialises in package tours from economic to 5-star budgets. Individuals are welcome to come in for advice on booking jungle trips to renting mountain bikes. Sacred Valley tours cost US$10 excluding lunch and groups are a maximum of 20 people. Ask in advance if you require guides with specific languages. Very informative and helpful.

Explorandes, Portal de Carnes 236, Plaza de Armas (next to *El Patio* restaurant, which is left of the cathedral), T/F244308, F233784, www.explorandes.com.pe English-speaking Natalia in the Cusco office can book only Inca trails. 5-day/4-night costs US$540; a 4-day/3-night up the Urubamba river avoiding most of the crowds is US$480 and a 2-day/1-night express costs US$345. Through the website you can book a 13-day/12-night trip down the Tambopata river, from mountains to rainforest, for US$1,495. Also arranges tours across Peru for lovers of orchids, ceramics or textiles.

Gatur Cusco, Puluchapata 140 (a small street off Av Sol 3rd block), T223496, F238645, gatur@terra.com.pe Esoteric, ecotourism, and general tours. Owner Dr José (Pepe) Altamirano is knowledgeable in Andean folk traditions, excellent conventional tours, bilingual guides and transportation. City tour US$10 (US$10 general entry ticket not included), Sacred Valley US$25 and includes lunch. 1-day 1st class train ride private trip to Machu Picchu is US$245 with lunch in the Machu Picchu Sanctuary Lodge Hotel. Guides speak English, French, Spanish and German. ***Inca Explorers***, Suecia 339, www.incaexplorers.com Inca Trail 4-day/3-night US$349 – excludes sleeping bag (US$14). Groups are small – between 4 and 8 people. Use dining and toilet tents. Good equipment. Departures on Mon, Tue, and Thu only. Excellent service for all types of arrangements including traditional tours, Tambopata, Manu and treks to Ausangate, good value.

Kantu Perú, Portal Carrizos 258, T246372, M 650202, kantuperu@wayna.rcp.net.pe Run by the enthusiastic, amiable Polack brothers who speak French and English. They organize all aspects of travel in Peru but specialize in adventure travel by trail bike and four-wheel drive vehicles. Trips can be as long as 16 days, or vehicles can be hired daily, with or without a guide. They have all the back-up and equipment you would expect from a company that won the best agency award in 2000, including satellite telephones. 4WD vehicles cost US$120-140/day with driver and full tank of fuel, 150 km free, then US$0.25 per extra km (extra for a guide). Trail bikes can be rented for US$45 for 250cc, US$55 for 600cc (extra for a guide). If you want to do the trip to the four mountain lakes and the Inca grass bridge (see) they can provide a vehicle with a guide/driver. They also specialize in mystic/religious tours and trips into Chile, Bolivia, Ecuador and Brazil. ***Kinjyo Travel Service***, Av Sol 761, T/F231121, F244605, tes3@latinmail.com An agency that also deals with group bookings from overseas but they will arrange personalized itineraries for groups. They will book all international/national flights. Includes treks to weaving villages.

Lima Tours, Av Machu Picchu D-24, Urb Mañuel Prado, T228431, www.limatours.com.pe. Offers a 5-day/4-night Inca Trail package for US$667 leaving every Tue Mar-Nov. Sleeping bags are not included. Also an Amex representative, gives travellers' cheques against Amex card, but no exchange, also DHL office, to receive a parcel you pay 35% of the marked value of customs tax. ***Liz´s Explorer***, Medio 114B, T/F246619, www.geocities.com/lizexplorer/ Inca Trail: 4-day/3-night US$145 (minimum group size 10, maximum 16), other lengths of trips available including 1 day for US$80. Liz gives a clearly laid-out list of what is and what is not included. Down sleeping bags are US$2.50 per day extra, fibre bags US$2. If you need a guide who speaks a language other than English let her know in advance. City tours US$5-8 (not including entry fees) and Sacred Valley US$10 (not including lunch). ***Luzma Tours***, Garcilaso 265, oficina 1, T245677, F242222, luzmatours@latinmail.com Wide range of treks around Cusco, plus longer (2 weeks and more) organized tours all over Peru and to Bolivia and Chile. Very experienced. Hotel reservations (with discounts), bus and air ticket bookings. City Tour in a group US$8, Sacred Valley in a group US$15, Machu Picchu one day: US$115 (luxury train), US$75 (backpacker). Also offers email, fax, phone and photocopying service – manager Luz Marina Anaya is very helpful.

Naty's Travel Agency Triunfo 338, 2nd floor, T/F239437, natystravel@terra.com.pe Inca Trail 4-day/3-night US$160 – excludes sleeping bag, bus from Machu Picchu to Aguas Calientes. Groups of 8-16 people. Guides speak English. Will organize all other trips including Puerto Maldonaldo and special fiestas. ***Peruvian Andean Treks***, Av Pardo 705,T225701, F238911, www.andeantreks.com Open Mon-Fri 0900-1300, 1500-1800, Sat 0900-1300, manager Tom Hendrickson has 5-day/4-night Inca Trail for US$440 using high-quality equipment and satellite phones. His 7-day/6-night Vilcanota Llama Trek to Ausangate (the mountain visible from Cusco) costs US$619 and includes a collapsible pressure chamber for altitude sickness. Incas and Llamas tour attaches this to Inca Trail for a total of US$1,452. ***Q'ente***, Plateros 325, 2nd floor, T247836, www.qente.com Inca Trail, 4-day/3-night, US$175 – excludes sleeping bag (rent fibre bag for US$8). They will organize private treks to Salkantay, Ausangate, Choquequirao, Vilcabamba and Q'eros. Prices depend on group size. Sacred Valley Tours US$25, tours to Piquillacta and Tipón US$25, to Moras and Moray US$25. Horseriding to local ruins costs US$25 for 4-5 hrs. Rafting on Urubamba 1-day, US$25 – excludes wetsuits (US$4). Very good, especially with children.

Servicios Aéreos AQP SA, T/F243229, 24 hrs T620585, aqpsa-cusco@mail.interplace.com.pe Offers a wide variety of tours within the country, agents for American, Continental, LAB and other airlines; head office in Lima, Los Castaños 347, San Isidro, T2223312, F2225910. ***Sky Travel***, Santa Catalina Ancha 366, interior 3-C (down alleyway next to *Rosie O´Grady´s* pub) T261818, F261414. English spoken. General tours around city (US$8, not including entry tickets) and Sacred Valley (US$18 including buffet lunch). Prides itself on leaving 30 mins before other groups, thus reaching sights and the lunch spot (!) before anyone else. 4-day/3-night Inca Trail is US$215 in good-sized double tents and a dinner tent. Continuing with the theme of concern for food, the group is asked what it would like on the menu 2 days before departure. Other trips include Vilcabamba and Ausangate (trekking only). ***Southern Cross Adventures***, Portal de Panes 123, oficina 301, Plaza de Armas, T237649, F239447 southerncrosspaullo@terra.com.pe This is mainly a receptive agency which deals with group bookings from overseas. However they will organize city tours for US$10 and Sacred Valley tours for US$15. If you require a tour in a language other than English or Spanish you need to ask for this in well in advance. They can book all international/national flights and tours. They will organize horse riding and rafting activities.

SAS Travel, Portal de Panes 143, T/F237292 (staff in a second office at Medio 137, mainly deal with jungle information and only speak Spanish), www.sastravel.com Discount for SAE members and students. Inca Trail 4-day/3-night US$195 excludes sleeping bags (can rent down bags for US$12, fibre bags for US$8), the bus down from Machu Picchu to Aguas Calientes and lunch on the last day. Group sizes are between 8 and 16 people. To go in a smaller group, costs rise to US$250. A personal porter costs US$8.50 1 day or US$30 for entire trip. They carry a cooking, dining and toilet tent. Before setting off they ensure you are told everything that is included and give advice on what personal items should be taken. They have their own hostel in Aguas Calientes, or will book other hostels for customers. Manu 8-day/7-night US$540, combination of platform camping and lodges. Also mountain bike, horse riding and rafting trips can be organized. All guides speak English (some better than others). Booking is available by email at no extra charge. They can book internal flights at much cheaper rates than booking from overseas. Robyn is Australian and very helpful. Responsible, good equipment and food.

Tambo Tours, www.2GOPERU.com T(281) 528-9448 (Lima), F(281)528-7378 (Lima). Has offices around the world but nowhere open to the public in Cusco. Offers daily departures to Machu Picchu and the Inca Trail (US$400-780 per person), as well as river rafting (US$50/day), fly fishing (US$125), horse riding (US$50) and Sacred Valley trips. *Top Vacations*, Portal Confiturías 265, interior, T/F263278, topvacations@terra.com.pe Inca Trail 4-day/3-night US$130 excludes sleeping bag (rent fibre bags for US$6), a personal porter costs US$40. Group sizes from 8 to 16. Groups can organize trekking to: Choquequirao, Ausangate, Salkantay, Vilcabamba and elsewhere, good guides and arrangements. Sacred Valley Tours US$8, City Tours US$5 (groups can be up to 35 people), check that the guide will speak English and ask well in advance for other languages. ***Trekperu***, Pumacahua C-10, Wanchac, T252899, F238591, www.trekperu.com Experienced trek operator as well as other adventure sports and mountain biking. Offers "culturally-sensitive" tours. US$480, 5-day/4-night Cusco Biking Adventure visits Tipón ruins, Huacarpa lake, Ninamarca burial towers, Paucartambo, Tres Cruces (superb views over Manu) as well as Pisac and Cusco. Includes support vehicle and good camping gear. Need sleeping bag. Inca Trail (5-day/4-night) US$565.

United Mice, Plateros 351T/F221139, F238050. Inca Trail, 4-day/3-night, US$185 – excludes sleeping bag (US$9), bus back from Machu Picchu. Private porter costs US$50. Good English-speaking guides; Salustio speaks Italian and Portuguese. Discount with student card, good food and equipment. City Tours US$6 in Spanish and English, US$7 only in English, Sacred Valley Tours US$8.50 in Spanish and English, US$11.50 only in English. Staff speak English.

River rafting, mountain biking & trekking

Much of the advice given on page 114 also applies here; also see the Sports and special interest section, pages 52 and 57

For **rafting**, unless you are on a tight budget, *Amazonas Explorers* come highly recommended. Among the other budget operators, *Mayuc* receives good reports. Having said this, all the agencies we list below have received favourable reports.

Amazonas Explorers, PO Box 722, Cusco, T/F 227137, www.amazonas-explorer.com Experts in rafting, hiking and biking; used by BBC. English owner Paul Cripps has great experience, but takes most bookings from overseas (T01874-658125 in England, Jan-Mar). However, he may be able to arrange a trip for travellers in Cusco. Rafting includes Río Apurímac (4-day/3-night, US$615) and Río Tambopata including Lake Titicaca and Cusco, all transfers from Lima (16-day/15-night, US$2,300). Also 5-day/4-night Inca Trail, return by helicopter (US$665). Rafting and trekking trips also combined. ***Apumayo***, C Garcilaso 265 interior 3 (Mon-Sat 0900-1300, 1600-2000),

T/F246018 (Lima: T/F444 2320), www.cuscoperu.com/apumayo Urubamba rafting (from 0800-1530 every day) US$25; 3 to 4-day Apurímac trip US$230. Also mountain biking (on Treks or GTs) for US$25 half-day to ruins around Cusco and US$40 for full-day trip to Maras and Moray in Sacred Valley. For Machu Picchu 4-day/3-night is US$230 (US$530 private trip) and US$290 for a 2-day/1-night private 1st class train trip there. This company also offers tours for disabled people, which even includes rafting.

Eric Adventures, Plateros 324, T/F228475, www.ericadventures.com Specialize in adventure activities. They clearly explain what equipment is included in their prices and what you will need to bring (they have no insurance so make sure your travel insurance covers you for these activities). Rafting: 1-day Río Urubamba, Class III from Jun-Dec, Class IV-V rest of year, US$25; 3-day/2-night Apurímac Canyon Class IV-V in high season (not viable in the low season) US$200; kayak course 3-day/2-night US$120; canyoning, level 1 – initiation course, 1-day, US$25, hydrospeed, 1-day in Río Urubamba Class II-III; mountain biking to Maras and Moray, 1-day, US$35; Inca Trail to Machu Picchu, 4-day/3-night, US$160. They also rent motorcross bikes for US$45 (guide is extra). Prices are more expensive if you book by email, you can get huge discounts if you book in the office. Good guides.

Instinct, Procuradores 50, T233451, www.instinct.es.vg Also at Plaza de Armas, Ollantaytambo, T204045. 1 day Río Ollanta , Class II, III & IV US$25 – includes food, wetsuit and transport; 4-day/3-night Río Apurímac, up to class V, US$160. Inca Trail 4-day/3-night US$ 210. Mountain biking in the Sacred Valley, US$25 also hire mountain bikes. Juan and Benjamín Muñiz speak good English and are recommended. ***Loreto Tours***, Medio 111, T228264, F236331. Rafting tours on Urubamba only (US$25). Also mountain biking on GT cycles to Maras salt mines and Moray agricultural terracing in the Sacred Valley (US$30, includes lunch groups of 4-20).

Mayuc Expediciones, Portal Confiturías 211, Plaza de Armas, T/F232666, chando@mayuc.com (online reservations), www.mayuc.com One of the major river rafting adventure companies in Cusco. Rafting: 1-day Río Urubamba Class III US$20; 4-day/3-night Río Apurímac Class III-V US$200 , 6-day/5-night Tambopata-Candamo jungle expedition Class III-IV US$790 (6-7 people), US$690 (8 or more people). Fixed departures are on the first and third Sun of every month from May until Nov. Qualified guides with Advanced Swiftwater Association level 3 diplomas and first aid training. Safety-oriented and family-friendly. Trekking: Inca Trail 4-day/3-night Premium service US$337 (4-7 people), economic service US$180 (4-7 people), they also offer an alternative route into Machu Picchu via Salcantay 7-day/6-day US$499 (for 6-7 people). An all-inclusive trip, 8-day/9-night, which includes a city tour, Sacred Valley tour, Inca Trail and all hotel accommodation is good value at US$567. A combination of horse-trekking and walking can be organized in the highlands of Peru. The helpful, English speaking staff will organize any itinerary in Peru for their clients.

Pony's Expeditions, Santa Catalina Ancha 353, 1 block from Plaza de Armas, at *Hotel Casa Grande*, T234887, www.ponyexpeditions.com New branch of established trekking and bike tour company from Caraz in the Callejón de Huaylas, open Mon-Sat 0900-1300, 1600-2000. Organizes and provides information for trekking in Salkantay, Ausangate and Inca Trail areas. Ausangate route can include a climb (optional) on Jampa Pampa (5,200 m, rock and ice, easy) or Sorimana (5,300 m, rock, ice, easy, more interesting). Also runs mountain bike tours to rarely-visited sights of Laguna Huaypo, Maras terraces and salt mines of Maras, then Urubamba in Sacred Valley (1-day, US$30, all off-road, minimum 4 people) and Paucartambo-Tres Cruces (3-day/2-night). Good quality camping gear for hire or sale; bikes are all USA-made Fuji with front suspension and packages include helmet, gloves, snack and water.

Jungle tours

For more details of tours to Manu, see page 205; for tours to Tambopata, see page 214

For Manu you're unlikely to go wrong. The pristine reserve area within the park (where hunting is prohibited) is worked by only 10 licensed operators. Those which have received favourable reports are all listed below. If any other agency is offering Manu, they will be taking you only to the culture area within the park, which is less protected. If you see Manu promoted in the many agencies along Plateros for US$300/400 that will be a trip to the culture area – whatever they tell you. This doesn´t mean you are in for a bad trip, but the destination and the experience will not be the same.

Expediciones Vilca, Plateros 363, T/F251872, www.cbc.org.pe/manuvilca/ Manu jungle tours: 8-day/7-night, US$620, other lengths of stay are available. Will supply sleeping bags at no extra cost. Minimum 5 people, maximum 10 per guide. They give clients a copy of the full-colour, *Manu Nature's Paradise*, by Finnish author Arto Ovaska. He works as a guide for *Vilca* so if you want a Finnish guide – ask! This is the only economical tour which camps at the Otorongo camp, which is supposedly quieter than Salvador where many agencies camp. There are discounts for students and members of SAE. In the low season they will organize all other tours.

InkaNatura Travel, Plateros 361, 1st floor, T/F251173 (in Lima: Manuel Bañon 461, San Isidro, T440 2022), www.inkanatura.com InkaNatura states that it is a non-profit organization where all proceeds are directed back into projects on sustainable tourism and conservation. 4-day/3-night trip to the Manu Reserved Zone, US$699 (promotional price), a 2-night extension costs a further US$490; Manu Wildlife Centre 4-day/3-night, US$990 (2-4 people), The Biotrip, 6-day/5-night, USD$1,290 (for 2-4 people) which takes you through the Andes to lowland jungle; Sandoval Lake Lodge in Tambopata, 4-day/3-night, US$250 (2-4 people), and also a unique tour into Machiguenga Indian territory, including the Pongo de Mainique, 4-day/3-night, US$590 (promotional price – normal price US$1,290). Trips can get booked up months in advance so contact them early on in your plans. Having said that they guarantee departures even if they only have 1 passenger, so don't rule out booking with them once you are in Cusco. In the office they sell copies of a book called *Peru's Amazonian Eden – Manu* for US$80 where proceeds are invested in the projects, it can be found in other bookshops at a much inflated price. 10% discount on all trips for Footprint Handbook readers.

Manu Ecological Adventures, Plateros 356, T261640, F225562, www.manuadventures.com Manu jungle tours, 8-day/7-night, US$550, economical tour in and out overland, 7-day/6-night, US$646 in by land, out by plane, giving you the longest time in the jungle, both leave on Sun. Other lengths of stay are available leaving on Mon and Tue. They operate with a minimum of 4 people and a maximum of 10 people per guide. With a minimum of 8 people they will operate specialized programmes.

Manu Expeditions, Av Pardo 895, PO Box 606, T226671, F236706, www.ManuExpeditions.com English spoken, open Mon-Fri 0900-1300, 1500-1900; Sat 0900-1300. Run by ornithologist and British Consul Barry Walker of the Cross Keys Pub. Three trips available: US$1,595, 9-day/8-night (leaves Sun), visits reserve and Manu Wildlife Centre; US$1,235, 6-day/5-night (leaves Sun), takes passengers to the reserve only and US$1,199, 4-day/3-night (leaves Fri), goes only to wildlife centre. The first 2 trips visit a lodge run by Machiguenga people on the first Sun of every month and cost an extra US$150. Also runs tailor-made bird trips in cloud and rainforest around Cusco and Peru. Also has horseriding and a 9-day/8-night trip to Machu Picchu along a different route from the Inca Trail, rejoining at Sun Gate. Highly recommended.

Manu Nature Tours, Av Pardo 1046, T252721, F234793, www.manuperu.com Owned by Boris Gómez Luna. English spoken. This agency has 2 lodges in the cloud forest and reserve. US$1,879, 8-day/7-night option, visits both as does US$710, 7-day/6-night, staying in a tent in reserve; macaw clay lick costs US$505 extra. US$1,532 for 5-day/4-night in reserve lodge only; US$1,311 for 4-day/3-night. Cloud forest lodge is US$465 for 3-day/2-night; US$309 for 2-day/1-night.

Pantiacolla Tours, Plateros 360, T238323, F252696, www.pantiacolla.com Manu jungle tours: 5-day, US$725; 7-day, US$795; 9-day US$765. The 5- and 7-day trips include return flights, the 9-day trip is an overland return. Guaranteed departure dates regardless of number, maximum 10 people with 1 guide. The trips involve a combination of camping, platform camping and lodges. All clients are given a booklet entitled, *Talking About Manu*, written by the Dutch owner, Marianne van Vlaardingen, who is a biologist who studied Tamarind monkeys at the biological station of Manu. She is extremely friendly and helpful. If you are lucky you may get her as a guide! Marianne and her Peruvian husband are working with the Yine Indians to open a lodge in Manu. In 10 years time the aim is for the Yine to run the lodge independently, but in the meantime they are looking for professional and/or mature volunteers who can dedicate 2 months to the project. For further details contact Marianne.

Peruvian Field Guides, Plateros 362, T/F243475, www.peruvianfieldguides.com .Only organizes trips to Manu. 5-day/4-night US$520, 7-day/6-night US$350, 8-day/7-night US$400. The 5-day includes a return flight, the others return by bus. Optional return flights cost US$120. Group size to 1 guide is between 5-10 people. Three days are in a lodge and the rest are platform camping. They use 4-man tents for 2 people and provide thick mattresses. Well-organized and professional. Guides speak English and office staff speak English and German.

For Tambopata the picture is not so clear because operators there do not have to be licensed. However, the market does not appear to be unscrupulous in the manner of the Inca Trail firms. Use one of the firms listed below, ask the right questions and you should be fine.

Peruvian Safaris, Plateros 365, T/F235342, www.peruviansafaris.com For reservations for the *Explorer's Inn,* 3-day/2-night US$180 – excluding park entrance fees and flights. Also see ***Explorandes***, ***Apu Expeditions***, ***Inca Explorers***, ***Mayuc*** and ***IncaNatura*** which are all listed above.

Cultural tours

Milla Tourism, Av Pardo 689, T231710, F231388, millaturismo+@amauta.rcp.net.pe Open Mon-Fri 0800-1300, 1500-1900, Sat 0800-1300. Mystical tours to Cusco´s Inca ceremonial sites, such as Pumamarca and The Temple of the Moon. Guide said to bring to life the Incas´ spiritual culture. Guide speaks only basic English. City tour US$18 (includes entry tickets), Sacred Valley tour US$20 (includes lunch) and Inca Trail: 4-day/3-night US$250 (minimum 10 people, maximum 15); 1-day backpacker US$85 and 1-day 1st class US$125. Also private tours arranged to Maray agricultural terracing and Maras salt mines in Sacred Valley, US$150 for car and guide, can be split. ***Mystic Inca Trail***, Unidad Vecinal de Santiago, bloque 9, dpto 301, T/F221358, ivanndp@terra.com.pe Specialize in tours of sacred Inca sites and study of Andean spirituality. This is takes 10 days, but it is possible to have shorter "experiences".

Personal Travel Service, Portal de Panes 123, oficina 109, T225518, F244036 , ititoss@terra.com.pe Mainly deals with group bookings and package holidays. They will organise a personalized itinerary for individuals and groups including international and national flights. They specialize in cultural tours in the Urubamba valley

Shamans & drug experiences

San Pedro and ayahuasca have been used for years by the locals, but it is best only to use a reputable agency/shaman if you want to try it and always to have a friend who is not taking it with you in case someone tries to rip you off, you react badly or you react well and take forever to come down. We also recommend not to try and take San Pedro and ayahuasca yourself as they can both be highly toxic if not prepared properly.

We suggest the following, whom we know to be legitimate: ***Casa de la serenidad***, T222851, www.shamanspirit.net It's a shamanic therapy centre run by a Swiss-American healer and Reiki Master who works together with local shamans. It al so has bed and breakfast accommodation and has received very good reports. ***Eleana Mollina***, T2636647, has also been recommended for both plants.

Paragliding

If you fancy a condor's-eye view of the Sacred Valley call ***Richard Pethigal*** on T942367 (cloudwalker@another.com). From May-Sep he runs half-day tandem paraglider flights from Cusco. He is licensed and charges US$60.

Private guides

All of those listed are bilingual and recommended. At the end of 2000 new laws stated that guides may only operate through a registered agency, or independently after paying a high registration fee

Standard tours Set prices: city tour US$15-20 per day; Urubamba/Sacred Valley US$25-30, Machu Picchu and other ruins US$40-50 per day.

Juana Pancorbo, Av Los Pinos D-2, T227482. ***Aydee Mogrovejo***, T221907, Aymoa@hotmail.com ***Mariella Lazo***, T264210, speaks German, experienced, also offers river rafting. ***José Cuba and Alejandra Cuba***, T226179, alecuba@Chaski.unsaac.edu.pe both speak English, Alejandra speaks German and French, very good tours. ***Satoshi Shinoda***, T227861 and ***Michiko Nakazahua***, T226185, both Japanese-speaking guides. ***Victoria Morales Condori***, San Juan de Dios 229, T235204. ***Boris Cárdenas***, boriscar@telser.com.pe Esoteric and cultural tours. ***Mireya Bocángel***, mireyabocangel@latinmail.com Recommended. ***Roberto Dargent***, Urb Zarumilla 5B-102, T247424, M 622080, turismo_inca @LatinMail.com Very helpful.

Adventure trips: *Roger Valencia Espinoza*, José Gabriel Cosio 307, T251278, F235334, vroger@qenqo.rcp.net.pe ***Tino Aucca***, Urb Titio Q-1-13 Wanchaq, T235850, a biologist studying the birds of the Polylepis forest. Victor Estrada, Parque España E-3, Urb Ucchullo Grande, T224049, is a shaman and spiritual guide who is also very knowledgeable about local history, architecture, etc, US$75 per day. ***Lic Rómulo Lizarraga***, *T239157. For spiritual tours and trekking.*

Transport

Bus

A new bus terminal, the Terminal Terrestre, has been opened on Prolongación Pachacútec

Long-distance All direct buses to **Lima** (22-24 hrs) now go via **Abancay** (Department of Apurímac), 195 km, 5 hrs (longer in the rainy season), paved to within an hour of Abancay, and **Nasca** (Department of Ica), on the Panamerican Highway. If prone to carsickness, be prepared on the road to Abancay, there are many, many curves, but the scenery is magnificent (it also happens to be a great route for cycling). From Abancay to Nasca via Puquío (Deaprtment of Ayacucho), the road is paved from Chalhuanca to Nasca and where it is unpaved it's mostly good; a safe journey these days with some stunning scenery through the mountains. At Abancay, the road forks, the other branch going to **Andahuaylas**, a further 138 km, 10-11 hrs from Cusco, and **Ayacucho** in the Central Highlands, another 261 km, 20 hrs from Cusco. On both routes at night, take a blanket or sleeping bag to ward off the cold. All buses leave daily from the Terminal Terrestre. ***Molina***, who also have an office on Av Pachacútec, just past the railway station, and ***Expreso Wari*** have buses on both routes. ***Molina*** to 0800 and 1400 to Abancay, Nasca and Lima, 1900 to Abancay and Andahuaylas; ***Wari*** at 0800, 1400 and 2000 to Abancay, Nasca and Lima, 1900 to Abancay, Andahuaylas and Ayacucho. ***San Jerónimo*** has buses to Abancay, Andahuaylas and Ayacucho at 1800. ***Turismo Ampay*** goes to Abancay at 0630, 1300 and 2000, ***Turismo Abancay*** at 0600, 1300 and 2000, and ***Expreso Huamanga*** at 0800. Fares: Abancay US$4.30, Andahuaylas US$5.75-7.20 (***Molina***), Ayacucho US$14.40, Nasca US$17, US$20 (***Imperial***), Lima US$21.60. After 2½ hrs buses pass a checkpoint at the Cusco/Apurímac departmental border. All foreigners must get out and show their passport. In Cusco you may be told that there are no buses in the day from Abancay to Andahuaylas; this is not so as ***Señor de Huanca*** does so. If you leave Cusco before 0800, with luck you'll make the onward connection at 1300, which is worth it for the scenery.

To Lake Titicaca and Bolivia: To **Juliaca**, 344 km, 5-6 hrs, US$10, ***Imexco***, day and night buses, and ***Tour Perú***, night buses, US$8. The road is fully paved, but after heavy rain buses may not run. To **Puno**, 44 km from Juliaca, there is a new service with ***First Class*** (Garcilaso 210, of 106, T240408, firstclass@goalsnet.com.pe) and ***Inka Express***, daily, 0700 or 0800, 9½ hrs, interesting stops en route, US$25. Other services are run by ***Imexco*** (daytime), ***Tour Perú*** and ***Libertad*** (both at night), US$12.60, 6½-8 hrs. For services between Peru and Bolivia, call ***Litoral***, T248989, which runs buses between the two countries, leaving Cusco at 2200, arriving La Paz 1200, US$30, including breakfast on the bus and a/c. Travel agencies also sell this ticket.

To **Arequipa**, 521 km, 10-12 hrs direct, US$7.75 (eg ***Carhuamayo***, 3 a day). The new road leaves the Cusco-Puno road at Sicuani and runs close to the Colca Canyon, via Chivay; it is very rough in parts. Buses travel mostly at night and it's a very cold journey, so take a blanket. Some buses, eg ***Cruz del Sur***, go via Puno, US$8.85.

Car hire

Caparó Rental, Sr Javier Caparó, Av Los Incas 916, T231473, rent4x4@eudoramail.com They rent mostly 4WD vehicles, but Sr Caparó can get small cars on request and with prior reservation. Rate is US$ 70 plus 18% sales tax per day including a driver and a full tank of fuel, 150 km free per day plus US$ 0.40 per extra km. ***Kantu Perú*** also rents 4WD and trail bikes (see page 116).

To rent a minibus for the day costs US$60-70 (US$30 for a half-day), including guide (less without guide), maximum 10 people. For transport contact ***Orellana Tours***, Garcilaso 206, T243717, M 621758. ***Julio Castro***, T232081, ***Agustín Pozo***, T223099, (Mob T688491), ***Marco Olivares***, T240300, Mob T650412 (speaks English, good for information on Inca history, geography, etc), Pepe Valdivia, Mob T651763, all are experienced and knowledgeable. ***Gabriel González***, T221460, Mob T624813. For larger buses, ***Super Tours***, Av Industrial 567, Huanccaro, T239211, ***Trans Tours Challco***, Villa María B 1-A, T232219, M ob T623468, and ***Wayna***, Huaynapata 369, T228034.

Those who find the hills and altitude too daunting can hire a **scooter** for the day from ***Los Perros Bar***, Tecseccocha 436 (see page 107). All-inclusive they may seem fairly steep at US$50 a day (half day US$25), but they provide a picnic, maps and routes plus helmets and the bikes are good.

Trains

All details of the train services out of Cusco can be found on www.perurail.com

The train to **Juliaca and Puno** leaves at 0800, on Mon, Wed, Fri and Sat, arriving in Juliaca at 1545 and Puno at 1645 (sit on the left for the best views). The train makes a stop to view the scenery at La Raya. Trains return from Puno on Mon, Wed, Thu and Sat at 0800, arriving in Cusco at 1645. Fares: Tourist class, US$19, Inka US$30. There is an *Económico* service from Cusco to Puno on Thu, 0830, arriving in Juliaca at 1510 and Puno at 1900. It returns on Tue at 0830, arriving in Cusco at 1730. The fare is US$7.25.

At Juliaca you can change trains for the service to **Arequipa**, which runs on Mon, Thu and Sun.

Tickets can be bought up to 5 days in advance. The ticket office at Wanchac station is open Mon-Fri 0800-1700, Sat 0900-1200. Tickets sell out quickly and there are queues from 0400 before holidays in the dry season. In the low season tickets to Puno can be bought on the day of departure. You can buy tickets through a travel agent, but check the date and seat number. Meals are served on the train. Always check on whether the train is running, especially in the rainy season, when services may be cancelled.

Directory

Airline offices

Aero Continente, Portal de Carnes 254, Plaza de Armas, T235666, airport T235696 (toll free T0800-42420). ***American Airlines***, Saphi 848, T248282 (toll free T0800-40350), reconfirm 72 hrs in advance, represented by *Cóndor Travel*. ***LAB***, Santa Catalina Angosta

160, T222920, F222279, airportT 229220. ***Lan Perú***, Portal Mantas 114, T225552. ***Taca***, Av Sol 226, T249921, airport T246858 (national and international reservations T0800-48222), good service. ***Tans***, San Agustín 315-317, T251000, open 0900-1930.

Banks

Most of the banks are along Av Sol and all have ATMs from which you can withdraw dollars or soles. Whether you use the counter or an ATM, choose your time carefully as there can be long queues at either. Most banks are closed between 1300 and 1600

Banco de Crédito, Av Sol 189. Gives cash advances on Visa and changes TCs to soles with no commission, 3% to dollars. It has an ATM for Visa. It also handles Amex. ***Interbank***, Av Sol y Puluchapata. Charges no commission on TCs and has a Visa ATM which gives dollars as well as soles. Next door is ***Banco Continental***, also has a Visa ATM and charges US$5 commission on TCs. ***Banco Santander***, Av Sol 459. Changes Amex TCs at reasonable rates. Has Red Unicard ATM for Visa/Plus and MasterCard. ***Banco Latino***, Almagro 125 and Av Sol 395. Has ATMs for MasterCard. ***Banco Wiese***, on Maruri between Pampa del Castillo and Pomeritos. Gives cash advances on MasterCard, in dollars. Emergency number for lost or stolen Visa cards, 0800-13333. ***Western Union*** at Sta Catalina Ancha 165, T233727. Money transfers in 10 mins; also at ***DHL***, see Communications below.

Many travel agencies and *casas de cambio* change dollars. Some of them change TCs as well, but charge 4-5% commission. There are many *cambios* on the west side of the Plaza de Armas (eg Portal Comercio Nos 107 and 148) and on the west side of Av Sol, most change TCs (best rates in the *cambios* at the top of Av Sol). The street changers hang around Av Sol, blocks 2-3, every day and are a pleasure to do business with. Some of them will also change TCs. In banks and on the street check the notes.

Communications

Internet There are lots of places in the area around the Plaza de Armas. All offer the same price (US$0.70/hr) except for ***Ukuku´s***, which has machines for US$0.60 in the morning. ***Speed-X***, Tecsecocha 400 (owner here speaks excellent English and is very knowledgeable with computers), Tecsecocha 420 and Procuradores 50 (in patio), all have Word, daily 0800-2400. ***@Internet***, Portal de Panes 123, Plaza de Armas at C Procuradores, oficina 105. ***Internet Perú***, Portal de Comercio 141, Plaza de Armas. 10 computers, fast connection, helpful, spacious. ***Internet Cusco***, at Galerías UNSAAC, Av Sol, beside Banco de Crédito, T238173. Open daily 0800-2400, 20 machines, no problem if you want more than an hour. ***Los Togas***, Portal de Carnes 258, Plaza de Armas, lostogas@latinmail.com Internet and coffee bar. ***Telser***, at Telefónica del Perú, C del Medio 117, T242424, F242222. 15 machines, popular, lower prices after 2100, difficult to get more than an hour, they have a café if you have to wait; also at Plazoleta Limacpampa, at Av Tullumayo and Arcopunco, T245505. ***Red Científica Peruana***, Portal Comercio 148, p 2, daily 0800-2400. ***DSI-Cyber Café***, Av Sol 226, daily 0800-2400. ***Worldnet***, Santa Catalina Ancha 315. Open 0800-2200, café, bar, music, net to phone, games, etc. Many more south of Plaza de Armas, rates all US$0.70 per hr.

Post Office Central office on Av Sol at the bottom end of block 5, T225232. Open Mon-Sat 0730-2000, 0800-1400 Sun and holidays. *Poste restante* is free and helpful. Sending packages from Cusco is not cheap. For sending packages or money overseas, DHL, Av Sol 627, T244167.

Telephones *Telefónica*, Av del Sol 386. For telephone and fax, open Mon-Sat 0700-2300, 0700-1200 Sun and holidays. International calls can be made by pay phone or go through the operator – a long wait is possible and a deposit is required. To send a fax costs (per page): US$4.75 to Europe and Israel; US$2.80 to North America. To receive a fax costs US$0.70 per page; the number is (084) 241111.

Radio messages *Radio Tawantinsuyo*, Av Sol 806. Open Mon-Sat 0600-1900, Sun 0600-1600, messages are sent out between 0500 and 2100 (you can choose the time), in Spanish or Quechua, price per message is US$1. This is sometimes helpful if things are stolen and you want them back. *Radio Comercial*, Av Sol 457, oficina 406, T231381. Open daily 0900-1200, 1600-1900, or making contact with other radio-users in Cusco and the jungle area. This is helpful if you wish to contact people in Manu and costs US$1.50 for 5 mins.

Embassies & consulates Belgium, Av Sol 959, T221098, F221100. **France**, Jorge Escobar, C Micaela Bastidas 101, p 4, T233610. **Germany**, Sra Maria-Sophia Júrgens de Hermoza, San Agustín 307, T235459, Casilla Postal 1128, Correo Central. Open Mon-Fri, 1000-1200, appointments may be made by phone, it also has a book exchange. **UK**, Barry Walker, Av Pardo 895, T239974, F236706, bwalker@amauta.rcp.net.pe **US Agent**, Olga Villagarcía, Apdo 949, Cusco, T222183, F233541, or at the Binational Center (ICPNA), Av Tullumayo 125, Huanchacc.

Language classes *Excel*, Cruz Verde 336, T235298, F232272, http://excel-spanishlanguageprograms-peru.org Very professional, US$3.50-7 per hr, depending on group size. The school can arrange accommodation with local families. *Amauta*, Suecia 480, 2nd floor, T/F241422, PO Box 1164, www.amautaspanish.com Same owners as *La Tertulia* and *Hostal Casa de Campo*. Spanish classes, one-to-one or in small groups, also Quechua classes and workshops in Peruvian cuisine, dance and music, US$6 per hr one-to-one, US$175 per week including accommodation. For one-to-one classes in your hotel, T270302.They have apartments to rent, arrange excursions and can help find voluntary work. They also have a school in Urubamba. Spanish classes are run by the Acupari, the German-Peruvian Cultural Association, San Agustín 307. *Inca's Language School*, Saphi 652, http://orbita.starmedia.com/~incaslanguage Reliable and professional, can arrange lodging with families, salsa classes and other extras. *English School,* Purgatorio 395, corner with Huaynapata, T235830/235903. US$5 per hr for one-to-one classes. Recommended. *Casa de Lenguas*, www.casadelenguas.com *Cusco Spanish School*, Garcilaso 265, oficina 6, T226928, www.webcusco.com/cuscospan or www.geocities.com/cuscospan School offers homestays, optional activities including dance and music classes, cookery courses, ceramics, Quechua, hiking and volunteer programmes. They also offer courses on a *hacienda* at Cusipata in the Vilcanota valley, east of Cusco. Excellent.

Laundry *Dana's Laundry*, Nueva Baja y Unión. US$2.10 per kg, takes about 6 hrs. *Lavandería Louis*, Choquechaca 264, San Blas. US$0.85 per kg, fresh, clean, good value. *Lavandería T'aqsana Wasi*, Santa Catalina Ancha 345. Same day service, they also iron clothes, US$2 per kg, good service, speak English, German, Italian and French, open Mon-Fri 0900-2030, Sat 0900-1900. *Lavandería* at Saphi 578. Open 0800-2000 Mon-Sat, 0800-1300 Sun, good, fast service, US$1 [S/.3] per kg. String markers will be attached to clothes if they have no label.

There are several cheap laundries on Procuradores, and also on Suecia and Tecseccocha

Medical services **Clinics and doctors** *Clínica Panamericana*, Av Infancia 508, Huanchacc, T222644, Mob T651552. 24-hr emergency and medical attention. *Clínica Pardo*, Av de la Cultura 710, T240387, Mob T930063, www.clinicapardocusco.com 24-hr emergency and hospitalization/medical attention, international department, trained bilingual personnel, handles complete medical assistance coverage with international insurance companies, free ambulance service, visit to hotel, discount in pharmacy, dental service, X rays, laboratory, full medical specialization. The best regarded and highly recommeded clinic in Cusco. Director: Dr Alcides Vargas. *Clínica Paredes*, C Lechugal 405, T 225265. Newly expanded premises and medical attention. Director: Dr Milagros Paredes, whose speciality is gynaecology. *Hospital Regional*, Av de la Cultura, T227661, emergencies 223691. *Dr Ilya Gomon*, Av de la Cultura, Edif Santa Fe, of 207, Mob T651906. Canadian chiropractor, good, reasonable prices, available for hotel or home visits. *Dr Gilbert Espejo* and *Dr Boris Espejo Muñoz*, both in the Centro Comercial Cusco, oficina 7, T228074 and T231918 respectively. If you need a yellow fever vaccination (for the jungle lowlands, or for travel to Bolivia or Brazil where it is required), it is available at the paediatric department of the ***Hospital Antonio Lorena*** from 0830 on Mon, Wed and Fri; they are free and include the international vaccination certificate.

Dentists *Dr Eduardo Franco*, Av de la Cultura, Edif Santa Fe, of 310, T242207, Mob T650179. 24-hr attention.

Public conveniences

Desperate for the loo and can´t face that in the internet café? New conveniences have been opened at the top of Plateros, at its junction with Saphi. They are fantastic. US$0.50.

Useful information

Immigration: Av Sol block 6 close to Post Office, T222740. Open Mon-Fri 0800-1300. Reported as not very helpful. **Motorcycle mechanics:** Eric and Oscar Antonio Aranzábal, Ejercicios 202, Tahuantinsuyo, T223397. Highly recommended for repairs. Also ***Autocusa***, Av de la Cultura 730 (Sr Marco Tomaycouza), T240378. **Bicycle repair:** A good mechanic is Eddy, whose workshop is off Av Garcilaso (street between Tacna and Manco Inca). He welds, builds wheels, etc, but has no spares. For parts, cyclists must go to Lima or Arequipa, or try to use local parts.

Walks around Sacsahuaman

Sacsayhuaman to Tambo Machay

From Sacsayhuaman, the route leads east by northeast, part of the way along the modern paved highway, until reaching the turnoff for Qenqo, about 2 km away. First pass lower **Qenqo** (Kenko Chico) and then Qenqo Grande (see also page 89). Following the exit road out of Qenqo and just before it joins the main paved highway running to the northeast, another smaller road feeds into it from the right. Follow this road which will soon curve left before reaching a large group of houses (Villa San Blas), about 200 m away, on the other side of a gully.

In the immediate vicinity of Villa San Blas, the paved road circles around a small rock outcropping with finely cut and polished niches and small platforms, a huaca (shrine). From that point, an older dirt track heads off in a northerly direction. Continue along this track for about 50 m, enough to steer comfortably clear of the houses, the children and the dogs, and then leave this secondary road altogether, striking off at right angles to the right of it and begin hiking east, skirting around fields and depressions (the remains of reservoirs), following any of several footpaths, but always maintaining a fairly straight course.

About 400 m away, there is a gentle descent into a shallow creek bed. After crossing it and walking on for almost 100 m, you will find some Inca stone walls. This marks the beginning of a semi-subterranean archaeological site similar to Qenqo. Because it does not protrude significantly above the level of the surrounding terrain, it is not easy to distinguish from many other rocky outcrops scattered throughout the area. It is, however, a conglomeration of large boulders with walkways and interconnecting galleries between them. The rocks are extensively sculpted with the usual array of niches and platforms and a great rofusion of carvings, many of which represent monkeys and snakes, as well as what is thought to have been a large sculpted stone representing a toad. There are also remains of a liturgical fountain and a very battered, partially defaced but still clearly perceptible stone sculpture of a large feline, possibly a puma, perhaps a jaguar (a plausible explanation given the presence of other examples of jungle fauna, the monkeys and snakes). This was once a huaca of great importance. The name given to this site is **Cusilluchayoc** ("place of the monkeys", from *kusillo*: monkey in quechua). In Spanish it is sometimes called "Templo de los Monos". The original Inca name is unknown.

Also unknown is the reason why so many of these huacas are partially or almost totally buried. Archaeological research has revealed as much as three metres of niches, pedestals, carvings and masonry below present ground level. Throughout the Sacsayhuaman archaeological park all the lower sections of the various huacas uncovered over the last 25 years are much lighter in colour, in many cases almost white, in marked contrast with the weathered grey patina of the parts exposed for hundreds of years. The lower levels retain the original luminosity of the polished limestone, traces of what must have been a dazzling landscape. Did the Incas themselves attempt to conceal their religious shrines from the conquistadores? Or was it the fanatic persecution of heathen idolatry undertaken by the Christians during and after the conquest that entombed the native places of worship? Alternatively, the consistency of the landfill and uniformity of the depth throughout the area could suggest a natural or geological cause. Landslides brought about by earthquake or flooding are possibilities. Although records from the last 500 years detail devastating earthquakes in the Cusco region, as well as floods and similar natural disasters, there are no specific references to great displacements of earth having obliterated this area.

After walking through Cusilluchayoc, you reach a well-defined, straight dirt track, flanked by sections of adobe walls with cacti and agave growing on them. This is a section of the ancient **Inca road** from Cusco to Pisac, still used by highland folk descending from the hills to Cusco. Turn left on this road and head northeast (away from Cusco) for about 300 m, towards a very prominent rock outcrop rising some 40 m above the surrounding fields. This is yet another important Inca huaca, currently known as **Laqo** (although the original Inca name is unknown). "Laqo" has more than one meaning in Quechua: it can be interpreted as "confusing, misleading, enigmatic", but it is also the

Walks around Sacsayhuaman

name of an algae found along Andean streams and marshes. And such a stream runs just below the site and so the place name would seem to derive from that. Still, it is also an enigmatic place. The name more commonly used by the local inhabitants is **Salonniyuc**, a hybrid Spanish-Quechua word roughly meaning "(place)...of the salon (hall, room in Spanish)". Another name is "Salapunku" or "Salonpunku", with the same Spanish noun plus the Quechua "punku" (door, doorway). It is always Laqo on maps.

Laqo is a formation of grey, porous limestone, some 50 m high. A split, large enough to walk through, cuts into the rock. There are two large caves with remains of zoomorphic sculptures similar to those in Cusilluchayoc. Carved in the rock are niches and an altar upon which sunlight and moonlight fall at certain times of the year, filtered through the fissure above. (Hence another name for the place, "Templo de la Luna" – Temple of the Moon.) The external surfaces also have carvings, sculptures, niches, stairways and the remains of a sundial, similar to the intihuatanas at Machu Picchu and Pisac.

Laqo has always been an observatory. Standing at the summit it is easy to appreciate why. It is the best single vantage point from which to view not only the Cusco countryside, but also to see through the fabric of Andean time. To the southeast, about 100 km away as the crow flies, rises the great snowy peak of **Ausangate** ("the one that pulls – or herds – the others"), 6,350 m above sea level, revered Apu of the eastern Andes and grandfather of mountains. Some 70 km closer, in the same direction, loom the dark, jagged crags of **Pachatusan** ("pillar – or fulcrum – of the earth"), 4,950 m, one of the children of Ausangate. And only 10 km away, aligned with father and grandfather, the young and green **Pikol**, one of the local Apus, 4,200 m high. Every Apu possesses its individual identity and name. Every mountain, every hill, is an Apu. The Apus are masculine and they all belong to a hierarchical order. At the same time, each Apu is both offspring and consort of Mother Earth, Pachamama, source of all life, the indivisible and fundamental feminine element in nature.

Almost all the limestone outcroppings scattered throughout the countryside are in effect huacas, all intricately carved and sculpted. But there are also groves of eucalyptus trees, imported to Peru from Australia (via California) in the mid-19th century; adobe walls belonging to kilns and brickworks from colonial times; ancient irrigation canals contouring many kilometres of mountain slopes; fields of native amaranth, maize, beans and potatoes interspersed with other fields sown with cereals of European origin, such as wheat, barley and oats.

At the northern end of Laqo, there is a dirt road, about 10 m wide, running east to west. Beyond it, lies a flat open field about 50 m long, which culminates on the side of a steep ravine with a shallow stream descending from the north. This runs through the many carved limestone outcrops, turns slightly to the southeast and flows on in the direction of Cusco. The same Inca road followed from Cusilluchayoc to Laqo descends into this ravine, crosses the stream and continues its northeasterly course, gradually climbing and skirting around the southeastern flanks of the mountains, crossing into a small valley and then into a larger one, eventually reaching the village of **Chilcapuquio**, about 2 km from Laqo. The cliffs and rocky canyon walls along this section display many overhangs and cave-like openings, some at ground level and others many metres higher. These are the remains of burials dating back to Inca times. It is not uncommon to find remains of ceremonial offerings, such as bouquets of flowers, candles, coca leaves and tobacco, tributes by the people of today to the eternal spirits of the mountains.

Beyond Chilcapuquio, the main trail swerves to the right and gradually begins heading eastward, climbing about 100 m towards **Yuncaypata**, another, larger, community. Before the main trail comes to and crosses another stream, called the Ccorimayo on maps, it is best to strike away from it, following any of several smaller trails which will be found on the left heading north. These paths follow the course of the Ccorimayu, always on the left side of its ravine, gradually pulling away from it and climbing above it. About 2 km to the north of the point where one has struck off the main trail, and 200 m higher, poised atop a prominent rock buttress, lies the site of Puka Pukara and, a further km beyond it, crossing the modern paved road from Cusco to Pisac, are the ruins of Tambo Machay and the finishing point of this hike (see page 89).

The return from Tambo Machay

You can return from Tambo Machay to Cusco by simply following the main paved road. There is also (time permitting) an interesting off-road alternative. Begin by following the main paved road going back to Cusco, retracing your steps past Puka Pukara and continuing for another 400 m. The road soon reaches the vicinity of the modern community of **Huayllacocha**. On the left side of the road, a small ravine can be seen, descending southward. This is the **Qenqomayu**, the zigzagging river, the same which eventually flows 50 m past the northern end of Laqo and which the trail from there to Chilcapuquio and Puka Pukara earlier crosses. Several footpaths, along either the left or right slopes of the gully, descend for about 3 km to reach the vicinity of Laqo.

About 500 m after starting the descent there is a notable feature on the right bank of the canyon: the western canyon walls become vertical cliffs, extensively pockmarked with open holes, most of them many metres above ground level. They are all graves (all looted) dating back to Inca times and representing one of the largest cemeteries in the department of Cusco. A similar one can be seen opposite the northern side of the ruins of Pisac. Facing the vertical necropolis in the Qencomayu gully is an Inca wall, of fine masonry, running for about 100 m. Its function is not known but it may indicate a shrine buried in the hill behind it, or some kind of canalization of the Qencomayu, channeling its course toward Cusco.

You approach Laqo, but to avoid visiting the site again, gradually climb above and away from the Qencomayu, at a southwesterly angle, eventually to descend and meet the dirt road which runs in front of the northern end of Laqo from east to west. Once on this road, head left (west) for about 1 km, until rejoining the main paved highway from Pisac to Cusco, now heading south toward Cusco. Cross the highway, turn left, and less than 50 m south there is turnoff to the right (west). Directly above, lies another limestone promontory containing another enigmatic huaca. The outer surface displays many carvings, though none as fine as the ones in Laqo or Cusilluchayoc. But the inner part of the huaca is a labyrinth of passageways and narrow caves. The official name of this site is **Lanlacuyoc**, which roughly translates as "that which has an evil (or mischievous) spirit". Its more popular name is "Zona X", no doubt bestowed upon it 25 years ago during Cusco's Hippy period (the Katmandu of the west, as it was called), when this particular archaeological site acquired a keen degree of interest.

Leaving the recent and ancient past behind, follow the paved road for about 3 km, past the ruins of a colonial kiln, an Inca quarry, countless clumps of intricately carved limestone and occasional parked cars with romantic couples in pursuit of the timeless ritual. Soon after the first few turns, Sacsayhuaman comes into view. Any options for getting off the road, as long as they are on the left and head down towards Sacsayhuaman, are good.

Ceques – the cosmic dial

To understand the basis on which many Inca roads were laid out, one needs to know a little about the ceque system. This involves a complex series of lines and associated huacas (shrines) that radiated out from Cusco and had astronomical, calendric, and sacred connotations. The centre point of this giant dial is generally taken to be the Qoricancha, although some say a pillar and the tower of the Suntur Huasi on the Huacaypata (the Plaza de Armas) were the sighting points. Forty one lines emanated from the hub, some hundreds of kilometres long. The lines were not necessarily marked on the ground, but ran dead straight towards the horizon. Four were the intercardinal roads to the four quarters of Tahuantinsuyo, others aimed at the equinox and solstice points, others to the points where different stars and constellations rise. On or near these rays, about 328 huacas pillars, and survey points were distributed.The lines served various purposes. They were used for tracking the movements of sun and stars; they helped predict the best time for planting crops; they were instumental in irrigation (about a third pointed to springs and other water sources). Certain ceques and their huacas were under the jurisdiction of particular panacas (clans). As well as delineating panaca property, the lines helped to define the organization of land, water and work and the rituals and ceremonies which began and closed work cycles.

Variations on the route

Both of these hiking routes can be undertaken in reverse. It is also possible to hike from Laqo, after coming there from Cusilluchayoc, northward, following the course of the Qenkomayu upward for about 3 km eventually reaching Huayllacocha on the main paved Cusco-Pisac highway, a few hundred metres before Puka Pukara. This avoids the longer roundabout way from Laqo to Chilcapuquio. The routes can be modified and combined according to time limitations and weather conditions. Likewise, it is possible to take motor transport to the furthest point, in this case Tambo Machay, and from there begin walking back in the direction of Sacsayhuaman and Cusco.

Most of these hiking routes can also be done on horseback and perhaps as many can be ridden on a mountain bike. Hiring of horses and rental of mountain bikes are readily available.

An alternative route Laqo-Cusco

After walking 1 km beyond Laqo, head northeast along the Inca road from Cusilluchayoc (which goes to Pisac) and follow it uphill to the right of the hill. The trail crosses from a narrow valley to a wider valley. After a grove of eucalyptus you will see well-preserved Inca terraces, to the right of which is **Inkiltambo**. Here is a vast area of carved niches,which housed the mummies of the ancestors of the Inca community that looked after the huaca.

From Inkiltambo you go down the quebrada of **Choquequirau**, taking the trail on the right side of the stream. You pass colonial kilns and then take a trail that goes up the right side of the valley, leading to a superb view of the Huatanay valley and San Jerónimo (see page 182). The outskirts of Cusco are reached through a gap in the ridge. A dirt track crosses the hillside towards Cusco to meet the paved road, which you follow to the right for about 100 m until you find the path again on the opposite side. This leads to **Titicaca** (or Tetekaka) huaca, which now has a cross and chapel. The shrine stands on the ceque (see above) of the winter solstice and Peter Frost (in his *Exploring Cusco*) associates this fact with the alignment of the huaca with the legendary birthplace of the sun in Lake Titicaca. Above the shrine, the path splits; take the upper fork and continue to the huaca called

Mesa Redonda, so called for its flat, table-like rock. Beyond, you go downhill into the city.

Hike to Chacán from Sacsayhuaman

You can reach the paved perimeter road around the north side of Sacsayhuaman from the centre of Cusco on foot. From the Plaza de Armas walk up Calle Suecia (straight up from the Portal de Carnes), or up Cuesta del Almirante to Plaza Nazarenas (turn left onto Calle Pumacurco), or via Calle Saphi and any of the pedestrian streets to the right of this street (eg Resbalosa, or Amargura staircase). All of these will lead you to a small ticket booth just a few metres above San Cristóbal church. Leave the paved road at the booth to climb a wide path heading north to the Sacsayhuaman archaeological site. Cross the esplanade of Sacsayhuaman, cross the paved road and you will find traces of an Inca road on the left of the modern trail. This will bring you to an irrigation channel made of concrete. Do not miss this channel, as it leads directly to **Chacán**. Follow the channel upstream for 2 km, where it meets the Tica Tica valley. Here a natural bridge (Chacán means "bridge place") carries the channel across the gorge while the stream runs 25 to 30 m below. Above this exceptional barrier stands a large carved rock built between stone walls. This is another of Cusco's sacred huacas. If you cross the bridge and go down to your right towards the edge of the cliff, you will reach a lookout point at the front of a cave, which has Inca carvings. Below you can see the Río Tica Tica emerging from another cave, which runs beneath Chacán.

One kilometre upstream from Chacán are the ruins of **Ñustapacana**. The surroundings of this site are full of fine terraces, stone walls and another huaca.

Back at Chacán, walk west on the high trail above the river. Look for a eucalyptus plantation (or the remains of it if it has been cut down), on the opposite side of the river. Walk down to the river at this point and cross over. Along this path you will see rocks carved in the shape of pyramids and other Andean religious motifs. Most prominent is a rock, some 2 ½ m in height, whose central symbol has been defaced. This is **Quispe Wara** (Crystal Loincloth). Associated with this shrine are high quality Inca walls and aqueducts, which can be seen on the return to Cucso. Stay on the left bank of the river at Quispe Wara and climb straight uphill until you reach a narrow road. A leisurely 2-km descent passes, as a point of reference, the *InkatamboHotel* on your left. After this, turn left for 100 m to get back to the paved road at the bend just below Sacsayhuaman.

The Sacred Valley

The Sacred Valley

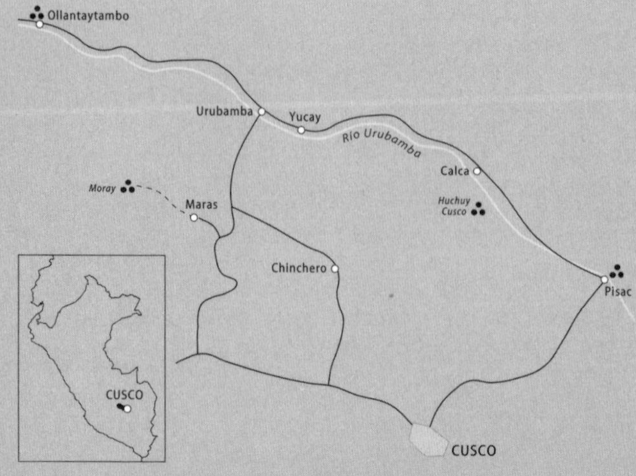

The Río Urubamba cuts its way through fields and rocky gorges beneath the high peaks of the Cordillera. The presence of giants such as Pitusiray and La Verónica is a constant reminder that to the Incas such mountains were apus, beings to be worshipped. The landscape is forever changing as shafts of sunlight fall upon plantations of corn, precipitous Inca terraces, tiled roofs, or the waters of the river itself. Brown hills, covered in wheat fields, separate Cusco from this beautiful high valley. Major Inca ruins command the heights – Pisac, Huchuy Cusco and Ollantaytambo are the best examples – and traditional villages guard the bridges or stand on the highlands.

The road from Cusco climbs up to a pass, then continues over the pampa before descending into the densely populated Urubamba valley, which stretches from Sicuani (on the railway to Puno) to the gorge of Torontoi, 600 m lower, to the northwest of Cusco. Upstream from Pisac, the river is usually called the Vilcanota, downstream it is the Urubamba. Beyond Ollantaytambo, the river begins its descent to the Amazonian lowlands, becoming wilder as it leaves the valley behind. That the river was of great significance to the Incas can be seen in the number of strategic sites they built above it. These enhanced the valley's fertility by building vast stretches of terraces on the mountain flanks and the Inca rulers had their royal estates here. It is from the Incas' own name for the river that the section from Pisac to Ollantaytambo is called Sacred today.

Things to do in The Sacred Valley

- Start the day in Pisac with a good breakfast at the *Hostal Pisaq* on the plaza, or at the *Beho*.
- At Pisac, walk up to the ruins. It's quite hard work, but worth it. As you climb, the views of the Urubamba Valley just get better and better.
- Visit the pottery workshop of *Seminario-Behar* in the town of Urubamba. They use precolumbian techniques and designs to make very desirable ceramics.
- Take a trip to Moray, in the hills above Urubamba, passing the village of Maras. Moray's three large depressions, converted into terraced crop laboratories, show the Incas' thorough understanding of their environment to perfection.
- Ollantaytambo, at the end of the Valley, is dominated by its Inca ruin, but don't overlook the town. Half of it retains its Inca layout (the *llaqta*). The town's museum should also not be missed.
- Don't take with a pinch of salt the recommendation to visit the spectacular salt pans at Pichingoto

Ins and outs

Getting there

Bus Buses to the Sacred Valley leave from the outskirts of Cusco, near the Clorindo Matto de Turner school and Av de la Cultura. To **Pisac**, 32 km, 1 hr, US$0.65; to **Calca**, a further 18 km, 30 mins, US$0.10; to **Urubamba** a further 22 km, 45 mins, US$0.40. To **Ollantaytambo**, there is a new direct service twice a day, in the morning and evening (0745 and 1945 from Ollantaytambo), otherwise take a bus to Urubamba and change there to a colectivo for the last 30 mins of the journey. Colectivos, minibuses and buses leave whenever they are full, between 0600 and 1600; also trucks and pick-ups. Buses returning from Pisac are often full. The last one back leaves around 2000.

Don't hurry through the Valley; most organized tours are too fast. Explore it on foot, by bike or on horseback

Car The road from Cusco which runs past Sacsayhuaman and on to Tambo Machay (see page 89) climbs up to a pass, then continues over the pampa before descending into the densely populated Urubamba valley. As the road drops from the heights above Cusco, there are two viewpoints, Mirador C'orao and Mirador Taray, over the plain around Pisac and, beyond, the Pitusiray and Sawasiray mountains. This road then crosses the Urubamba river by a bridge at Pisac and follows the north bank to the end of the paved road at Ollantaytambo. It passes through Calca, Yucay and Urubamba, which can also reached from Cusco by the beautiful, direct road through Chinchero (see page 147).

Combis & colectivos Combis and colectivos leave from 300 block of Av Grau, near Av Centenario for **Chinchero**, 23 km, 45 mins, US$0.45; and for **Urubamba** a further 25 km, 45 mins, US$0.45 (or US$0.85 Cusco-Urubamba direct, US$1.15 for a seat in a colectivo taxi).

Organized tours An organized tour to Chinchero, Urubamba and Ollantaytambo can be fixed up anytime with a Cusco tour operator for US$5-6 per person. Usually only day tours are offered. For a list of tour operators, see page 115. But note that using public transport and staying overnight in Urubamba, Ollantaytambo or Pisac will allow much more time to see the ruins and markets.

Taxi

A taxi costs US$20-25 for the round trip up the valley and back to Cusco

To organize your own Sacred Valley transport, try one of these taxi drivers, recommended by South America Explorers: ***Ferdinand Pinares***, Yuracpunco 155, Tahuantinsuyo, T225914 (speaks English, French and Spanish); ***Manuel Calanche***, T227368; or ***Carlos Hinojosa***, T251160. Other recommended taxi drivers are: ***Angel Marcavillaca Palomino***, Av Regional 877, T251822, amarcavillaca@yahoo.com Helpful, patient, reasonable prices. ***Angel Salazar***, Marcavalle I-4 Huanchac, T224679 to leave messages. He is English speaking and arranges good tours, very knowledgeable and enthusiastic. ***Milton Velásquez***, T222638, M 680730. He is also an anthropologist and tour guide and speaks English. ***David Quispe***, M 621947. He has a Toyota minibus which holds 10. ***Movilidad Inmediata***, M 623821, run local tours with an English-speaking guide.

Orientation and information

For the visitor, paved roads, plentiful transport and a good selection of hotels and eating places make this a straighforward place to explore. You can choose either a quick visit from the city or, better still, linger for a few days, savouring the sights and atmosphere. The valley itself is great for cycling and there are plenty of walking trails for one to two-day excursions. Horse riding and rafting are also popular in this most visitor-friendly of tourist destinations. If the altitude of Cusco itself is too much, you can hop on a minibus down to the Urubamba Valley. The 500 m difference can do wonders for your health.The best time to visit this area is Apr-May or Oct-Nov. The high season is Jun-Sep, but the rainy season, from Dec to Mar, is cheaper and pleasant enough

Pisac

Phone code: 084
Colour map 2, grid B3

Only 30 km north of Cusco is little village of Pisac, which is well worth a visit for its superb Inca ruins, perched precariously on the mountainside, high above the town and considered to be amongst the very finest Inca ruins in the valley. Strange as it may seem, however, most visitors don't come to Pisac for the ruins. They come instead, by the bus-load, for its Sunday morning market.

Ins & outs

Pisac is usually visited as part of a tour from Cusco. You can continue the Sun morning tour to Pisac along the Urubamba valley to Ollantaytambo, with lunch at Yucay or in Urubamba. Tours from Cusco usually allow only 1 ½ hrs at Pisac. This is not enough time to take in the ruins and splendid scenery. Apart from Sun when Pisac is crowded, there are very few tourists. If you're not interested in the market, it would be a good idea to ask the driver to do the tour clockwise, Chinchero, Ollantaytambo, then Pisac, thereby missing the crowds.

Sights

A local fiesta is held on 15 Jul

The **market** is described variously as colourful and interesting, or touristy and expensive, which is in part explained by the fact that it contains both sections for the tourist and sections for the local community. Traditionally, Sunday is the day when the people of the highlands come down to sell their produce (potatoes, corn, beans, vegetables, weavings, pottery, etc). These are traded for essentials such as salt, sugar, rice, noodles, fruit, medicines, plastic goods and tools. The market comes to life after the arrival of tourist buses around 1000, and is usually over by 1500. However, there is also an important ceremony every Sunday, in which the Varayocs (village mayors) from the surrounding and highland villages participate in a Quechua Catholic mass in

Pisac church. It is a good example of the merging of, and respect for, different religious cultures. This aspect of the traditional Pisac Sunday market is still celebrated at 1200 sharp. Pisac has other, somewhat less crowded, less expensive markets on Tuesday and Thursday morning. It's best to get there before 0900.

On the plaza, which has several large *pisonay* trees, are the church and a small interesting **Museo Folklórico**. The town, with its narrow streets, is worth strolling around, and while you're doing so, look for the fine façade at Grau 485. There are many souvenir shops on Bolognesi.

Inca ruins

The ruins of Inca Pisac stand on a spur between the Urubamba river to the south and the smaller Chongo to the east. It is not difficult to imagine why this stunning location was chosen, as it provides an ideal vantage point over the flat plain of the Urubamba here, the terraces below and the terraced hillsides across the eastern valley. In *The Conquest of the Incas*, John Hemming describes Pisac as one of the Incas' "pleasure houses" in the Yucay valley (another name for this stretch of the Urubamba). If it were merely that, it would have been some country estate. There were, however, many other facets to the site, defensive, religious and agricultural, all contributing to one of the largest Inca ruins in the vicinity of Cusco. The main buildings that can be seen today have been dated to the reign of Pachacútec, to whom, it is said, the estate belonged. To appreciate the site fully, allow five or six hours if going on foot. Even if going by car, do not rush as there is a lot to see and a lot of walking to do.

The walk up to the ruins begins from the plaza, passing the Centro de Salud and a new control post. The path goes through working terraces, giving the ruins a context. The first group of buildings is *Pisaqa*, with a fine curving wall. Climb up to the central part of the ruins, the *Intihuatana* group of temples and rock outcrops in the most magnificent Inca masonry. Here are the *Reloj Solar* ('Hitching Post of the Sun') – now closed because thieves stole a piece from it, palaces of the moon and stars, solstice markers, baths and water channels. From *Intihuatana*, a path leads around the hillside through a tunnel to *Q'Allaqasa*, the 'military area'. Across the valley at this point, a large area of Inca tombs in holes in the hillside can be seen. The end of the site is *Kanchiracay*, where the agricultural workers were housed. Road transport approaches from this end.

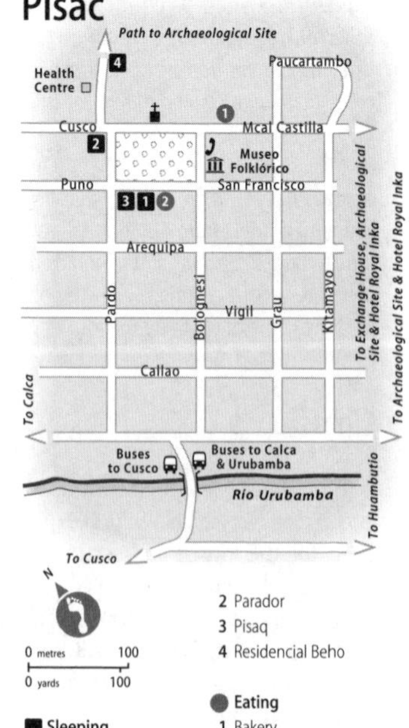

The drive up from town takes about 20 minutes. There are two stopping places, upper and lower. Tourist vehicles will often drop passengers at one point and arrange to meet them at the other after visiting the ruins.

The descent takes 30 minutes. At dusk you will hear, if not see, the *pisaca* (partridges), after which the place is named. If lucky you will also see deer.

A market for beads

A major feature of Pisac's popular market is the huge and varied collection of multi-coloured beads on sale. Though commonly called 'Inca beads', this is something of a misnomer. For although the Incas were highly talented potters and decorated their ware with detailed geometric motifs, they are not known to have made ceramic beads.

These attractive items have become popular relatively recently. They used to be rolled individually by hand and were very time-consuming to produce. Now, in a major concession to consumerism, they are machine-made and produced in quantity, then hand-painted and glazed.

Today, the clay beads are produced in countless, often family-run, workshops in Cusco and Pisac. Some are made into earrings, necklaces and bracelets, but many thousands are sold loose.

■ *The site is open 0700-1730. If you go early (before 1000) you'll have the ruins to yourself. If you do not show your multi-site ticket, or pay US$2.25, on the way up, you will be asked to do so by the warden. Guides charge US$5, but the wardens on site are very helpful and don't charge anything to give out information. There is transport up to the Inca ruins on market days. At other times you'll have to walk which, although tiring, is recommended for the views and location. It's at least one hour uphill all the way. Horses are available for US$3 per person, but a new riding route is planned because the local community does not want horses to use the current route. Expect prices to rise. Travellers with US$3 to spare could get a taxi from near the bridge up to the ruins (they run every day) and walk back down (if you want the taxi to take you back down negotiate a fare). Another way down is to walk back from the car parks to the road junction (about 500 m) and wait for a bus going down to Pisac (schedules unknown).*

Essentials

Sleeping

AL ***Royal Inca Pisac***, Carretera Ruinas Km 1.5, T203064, F203067, royalin@terra.com.pe In the same chain as the *Royal Incas I* and *II* in Cusco, this hotel can be reached by the hotels' own bus service. It is a short distance out of town, on the road that goes up to the ruins, a taxi ride after dark. Price includes taxes and breakfast. Camping is available for US$5 per person. A guide for the ruins can be provided. The rooms are comfortable, in a number of blocks in the grounds of a converted hacienda; they are pleasantly furnished, with all conveniences. There is a pool, sauna and jacuzzi (US$7), tennis court, horse riding and bicycle rental. The restaurant is good and there is a bar. the hotel is popular with day-trippers from Cusco. In the public area a rescued owl sits on a perch, casting an eye over the guests. A small deer wanders around the property, but there is also a puma in a cage. Staff are very helpful and accommodating.

F per person ***Pisaq***, at the corner of Pardo, on the Plaza in front of the church and marketplace, Casilla Postal 1179, Cusco, T203062, htpisaq@terra.com.pe There is one room with bath, priced in our **C** range. All others share bathrooms, which are spotless. Breakfast is US$2.50 extra (a bit more if you have eggs). Excellent brownies are on sale and pizza is served on Sun. Expansion was carried out in 2000. There is hot water 24 hrs, pleasant decor, and a sauna. Being right on the plaza, there is no parking for cars. fFriendly and knowledgeable staff. Recommended. **F** ***Residencial Beho***, Intihuatana 642, 50 m from the Plaza, T/F203001. Up the hill from the plaza; ask for a room in the main building. They serve a good breakfast for US$1. The hostal has a shop selling local handicrafts including masks. The owner's son will act as a guide to the ruins at the weekend.

G per person ***Parador***, on the Plaza, T203061. All rooms share bathrooms, which have hot water. Breakfast is not included in the price, but the restaurant serves other meals. **G** per person ***Hospedaje Familiar Kinsa Ccocha***, also on the Plaza. The rooms are basic and none has bath. You pay les if you do not use hot water. **G *Hospedaje Chihuanco***, on the road out town towards Calca and Urubamba. Basic but clean accommodation in rooms with shared bath and cold showers. Motorcycles and bikes and can be parked in the courtyard.

Eating Good, cheap trout is available in many restaurants. Good, cheap food can be bought on market day. ***Doña Clorinda***, on the Plaza opposite the church, doesn't look very inviting but cooks very tasty food, including vegetarian options. A very friendly place. The bakery at Mcal Castilla 372 sells excellent cheese and onion *empanadas* for US$0.25, suitable for vegetarians, and good wholemeal bread. The oven is tremendous – take a look even if you aren't hungry for bread or a snack. ***Valle Sagrado***, is just out of town along from the bridge going towards Urubamba. Meals are not cheap, but the helpings are huge and good value. Recommended, especially for the fish.

Directory On the same side of the Plaza as the museum are the municipal building with a **computer centre** (internet for US$0.75 per hour, closed Sunday morning) and a **public phone booth**. If you need to **change money**, there is a shop on M Castilla, heading away form the Plaza, near where the road bends; it will change travellers' cheques.

Pisac to Urubamba

At **Coya**, the first village on the road from Pisac towards Urubamba, the *Fiesta de la Vírgen Asunta* is held on 15-16 August. Next is **Lamay**, near which are warm springs, which are highly regarded locally for their medicinal properties. There is a new, rather nice little *hostal* beside the springs called *Jerseyhuasi* (**F** including breakfast, with generous portions of good food at other meals, clean and comfortable rooms). They also have camping possibilities.

Calca

There is a festival on 15 Aug

Eighteen kilometres beyond Pisac is Calca at 2,900 m. This was the headquarters of Manco Inca at the beginning of his uprising against the Spaniards in 1536. Today it is a busy hub in the valley, with a plaza which is divided into two parts. Urubamba buses stop on one side, and Cusco and Pisac buses on the other side of the dividing strip. Look out for the *api* sellers with their bicycles loaded with a steaming kettle and assortment of bottles, glasses and tubs. The municipal library has internet connection.

It is a two day hike from Cusco to Calca, via Sacsayhuaman, Qenqo, Puka Pukara, Tambo Machay and Huchuy Cusco with excellent views of the Eastern Cordilleras, past small villages and along beautifully built Inca paths. There are many places to camp, but take water.

There are mineral baths (cold) at **Minas Maco**, 30 minutes walk along the Urubamba river, and at **Machacancha**, 8 km east of Calca. These springs are indoors, pleasantly warm and will open at night for groups. They are half an hour by taxi from town. If you continue past Minas Maco, and bear right up a small footpath leading by a clump of trees, the first house you come to after crossing a small stream and climbing a hill is a Pre-Columbian ruin. About 3 km beyond Machacancha are the Inca ruins of **Arquasmarca**.

Sleeping and eating There are a couple of very basic hotels. One is opposite the market place, 1 block from the plaza, **G *Hostal Martín***, dirty, cold water only. Also **E *Hostal Pitusiray***, on the edge of town. There are some basic restaurants around the plaza.

Transport Walter Góngora Arizábal, T202124, is a combi driver who does private trips. He charges around US$30 to Cusco, and US$18 to Pisac, including wait.

Huchuy Cusco

The ruins of a small Inca town, Huchuy Cusco, are across the Río Urubamba and up a stiff 3-4 hour climb. Huchuy Cusco (also spelt) Qosqo, which in Quechua means "Little Cusco", was the name given to this impressive Inca site some time in the 20th century. Its original name was Kakya Qawani, which translates as "from where the lightning can be seen". According to the Spanish chronicler Pedro de Cieza De León, the palaces and temples at Huchuy Cusco were built by the eighth Inca, Viracocha, who conquered the area by defeating the ethnic groups already settled there.

Huchuy Cusco is dramatically located on a flat esplanade almost 600 m above the villages of Lamay and Calca in the Sacred Valley. The views from the site are magnificent, with the Urubamba river far below meandering through fertile fields, and the sombre Pitusiray massif opposite, surrounded by other snowy peaks.

The ruins themselves consist of extensive agricultural terraces with high retaining walls and several buildings made from both the finely-wrought stonework the Incas reserved for their most important constructions, and adobe mud bricks. The Peruvian National Culture Institute (INC) began restoration work at the site in July 2001.

There are several ways to reach Huchuy Cusco. The ruins can be accessed most easily by following the steep trail behind the village of Lamay, which is reached by crossing the bridge over the river. There is also a clearly marked trail from the village of Calca. Another longer route leads to Huchuy Cusco from Tambomachay near Cusco, a magnificent one- or two-day trek along the route once taken by the Inca from his capital to his country estate at Huchuy Cusco, where some sections of the original Inca highway remain intact.

Yucay

A few kilometres east of Urubamba, Yucay has two large, grassy plazas divided by the restored colonial church of Santiago Apóstol, with its oil paintings and fine altars. On the opposite side from Plaza Manco II is the adobe palace built for Sayri Túpac (Manco's son) when he emerged from Vilcabamba in 1558. In Yucay monks sell fresh milk, ham, eggs and other dairy produce from their farm on the hillside.

Back along the road towards Yucay a bridge crosses the river to the village of **Huayllabamba**. If you are not dashing along the road at the speed of a local minibus, it is pleasant to cross the river and amble along the quieter bank, through farmland and small communities.

Sleeping **L-AL** *Sonesta Posadas del Inca*, on Plaza Manco II de Yucay 123, T201414, F201345 (Lima: T222 4777, F422 4345), www.posadas.com.pe The price includes taxes and buffet breakfast. A converted 300-year-old monastery is now a hotel which is like a little village with plazas, lovely gardens, a chapel, and many different types of room (one even has its own ghost – ask for room 111 if you want to be spooked). As well as rooms in the old part, there are recent additions, which are comfortable and well-appoointed. The restaurant serves an excellent buffet lunch. There is a conference centre. Highly recommended.

In the same chain and just a short way from this hotel is the **AL** *Sonesta Posada del Inca Yucay II* (also called *Posada del Inca Libertador*, or *Casona*), Plaza Manco II 104, T201107, F201345. Previously called the *Posada del Libertador*, this colonial house was where Simón Bolívar stayed during his liberation campaign in 1824. The price includes taxes and breakfast. The 39 rooms have heating and, outside, there are 2 patios and gardens. There is a restaurant and pizzería. Various activities can be arranged: canoeing, horse riding, mountain biking and guided treks and tours.

Also on the plaza is **B-C *Hostal Y'Llary***, T201112. The price includes bathroom and breakfast.

Urubamba

Phone code: 084
Altitude: 2,863 m
Colour map 2, grid B2

Like many places along the valley, Urubamba is in a fine setting with snow-capped peaks in view and enjoys a mild climate. The main plaza, with a fountain capped by a maize cob, is surrounded by buildings painted blue. Calle Berriózabal, on the west edge of town, is lined with pisonay trees. The large market square is one block west of the main plaza. The main road skirts the town and the bridge for the road to Chinchero is just to the east of town.

Ins and outs

Getting there

Buses and combis to all destinations can be caught at the new bus terminal, just west of town on the main road. Buses run from Urubamba to **Calca**, **Pisac** (US$0.80, 1 hr) and **Cusco** (2 hrs, US$1), from 0530 onwards. There are also buses to Cusco via Chinchero. **Colectivos** to Cusco can be caught outside the terminal and on the

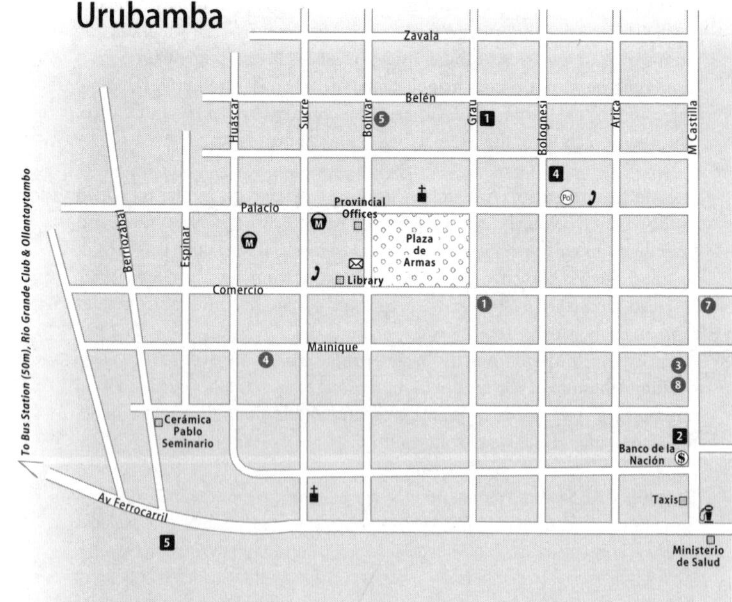

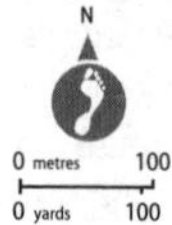

Sleeping
1 Capulí
2 El Señor de Torrechayoc
3 Hospedaje Perla de Vilcanot
4 Hostal Urubamba
5 Incaland

Eating
1 Chez Mary
2 El Maizal
3 El Retorno
4 El Viejo Sauco

main road, US$1.15. Combis run to **Ollantaytambo**, 45 mins, US$0.30. There are buses to **Quillabamba**.

Sights

A visit to the **Seminario-Behar Ceramic Studio** is highly recommended. Founded in 1980, the studio is now located in the beautiful grounds of the former Hostal Urpihuasi, at Calle Berriózabal 111, a right turn off the main road to Ollantaytambo. Seminario has investigated the techniques and designs of Pre-Clumbian Peruvian cultures and has created a style with strong links to the past. Each piece is hand made and painted, using ancient glazes and minerals, and is then fired in reproduction precolumbian kilns. The resulting pieces are very attractive. Reservations to visit the studio and a personal appointment with the artists (Pablo and Marilú) are welcomed. ■ *The art gallery and shop are open every day, just ring the bell. T201002, kupa@terra.com.pe*

Five kilometres west of Urubamba is the village of **Tarabamba**, where a bridge crosses the Río Urubamba. If you turn right after the bridge you'll come to **Pichingoto**, a tumbled-down village built under an overhanging cliff. Also, just over the bridge and before the town to the left of a small, walled cemetery is a salt stream. Follow the footpath beside the stream and you'll come to **Salinas**, a small village below which are a mass of terraced Inca salt pans (*salineras*), which are still in production after thousands of years. It's a very spectacular sight as there are over 5,000. These are now a fixture on the tourist circuit and can become congested with buses. The walk to the salt pans takes about 30 minutes. Take water as this side of the valley can be very hot and dry.

9 de Noviembre
3
To Hotel San Agustín Urubamba, Yucay & Cusco via Calca
2
6
Coliseo Municipal
To Cusco via Chinchero

5 La Casa de la Abuela
6 Quinta los Geranios
7 Tiwinza
8 Vilcanota

Essentials

Sleeping

AL ***Incaland Hotel and Conference Center***, Av Ferrocarril sin número, 5 mins' walk from the centre, T201126, F201071, www.incalandperu.com Special rates are also available. Originally a state-run hotel, this has been converted into a collection of 65 comfortable, spacious bungalows set in extensive gardens. The bungalows have a bathroom and sitting area as well as the bedroom. The hotel, which is often booked by groups, is English-owned. The restaurant, in a large hall, serves good buffet meals. There is a bar, disco, 2 swimming pools. Also available are horse riding (eg to Moray), mountain biking, kayaking and rafting. The staff are helpful and service is good.

AL-A ***San Agustín Urubamba***, Km 71, T201443, 20 mins' walk from town, towards Yucay. A member of the San Agustín chain, reservations can be made at *San Agustín Internacional* in Cusco. A comfortable hotel with a restaurant which serves a buffet on Tue, Thu and Sun for US$3.50. There is room service, and a small pool.

B ***El Maizal***, just over 1 km west of the service station. Breakfast isincluded in the price; rates are cheaper in low season. Rooms with bath are comfortable and have no TV. Restaurant is good but overpriced (not to be confused with the restaurant of the same name, but same owners, see below).

B ***Río Grande Club Hotel***, Rumichaca sin número, at Km 75 on the main road between Urubamba and Ollantaytambo, T/F201528, jotacha@hotmail.com This beautiful old farm, where visitors can relax in the countryside, belongs to the Chávez family. All rooms have bath. A country-style breakfast is included in the price, also 24-hr hot water. The swimming pool is solar heated, and there are children's play grounds and a natural eucalyptus sauna. The lake is stocked with Urubamba rainbow trout, which are bred and can be fished. The hotel can customize hikes in the area (for instance to the colonial salt mines of Pichingoto and other interesting Inca remains), horse riding, birdwatching. All credit cards welcome. Recommended. (See also *Perol Chico* under Sports, below.)

In town: **E** ***El Señor de Torrechayoc***, M Castilla 2nd block, T201033. A new hotel, modern design, with rooms with bath and hot water. It has a restaurant. **F** per person ***Capulí***, Grau 222. Rooms have bath, hot water and TV., Or you can pay **G** per bed in a room with shared bath. **F*Las Tres Marías***, Zavala 307, T201004 (Cusco 225252). Another new hotel, it has beautiful gardens and is welcoming. Hot water is available. Recommended. **F** ***Hostal Urubamba***, Bolognesi 605. Basic, but pleasant lodging in rooms with bath and cold water., Price is **G** for a room without bath. **G** ***Hospedaje Perla de Vilcanota***, on 9 de Noviembre, T201135. Price is per bed, without bath, but hot water in the shared bathrooms. There are even cheaper rooms in this basic place.

Eating *La Casa de la Abuela*, Bolívar 272, 2 blocks up from the Plaza de Armas, T622975. Excellent restaurant with rooms grouped around a small courtyard. The trout is fantastic and food is served with baskets of roasted potatoes and salad. Recommended. ***Chez Mary***, Comercio y Grau, corner of main Plaza, T201003. Mary Cuba, the owner, is a local *Urubambina*, very pleasant and helpful, she speaks good English. She serves excellent food, good pasta and pizzas, and the atmosphere is very cosy and comfortable, with smart decor and good music. At night the bar has live music. ***El Fogón***, Parque Pintacha, T201534. Recommended for Peruvian food. ***El Viejo Sauco***, Mainique 629. Café, restaurant and bar.

There are several restaurants on M Castilla such as ***Tiwinza***, which calls itself a *pollería, bar, restaurante turístico, ecológico*, ***El Retorno*** restaurant and pizzería, which serves good food, and ***Vilcanota***. On the main road, before the bridge, are: ***Quinta los Geranios***, T201043. Specializing in regional dishes, lunch is excellent, with more than enough food, average price US$13 per person; and ***El Maizal***, T201454. A country-style restaurant with a good reputation in the Urubamba Valley, it offers buffet service with a variety of typical Novo Andino dishes, plus international choices. There are beautiful gardens with native flowers and fruit trees. Recommended. Two other places in this part of town are ***El Bosque*** and ***Del Inka***.

Local festivals **May** and **Jun** are the harvest months, with many processions following mysterious ancient schedules. Urubamba's main festival, ***El Señor de Torrechayoc***, takes place during the **first week of Jun**.

Sports **Horse riding** *Perol Chico Tours*, Casilla postal 59, Correo Central, T695188, www.perolchico.com Owned and operated by Eddy van Brunschot (Dutch/Peruvian), who offers 1 to 12-day trips out of Urubamba, using good horses. Riding is Peruvian Paso style. A 1-day trip to Moray and the salt pans costs US$60 (6 hrs). He also has accommodation in private bungalows with fireplace and kitchen on the ranch . Recommended. Also contact through ***SAS Travel*** in Cusco.

Directory

Banks *Banco de la Nación* is on M Castilla at the start of the 2nd block. **Communications** *Serpost*, post office, is on the Plaza de Armas. There are several phone booths around the centre. The one outside *Hostal Urubamba* can make international calls.

Chinchero

Altitude: 3,762 m
Colour map 2, grid B3

Chinchero is northwest from Cusco, high on the pampa just off a direct road to Urubamba. The streets of the village wind up from the lower sections, where transport stops, to the plaza, which is reached through an archway. The great square appears to be stepped, with a magnificent Inca wall separating the two levels. Let into the wall is a row of trapezoidal niches, each much taller than a man. From the lower section, which is paved, another arch leads to upper terrace, upon which the Spaniards built an attractive church, recently painted white. The interior has been restored to reveal the paintings in all their glory. The ceiling, beams and walls are covered in beautiful floral and religious designs. The altar, too, is fine. The church is open on Sunday for mass and at festivals. Ask in the tourist office in Cusco if it is open at other times as it is worth spending a quiet moment or two inside. From the upper square, which is of earth and grass, there are superb views over the mountain ranges. Opposite the church is a small local museum. Recent excavations there have revealed many Inca walls, terraces and other features.

■ *The site is open daily, 0700-1730, and can be visited on the combined entrance ticket (see page 74).*

The local produce market on Sunday morning is fascinating and very colourful, and best before the tour groups arrive. It's on your left as you come into town. There's also a small handicraft market, also on Sunday, up by the church. Chinchero attracts few tourists, except on Sunday. The town celebrates the day of the Virgin, on 8 September.

Sleeping There's accommodation in town at **F** *Hotel Inca*, which also has a restaurant.

Chinchero to Huayllabamba hike

There is a scenic path from Chinchero to Huayllabamba, the village on the left bank of the Río Urubamba between Yucay and Calca (see above). The hike is quite beautiful, with fine views of the peaks of the Urubamba range, and takes about three to four hours. Follow the old Chinchero-Urubamba dirt road, to the left of the new paved road. Ask the locals when you are not sure. It runs over the pampa, with a good view of Chinchero, then drops down to the Urubamba valley. The end of the hike is about 10 km before the town of Urubamba. You can either proceed to Urubamaba or back to Cusco.

An alternative hike from Chinchero follows the spectacular Maras-Moray-Pichingoto salt mines route. This brings you to the main Urubamba valley road, about 10-12 km beyond the town of Urubamba. You could also take the more direct main road from Chinchero to Urubamba, with occasional shortcuts, but this route is a lot less interesting.

Moray

This remote but beautiful site lies 9 km to the west of the little town of **Maras** and is well worth a visit. There are three 'colosseums', used by the Incas as a sort of open-air crop laboratory, known locally as the greenhouses of the

Incas. The great depressions are terraced and it is said that each terrace has a different microclimate from those above and below. There are no great structures here to impress visually. Moray requires an active imagination and an affinity with ancient beliefs to fully appreciate its qualites. The scenery around here is absolutely stunning. As you leave Maras, look back to the village with its church, tiled roofs and adobe walls framed by snowy mountains.

All around are fields of wheat and other crops, such as kiwicha, whose tall, thin, violet-coloured flowers produce a protein-rich grain. At harvest-time the whole area turns from rich green to every shade of gold and brown imaginable. To the northwest stands the majestic white peak of La Verónica. The light is wonderful in the late afternoon, but for photography it's best to arrive in the morning. The road eventually arrives the guardian's hut, but there is little indication of the scale of the colosseums until you reach the rim. ■ *Entry to Moray costs US$1.45.*

About 1½ km below Maras are the spectacualr *Salineras* (salt pans) at Pichingoto, which are well worth a visit. The cascade of centuries-old rectangular basins is like a giant artwork by a Cubist painter obsessed by the colour white. At **Tiobamba**, near Maras, a fascinating indigenous market-festival is held on 15 August, where Sacred Valley yellow maize is exchanged for pottery from Lake Titicaca.

Transport There is a paved road from the main road between Chinchero and Urubamba to Maras and from there an unmade road in good condition leads to Moray. There is public transport from Chinchero to Maras and regular pick-up trucks which carry people and produce in and out. Maras and Moray are visited most easily via Chinchero nowadays. Transport stops running between 1700 and 1800; it costs between US$0.60-1.

The most interesting way to get to Moray is from Urubamba via the Pichingoto bridge over the Río Urubamba. The climb up from the bridge is fairly steep but easy, with great views of Nevado Chicón. The path passes by the spectacular salt pans (see above) . Moray is about 1 ½ hrs further on. If you cannot get transport into Maras, take any combi going between Urubamba and Chinchero, get out at the junction for Maras and walk from there. It's 30 mins to Maras; once through the village, bear left a little, and ask directions to Moray. It's 1 ½ hrs walk in total. Hitching back to Urubamba is quite easy, but there are no hotels at all in the area, so take care not to be stranded. The *Hotel Incaland* in Urubamba can arrange horses and guide and a pick-up truck for the return, all for US$30-40 per person (see page 145). Another option is to hire a taxi with driver to take you all the way to Moray.

Ollantaytambo

Phone code: 084
Altitude: 2,800 m
Colour map 2, grid A2

A trip to Ollantaytambo is a journey into the past, to a world governed by a concept of time very different to the one which holds sway nowadays. Today, the descendants of the people who founded Ollantaytambo continue to live there, watched over still by the sacred mountains of Verónica and Alankoma. They work the land as they have always done, with the same patience and skill that their ancestors employed to shape and then move the huge blocks of stone with which they built both their homes and the temples in which they worshipped. The attractive little town now sits at the foot of some spectacular Inca ruins and terraces, and is built directly on top of the original Inca town.

Ins and outs

There is a direct bus service from Ollantaytambo to Cusco at 0715 and 1945; the fare is less than US$2. The station is 10-15 mins walk from the plaza. There are colectivos at the plaza for the station when trains are due. Also, a bus leaves the station at 0900 for Urubamba and Chinchero, US$1.50. Check in advance the time trains pass through here (see also under trains to and from Machu Picchu, page 161). You won't be allowed on the station unless you have previously bought a ticket for the train. The gates are locked and only those with tickets can enter. For those travelling by car and intending to go to Machu Picchu, it is recommended to leave the car at Ollantaytambo railway station, which costs US$1 a day. Ask Wendy Weeks at *El Albergue* for details (see Sleeping, below).

History

The Tambo Valley, as the Spanish chroniclers called it, is a fertile stretch of land sown with fields of maize which hug the banks of the Urubamba (Vilcanota) river from Ollantaytambo to Machu Picchu. Long before the arrival of the Incas, the valley was inhabited by the Ayarmaca, who had migrated from Lake Titicaca, far to the southeast. On their long journey, this race of farmers followed the course of the Vilcanota, abandoning the harsh *altiplano* in their search for a better climate for their agricultural activities. The Ayarmacas, known in the Spanish chronicles as Tampus, came from the same ethnic stock as the Incas of Cusco, and maintained with them many cultural, linguistic and family ties which would ensure them, at least for a while, a degree of regional autonomy during the period of Inca imperial expansion. When Inca Pachacútec did begin to take control of neighbouring areas (see **History** section in Background), one of his first conquests was the Tambo valley. The chronicles tell of two *curacas*, or local chieftains, Paucar Ancho and Tokori Tupa, who led the resistance against the Inca, only to be defeated in the mid-15th century. Pachacútec sacked their town, subjugated its people and made their lands his royal estate.

Upon the death of Pachacútec in 1471, his properties were passed to the members of his royal household, or *panaca*, the Hatun Ayllu (Great Clan). This was the Inca's extended family and formed the social, political and religious elite from whose ranks the new Inca would emerge. The Hatun Ayllu set about converting Ollantaytambo into a great agricultural complex by extending its terraces beyond the town. To reclaim still more land for cultivation, they straightened a 3-km stretch of the river, as well as building canals and irrigation channels to bring fresh water from the area's snow-capped peaks and highland lakes. They ordered the construction of *qolqas* (barns), to store the harvest, as well as establishing checkpoints to control access to the residential and religious centre known today as Ollantaytambo. To link Ollantaytambo to the rest of their empire via the Royal Inca Highway (*Capac Ñan*), the Incas built a tremendous suspension bridge across the river. Undiminished after more than five centuries, the single supporting central buttress of that ancient bridge now supports a modern metal structure.

When Manco Inca decided to rebel against the Spaniards in 1536, he fell back to Ollantaytambo from Calca to stage one of the greatest acts of resistance to the *conquistadores*. Hernando Pizarro led his troops to the foot of the Inca's stronghold which, later, Hernando's brother Pedro described as "so well fortified that it was a thing of horror". Under fierce fire, Pizarro's men failed to capture Manco and retreated to Cusco, but Manco could not press home any

The Inn of Origin

One of the Incas' three creation stories is the Inn of Origin. This legend tells of Pacaritambo, the Inn, or House of Origin, which is also associated with another name, Tambotocco, the Place of the Hole. Like the Children of the Sun story, (see page 242), there are variations on the basic theme, which relates that four brothers and four sisters (three of each in some versions) emerged from the central cave of three in a cliff. The names of the brothers and sisters vary, but usually the men were called Ayar Cachi, Ayar Manco, Ayar Uchu and Ayar Sauca, and the women Mama Huaco, Mama Ocllo, Mama Coya and Mama Rahua. The brothers and sisters set out in search of good land on which to settle and on the way fell out with Ayar Cachi, who was much stronger, more violent and more arrogant than the others. They lured him back to the cave and walled him up inside before recommencing their journey. Soon, though, Ayar Cachi miraculously reappeared, telling them to move on to the valley of Cusco and found the city. He then went to the mountain of Huanacauri where his spirit remained, becoming a place of veneration for the Incas. In return for them worshipping him on the mountain, Ayar Cachi would intercede on their behalf to the gods to ensure prosperity and success in war. Ayar Manco then proceeded with his sisters to Cusco, where, according to some versions, he built Qoricancha as his first house and quickly earned the respect of the local Indians. A bloody twist to this story recounts how one of the four sisters, on the lookout for the ideal land, came to Cusco and petrified the inhabitants by killing an Indian, ripping out his lungs and blowing them up as she entered the village.

This myth has several elements in common with the Children of the Sun: siblings teaching the unenlightened people and founding Cusco and the Inca dynasty; the discover y of fertile land on which to base the kingdom; the role of Huanacauri mountain. Whereas the Children of the Sun borrows from the Lake Titicaca creation myth, the Inn of Origin borrows from another major American tradition; ancestors, especially brothers, coming out of rocks or the ground.
For the sake of completeness, the third main creation story concerns a Shining Mantle, the brightness of which as it reflected the sun's rays so dazzled the people that the wearer deceived them into believing him descended from the Sun. Some versions say that Ayar Manco was the instigator of this trickery after he and his brothers emerged from Pacaritambo. He used sheets of silver strapped to his body to flash in the sun as a he strode along a hilltop. An alternative version says that it was Sinchi Roca, Manco's successor, who was dressed in this magnificent robe by his mother. She thus led the people to believe that the boy was a ruler sent by the Sun.

advantage. The Inca siege of the Spaniards in Cusco turned into stalemate and Manco was unable to capitalise on the arrival of Diego de Almagro's army from Chile to threaten the Pizarro brothers' hold on Cusco. In 1537, feeling vulnerable to further attacks, Manco left Ollantaytambo for Vilcabamba.

It is easy to see, even today, how daunting an assault on the Inca's defences must have seemed to Pizarro. Great walled terraces of fine masonry climb the hillside, at the top of which is an unassailable sanctuary. The entire construction is superb, including the curving terraces following the contours of the rocks overlooking the Urubamba. It was these terraces which were successfully defended by Manco Inca's warriors. Manco built the defensive wall above the site and another wall closing the Yucay valley against attack from Cusco. These are still visible on either side of the valley. Walking up the terraces is taxing enough, but imagine how impossible it must have been for armed *conquistadores* trying to scale the hill under a hail of missiles.

Sights

The guide book 'Ollantaytambo' by Víctor Angles Vargas is available in Cusco bookshops. Ask for Dr Hernán Amat Olazábal, a leading Inca-ologist, at the community museum for further explanation

Entering Ollantaytambo from Urubamba, the road is built along the long wall of 100 niches. Note the inclination of the wall: it leans towards the road. Since it was the Incas' practice to build with the walls leaning towards the interiors of the buildings, it has been deduced that the road, much narrower then, was built inside a succession of buildings. The road leads into the main plaza, in the middle of which is a fountain on whose top rim stand the statues of two white geese. Public transport congregates in the centre of the square and there is a small church in the south east corner. The original Inca town is behind the north side of the plaza and you can enter it by taking any of the streets, or the street that runs beside the Río Patacancha. The road out of the northwest corner of the plaza looks straight up to the Inca temple, but to get there you have to cross the river bridge and go down to the colonial church with its enclosed *recinto*. Beyond is a grand plaza (and car park) with entrances to the archaeological site.

The Fortress

The ruins, known as "the fortress", were, in fact, a religious complex, with temples dedicated to the many divinities which comprised the Inca pantheon. The gods the Incas worshipped represented the forces of nature, and were seen, therefore, to control the agricultural life of the community. At the fortress, we find the temple of Viracocha, the creator god, as well as those devoted to the sun, water, earth and lightning. The magnificent terraces which lead up to the temple site were almost certainly used by astronomer-priests for the cultivation of corn for ceremonial purposes; the maize they grew there would mark the seasons for planting and harvesting for the rest of the community.

The visitor to Ollantaytambo is confronted by a series of sixteen massive, stepped terraces of the very finest stonework after crossing the great high-walled trapezoidal esplanade known as *Mañariki*. Beyond these imposing terraces lies the so-called "Temple of Ten Niches", a funeral chamber once dedicated to the worship of the Pachacútec *panaca*. Immediately above this are is the site popularly known as "The Temple of the Sun", although it is not known for certain whether it was ever intended for that purpose. The remains of this temple consist of six monolithic upright blocks of rose-coloured rhyolite, forming a wall which, in common with other Inca temples, runs from east to west. A narrow, vertical course, like stone beading, separates the giant monoliths, on which traces of relief carving can be seen. Typical Andean motifs like the *chakana*, or Andean cross, as well as other zoomorphic figures are just legible. These designs were defaced by the Spanish shortly after the conquest, as part of a systematic campaign by the victors physically to erase the indigenous religion. They have also suffered, though, from erosion; sketches by the American traveller Ephrain George Squier, who visited Ollantaytambo in the 1870s, show that the figures were much more complete then. Below the "Temple of the Sun", the dark grey stone is embellished today with bright orange lichen. Note how most of the stones have one or two protrusions at the bottom edge, a feature you will not see in Cusco or Pisac.

You can either descend by the route you came up, or follow the terracing round to the left (as you face the town) and work your way down to the valley of the Patacancha. Here are more Inca ruins in the small area between the town and the temple fortress, behind the church. Most impressive is the **Baño de la Ñusta** (Bath of the Princess), a grey granite rock, about waist high, beneath which is the bath itself. It is delicately finished with a three-dimensional *chakana* motif. The water falls over the relief arch into the pool, which was probably used for the worship of water in the form of ritual bathing. Some 200 m behind the Baño de la Ñusta along the face of the mountain are some small ruins known as **Inca Misanca**, believed to have been a small temple or observatory. A series of steps, seats and niches have been carved out of the cliff. There is a complete irrigation system, including a canal at shoulder level, some 15 cm deep, cut out of the sheer rock face.

■ *0700-1730. Admission is by combined entrance ticket, which can be bought at the site. Otherwise it's US$2. If possible arrive very early, 0700, before the tourists. Guides at the entrance charge US$2. Avoid Sun afternoons, when tour groups from Pisac descend in their hundreds.*

The town Tucked away below its more famous ruins and rarely visited, the town of Ollantaytambo gives those few travellers who do wander its narrow streets, unchanged for 500 years, a much clearer idea of what life must have been like under Inca rule. Unlike modern cities, Inca towns, or *llaqtas*, were not designed to house large, economically active populations. Inca society was essentially agrarian and, among the common people, almost everyone worked and lived on the land. The towns and cities that the Incas did build were meant to serve as residential areas for the state's administrative and religious elite.

Throughout the Inca empire of Tawantinsuyo, the *llaqtas* were divided into two zones, along blood lines, between the two principal *ayllus*, of Hanan and Urin. In Ollantaytambo, the Urin occupied the area which today corresponds to the present-day village. Called *Qosqo Ayllu*, it was both an administrative centre and the home of the Pachacútec *panaca*. The streets were laid out in a simple grid pattern, with the whole forming the Inca trapezoid (see page 247). These streets, whose corners are marked with huge stone blocks, surround *canchas*, communal enclosures which house many families. Each *cancha* occupies half a block, with just one entrance on those streets which run parallel to the Río Patacancha. It is clear, from the elaborate double-jamb porticos which form their entrances, that these *canchas* were built for members of the Incas' social and religious élite. The Inca nobility did not work on the land, their *yanaconas*, or servants did it for them, and the remains of the homes of this servant class, built from much simpler materials, have been found in the northern part of the town.

El Museo Catcco (Centro Andino de Tecnología de las Comunidades de Ollantaytambo) is one block from the plaza, in the Casa Horno, on Patacalle. It has displays of textiles as well as ethnographic and archaeological information and findings from local ruins, run by Sra Rosa de Alamo. The museum is well worth a visit and has the only **internet café** in town. Note the guttering down the middle of the street outside the museum. ■ *Tue-Sun 1000-1300, 1500-1800, entry US$1.50 (children free). Tourist information is available in the museum. T/F204024. Information on the museum and other aspects of Ollantaytambo can be found in Spanish on www.cbc.org.pe/rao/index.htm*

Recently a 'pyramid' has been identified on the west side of the main ruins of Ollantaytambo. Its discoverers, Fernando and Edgar Elorietta, claim it is the real Pacaritambo, from where the four original Inca brothers emerged to found their empire (see page 150). Whether this is the case or not, it is still a first-class piece of engineering with great terraced fields and a fine 750-m wall creating the optical illusion of a pyramid. The wall is aligned with the rays of the winter solstice, on 21 June. People gather at mid-winter dawn to watch this event.

getaway tonight on

www.exodus.co.uk

exodus
9 Weir Road
LONDON
SW12 0BR

2

BUSINESS REPLY SERVICE
Licence No SW4909

The mysterious 'pyramid', which covers 50-60 ha, can be seen properly from the other side of the river. This is a pleasant, easy one-hour walk, west from the Puente Inca, just outside the town. You'll also be rewarded with great views of the Sacred Valley and the river, with the snowy peaks of the Verónica massif as a backdrop.

Essentials

Sleeping

AL ***Pakaritampu***, C Ferrocarril sin número, T204104, F204105, www.pakaritampu.com The price includes breakfast and taxes. This modern, 3-star hotel has 20 rooms with bath and views. There is a TV room, restaurant and bar, internet service for guests, laundry, safe and room service. Adventure sports such as rafting, climbing, trekking, mountain biking and riding can be arranged. Meals are extra: buffet US$13, dinner US$15. Excellent quality and service.

On the road to the station is **B** ***Hostal Munay Tika***, T204111, tika@latinmail.com Price includes breakfast and bath; price without bath is **C.** Dinner is served by arrangement. To use the sauna costs US$3 with prior notice.Also has a nice garden, new and good.

C ***Albergue Kapuly***, at the end of the station road, T204017. Prices are lower in the off season. A quiet place with spacious rooms, some with and some without bath. The garden is nice. Recommended.

D per person *El Albergue Ollantaytambo*, within the railway station gates, T/F204014. Owned by North American Wendy Weeks, the *Albergue* has 6 rooms with shared bathrooms. Breakfast costs US$3, box lunch US$5, full dinner US$10. The rooms are full of character and are set in buildings around a courtyard and lovely gardens. Great showers and a eucalyptus steam sauna. The whole place is charming, very relaxing and homely. See the office-cum-shop-cum-exhibition where interesting handicrafts can be bought. It's very convenient for the Machu Picchu train and good place for information. Private transport can be arranged to the salt mines, Moray, Abra Málaga for birdwatching and taxi transfers to the airport. Highly recommended.

E per person ***Las Orquídeas***, near the start of the road to the station, T204032. Good accommodation at this hostal, and meals are available. **E** ***Hostal La Ñusta***, Plaza de Armas, T204035/077. This is a very good place to stay on the square. Proprietor Rubén

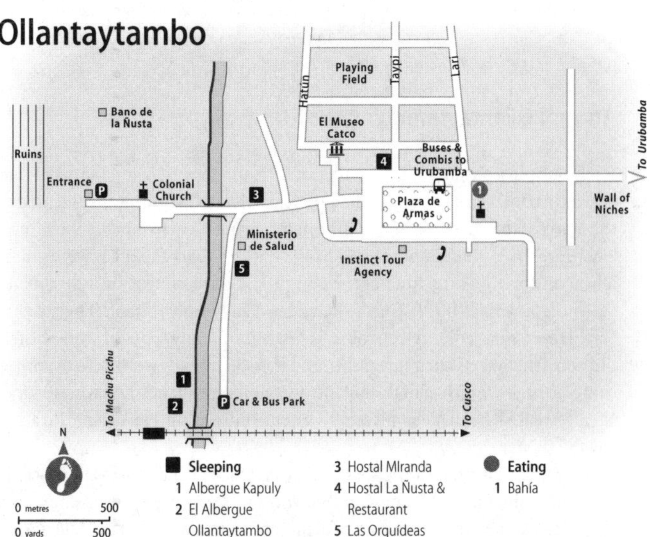

Ponce loves to share his knowledge of the ruins with guests. You get a good view from the balcony. See below for the restaurant.

F ***Hostal Chuza***, just below the main plaza in town, T204038. Very clean and friendly with safe motorcycle parking. Recommended. **F** ***Hostal Miranda***, between the main plaza and the ruins, T204091. A basic hostal with shower included. It's very friendly and clean.

G per person ***Alojamiento Yavar***, 1½ blocks from the main plaza. Another basic, but friendly place. If they're full, they'll let you sleep on the floor for free. There is no water in the evening. They have information on horse riding in the area.

Eating There are several restaurants on the Plaza, such as ***La Ñusta***, see above, which is popular and serves good food; snacks available. Also ***Bahía***, on the east side of the Plaza. Very friendly, vegetarian dishes served on request. ***Del Sol***, esquina Plaza de Ruinas, T204009. An inviting new restaurant run by an American chef called Irini. The fresh food includes soups, salads, vegetables, fish and meat; medium-priced, small wine list, open for lunch and dinner. Recommended. ***Mayupata***, Jr Convención sin número, across the bridge on the way to the ruins, on the left, T204083 (Cusco). Serving international choices and a selection of Peruvian dishes, desserts, sandwiches and coffee. It opens at 0600 for breakfast, and serves lunch and dinner. The bar has a fireplace; river view, relaxing atmosphere.

Festivals On **6 Jan** there is the ***Bajada de Reyes Magos*** (the Magi), at which indigenous people from the highland communities bring down to Ollantaytambo the Niño Jesús, dressed in a poncho etc. There is some traditional dancing, a bull fight, local food and a fair. The ***Fiesta de Compadres***, a moveable feast 10 days before *Carnavales* and 13 days before Ash Wednesday, is celebrated in the small, indigenous pueblo of Marcacocha, close to Ollantaytambo by local transport or on foot. There is a delghtful chapel on an Inca site, the dance of the *huayllata* (Andean goose), a mass and a bullfight inthe smallest bullring imaginable, all in beautiful surroundings. As elsewhere, ***Semana Santa***, the week before Easter, is a lovely time of year. **End-May/early-Jun**: ***Pentecostes***, 50 days after Easter, is the ***Fiesta del Señor de Choquekillca***, patron saint of Ollantaytambo. There are several days of dancing, weddings, processions, masses, feasting and drinking (the last opportunity to see traditional Cusqueño dancing). On **29 Jun**, following *Inti Raymi* in Cusco, there is a colourful festival, the ***Ollanta-Raymi***, at which the Quechua drama, *Ollantay*, is reenacted. **29 Oct** is the ***Aniversario de Ollantaytambo***, a festival with dancing in traditional costume and many local delicacies for sale.

Around Ollantaytambo

Inca quarries at Cachiccata It takes about a day to walk to the Inca quarries on the opposite side of the river and return to Ollantaytambo. The stone quarries of **Cachiccata** are located on the lands of the hacienda of the same name, some 9 km from Ollantaytambo. There are three quarries at the site: Molle Puqro, which the Incas were gradually abandoning at the time of the conquest; Sirkusirkuyoc and the smaller Cachiccata, which both seem to have been fully operational. The stone at Cachiccata, rose-coloured rhyolite, is just one of many types of stone used in the construction of Ollantaytambo, and it is still not known where the others came from. It would seem that all the quarries were abandoned when Manco Inca retreated from Ollantaytambo after confronting Hernando Pizarro's cavalry there in 1537.

Standing to the left of the six monolithic blocks which form the so-called Temple of the Sun at Ollantaytambo, you can see, looking west-south-west across the valley, the quarries of Cachiccata, below a mountain called Yana

Urco. From here, you can appreciate the Herculean nature of the task that the builders of Ollantaytambo's magnificent temples set themselves. Several generations of stonemasons and labourers must have worked in their thousands to quarry the huge blocks that the Incas used in the construction of the Temple of the Sun and the Royal House of the Sun. Once extracted, the stones would have been roughly shaped before being transported to the building site. Possibly using rollers, or more probably using the simple brute force of the thousands of men that the Incas' highly organized society would have been able to dedicate to the task, the blocks were then dragged for more that 6 km across open country.

The Incas would have only been able to cross the Urubamba river in winter, when its waters are at their lowest ebb, and even then they could probably have only done so by diverting the river's course. It is thought that they dug two channels; the stones would then have been dragged across the dry left-hand channel while the river was being diverted through the right-hand one. This right-hand channel would then be drained in its turn to allow the stones to continue their painstaking progress.

The next task was to raise the rhyolite blocks from the valley floor up to the site known as the fortress and to accomplish this, the Incas' engineers built a great ramp. Looking down from the Temple of the Sun, to the left of the six monoliths, the remains of this ramp can still be seen, and they are even more clearly visible when you look up at the ruins from the valley floor. It is difficult to appreciate from today's highly-mechanised perspective just how hard the Incas laboured to build Ollantaytambo, employing as they did a patience and skill born of a concept of time very different to our own. The stones were found near the summit of a mountain on the other side of the river valley after a prolonged search. They then had to be quarried, hewn into a rough shape, and hauled across the valley floor and up to the temple. Once there, they were sculpted by the master masons to fit together perfectly, to the design of an architect, or architects, of consummate skill.

Between the ruins and the quarries of Cachiccata more that 50 enormous stones that never reached their destination lie abandoned. The inhabitants of the area call them *las piedras cansadas*, or "the tired stones". It is still not known whether work on the temples cease when the Spanish arrived, or did it stop during the civil war between Atahualpa and Huascar? The thousands of workers who were involved in the construction of Ollantaytambo, over a period of generations, almost certainly worked under the mit'a system (see page 243). For several months of each year they would have to leave their work to tend their crops, and in times of war construction would have been abandoned and the workers integrated into the enormous conscript armies upon which the Inca state depended. Another suggestion is that Colla Indians from Lake Titicaca were employed in the construction of the site. This conclusion has been drawn from the similarities of the monoliths facing the central platform with the Tiahuanaco remains. According to this theory, the Colla are believed to have deserted half-way through the work, leaving behind all the unfinished blocks visible today. While most experts agree that the work on Ollantaytambo was begun under Pachacútec, it will probably never be known for certain exactly when Cachiccata's great stones great stones first began to tire.

Pinkuylluna

Pinkuylluna hill, on the western edge of Ollantaytambo, is home to the Sacred Valley's most impressive collection of storehouses, or *qolqas*, structures which have often (and erroneously) been called prisons by local guides. The reason why these granaries were built so high up on the hillside is given by the 17th century Spanish chronicler Bernabé Cobo: the Incas "built their storehouses outside their towns, in the high places that were fresh and well-ventilated...". It is impossible to know with any certainty what kinds of produce were stored at Pinkuylluna, but the main harvest was certainly maize, which was probably stored alongside other crops. Many observers take the gigantic image, known locally as the Tunupa, which appears on the hillside when viewed from the bridge in front of the ruins, to be a carved likeness of the Inca creator god Viracocha.

Pinculluna The Pinculluna mountain can be climbed with no mountaineering experience, although there are some difficult stretches – allow 2-3 hours going up. The path is difficult to make out, so it's best not to go on your own. Walk up the valley to the left of the mountain, which is very beautiful and impressive, with Inca terraces after 4 km.

Pumamarca Hidden away in the hills beyond the historic town, Pumamarca lies about two hours on foot from Ollantaytambo through fertile countryside sculpted long ago into a magnificent series of agricultural terraces which to this day are sown with corn and kiwicha. Pumamarca is a small, well-preserved Inca citadel some 7 km north of, and 800 m above, Ollantaytambo. It lies at the confluence of the Patacancha river and its tributary, the Yuracmayo (or White River). From there it dominates a strategic point, commanding a privileged view of both valleys, which would have once controlled access to Ollantaytambo from that direction, as well as guarding the canal which bears its name.

The ruins' high surrounding wall with its numerous zig-zags suggests that the site was a fortress, although (as at Ollantaytambo) all the *qolqas*, or foodstores, were built outside the main complex. Nobody knows for sure exactly when this citadel was built. Some researchers believe that it may have been another checkpoint, designed to limit access to Ollantaytambo from Antisuyo, the eastern *suyo* (quarter) of the Inca empire. But the impressive nature of Pumamarca, built in classic Inca style, leads many scholars to conclude that it may have been one of the first Inca settlements in the area, and not just a simple outpost of Ollantaytambo.

The path to Pumamarca passes through the village of Munaypata and follows the Patacancha river. Up the same valley are the indigenous villages of Marcacocha, Huilloc and Patacancha.

Cusichaca Valley A major excavation project has been carried out since 1977 under the direction of Ann Kendall in the Cusichaca valley, 26 km from Ollantaytambo, at the intersection of the Inca routes. Only 9 km of this road are passable by ordinary car. The Inca fort, **Huillca Raccay**, was excavated in 1978-80, and work is now concentrated on Llactapata, a site of domestic buildings. Ann Kendall is now working in the Patacancha valley northeast of Ollantaytambo. Excavations are being carried out in parallel with the restoration of Inca canals to bring fresh clean water to the settlements in the valley.

5 Machu Picchu & the Inca Trail

Machu Picchu & the Inca Trail

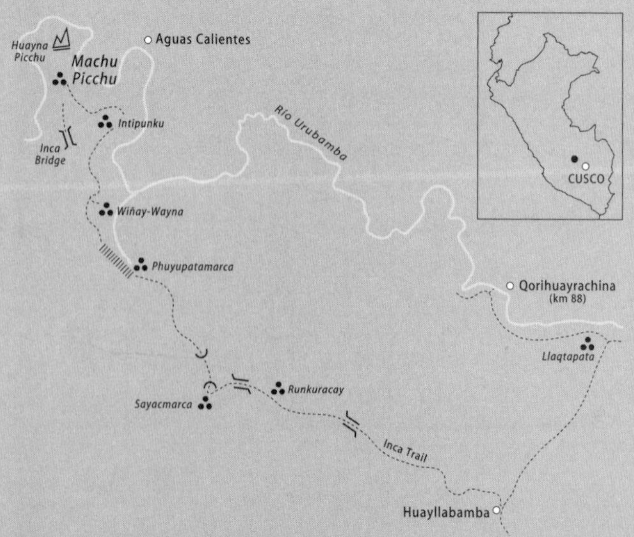

To almost anyone looking for a picture that sums up South America, Machu Picchu is usually what first springs to mind. On the television, in brochures, on packets of coffee, you name it, Machu Picchu has become a kind of shorthand for lost civilizations, the thrill of discovery, exotic travel and, above all, the mystery that can still be found in an increasingly technological world. There is a tremendous feeling of awe on first witnessing this incredible sight. The ancient citadel (42 km from Ollantaytambo by rail) straddles the saddle of a high mountain with steep terraced slopes falling away to the fast-flowing Urubamba river snaking its hairpin course far below in the valley floor. Towering overhead is Huayna Picchu, and green jungle peaks provide the backdrop for the whole majestic scene. In comparison with many archaeological ruins, there are so many standing buildings that it requires no stretch of the imagination to work out what the city looked like. What function some of those buildings had and the meaning of their enigmatic symbols is harder to guess at, but this only adds to the allure of the place.

Getting the most out of Machu Picchu

- Not everyone has the time, or the stamina to trek into Machu Picchu. There is still a thriving business in one- or two-day trips, but a quick visit hardly gives you time to recover from the initial sense of awe. It takes at least a day to appreciate the ruins and their surroundings fully.
- Do find time to peer into corners, investigate the angles of stones, the weight of lintels, the outlook of windows. See how rocks and openings align themselves with peaks across the valley.
- Try to be there for dawn or dusk to enjoy the changing of the light. A good time to visit is before 0830, when the views are at their best.
- The Watchman's Hut is an ideal place to spend the last few minutes of daylight.
- Monday and Friday are bad days because there is usually a crowd of people on guided tours who are going or have been to Pisac market on Sunday, and too many people all want lunch at the same time.
- The ruins are at their busiest in the morning, after the buses arrive bringing tourists up from the first train 0925.
- It is quieter in the afternoon, but a lot of people stay on to see the sun setting behind the mountains.

Ins and outs

Getting there

Air The quickest way to Machu Picchu is by helicopter. While not exactly following in the footsteps of the Incas, it does get you there in only 25 mins. Flights leave from Cusco airport daily at 0700 and return at 1700. US$90 one way, US$170 return; with ***HeliCusco***, C Triunfo 379, 2nd floor, T/F227283 (T445 6126, F444 8708; Lima), dfhr@amauta.rcp.net.pe www.rcp.net.pe/HELICUSCO/

Buses Buses leave Aguas Calientes for Machu Picchu every 30 mins from 0630 to 1300 and cost US$9 return, valid for 48 hrs. Buses run down from the ruins from 1200 to 1730. It is also possible to take a bus down between 0700 and 0900. The office for buying bus tickets is opposite the bus stop. Tickets can also be bought in advance at ***Consetur***, Santa Catalina Ancha, Cusco, which saves queuing when you arrive in Aguas Calientes.

The Inca Trail
See page 167 for further information

The only true way to get to Machu Picchu is to sling your rucksack on your back, and follow in the footsteps of the Incas. This way you are making a true pilgrimage and the sweat and struggle is all worth it when you set your eyes on this mystical site at sunrise from the Inca sun gate above the ruins. That way you see Machu Picchu in its proper context. Afterwards you recover in Aguas Calientes and soothe those aching limbs in the hot springs.

The introduction of new regulations for walking the Inca Trail in 2001 has opened up new possibilities, however constricting the rules may seem, or however loosely applied. You don't have to do the traditional Inca Trail any more. In fact, the old start point, Km 88 on the railway, is falling from favour. There are a number of options now, some shorter, some longer than the old route, so if you fancy widening the perspective of how the Incas walked to their sacred city, ask your chosen tour operator to show you the alternatives.

Trains

Tickets for all trains should be bought at Wanchac station in Cusco, on Av Pachacútec. They can be bought up to 5 days in advance

The ***PerúRail*** trains to Machu Picchu run from San Pedro station in Cusco. They pass through Poroy and Ollantaytambo to Aguas Calientes (the official name of this station is 'Machu Picchu'). There is a new train station for the tourist trains at Aguas Calientes – it is on the outskirts of town, 200 m from *Machu Picchu Pueblo Hotel* and 50 m from where buses leave for Machu Picchu ruins. The ticket office is open 0630-1730; there is a guard on the gate. Trains do not go on to Machu Picchu station (officially called 'Puente Ruinas'). The railway continues to Quillabamba, but this section has been closed since 1998. There is a paved road in poor condition between Aguas Calientes and 'Puente Ruinas' station, which is at the foot of the road up to the ruins.

There are 4 classes of tourist train: *Autovagón*, *Inka*, *Ferrostal* and *Backpacker*. The *Autovagón* and *Inka* tickets cost US$70 return; the *Backpacker* costs US$30 return. These trains depart from Cusco. The *Ferrostal* service is from Ollantaytambo to Machu Picchu and costs US$55 return, while the *Backpacker Cerrojo* runs from Ollantaytambo to Machu Picchu and costs US$25 return. The *Autovagón* leaves Cusco daily at 0600, stopping at Poroy at 0640, Ollantaytambo at 0805 and Machu Picchu at 0925. It returns from Machu Picchu at 1500, passing Ollantaytambo at 1630, reaching Cusco at 1840. The *Inka* leaves at 0610, passing Poroy at 0700, Ollantaytambo at 0825, reaching Machu Picchu at 1000. It returns at 1520, passing Ollantaytambo at 1650, getting to Cusco at 1915. The *Backpacker* leaves Cusco at 0730, passing Poroy at 0820, Ollantaytambo at 0955 and Machu Picchu at 1125. It returns at 1630, passing Ollantaytambo at 1810, getting to Cusco at 2045.The *Ferrostal* trains leave Ollantaytambo at 0630 and 1550, arriving at Machu Picchu at 0740 and 1705; they return at 0800 and 1730, arriving back in Ollantaytambo at 0920 and 1845. *Backpacker Cerrojo* leaves Ollantaytambo at 1045, arriving at Machu Picchu at 1210, returning at 1830, reaching Ollantaytambo at 2005.

Seats can be reserved even if you're not returning the same day. The *Autovagón* and *Inka* tickets include food in the price. These trains have toilets, video, snacks and drinks for sale. Many people return by bus from Ollantaytambo, leaving the trains emptier for the return trip to Cusco. Tour agencies in Cusco sell various tourist tickets which include train fare, round trip by bus up to the ruins, entrance fee and guide. They will pick you up from your hotel in Cusco and take you to the train station.

There are also local trains: the *Tren Local* or *Servicio Social* from Cusco and the *Cerrojo Social* from Ollantaytambo. These trains are only for people who live along the route of the railway, Peruvian students and retired Peruvians. Tourists cannot buy tickets for these trains, as national identity has to be proved. If tourists do buy these tickets and are found on board they will be sent back at their own expense. This may seem a harsh measure, but these trains are run by ***PerúRail*** as a public service, to support the local communities, and tourists purchasing seats will be depriving local people of their only means of transport.

Advice and information

The site is open from 0700 to 1730. Entrance fee is US$20. A second day ticket is half price if you pay in dollars, more than half price if you pay in soles. It is possible to pay in dollars, but only clean, undamaged notes will be accepted. You can deposit your luggage at the entrance for US$0.50. Guides are available at the site, they are often very knowledgeable and worthwhile, and charge US$15 for 2½ hrs.

The hotel is located next to the entrance, with a restaurant serving buffet lunch. Beside the entrance and luggage store is a snack bar. Neither place is cheap so it's best to take your own food and drink, and take plenty of drinking water. Note that food is not officially allowed into the site.

Permission to enter the ruins before 0630 to watch the sunrise over the Andes, which is a spectacular experience, can be obtained from the ***Instituto Nacional de***

Cultura (INC) in Cusco, but it is often possible if you talk to the guards at the gate. They are also quieter after 1530, but don't forget that the last bus down from the ruins leaves at 1730. The walk up takes 2-2 ½ hrs, following the Inca path. Walking down to Aguas Calientes, if staying the night there, takes 30 mins-1 hr.

You are not allowed to walk back along the trail, though you can pay US$4.50 at Intipunku to be allowed to walk back as far as Wiñay-Wayna. You cannot take backpacks into Machu Picchu; leave them at ticket office. In the dry season sandflies can be a problem, so take insect repellent and wear long clothing.

Recommended reading *Lost City of the Incas* by Hiram Bingham (available in Lima and Cusco). *A Walking Tour of Machu Picchu* by Pedro Sueldo Nava – in several languages, available in Cusco. The Tourist Hotel sells guides, although at a rather inflated price. South American Explorers in Lima and Cusco have detailed information on walks here.

History

For centuries Machu Picchu was buried in jungle, until Hiram Bingham stumbled upon it in July 1911. It was then explored by an archaeological expedition sent by Yale University. Machu Picchu was a stunning archaeological find. The only major Inca site to escape 400 years of looting and destruction, it was remarkably well preserved. And it was no ordinary Inca settlement. It sat in an inaccessible location above the Urubamba gorge, and contained so many fine buildings that people have puzzled over its meaning ever since.

Bingham claimed he had discovered the lost city of Vilcabamba, and for 50 years everyone believed him. But he was proved wrong, and the mystery deepened. Later discoveries have revealed that Machu Picchu was the centre of an extensive Inca province. Many finely preserved satellite sites and highways also survive. This is craggy terrain and the value of a province with no mines and little agricultural land – it was not even self-sufficient – is hard to determine. Bingham postulated it was a defensive citadel on the fringes of the Amazon. But the architecture fails to convince us, and in any case, defense against whom?

The Incas were the first to build permanent structures in this region, which was unusual because they arrived at the tail end of 4,000 years of Andean civilization. 16th-century land titles discovered in the 1980s revealed that Machu Picchu was built by the Inca Pachacútec, founding father of the Inca empire. But they do not tell us why he built it. One reasonable speculation is that this area provided access to coca plantations in the lower Urubamba valley. However, the fine architecture of Machu Picchu cannot be explained away simply as a coca-collecting station.

Recent studies have shown that the 'torreón' was an observatory for the solstice sunrise, and that the 'Intihuatana' stela is the centre-point between cardinal alignments of nearby sacred peaks. The Incas worshipped nature: the celestial bodies, mountains, lightning, rainbows, rocks – anything, in fact, that was imbued with 'huaca', or spiritual power. And here Pachacútec found 'huaca' in unusual abundance.

This spiritual component is the key to understanding Machu Picchu. The Bingham expedition identified 75% of the human remains as female, and a common belief is that Machu Picchu was a refuge of the Inca 'Virgins of the Sun'. However, the skeletons were re-examined in the 1980s using modern technology, and the latest conclusion is that the gender split was roughly 50/50.

Machu Picchu was deliberately abandoned by its inhabitants – when, we do not know. This may have happened even before the Spanish invasion, perhaps as a result of the Inca civil wars, or the epidemics of European diseases which ran like brushfires ahead of the Spanish in the New World. One theory proposes that the city ran dry in a period of drought, another suggests a devastating fire. Or the city may have been evacuated during the period of Inca resistance to the Spanish, which lasted nearly 40 years and was concentrated not far west of Machu Picchu.

Machu Picchu

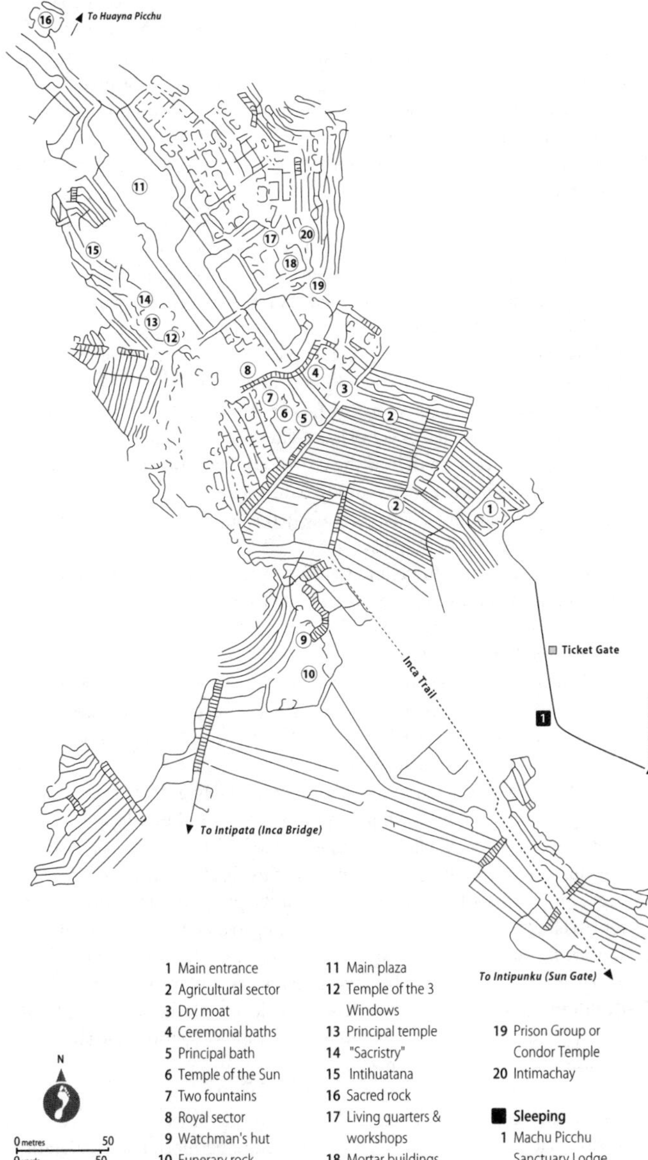

The site

Colour map 2, grid A2
Altitude: 2,380 m
Before doing any trekking around Machu Picchu, check with an official which paths may be used, or which are one way

Once you have passed through the ticket gate you follow a path to a small complex of buildings which now acts as the main entrance to the ruins. It is set at the eastern end of the extensive terracing which must have supplied the crops for the city. Above this point, turning back on yourself, is the final stretch of the Inca Trail leading down from Intipunku (see below). From a promontory here, on which stands the building called the **Watchman's Hut**, you get *the* perfect view of the city (the one you've seen on all the postcards), laid out before you with Huayna Picchu rising above the farthest extremity. Go round the promontory and head south for the Inca bridge (see also below). The main path into the ruins comes to a dry moat, which cuts right across the site. At the moat you can either climb the long staircase which goes to the upper reaches of the city, or you can enter the city by the baths and Temple of the Sun.

The more strenuous way into the city is by the former route, which takes you past quarries, on your left as you look down to the Urubamba on the west flank of the mountain. To your right are roofless buildings where you can see in close up the general construction methods used in the city. Proceeding along this level, above the main plazas, you reach the **Temple of the Three Windows** and the **Principal Temple**, which has an associated smaller building called the **Sacristy**. The two main buildings are three-sided and were clearly of great importance, given the fine stonework involved. The wall containing the three windows is built onto a single rock, one of the many instances in the city where the architects did not merely put their construction on a convenient piece of land. They used and fashioned its features to suit their conception of how the city should be tied to the mountain, its forces and the alignment of its stones to the surrounding peaks. In the Principal Temple, a diamond-shaped stone in the floor is said to depict the constellation of the Southern Cross.

Continue on the path behind the Sacristy to reach the **Intihuatana**, the 'hitching-post of the sun'. The name comes from the theory that such carved rocks (gnomons), found at all major Inca sites, were the point to which the sun was symbolically 'tied' at the winter solstice, before being freed to rise again on its annual ascent towards the summer solstice. The steps, angles and planes of this sculpted block appear to indicate a purpose beyond simple decoration and researchers, such as Johan Reinhard in *The Sacred Center*, have sought the trajectory of each alignment. Whatever the motivation behind this magnificent carving, it is undoubtedly one of the highlights of Machu Picchu.

Climb down from the Intihuatana's mound to the **Main Plaza**. Beyond its northern end is a small plaza with open-sided buildings on two sides and on the third, the **Sacred Rock**. The outline of this gigantic, flat stone echoes that of the mountains behind it. From here you can proceed to the entrance to the trail to Huayna Picchu (see below). Returning to the Main Plaza and heading southeast you pass, on your left, several groups of closely-packed buildings which have been taken to be **Living Quarters and Workshops**, **Mortar Buildings** (look for the house with two discs let into the floor) and the **Prison Group**, one of whose constructions is known as the **Condor Temple**. Also in this area is a cave called **Intimachay**.

A short distance from the Condor Temple is the lower end of a series of **Ceremonial Baths** or fountains. They were probably used for ritual bathing and the water still flows down them today. The uppermost, **Principal Bath**, is the most elaborate. Next to it is the **Temple of the Sun**, or Torreón. This

Killing the goose?

In September 2000, the Intihuatana was chipped when a television commercial was being filmed around it. No doubt it was an accident, but a gross piece of desecration nevertheless, especially bearing in mind that the stone was the only such shrine to survive the destruction of the Spaniards. Not only the Peruvians were furious about this, but also UNESCO, as it is a World Heritage site. This was just one of a series of controversies which has surrounded Machu Picchu in recent years, controversies at whose root is the problem that the Incas did not build a site to accommodate thousands of tourists.

The Instituto Nacional de Cultura (INC) led a campaign in 2001 to have Machu Picchu included in a UNESCO promotion, the New Seven Wonders of the World. People were asked to vote on the Internet for places ancient and modern and the Inca city was competing against such treasures as the Taj Mahal, Chichén Itzá and the Great Wall of China. To vote, visit www.newsevenwonders.com/s/voting.php While the INC was eager to promote its Peruvian heritage, some argue that the rebuilding and addition of roofs to buildings at the site is inappropriate. In 2001, a new debate arose following the publication of a survey by Japanese geologist Kyoji Sassa which suggested that Machu Picchu was at risk of slipping off its mountain because of increasing instability in the ground beneath it. Press reports and statements by experts quickly followed, all expressing the fear that the loss of Machu Picchu was imminent. Sassa responded that his report had been misrepresented. His study, he said, had not looked at deep structures and had not covered a long enough period, so much more detailed monitoring is required.

There is one issue, however, which stands out above all others, a cable car from the Río Urubamba to Machu Picchu. This project was first proposed in the 1970s, before Machu Picchu became a World Heritage site in 1983. Although no work had been done on a cable car, objections gathered momentum on the grounds that the project would be a violation of Peru's World Heritage obligations. In 2001, the plan was scrapped and newly-elected President Toledo pledged to safeguard Machu Picchu. Nevertheless, a new cable car scheme has been proposed and has met with opposition since Toledo came to office. Among the considerations are the exact location of the cable's termini, the effect it will have on Aguas Calientes' tourist trade, the construction of more hotel facilities at the summit and, returning to Kyoji Sasso's survey, will a cable car be a stable proposition? Even if a cable car is not a viable option, there are those who ask if the constant stream of buses from the river up to the entrance is not equally damaging to the environment. Clearly Machu Picchu is a "good earner" and Peru would not wish to reduce the income it derives from the site until tourism of an equivalent capacity can be developed elsewhere in the country. But there are genuine concerns about the sustainability of tourism here, which hasty decisions are not going to solve. The Save Machu Picchi website is http://mpicchu.org on which most sides of the arguments are given space. See also the INC's site, www.inc.perucultural.org.pe/proy2x.htm

singular building has one straight wall from which another wall curves around and back to meet the straight one, but for the doorway. From above it looks like an incomplete letter P. It is another example of the architecture being at one with its environment as the interior is taken up by the partly-worked summit of the outcrop onto which the building is placed. All indications are that this temple was used for astronomical purposes. Underneath the Torreón a cave-like opening has been formed by an oblique gash in the rock. Fine masonry has been added to the opposing wall, making a second side of a

Trail tribulations

In 2000 it was decided that the Inca Trail was becoming too seriously degraded because of the number of people using it. Figures for 1998 show that 66,000 people walked the Trail, compared with 300,000 visiting Machu Picchu. On an average day in the high season, 180 people arrived at Machu Picchu having walked the Trail, while 1,680 arrived by train and 50 by helicopter. The authorities proposed therefore to introduce limits on the number of people using the Trail. The regulations are detailed below, but the main change is that no one may walk the Inca Trail independently. Access is therefore only permissable with a licensed agent. This ruling applies wherever you decide to start the Trail.

triangle, which contrasts with the rough edge of the split rock. But the blocks of masonry appear to have been slotted behind another sculpted piece of natural stone, which has been cut into a four-stepped buttress. Immediately behind this is a two-stepped buttress. This strange combination of the natural and the manmade has been called the Tomb or Palace of the Princess. Across the stairway from the complex which includes the Torreón is the group of buildings known as the **Royal Sector**.

Huayna Picchu Synonymous with the ruins themselves is Huayna Picchu, the verdant mountain overlooking the site. There are also ruins on the mountain itself, and steps to the top for a superlative view of the whole magnificent scene, but this is not for those who are afraid of heights. The climb takes up to 90 minutes but the steps are dangerous after bad weather and you shouldn't leave the path, which is open 0700-1300, with the latest return time being 1500. You must register at a hut at the beginning of the trail.

The other trail to Huayna Picchu, down near the Urubamba, is via the Temple of the Moon, in two caves, one above the other, with superb Inca niches inside, which have sadly been blemished by graffiti. To reach the Temple of the Moon from the path to Huayna Picchu, take the marked trail to the left; it is in good shape. It descends further than you think it should. After the Temple you may proceed to Huayna Picchu, but this path is overgrown, slippery in the wet and has a crooked ladder on an exposed part about 10 minutes before reaching the top (not for the faint-hearted). It is safer to return to the main trail to Huayna Picchu, although this adds about 30 minutes to the climb. The round trip takes about four hours.

Intipata The famous Inca bridge – Intipata – is about 45 minutes along a well-marked trail south of the Royal Sector. The bridge – which is actually a couple of logs – is spectacularly sited, carved into a vertiginous cliff-face. East of the Agricultural Sector is the path leading up to Intipunku. It's a 45-minute walk and well worth it for the fine views alone. It's also amusing to watch people putting on a brave face as they stand on the precariously-placed logs to have their picture taken, smiling nervously and trying not to look down.

Essentials

Sleeping & eating **LL** *Machu Picchu Sanctuary Lodge*, for reservations the details are the same as for the *Hotel Monasterio* in Cusco, which is under the same management (Peru Orient Express Hotels) T241777, F237111, http://monasterio.orient-express.com/index.html This hotel, at the entrance to the ruins, was completely refurbished in 2001 and has included some environmentally-friendly features. They will accept American Express traveller's cheques at the official rate. The rooms are comfortable, the service is good and the staff helpful. Electricity and water are available 24 hrs a day. Food in the restaurant is well-cooked and presented;. the restaurant is for residents only in the evening, but the buffet lunch is open to all. The hotel is usually fully booked well in advance, try Sun night as other tourists find Pisac market a greater attraction.

Camping is not allowed at Intipunku; guards may confiscate your tent. There is a free campsite down beside the rail tracks at Puente Ruinas station.

The Inca Trail

The wonder of Machu Picchu has been well documented over the years. Equally impressive is the centuries-old Inca Trail that winds its way from the Sacred Valley near Ollantaytambo, taking three to four days. What makes this hike so special is the stunning combination of Inca ruins, unforgettable views, magnificent mountains, exotic vegetation and extraordinary ecological variety. The government acknowledged this uniqueness in 1981 by including the trail in a 325 sq-km national park, the Machu Picchu Historical Sanctuary. Machu Picchu itself cannot be understood without the Inca Trail. Its principal sites are ceremonial in character, apparently in ascending hierarchical order. This Inca province was a unique area of elite access. The trail is essentially a work of spiritual art, like a gothic cathedral, and walking it was formerly an act of devotion.

Ins and outs

Entrance tickets

An entrance ticket for the trail or its variations must be bought at the *INC* office in Cusco: no tickets are sold at the entrance gates. Furthermore, tickets are only sold on presentation of a letter from a licensed tour operator on behalf of the visitor. There is a 50% discount for students, but note that officials are very strict, only an ISIC card will be accepted as proof of status. Tickets are checked at Km 82, Huayllabamba and Wiñay Wayna.

On all hiking trails (Km 82 or Km 88 to Machu Picchu, Salkantay to Machu Picchu, and Km 82 or 88 to Machu Picchu via Km 104) adults must pay US$50, students and children under 15 US$25. On the Camino Real de los Inkas from Km 104 to Wiñay Wayna and Machu Picchu the fee is US$25 per adult, US$15 for students and children (or US$20 and US$10 respectively if you don't camp at Wiñay Wayna).

New regulations & tours

Tour Agencies in Cusco will arrange transport to the start, equipment, food, etc, for an all-in price, averaging around US$120 per person. From the start of 2001 all agencies are subject to strict new rules and all must be licensed. Groups of up to 10 independent travellers who do not wish to use a tour operator will be allowed to hike the trails if they contact an independent, licensed guide to accompany them, as long as they do not contract any other persons such as porters or cooks. There will be a maximum of 500 visitors per day allowed on the Trail. Operators will pay US$10 for each porter and other trail staff; porters will not be permitted to carry more than 25 kg. Littering is banned, as is carrying plastic water bottles (canteens only may be carried). Pets and pack animals are prohibited, but llamas are allowed as far as the first pass. Groups have to use approved campsites; on the routes from Km 82, Km 88 and Salkantay, the campsites may be changed with prior authorization (Llulluchayoc, Llulluchapampa, Pacaymayo valley, Runkurakay, or Phuyupatamarca).

As of August 2001, the only regulations that were being enforced with any certainty were the new prices and the rule that trekkers have to go with a licensed operator. Other aspects, such as limits on groups size, carrying medical kits with oxygen, responsible disposal of waste, were only being applied haphazardly. The best advice is to check in advance with a reputable tour company in Cusco (see the list given on page 115), with ***South American Explorers***, or with a government agency such as ***PromPerú*** (www.promperu.org or via www.peruonline.net) or the ***Ministry of Tourism***.

Advice & information

For advice on trekking and camping equipment, see page 171

Leave all your valuables in Cusco and keep everything inside your tent, even your shoes. Security has, however, improved in recent years, but not 100 %. Avoid the Jul-Aug high season and the rainy season from Nov to Apr (note that this can change, so check in advance). In the wet it is cloudy and the paths are very muddy and difficult. Also watch out for coral snakes in this area (black, red, yellow bands). Please remove all your rubbish, including toilet paper, or use the pits provided. Do not light open fires as they can get out of control. ***The Earth Preservation Fund*** sponsors an annual clean-up Jul-Aug: volunteers should write to EPF, Inca Trail Project, Box 7545, Ann Arbor, Michigan 48107, USA. In Cusco, different agencies organize the clean-up each year

The Trek

Day 1 The trek to the sacred site begins either at Km 82, **Piscacucho**, or at Km 88, **Qorihuayrachina**, at 2,600 m. In order to reach Km 82 hikers are transported by their tour operator (see above) in a minibus on the road that goes to Quillabamba. From Piri onward the road follows the riverbank and ends at Km 82. Where there used to be an *oroya* (cable crossing), there is now a bridge. You can depart as early as you like and arrive at Km 82 faster than going by train. The Inca Trail equipment, food, fuel and field personnel reach Km 82 (depending on the tour operator's logistics) for the Inrena staff to weigh each bundle before the group arrives. When several groups are leaving on the same day, it is more convenient to arrive early. Km 88 can only be

Inca Trail

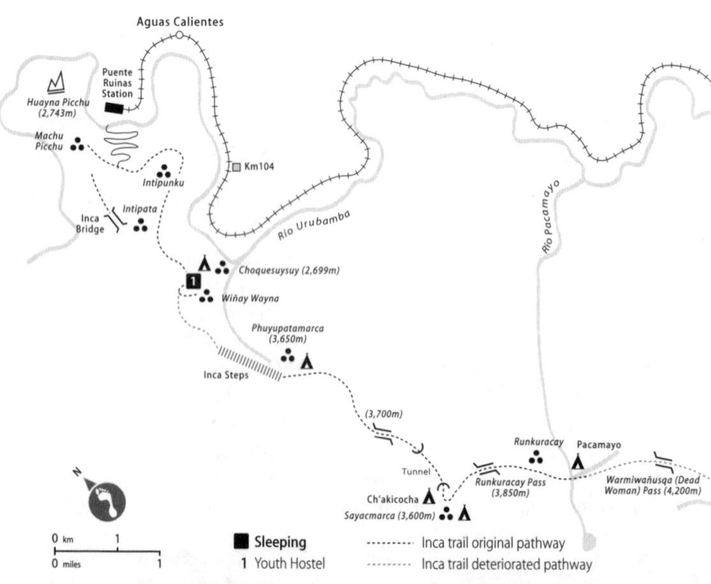

reached by train, subject to schedule and baggage limitations. The train goes slower than a bus, but you start your walk nearer to Llaqtapata and Huayllabamba. (See below for details of variations in starting points for the Inca Trail.)

The first ruin is **Llaqtapata**, near Km 88, the utilitarian centre of a large settlement of farming terraces which probably supplied the other Inca trail sites. From here, it is a relatively easy three-hour walk to the village of **Huayllabamba**. Note that the route from Km 82 goes via **Cusichaca**, the valley in which Ann Kendall worked (see page 156), rather than Llaqtapata.

A series of gentle climbs and descents leads along the Río Cusichaca, the ideal introduction to the trail. The village is a popular camping spot for tour groups, so it's a better idea to continue for about an hour up to the next site, **Llulluchayoc** – 'three white stones' – which is a patch of green beside a fast-flowing stream. It's a steep climb but you're pretty much guaranteed a decent pitch for the night. If you're feeling really energetic, you can go on to the next camping spot, a perfectly flat meadow, called **Llulluchapampa**. This means a punishing 1½-hour ascent through cloud forest, but it does leave you with a much easier second day. There's also the advantage of relative isolation and a magnificent view back down the valley.

Day 2

For most people the second day is by far the toughest. It's a steep climb to the meadow, followed by an exhausting 2½-hour haul up to the first pass – aptly named **Warmiwañusqa** (Dead Woman) – at 4,200 m. The feeling of relief on reaching the top is immense and there's the added, sadistic pleasure of watching your fellow sufferers struggling in your wake. After a well-earned break it's a sharp descent on a treacherous path down to the Pacamayo valley, where there are a few flat camping spots near a stream if you're too weary to continue.

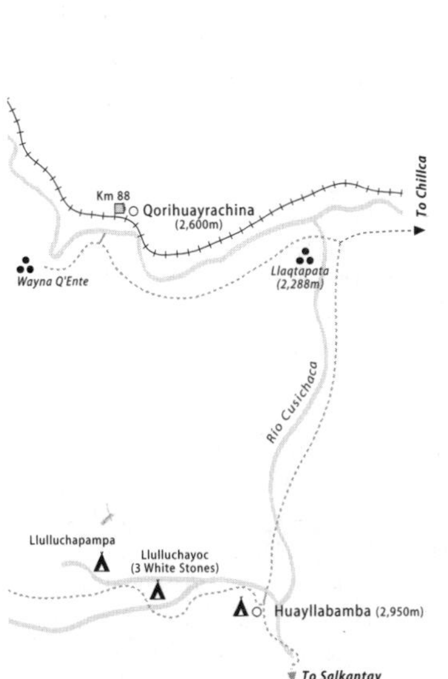

Day2/3

If you're feeling energetic, you can proceed to the second. Halfway up comes the ruin of **Runkuracay**, which was probably an Inca tambo, or post-house. It is no longer permitted to camp here. A steep climb up an Inca staircase leads to the next pass, at 3,850 m, with spectacular views of Pumasillo (6,246 m) and the Vilcabamba range. The trail then desends to **Sayacmarca** (Inaccessible town), a spectacular site overlooking the Aobamba valley, where it's possible to camp. Just below Sayacmarca lies **Conchamarca** (Shell town), a small group of buildings standing on rounded terraces – perhaps another tambo.

Day 3

A blissfully gentle two hours climb on a fine stone highway, leads through an Inca tunnel and along the enchanted fringes of the cloud forest, to the third pass. This is the most rewarding part of the trail, with spectacular views of the entire Vilcabamba range, and it's worth taking the time to dwell on the wonders of nature. Then it's down to the extensive ruins of **Phuyupatamarca** (Cloud-level town), at 3,650 m, where adjacent Inca observation platforms offer awesome views of nearby Salkantay (6,270 m) and surrounding peaks. There is a 'tourist bathroom' here, where water can be collected, but purify it before drinking.

From here an Inca stairway of white granite plunges more than 1,000 m to the spectacularly-sited and impressive ruins of **Wiñay-Wayna** (Forever Young), offering views of newly uncovered agricultural terraces at **Intipata** (Sun place). A trail, not easily visible, goes from Wiñay-Wayna to the newly-discovered terracing. There is a youth hostel at Wiñay-Wayna, with bunk beds (**G** per person), showers and a small restaurant, but the place is often fully booked. You can sleep on the floor of the restaurant more cheaply, but it is open for diners until 2300. There are also spaces for a few tents, but they get snapped up quickly. The hostel's door is closed at 1730. After Wiñay-Wayna there is no water, and no place to camp, until Machu Picchu. A gate by Wiñay-Wayna is locked between 1530 and 0500, preventing access to the path to Machu Picchu at night.

Day 4 From Wiñay-Wayna it is a gentle hour's walk through another type of forest, with larger trees and giant ferns, to a steep Inca staircase which leads up to **Intipunku** (Sun gate), where you look down at last upon Machu Picchu, basking in all her reflective glory. Aching muscles are quickly forgotten and even the presence of the functional hotel building cannot detract from one of the most magical sights in all the Americas.

Alternative Inca routes

The Inca Trail from Km 104 A short Inca trail, the Camino Real de los Inkas, is used by those who don't want to endure the full hike. It starts at Km 104, where a footbridge gives access to the ruins of Chachabamba and the trail which ascends through the ruins of Choquesuysuy, lately cleaned up, to connect with the main trail at Wiñay-Wayna. This first part is a steady, continuous ascent of three hours (take water) and the trail is narrow and exposed in parts. About 15 minutes before Wiñay-Wayna is a waterfall where fresh water can be obtained (best to purify it before drinking).

Salkantay to Machu Picchu
This route takes 3 nights

A trek from **Salkantay** joins the Inca Trail at Huayllabamba, then proceeds as before on the main Trail through Wiñay Wayna to Machu Picchu. There is no checkpoint at Salkantay for verifying that the relevant fees have been paid, but you will get checked at Huayllabamba. To get to Salkantay, you have to start the trek in Mollepata, northwest of Cusco in the Apurímac valley. Buses of the *Ampay* company run from Arcopata on the Chinchero road, or you can take private transport to Mollepata (three hours from Cusco). It is down an unpaved road which turns off the main road after Limatambo. From Mollepata it's an all-day trek to Salkantay Pampa, also called Soraypampa. Camp below Salkantay (6,271 m). From Salkantay Pampa a very demanding ascent leads to the Incachiriaska Pass (4,900 m). Descend to camp at Sisaypampa. From there, trek to Pampacahuana, an outstanding and seldom-visited Inca ruin. The remains of an Inca road then go down to the singular Inca ruins of Paucarcancha. This entire section is done with mules and/or horses. There is an obligatory change from animals to porters before you reach Huayllabamba.

An alternative from Salkantay is to go to Huayllabamba, then down to Km 88, from where you can take the train to Aguas Calientes, or back to Cusco. There is an entrance fee of US$15 for this hike, but it does not include the entrance to Machu Picchu. If you combine this route with the short Inca Trail from Km 104, you have to pay the US$ 25 trail fee (see above for full details on prices).

Paucarcancha to Machu Picchu

A four-night trek from Paucarcancha to Huayllabamba, then on the traditional Trail to Machu Picchu. Paucarcancha is an abandoned set of ruins on the descent from Pampacahuana, before the village of Huayllabamba on the main Inca Trail. Paucarcancha is also shown as Incarakay on some maps. Nearby there are some hot springs. Paucarcancha is an important camping site on the trek from Salkantay, or from Ancascocha Lake pass on the route from the Sillque valley. As an alternative to the Inca Trail, there is a trek from Paucarcancha to the Palcaycasa Pass between the Salkantay and Palcay snow peaks. From the pass you can walk on a wide, well-preserved Inca trail to Aobamba or the hydroelectric station.

Other routes

There are other routes which approach the Inca Trails to Machu Picchu, such as Km 77, Chillca, up the Sillque ravine in the Qente valley, which is commonly called the Lago Ancascocha route. Then there is another access through the Millpo Valley in the Salkantay area. From the Vilcabamba mountain range, you can reach Machu Picchu by hiking down from Huancacalle to Chaulla by road, getting to Santa Teresa and walking to the hydroelectric (Aobamba) train station. Then it's an hour's train ride on the local train to Aguas Calientes (tourists are allowed to ride the local train for this short section).

A three-night trek goes from Km 82 to Km 88, then along the Río Urubamba to Pacaymayo Bajo and Km 104, from where you take the trail described above to Wiñay Wayna and Machu Picchu.

Also, good hiking trails from Aguas Calientes have been opened along the left bank of the Urubamba, for day hikes crossing the bridge of the hydroelectric plant to Choquesuysuy.

Essentials

Equipment

While hiking the Inca Trail note that it is cold at night, and weather conditions change rapidly, so it is important to take strong footwear, rain gear and warm clothing (this includes long johns if you want to sleep rather than freeze at night): dress in layers. Also take food, water, water purification tablets, insect repellent, sunscreen, a hat and sunglasses, a supply of plastic bags, coverings, a good sleeping bag, a torch/flashlight and a stove for preparing hot food and drink to ward off the cold at night. It is worth paying extra to hire a down sleeping bag if you haven´t brought your own. A stove using paraffin (kerosene) is preferable, as fuel can be bought in small quantities in markets.

A tent is essential, but if you're hiring one in Cusco, check carefully for leaks. Walkers who have not taken adequate equipment have died of exposure. Caves marked on some maps are little better than overhangs and are not sufficient shelter to sleep in. You could also take a first-aid kit; if you don't need it the porters probably will, given their rather basic footwear.

It is now forbidden to use trekking poles because the metal tips are damaging the trail. Leave them at home and buy a carved wooden stick on sale in the main plaza in Ollantaytambo or at the trail head. Many will need this for the steep descents on the path. If you need knee/ankle/thigh supports go to ***Ayala***, a shop down a small arcade in Cusco, to the right of Taca Peru, opposite the Palacio de Justicia near the top of Av Sol.

All the necessary equipment can be rented in Cusco (see page 115). Good maps of the Trail and area can be bought from South American Explorers in Lima or Cusco. If you have any doubts about carrying your own pack, porters/guides are available through Cusco agencies. Carry a day-pack, water and snacks in case you walk faster or slower than the porters and you have to wait for them to catch you up or you have to catch them up.

Take around US$30 extra per person for tips and a drink at the end of the trail. If you´re carrying your own gear it´s wise to take another US$60 for when you realise the climb and altitude really is too much; freelance porters are everywhere on the trail and will carry your bags for US$8-15 per day.

Aguas Calientes

Phone code: 084
Colour map 2, grid A2

Only 1 ½ km back along the railway from Puente Ruinas, this is a popular resting place for those recovering from the rigours of the Inca Trail. It is called Aguas Calientes after the hot springs above the town. It is also called the town of Machu Picchu. Most activity is centred around the old railway station, on the plaza, or on Avenida Pachacútec, which leads from the plaza to the thermal baths.

The baths consist of a rather smelly communal pool, 10 minutes' walk from the town. You can rent towels and bathing costumes for US$0.65 at several places on the road to the baths. There are basic toilets and changing facilities and showers for washing *before* entering the baths. Take soap and shampoo and keep an eye on your valuables. ■ *Open 0500-2030. Entry US$1.50.*

Sleeping
■ *on map*

LL ***Machu Picchu Pueblo Hotel,*** Km 110, 5 mins walk along the railway from the town. For reservations: Jr Andalucia 174, San Isidro, Lima, T(01)422 6574, F422 4701; in Cusco at Julio C Tello C-13, Urb Santa Mónica, T245314, F244669, www.inkaterra.com.pe Beautiful colonial-style bungalows have been built in a village compound surrounded by cloud forest. The hotel has lovely gardens in which there are many species of birds, butterflies and orchids. There is a pool, an expensive restaurant, but also a campsite with hot showers at good rates. It offers tours to Machu Picchu, several guided walks on the property. The buffet breakfasts for US$12 are great. It also has the *Café Amazónico* by the railway line. Recommended, but there are a lot of steps between the public areas and rooms.

L ***Hatuchay Tower***, Carretera Puente Ruinas block 4, T211200, F211202 (in Lima 447 8170, in Cusco 244272), www.hatuchaytower.com.pe At this smart new hotel, the price includes American breakfast, but not tax and service. There are standard rooms and luxury suites. It is below the old station.

AL-A ***Machu Picchu Inn***, Av Pachacútec 101, T211057, mapiinn@peruhotel.com.pe The price includes bathroom and breakfast. The rooms are comfortable and the overall service is good. It's also a friendly place.

B ***Gringo Bill's*** (***Hostal Q'oñi Unu***), Colla Raymi 104, T/F211046, gringobills@yahoo.com Price includes bathroom, but it is cheaper without bath. *Gringo Bill's* is an Aguas Calientes institution and they are to open a place with 18 rooms in Cusco. It's friendly and relaxed, with hot water, good beds, luggage store, laundry and money exchange. Don't stay in the rooms nearest the entrance as they flood during heavy rain. Good but expensive meals are served in *Villa Margarita* restaurant; breakfast starts at 0530 and they offer a US$2 packed lunch to take up to the ruins.

C ***Hostal Ima Sumac***, Av Pachacútec 173, 5 mins before the baths, so quite a climb up from the station, T211021. One of the posher places in town; they exchange money. **C** ***Presidente***, at the old station, T211034 (Cusco T/F244598). Next to *Hostal Machu Picchu*, see below, this is the more upmarkethalf of the establishment. Rooms without river view are cheaper, but the price includes breakfast and taxes.

D ***El Inka***, C Wiracocha, T211008. One of three hostales on this side street, the price includes bath and breakfast. **D** ***Hostal Continental***, near the old train station, T211065. Very clean rooms with good beds, hot showers. **D** ***Hostal Don Guiller***, Av Pachacútec 136, T211128 (Cusco T683620). Price includes breakfast and lunch *menú*. Rooms have bath and hot water. In the same building is the *Pizzería El Candamo*. **D** ***La Cabaña***, Av Pachacútec M20-3, T/F211048. Price includes bath. Rooms have hot water. There is a

Aguas Calientes

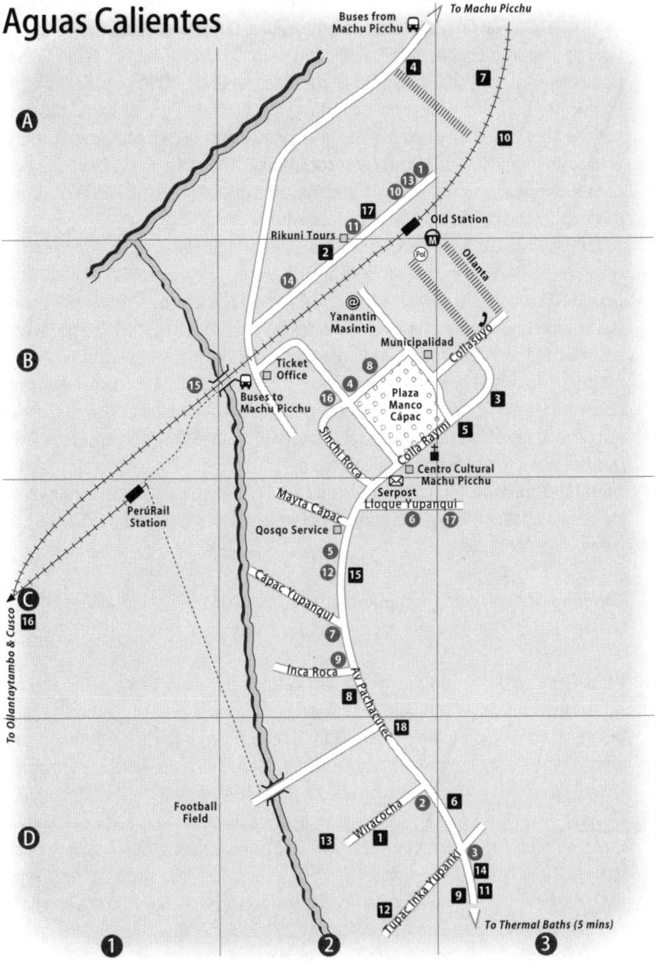

Sleeping

1 El Inka *D2*
2 El Tambo *B2*
3 Gringo Bill's (Hostal Q'oñi Unu) *B3*
4 Hatuchay Tower *A2*
5 Hospedaje Las Bromelias *B3*
6 Hospedaje Quilla *D3*
7 Hostal Continental *A3*
8 Hostal Don Guiller & Pizzería El Candamo *C2*
9 Hostal Ima Sumac *D3*
10 Hostal Los Caminantes *A3*
11 Hostal Pachakúteq *D3*
12 Hostal Samana Wasi *D2*
13 Hostal Wiracocha Inn *D2*
14 La Cabaña *D3*
15 Machu Picchu Inn *C2*
16 Machu Picchu Pueblo *C1*
17 Presidente & Hostal Machu Picchu *A2*
18 Sinchi Roca *D2*

Eating

1 Aiko *A2*
2 Clave de Sol *D2*
3 Govinda *D3*
4 Illary *B2*
5 Inca Wasi *C2*
6 Indio Feliz *C2*
7 Inka Machu Picchu *C2*
8 Inka's Pizza Pub *B2*
9 K'utchi *C2*
10 La Chosa Pizzería *A2*
11 Las Qenas *A2*
12 Machu Picchu *C2*
13 Pizzería Samana Wasi 1 *A2*
14 Pizzería Samana Wasi 2 *B2*
15 Toto's House *B1*
16 Tunqui *B2*
17 Waisicha Pub *C3*

café and laundry service. The hotel is popular with groups. **D *Las Orquídeas***, Urb Las Orquideas A-8, T211171. From Av Pachacútec, cross the bridge over the river to the football pitch and find a small dirt path on the right. Rooms have bath, and hot water and are clean. This is a quiet, pleasant place away from the main part of town. **D *Hostal Machu Picchu***, at the old station, T211212. Price includes breakfast and taxes. A clean, functional establishment, which is quiet and friendly, especially Wilber, the owner's son. There is hot water, a nice balcony over the Urubamba, a grocery store and travel information is available. Recommended. **D *Hostal Pachakúteq***, up the hill beyond *Hostal La Cabaña*, T211061. Rooms with bathroom and hot water 24 hrs. Good breakfast is on offer, quiet, family-run. Recommended. **D *Hospedaje Quilla***, Av Pachacútec between Wiracocha and Tupac Inka Yupanki. Price includes breakfast, bath and hot water. They rent bathing gear for the hot springs if you arrived without your costume and towel. **D *Hostal Wiracocha Inn***, C Wiracocha, T211088. Rooms with bath and hot water. Breakfast and soft drinks are available. There is a small garden at this friendly and helpful hostal. It's popular with European groups.

E *Hospedaje Las Bromelias*, Colla Raymi, just off the plaza before *Gringo Bill's*. A small place which has rooms with bath and hot water. It's cheaper without bath. **E** per person ***El Tambo***, at the old station, T211054. 4 rooms with bath and hot water, breakfast included in the price. It also has a bar, *cambio* and a restaurant serving pizzas and pasta. **E** per person ***Sinchi Roca***, Av Pachacútec block 22, no 2, T/F211033. Price is for a room with bath and hot water. Laundry service at the hostal. A modern, new *Sinchi Roca* can be found on Wiracocha. **F** per person ***Hostal Los Caminantes***, by the railway just beyond the old station. Price is for a room with bathroom; it's **G** per person without. Hot water available abd breakfast costs extra. It's basic, but friendly and clean. **F *Hostal Samana Wasi***, C Tupac Inka Yupanki, T211170, quillavane@hotmail.com Price includes bath and hot water 24 hrs. There are cheaper rooms without bath at this friendly, pleasant place.

Machu Picchu & the Inca Trail

Camping The only official campsite is in a field by the river, just below Puente Ruinas station. Do not leave your tent and belongings unattended.

Eating
● on map

Pizza seems to be the most common dish in town, but many of the pizzerías serve other types of food as well. The old station and Av Pachútec are lined with eating places. At the station (where staff will try to entice you into their restaurant), are, among others: ***Aiko***, which is recommended; ***La Chosa Pizzería***, with pleasant atmosphere, good value, some have reported poor food here (but not the author); ***Las Quenas***, which is a café and a baggage store (US$0.30 per locker); and 2 branches of ***Pizzería Samana Wasi***. ***Toto's House***, Av Imperio de los Incas, on the railway line. Good value and quality *menú*. ***Clave de Sol***, Av Pachacútec 156. Same owner as *Chez Maggy* in Cusco, serving good, cheap Italian food for under US$4, changes money, also has a vegetarian menu, great atmosphere, open 1200-1500, 1800-whenever. Also on this street: ***Govinda***, by the corner with Tupac Inka Yupanki, vegetarian restaurant with a cheap set lunch, rRecommended; ***Machu Picchu***, Good food in a friendly atmosphere; ***Inca Wasi***, very good; ***Inka Machu Picchu***, No 122, including vegetarian options; ***K'utchi*** pizzas and vegetarian; and others. ***Inka's Pizza Pub***, on the plaza. Good pizzas, changes money, accepts traveller's cheques. Next door is ***Illary***, popular, and across the street ***Tunqui***. On C Lloque Yupanqui are ***Waisicha Pub***, for good music and atmosphere, and ***Indio Feliz***, T/F211090, which has great French cuisine, excellent value and service, set 3-course meal for US$10, good pisco sours. Highly recommended.

Directory

Banks There are no banks in Aguas Calientes. Those businesses that change money will not do so at rates as favourable as you will find in Cusco. **Communications Internet** At *Yanantin Masintin* (US$3 per hr), which is part of the *Rikuni* group, as is ***Tea House***, which is opposite, Av Imperio de los Incas 119. Both serve coffees, teas, snacks etc. The town has electricity 24 hrs a day. Several hotels, restaurants, and other establishments, plus other information can be found at www.machupicchuperu.com **Post** ***Serpost*** (Post Office) agencies: just off the plaza, between the Centro Cultural Machu Picchu and *Galería de Arte Tunupa*, and next to HeliCusco office on the railway line. **Telephone** The telephone office is on C Collasuyo and there are plenty of phone booths around town. There are lots of places to choose from for exchange, shop around. Qosqo Service , at the corner of Av Pachacútec and Mayta Capac, has postal service, *cambio* and guiding service. **Travel agents** ***Rikuni Tours***, is at the old station, Av Imperio de los Incas 123, T/F211036, rikuni@chaski.unsaac.edu.pe Nydia is very helpful. They change money, have a postal service and sell postcards, maps and books (expensive).

Quillabamba

Colour map 2, grid A2

At Quillabamba there are few attractions for the tourist, but this is a good place to bask in the sun or take a swim in the river; ask the locals where the safe stretches are, as the current is quite rapid in places. There is also a clean market building and a football stadium. Unless you're here during the high season – June and July – you won't see many other tourists in these parts. There's also a Dominican mission here.

Macchu Picchu & the Inca Trail

Getting there

The railway from Machu Picchu used to continue for 79 km, through Chaullay, to Quillabamba, but there are no passenger services on this line any more as much of the track was severely damaged in 1998. As no trains run beyond Aguas Calientes, the only route is by road from Ollantaytambo. It passes through **Peña**, a place of great beauty. Once out of Peña, the road climbs on endless zig-zags and breathtaking views to reach the Abra Málaga pass. At **Chaullay**, the road meets the old railway to Quillabamba, Machu Picchu and Cusco and continues up the east bank of the river. Buses leave Cusco's new bus terminal for Quillabamba, taking 10 hrs for the 233 km. ***Ampay*** have a bus morning and evening, ***Carhuamayo*** in the evening only.

Sleeping

D ***Quillabamba***, Prolongación y M Grau 590, unmarked entrance next to the Autoservicio behind the market, T281369. The hotel has a roof terrace restaurant, a laundry service, and is genrally recommended. **E** ***Hostal Don Carlos***, Jr Libertad 556, T281371. A clean hotel with rooms with private shower. The water is usually hot. **F** ***Hostal Cusco***, with patio and roof terrace. Recommended. There is other accommodation, **G** and upwards, near the market.

Eating

Pub Don Sebas, Jr Espinar 235 on Plaza de Armas. Good, great sandwiches, run by Karen Molero who is very friendly and always ready for a chat. ***El Gordito***, on Espinar. A good place for chicken (US$3). There are many *heladerías*, which are much needed in the heat. The best of these is on the northwest corner of the Plaza de Armas.

Directory

Banks *Banco de Crédito* is good for TCs.

Huancacalle

At Chaullay, the historic Choquechaca bridge, built on Inca foundations, was wiped out by a landslide in 1998. Reconstruction is under way. When reopened, it will allow drivers to cross the river to get to the village of Huancacalle. A temporary bridge allows foot passengers across, but vehicles go 30 minutes downstream to Maranura, where a new bridge crosses the river. Then you have to backtrack down on the other side to get to Huancacalle

Ins & outs

Getting there Huancacalle can be reached from Quillabamba daily by truck and bus. The journey takes 4-7 hrs.

Huancacalle is the best base for exploring the nearby Inca ruins of **Vitcos**. Here is the palace of the last four Inca rulers from 1536 to 1572, and **Yurac Rumi**, the sacred white stone of the Incas. Both are now easily accessible and well worth the effort of a visit. Vitcos remains romantically overgrown by jungle, much as Dr Hiram Bingham found it (and Machu Picchu) in 1911, but unlike Machu Picchu it has all the documented historical associations which make a visit particularly interesting and rewarding. The Yurac Rumi, once the most sacred site in South America, is very large (8 m high by 20 m wide), with intricate and elaborately carvings. Lichens now cover its whiteness.

Allow plenty of time for hiking to, and visiting the ruins. It takes one hour to walk from Huancacalle to Vitcos, 45 minutes Vitcos-Yurac Rumi, and 45 minutes Yurac Rumi-Huancacalle. Horses can be hired if you wish.

You can also hike up to **Vilcabamba La Nueva** from Huancacalle. It's a three-hour walk through beautiful countryside with Inca ruins dotted around. There is a missionary building run by Italians, with electricity and running water, where you may be able to spend the night.

Sleeping

There are basic places to stay at Huancacalle (**G**), including a hostel opened by Vincent R Lee (see below). Alternatively villagers will accept travellers in their very basic homes (take a sleeping bag). The Cobo family permits travellers to put up their tents on their property. There are no restaurants, but a few shops.

Espíritu Pampa

Colour map 2, grid A1

Travellers with plenty time can hike from Huancacalle to Espíritu Pampa, the site of the **Vilcabamba Vieja** ruins, a vast pre-Inca ruin with a neo-Inca overlay set in deep jungle at 1,000 m. Here is a sister stone of the Yurac Rumi, and the surrounding jungle is full of wildlife and worth the trip on its own. Note, however, that a visit to Vilcabamba Vieja is a formidable undertaking, involving at least eight days of hiking over rough trails, taking all camping gear and food, etc.

Vilcabamba

The last Incas of Vilcabamba

After Pizarro killed Atahualpa in 1532 the Inca empire disintegrated rapidly, and it is often thought that native resistance ended there. But in fact it continued for 40 more years, beginning with Manco, a teenage half-brother of Atahualpa.

In 1536, Manco escaped from the Spanish and returned to lead a massive army against them. He besieged Cusco and Lima simultaneously, and came close to dislodging the Spaniards from Peru. Spanish reinforcements arrived and Manco fled to Vilcabamba, a mountainous forest region west of Cusco that was remote, but still fairly close to the Inca capital, which he always dreamed of recapturing.

The Spanish chased Manco deep into Vilcabamba but he managed to elude them and continued his guerrilla war, raiding Spanish commerce on the Lima highway, and keeping alive the Inca flame. Then, in 1544, Spanish outlaws to whom he had given refuge murdered him, ending the most active period of Inca resistance.

The Inca line passed to his sons. The first, a child too young to rule named Sayri Túpac, eventually yielded to Spanish enticements and emerged from Vilcabamba, taking up residence in Yucay, near Urubamba in 1558. He died mysteriously – possibly poisoned – three years later.

His brother Titu Cusi, who was still in Vilcabamba, now took up the Inca mantle. Astute and determined, he resumed raiding and fomenting rebellion against the Spanish. But in 1570, Titu Cusi fell ill and died suddenly. A Spanish priest was accused of murdering him. Anti-Spanish resentment erupted, and the priest and a Spanish viceregal envoy were killed. The Spanish Viceroy reacted immediately, and the Spanish invaded Vilcabamba for the third and last time in 1572.

A third brother, Túpac Amaru was now in charge. He lacked his brother's experience and acuity, and his destiny was to be the sacrificial last Inca. The Spanish overran the Inca's jungle capital, and dragged him back to Cusco in chains. There, Túpac Amaru, the last Inca, was publicly executed in Cusco's main plaza.

The location of the neo-Inca capital of Vilcabamba was forgotten over the centuries, and the search for it provoked Hiram Bingham's expeditions, and his discovery of Machu Picchu. Bingham did also discover Vilcabama the Old, without realizing it, but the true location at Espíritu Pampa was only pinpointed by Gene Savoy in the 1960s, and was not confirmed irrefutably until the work of Vincent Lee in the 1980s.

Ins & outs

Getting there The site is reached on foot or horseback from Pampaconas. From Chaullay, take a truck to Yupanca, Lucma or Pucyura, where you can rent horses or mules and travel through superb country to Espíritu Pampa. You can then continue to Koshireni on the Río San Miguel. Allow 5-8 days if going on foot.

Advice and information To visit this area you must register with the police in Pucyura. You are advised to seek full information before travelling. Distances are considerable – it is at least 100 km from Chaullay to Espíritu Pampa – the going is difficult and maps appear to be very poor. The best time of year is May-Oct. During the wet season it really does rain, so be prepared to get very wet and very muddy. Insect repellent is essential. Also take pain-killers and other basic medicines; these will be much appreciated by the local people should you need to take advantage of their hospitality.

Guides For Vilcabamba Vieja contact ***Vidal Albertes*** in Huancacalle, or ***Paulo Quispe Cusi*** in Yupanca. Another local guide in Pucyura is ***Gilberto Quintanilla***. Also try ***Adriel Garay*** at *White River Tours*, Plateros, Cusco, or C Bayoneta 739, Cusco, T234575.

Further reading If you intend to attempt this trip, you should first read *Sixpac Manco: travels among the Incas*, by Vincent R Lee, which is available in Cusco. It contains accurate maps of all the archaeological sites in this area, and describes two expeditions into the region by the author and his party in 1982 and 1984, following in the footsteps of Gene Savoy, who first identified the site in the 1960s. His book, *Antisuyo*, which describes his expeditions here and elsewhere in Peru, is also recommended reading.

Kiteni

At Kiteni you must register on arrival with the police. Take a torch/flashlight as there is no electricity

You can also go by boat to Kiteni from Koshireni and then by truck to Quillabamba (12-15 hours, US$5). There is basic accommodation at **G** *Hotel Kiteni*, and several restaurants. Irregular boats go to the Pongo de Mainique, where the river goes through the mountain with a rock wall of several hundred metres on either side, before descending into the jungle, where you can see many varieties of animals, birds, butterflies, snakes etc. This has been described by no less a traveller than Michael Palin (ex-Monty Python) as one of the most spectacular journeys anywhere on earth. It is two days from Quillabamba to Pongo. Seek advice in advance on the river conditions; at certain times it is too high.

South & west of Cusco

South & West of Cusco

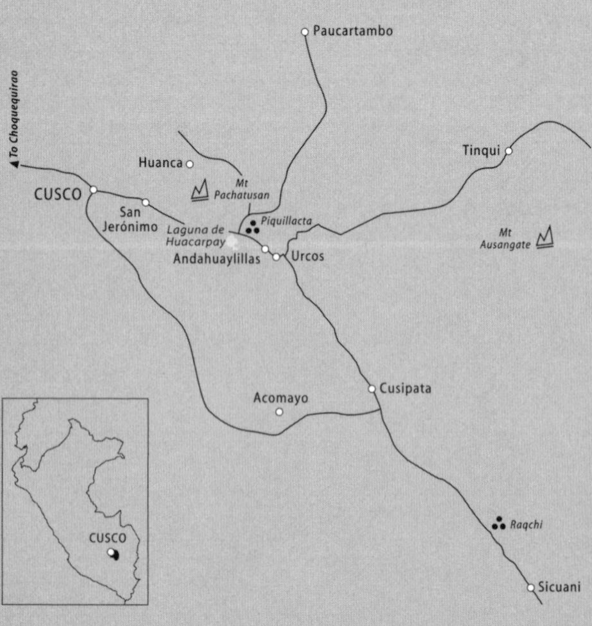

Most visitors to Cusco, after seeing the city, head to the Sacred Valley and Machu Picchu, but to the south are many equally tempting propositions. This part of the country is singularly off the beaten track in relation to the rest of the region. An area of myths, reputed to be where the founders of the Inca dynasty emerged into the world. Along or near the main road from Cusco to Lake Titicaca are a number of archaeological sites, the most prominent of which are Tipón and Raqchi, while the colonial churches at Andahuaylillas and Huaro are amongst the most fascinating in the whole region. There are beautiful lakes, too; four of them are near the village of Acomayo, while Huacarpay is an excellent place for walking and birdwatching. Also accessible from this road is the majestic Ausangate massif, where you can do some serious high-altitude trekking. And not be outdone, the southern part of the region also boasts its own 'lost city', at Choquequirao. As impressive as Machu Picchu, but in comparison hardly ever visited, this is a tremendous site, and getting there requires an expedition of six days or more.

Things to do south and west of Cusco

- Visit the Sistine Chapel of the Andes at Andahuaylillas. Nearby is the equally remarkable church at Huaro. For the best view, take a strong torch as they are not lit.
- Tired of ruins, churches, roads and people? Then take a trip to the four lakes near the village of Acomayo. Here you will find absolute peace at the water's edge.
- Cross the last Inca suspension bridge, at Qeswachaka, which is rebuilt annually in the only festival of its kind.
- Raqchi is a highly spiritual place which now contains the remnants of one of the tallest Inca buildings ever built, the temple to the creator god Viracocha. It is now a centre for the local ceramics industry .
- In mid July visit Paucartambo, on the road to Manu, when the festival of the Virgen del Carmen takes place, one of the highlights of the Cusco departmental calendar.
- Take a side trip to Tres Cruces to witness its famous sunrise, especially in June or July.

South of Cusco

Ins and outs

Getting around A newly-paved road runs southeast from Cusco to Sicuani, at the southeastern edge of the Department of Cusco. It continues to Puno, on the shores of Lake Titicaca, then on to the border with Bolivia. Combis run every 15-20 mins between Cusco and **Sicuani** (US$1.25), and more frequently to the villages and towns in between.

Transporte Vilcanota , from terminal on Av de la Cultura at the Paradero Hospital Regional (on a side street), run to **San Jerònimo, Saylla, Huasao, Tipón, Oropesa, Piquillacta/Huacarpay, Andahuaylillas** and on to **Urcos**. These buses run from 0500 to 2100, fare US$ 0.72 to Urcos.

To visit the 4 beautiful moutain lakes and Inca bridge accessible by rough mountain roads to the south of the paved road (see page 196), it would be worthwhile renting a 4WD for 2 days (*Kantu Perú Tours* in Cusco can organize this as well as a driver/guide for US$280, see page 115). It is just as feasible by combi, but will take longer.

South to Pacarijtambo

Pacarijtambo is a good starting point for the three to four hours walk to the ruins of **Maukallaqta**, which contain good examples of Inca stonework. From there, you can walk to **Pumaorca**, a high rock carved with steps, seats and a small puma in relief on top. Below this are more Inca ruins.

From Cusco, buses and trucks to Pacarijtambo take four hours, US$2. You can find lodging for the night in Pacarijtambo at the house of the Villacorta family and leave for Cusco by truck the next morning. On the way back, you'll pass the caves of Tambo Toco, where a legend says that the four original Inca brothers emerged into the world, in contradiction of the theory that the windows from which the brothers emerged were at Ollantaytambo (see page 150).

San Jerónimo to Huanca trek

Leaving Cusco, you will soon pass the condor monument (see page 87) of San Sebastián then enter the old colonial town of **San Jerónimo**, which has become almost a suburb of the sprawling city and is now home to Cusco´s wholesale Saturday morning food market. Porters struggle past carrying loads of up to 70 kg and there is a huge array of colourful fruit and vegetables, as well as campesinos in for the day to sell their produce and wares. Get there for 0800, but be aware that 'gringos' stick out like a sore thumb so take no valuables. San Jerónimo is the starting point for an excellent trek to Huanca, described below.

Ins & outs

Getting there *ET Leòn de San Jerònimo*, from Puquín District (on the road to Chinchero) to San Jerónimo; catch this minibus on the corner of C Ayacucho and Av Sol 3rd block. It goes through the downtown area, Wanchac district, Av de la Cultura all the way to San Jerònimo (final stop beyond the Plaza, at the corner of the Fé y Alegría and Santa Bernardita schools). ***Santiago Express***, from Plaza of Santiago district, a few blocks from La Virgen de Belén and the Antonio Lorena Hospital. Board this bus on 3rd block of Av Sol (near the Post Office); it turns left to Wanchac, then follows Av de la Cultura to San Jerónimo's main plaza. US$ 0.15. ***Chaska***, from Villa El Sol-Independencia in the Santiago district above Cusco to Jr Arica at the plaza in San Jerónimo. Best place in central Cusco is the corner of C Ayacucho and Av Sol (3rd block). US$0.15. All services run from 0530 to 2200. All pass in front the San Jerònimo Police station, from which C Clorinda Matto de Turner is 1 ½ blocks away (this is the street where the San Jerónimo main market is located, as well as the cemetery at the very end).

San Jerónimo to Huaccoto

A minimum of 4-5 hrs should be allowed for the ascent from San Jerónimo to Huaccoto

From San Jerónimo, head north along Calle Clorinda Matto de Turner (past the main produce market on the left and the *Andenes de Andrea* restaurant). Further along is the cemetery. The street becomes an unpaved road, swings to the right (east) for 500 m and then left (north) again on its definite course up the mountain. There is a four-wheel drive road which connects San Jerónimo with Huaccotto, laboriously winding its way for 15 km from 3,200 m up to 4,000 m. Much more interesting and worthwhile, is to follow the old Inca and spanish colonial treck, which ascends the quebrada of the Huacottomayu and is only about half as long and more direct, but also likewise steep in places. This is wide, very clearly marked and widely travelled road. Heading north by northwest, the pedestrian road leaves the narrow streets of the town. On the way out through the outskirts, the road winds past the remains of once great colonial *estancias*. Old adobe walls and the uprooted stumps of ancient eucalyptus trees mark the limits of farmfields and pastures.

San Jerónimo to Huanca Trek

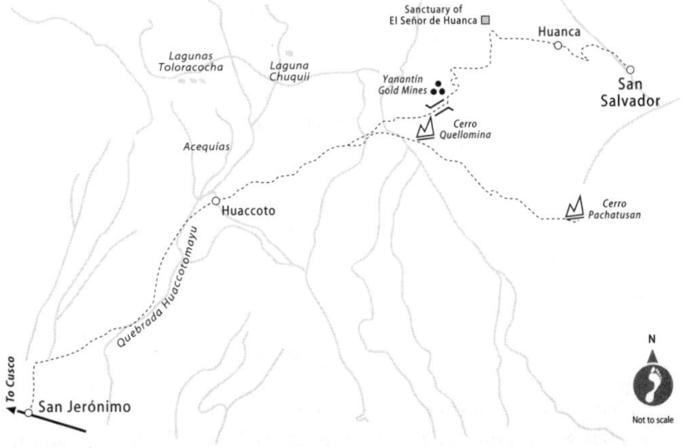

The most striking feature of the landscape are the thousands of eucalyptus trees covering the slopes of all the surrounding hillsides. Few truly old trees remain (the eucalyptus was first introduced to this region in the 1870-80s). There are large groves of 20-40 year old trees growing out of older and thicker stumps, harvested around the mid 20th century, intersperced with extensive patches much younger trees. The air is dense with that most envigorating and promising aroma of menthol.

Below are visible the red tiled roofs of the 500 year-old colonial town of San Jerónimo and the broader expanse of the valley of the Huatanay river, gradually making its way southeast toward its confluence with the Urubamba River – only 20 km distant from this point, but whose waters will eventually flow into the Amazonas region and on to the Atlantic Ocean, thousands of kilometers from here.

The broad trail climbs the mountainside, intersecting the many turns and twists of the little-used track. The walking trail pretty much follows the course of a fast flowing *acequía* (irrigation channel), no doubt originally channeled by the Incas or their predecessors, the Huari-Tiahuanacos, who built Piquillacta (see page 189). There are other canals and aqueducts, which distribute the water from the numerous *puquios* (natural springs), which sprout from the slopes and gullies of **Cerro Pachatusan** (the pillar, or pivot of the world), which, although its main peak and summit are not yet visible, we have been ascending since San Jerónimo.

As the eucalyptus groves begin to thin out (approaching the 3,700 m line), the ridgeline and highlands finally become visible. Due north, is the prominent, pyramidal summit of Pikol, a minor Apu (mountain) but an important landmark. Its name is clearly carved on its slopes. To the right of it, at roughly two o'clock, a short segment of jagged dark grey boulders and rocks can clearly be seen. This is the first hint of the Huaccoto quarries and the principal reference point to head for. In Inca times, remaining so throughout the colonial and republican periods, Huacotto was the site of an important stone quarry and a principal source of the building materials for the Inca temples and Spanish colonial mansions of Cusco. To the immediate right is the gully formed by the Río Huaccotomayu, which will somehow merge and vanish into the mountain slope a few hundred meters beyond and above.

The tree line is at about 3,700-3,800 m. You emerge from it into an altogether different world. The panorama is wide and very luminous (assuming, of course, that the weather is fine). The landscape is composed of rolling hills, dotted with tarns that can swell into flooding lakes during the rainy season Although the ever-growing African kikuyo grass (introducedto the area in the early 20th century) has already made headway into this last pocket of native highland flora, it is the native grasses – the ichu and its nearest relatives – which predominate, but only briefly. Soon is a landscape devoid of trees, with cushion plants, growing low to preserve heat and moisture. The most common is the yareta, a bright green bubble-like growth, reminiscent of coral, but often, incorrectly, referred to as tundra. Beyond the foreground of rolling hills of tundra and tarn are several cordilleras of great mountain peaks.

Huaccoto to Huanca

From Huaccoto it is possible to make a detour to the summit of Pachatusan, heading for the first of its many false summits (east, then south along the slope of the mountain), though this is only for experienced climbers. Instead, continue on the same well-worn path that brought you to this point. A gentle climb of a few more metres and 1 km further, veering slightly east by northeast, sets course towards an obvious breach between Pachatusan and its northwestern extension, known as Cerro Quellomina. This pass and a winding trail descend through a maze of impregnable crags, all the way down to the green valley of the Urubamba, which makes its way from southeast to northwest, splaying out into various branches and channels, creating islets and sand banks which disappear in the rainy season.

Along the crest, close to the pass, are numerous wooden crosses draped in long, flowing, veil-like cloths, many of them well over three metres tall. These have been erected by pilgrims and devotees and each year they are clad in fresh garments. A few hundred metres along the pass, on the left, is the entrance to what were once the famous Yanantín gold mines, belonging to the Marqués de Valleumbroso, which now yield only copper. The entire area was once known as the "Marquesado de Oropeza". The trail, very wide and easily recognizable, twists down through the rock spires. Another 200 m beyond is a small Inca fortress perched on one of the buttresses. Closer inspection reveals the remains of other observation points and Inca constructions among the rock towers. Just below this point, another major trail branches off to the left (northwest) climbing up to a well-marked pass. This is an original Inca road, leading back up to Ccoricocha and eventually Huchuy Cusco and on to Chinchero.

Soon , although still far below your present position, a large, relatively flat area with many buildings and cereal cultivation, as well as groves of very tall, old eucalyptus trees, comes into view. This green belt of fertility amid the seemingly relentless precipices of Pachatusan's northeastern face is **Huanca**, site of the famous sanctuary, one of the great religious shrines of the Andes. Its fame spreads far beyond its immediate vicinity. Devotees, belonging to branches and brotherhoods, come from as far as Ecuador and Bolivia.

The Sanctuary of El Señor de Huanca

The popular festival of El Señor de Huanca is held annually on 15 Sep

The Sanctuary of El Señor de Huanca stands above the clouds, surrounded by flower-filled gardens and trees of many kinds. It is a great gathering place of so many hopes and wishes for goodness, protected by the great misty crag, Pachatusan. From Huaccoto, three hours hiking, not counting the unavoidable stops to appreciate the scenery, should bring you to the grounds of the sanctuary. The Mercedarian fathers, though fewer than in the past, are still there to greet visitors. The Reverend Father Manuel Jesús Ampuero, Comendador Capellán, is currently in charge. He requests that all hikers descending from Huaccoto past the springs pick up all the garbage they can, as a contribution to the conservation of the sanctuary grounds. Lodging and meals are avilable for pilgrims and hikers: US$5.75 for bed and board, free for somewhere to sleep only (but you can cook). Both include full use of bath and toilet facilities. There is also a public telephone.

Ins & outs

Transport from Cusco to the Sanctuary leaves from the Coliseo Cerrado and the back of the Social Security Hospital compound, 2 blocks from the Hospital Regional main bus stop; to the right on Av de la Cultura going southeast. Buses run on weekends and daily during the Señor de Huanca celebrations, 14-21 Sep and the following pilgrimage season which goes on throughout Oct. Departs 0700 until midday and returns from midday to 1600. Taxis to the Sanctuary of Huanca are available for expreso rides, about US$10 one way, with waiting time and return trip US$20-25.

Note that there is always a ride available from the Sanctuary, as the priests are more than willing to help the faithful who need transport. Ring the bell of the private quarters of the Sanctuary and the resident priest will assist. The priests have their own private transport, which can be rented for a ride to the closest point for transport to Cusco or Pisac. Of course, a contribution to the Sanctuary will be appreciated.

History of the Sanctuary

We know from Spanish chroniclers of the mid 16th century, such as Pedro de Cieza de León and Juan Polo de Ondegardo, that the Apu Pachatusan was a major huaca (shrine) long before the conquest. It was the origin of the ashlars and stone used for building Imperial Cusco of Pachacútec. It had numerous springs, on both its western and eastern slopes. Last but not least, as the later exploitation of the rich mines of the Marqués de Valleumbroso confirmed, it was a source of gold, silver and copper, all of great importance in Pre-Columbian Peru, but of much greater value to the piratical economy of 16th-century Europe. The town of Oropesa ("where the Gold is weighed"), some 10 km beyond San Jerónimo (see next page) and close Piquillacta, founded by the Spaniards in the boom years of the late 16th century, was aptly named. Even before the Incas and Spaniards (as well as the Huari-Tiahuanacos of Piquillacta) two fundamental elements characterized the mountain: the abundance of fresh water springs, and a large population of pumas. Today the puma have disappeared, but the deer that must have constituted their prey can still be seen in groups in more isolated parts of the mountain.

Instead of succumbing to the more zealous approach of the early, crusading conquistadores, Pachatusan's sacredness was absorbed and adapted in the more enlightened approach of "religious syncretism" that prevailed in the mid-17th to late-18th century. How else were the Marqués de Valleumbroso going to get the locals to work the mines? At Huanca, the necessary Christian miracle took place in 1675, 25 years after the great earthquake of 1650. It was a time when miracles, no matter their provenance, were universally required.

In May that year, one Diego Quispe, a simple Indian from Chincheros working in the Yanantín mines, committed some grave disciplinary error as a result of which he was to be subjected to severe punishment next day. He fled into the crags and gullies of Apu Pachatusan, trusting more in the justice of the earth than that of his overlords. He crept into the furthest depths of an overhang and began to pray. As night fell and Quispe prepared to resume his flight to freedom, the miracle took place. Jesus appeared to him, wearing the crown of thorns and bleeding from the lashes on his back. And He spoke the words: "Diego, I have chosen this site to be a volcano of love and a pure spring of regeneration and forgiveness. Go to your home and let the local priest and all your people know. I shall await you here." Diego took a silver chain from his neck and laid it at the base of the rock where the apparition occurred (the first of many centuries of gifts and tributes to El Señor de Huanca).

Diego's life was spared, and more miracles followed. In the course of the next two generations, the boulder acquired a painting of Christ being whipped by a stylized, moorish-looking ruffian (an ironic echo of the treatment inflicted upon the mineworkers by the Marqués de Valleumbroso). In time, ownership of the land passed to the Religious Order of La Merced of Cusco (Mercedarios). A large sanctuary was built over the original boulder and among the devotees whos generosity contributed to its construction are various South American presidents, the elder Alessandri of Chile prominent among them.

Today, the boulder and traces of the painting are partially visible through glass. Nearly 400 years' accummulation of plaques, icons and messages are everywhere. People come on foot, horse and cars to fill empty coke bottles and glass jars wth the magic water that flows out of Apu Pachatusan just above the sanctuary.

San Jerónimo to Huambutío

Southeast from San Jerónimo the valley begins to narrow as you reach **Saylla**, famous for its *chicharones* – deep-fried pieces of pork. Between here and the next village of Oropesa are the extensive ruins of **Tipón.** They include baths, terraces, irrigation systems and a temple complex, accessible from a path leading from just above the last terrace, all in a fine setting. From the ruins you can go up to more ruins and an amazing Inca road with a deep irrigation channel which leads straight up into a mountain and the further sites of Pucará and Cruzmoco. Allow a full day to see them all. From Tipón village it's an hour's climb to the ruins; or take a taxi.

Farther on is **Oropesa**, which has been known as Cusco´s breadbasket since colonial times and and is the national capital of this staple diet. Try the large, delicious circular bread. The church here contains a fine ornately carved pulpit. Next comes the village of **Huacarpay**, near the shores of Laguna de Huacarpay, in the Piquillacta Archaeological Park. For details of Inca ruins and walks around this area, see page 189.

At **Huambutío**, north of Huacarpay, the road divides: northwest to Pisac (see page 139) and north to Paucartambo, on the eastern slope of Andes. The road from Huambutío northwest to Pisac (about 20 km) is fully paved. This is an access road for the first river-rafting section on the Río Urubamba, which also connects with another rafting route from Piñipampa. In the rainy season, and for less-experienced rafters, the Huambutío (Piñipampa) to Pisac river section is safer to run. The rapids are class II to III. The length of the rafting trip is 30-35 km with spectacular views of the Urubamba valley that are not seen in a conventional Valley tour. This part of the river offers views of the **Sanctuary of El Señor de Huanca** (see above).

Transport

To **Huambutío, San Salvador** and the **Sanctuary of Huanca**: *Empresa de Transportes Paucartambo y Pitusiray* Av Tullumayo 202 (lower part), southeast part of Cusco. About 3 km beyond **Oropesa** is a turning to the left; the higher road, called Carretera Carmen Bonita, goes to **Paucartambo** and on to Manu. To the left, following the river bank, the road passes **Huambutío** (see below), **Vilcabamba, San Salvador** and ends at **Pisac**, connecting with the road to the Sacred Valley of the Urubamba and the road back to Cusco via Sacsayhuaman. Relevant schedules are: Mon to Sat, Cusco to San Salvador, 1½ hrs, 0640 and 1300, US$0.75; San Salvador to Cusco 0800 and 1330, and from San Salvador to Pisac at 1400, 45 mins-1 hr, US$0.60.

Paucartambo

This once remote town, 80 km east of Cusco, is on the road to Pilcopata, Atalaya and Shintuya. This is now the overland route used by tour companies from Cusco into Manu National Park. Consequently, it has become a popular tourist destination. On 15-17 July, the festival of the *Virgen del Carmen* is a major attraction and well worth seeing. Masked dancers enact rituals and folk tales in the streets (see next page).

Getting there

Private car hire for a round trip from Cusco on 15-17 Jul costs US$30. Tour operators in Cusco can arrange this. A minibus leaves for Paucartambo from Av Huáscar in Cusco, every other day, US$4.50, 3-4 hrs; alternate days Paucartambo-Cusco. Trucks and a private bus leave from the Coliseo, behind Hospital Segura in Cusco; 5 hrs, US$2.50.

The fiesta of the Virgen del Carmen

In the highland village of Paucartambo, 80 km east of Cusco, a pagan-Christian festival celebrates the Virgen del Carmen every year on 15-17 July. Her feast days fall in the Quechua month of "Earthly Purification".

There are two popular myths surrounding the history of the Virgen del Carmen: the first tells how the Virgin appeared in Paucartambo. The story goes that a rich Ccollao woman called Felipa Begolla came to Paucartambo to trade goods. One day she was unloading her wares, when, in one of her earthenware pots, the head of a beautiful woman appeared and a sweet voice spoke to her, "Do not be afraid, my dear, my name is Carmen". The head shone like the rays of the sun. Felipa contracted a great cabinet maker in the town to carve a body made of fine wood on which to place that beautiful head. She brought the statue of the Virgin into the town's church and all the Ccollas celebrated since the Virgin had arrived in a pot from the Ccollao, an area beginning 150 km southeast of Cusco, beyond the Ausangate massif, covering the enormous highland plateau which includes Titicaca and stretching as far as northern Argentina. The inhabitants of this area, the Ccolla, swore to come every year on July 16 so that the Virgin would not feel sad at being away from her own land. The Virgin del Carmen festival became popular and so, each year, dancing groups dressed in colourful costumes with decorated masks came to reenact the old folk tales. (Sra Betty Yabar, Testimonio de Cheqec, 1971)

In the other popular myth, the Chontakirus, a tribe of jungle Indians, tell that the Ch'unchos, who in history and fables embody profanity and contempt for sacred things, stole the statue of the Virgin from the Ccollas of Puno who were taking it to Paucartambo for the Corpus celebrations. During the confrontation the Ch'unchos killed the Ccollas and threw the statue into the Amaru River (river of the serpent). From that day, the river was renamed the Madre de Dios, after the Mother of God. The statue was rescued from the waters and taken to the church in Paucartambo, where she remains. Scars from the arrows in her chest can still be seen. (Sra Alfonsina Barrionuevo, Cusco Màgico, 1968)

For the festival, the church is decorated, with the Mamacha Carmen dressed in fine clothes and she is visited by the dancing Comparsas. Some travel from far away, such as the Negritos who, in colonial times, came to dance for the Virgin, praying for their freedom. The Ch'unchos, her captors, are her main dancers and they guard her along the route of the procession. The party continues for the next two days with lots of dancing and music. Each dancing group has its own station in town and every year important people are named as Carguyocs, who are in charge of a particular dancing group at every ceremony. The Carguyocs cover all the costs of the festivity for the dancers and for all the people who visit. They provide lodging, food and drink.

The Mamacha Carmen is taken out on her final procession to the colonial stone bridge (built by King Carlos III of Spain in the 18th century). She then blesses the four Suyos, or cardinal points. The Saqras (demons) scurry over the rooftops trying to tempt her, but the Virgin with her kindness makes them repent. In the afternoon, a reenactment of the battle between the Ccollas and the Ch'unchos, called the Guerrilla, takes place. The whole town gets involved. During these events, the music, dancing and drinking continue.

Since colonial times this was on the route for produce brought from the jungle to the Sierra and thence to the coast. King Carlos III of Spain had a stone bridge built across the river here in the 18th century to replace the previous rope bridge. The locals claimed that the reason the King lost such a large proportion of the *diezmos reales* (tithes, or one-tenth tax on annual produce) due to him from the area was that the mule loads were too heavy for original bridge. They said that the old bridge was constantly deteriorating as a result of lack of maintenance and rain rotting the fibres, so the goods were lost in the river. The King believed the Indians were simply stealing his profits. To be fair to Carlos III, the stone bridge may have solved his tax problem, but it also furthered his aim of promoting the development of Paucartambo and encouraging scientific and exploratory expeditions in the region.

Sleeping

There are 2 basic places to stay: **G** *Quinta Rosa Marina*, near the bridge, and **G** *Albergue Municipal Carmen de la Virgen.*

You can walk from Paucartambo to the *chullpas* of **Machu Cruz** in about an hour, or to the *chullpas* of **Pijchu** (take a guide). You can also visit the Inca fortress of **Huatojto**, which has fine doorways and stonework. A car will take you as far as Ayre, from where the fortress is a two- hour walk. From Paucartambo, in the dry season, you can go 44 km to **Tres Cruces**, along the Pilcopata road, turning left after 25 km. Señor Cáceres in Paucartambo will arrange this trip for you. Tres Cruces gives a wonderful view of the sunrise in June and July: peculiar climactic conditions make it appear that three suns are rising. Tour operators in Cusco can arrange transport and lodging.

Around Laguna de Huacarpay

The **Piquillacta Archaeological Park** is 30 km southeast of Cusco, covering an area of 3,421 ha. Its nucleus is the remains of a lake, the Laguna de Huacarpay, now smaller than in ancient times when it was called Muyna. It is also known as Laguna de Lucre. The basin of the lake lies at an altitude of 3,200 m and is surrounded by several hills no higher than 3,350-3,400 m. Its shape is roughly circular and its circumference is presently about 8 km. Around it are a number of precolumbian archaeological remains, of which the principal ones are: Piquillacta, Choquepuquio, Kañaraqay, Urpicancha and Rumicolca.

Ins & outs

Getting there Buses to Lucre leave from the bus station on Calle Huáscar, in Wanchac district, on a side street ½ block from the market, 1 hr. Fare from Cusco to Oropesa is US$0.30 (passing by San Sebastián, San Jerónimo, Saylla, Huasao, Tipón); fare Cusco-Lucre is US$0.45. Small cars wait at the start of the 8 km circuit around the Huacarpay lake charging US$1.50 (Ruperto Valencia and Ernesto Arredondo recommended drivers).

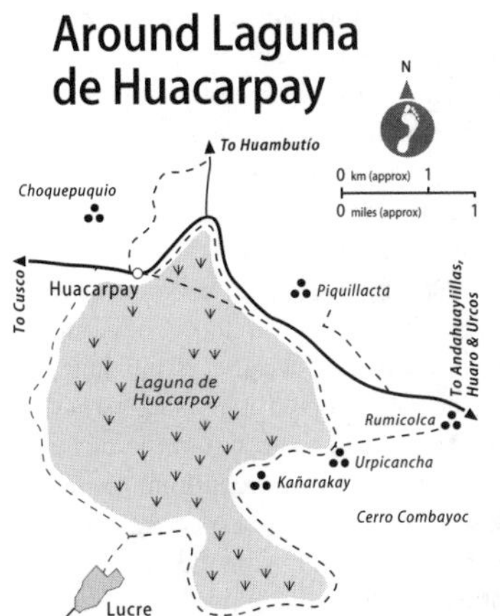

Sections of the lake are overgrown with thick beds of totora reeds and other Andean lakeside vegetation. As the lake is gradually drying up, the reeds are spreading and fragmenting the open water, but several relatively large sections of water remain. At the same time, water levels fluctuate dramatically between the so-called 'dry' and 'rainy' seasons and in other climatic events, such as El Niño. The village of Huacarpay, on its northern shore, can be subjected to damaging floods.

The Laguna de Huacarpay is habitat to a variety of birdlife. In the open water, flocks of puna teals, pochards and pintails, as well as more scattered individual Andean ruddy ducks, with their conspicuous blue beaks, can be seen. The totora reed banks are home to several varieties of gallinules and coots, the giant and the red-fronted being most noticeable. Along the shores of the lake and the neighbouring marshlands live puna ibis (though not in large numbers) and sometimes white-faced ibis; also some herons, occasional egrets. There are also lapwings, terns and Andean gulls. Most of these are present year-round. Huacarpay is probably the most readily accessible area from Cusco in which to observe a typical Andean highland lake environment.

The lake circuit A good way to see all this is to hike or cycle around the lake, on 8 km of level, paved secondary road, which few motor vehicles use. The main focus of this basic circuit is birdwatching and only two or three secondary archaeological sites, but the hike can be lengthened to include the majority of the archaeological sites built on the surrounding hills. Some can be visited independently, but on an anticlockwise circuit of the lake basin they can easily be taken in.

Starting from a point about 3-4 km due south of the Lucre turnoff on the main Cusco-Urcos highway, heading due south, you reach the southern end of the lake. The road begins to swing slightly to the left (east) and soon splits: right to the town of Lucre and left around the lake. **Lucre** has been associated with textiles from Inca times on. In the 1850s-60s, the area was owned by the Garmendia family who pioneered the first industrial production of textiles (worsteds, tweeds, alpaca and vicuña finished cloth) in this area, maybe in all Peru. To do this they imported a complete textile mill from England, the whole works, including the engineers and mechanics. It was shipped to Mollendo, thence to Arequipa and on over the Andes by mule. For many years it played a significant part in the local economy. But today, there is no sign of it.

The left hand fork continues east and shortly begins to climb a little and head northeast. Here a really nice hike starts. On some maps this is marked "Morada de Huascar", but its true name is **Kañarakay**. From this point, angling away and above the modern road, following the gently rising crest and the various converging trails and footpaths, you begin to glimpse the layers of history of this area. Looking north, some 5 km across the lake, as if moulded onto its hill, lies the rectilinear grid of Piquillacta. West of it and slightly lower are the less regular, but taller walls of Choqepuquio, while slightly lower but close by are the remains of a colonial hacienda, also named Choqepuquio. Much further away, 20-30 km north, is the unusual, stark profile of Cerro Pachatusan. Looking east from Piquillacta the gates of Rumicolca are visible, the irrigation canals contouring the mountains from distant, forgotten sources. Also visible is the unmistakable architectural harmony between structure and environment which characterizes Inca building, in this case, the terraces of Urpicancha. That's the entire hike which lies ahead.

Start hiking northeastward. What at first sight appears to be arid, rocky country interspersed with crumbling ridges and strewn with loose rocks and scree, is in fact the remnants of a vast network of roads, passageways, buildings, retaining walls and stairways. Several cities lie scattered here, successively inhabited, abandoned and repopulated. This is also the realm of the cactii: opuntia predominate, but also thin, elongated prickly pears, enormously tall flat nopales, small barrel cactii, some with enormous bright scarlet and yellow flowers. There are seven-pointed San Pedro cactii, with lily-white flowers which bud at dawn, blossom at noon and wither by sunset. Epyphitic bromeliads, most of them tsillandsias with bushy crowns of long thin leaves armed with sharp thorns, cling to ancient walls and grow in empty windows. And almost everywhere, blankets of Spanish moss. There are also aloes and agave. The fauna is limited to lizards and rodents, which keep the insect population under control. Most common are black widow spiders, which live under stones (it best to leave rocks where they are and watch carefully where you sit down for a break!). Kestrels and hawks streak overhead, but the most typical of local birds are the Andean flicker, a large bright yellow-greenish speckled ground woodpecker, fond of lizards, and the giant hummingbirds – Patagonia gigas – with their nests strategically placed among the thick branches of a thorny cactus.

After 1 km of this jumble of stone, you come to the ruins of **Urpicancha** (Urpi meaning dove, and cancha an enclosed field). Some legends say this was the birthplace of the Inca Huáscar, who waged war with his half-brother Atahualpa. Urpicancha is like a small oasis in the middle of the dusty environment surrounding the lake. It consists of a succession of a terraced hillside, descending almost to the lakeshore. At its base are two partial enclosures, made of well-fitted rocks which have acquired a striking orange hue from the lichen. A fresh-water spring descends the hillside, partially piped, and there's an old colonial house, closed down for some years now. It's a shady spot, with eucalyptus, willows and a few mature elderberry trees (sauco).

From here, the hike climbs up to Rumicolca. Several paths meander along the western slope of the large hill called Cerro Combayoc. All these trails will lead to Rumicolca. The closer to Urpicancha, or from Urpicancha itself, that you head up Combayoc, the more scenic the hike will be. The entire Muyna basin can be seen, and the eastern side of Combayoc, including 40 km of the Vilcanota river valley, Andahuaylillas and sections of the quarries of Rumicolca.

Rumicolca

Back on the main road to Sicuani and Puno, shortly after the turn-off to Piquillacta, you will see, on the right, the huge gateway of Rumicolca. You can walk around it for free. This was a Huari aqueduct, built across this narrow stretch of the valley, which the Incas clad in fine stonework to create this gateway. If you look at the top you can see the original walls, four tiers high. It is now being 'restored' which in Cusco means rebuilt; a highly controversial topic.

Rumicolca itself (the name means depository or storage site for rocks) was a control point and parallel set of gateways through which in Inca times all traffic between Cusco and Collasuyo (the southeastern quarter of the Inca dominions) had to pass. It is very imposing. The wall through which the gates pass is of common enough composition, rough-hewn rock bound by a hardened clay mortar. There is evidence that this was covered in stucco and painted in ochres and reds. The gateways, though, are some of the finest Inca masonry. Large, perfectly cut, polished andesite ashlars fit together exactly, without mortar, of a quality equal to anything in Cusco, Ollantaytambo or Pisac. The finely-dressed gateways probably date from the 14th century, contemporary with the monumental phase of Inca architecture in the era of Pachacútec or his successor Túpac Yupanqui. The wall which the gateway crosses is 600 to 800 years older and supported a Huari aqueduct which brought water to Piquillacta.

Piquillacta

Rumicolca is a few metres from the modern Cusco to Puno road. On the other side of the road, less than 50 m away, lies the entrance to the Huari adobe wall ruins of Piquillacta (which translates as the City of Fleas). Piquillacta is a large site, with some reconstruction in progress. It was an administrative centre at the southern end of the Huari empire. The Huari, who were contemporaneous with the Tiahuanaco culture (AD 600-1000), were based near present-day Ayacucho in the Central Highlands, almost 600 km by road north of Cusco.

Huari influence covered most of what we now know as Peru, from Cajamarca and the Pacific coast in the north to the borders of the Tiahuanaco in the south. Their system of regional storehouses, irrigation, roads and government was similar to, and was adopted by the Incas. Archaeological evidence from Piquillacta is confusing, but mostly suggests that this was not a place for permanent residents, more for storing supplies, for housing itinerant groups of workers, for tribute gathering and distribution and for ceremonies. The whole site is surrounded by a wall, there are many enclosed compounds with buildings of over one storey and it appears that the walls were plastered and finished with a layer of lime. ■ *Open daily, 0700-1730, entry by BTU tourist ticket. Buses to Urcos from Av Huáscar in Cusco will drop you at the entrance on the north side of the complex, though this is not the official entry.*

From Piquillacta, head west into a valley through which the paved road from Cusco to Paucartambo runs. Cross it and continue for about 50 m until you come to the remains of the old dirt road which runs parallel to the modern one for a short stretch and then veers left, crossing an old bridge. Over the bridge head west by southwest, past the site of a lime crusher (some houses, a small adobe factory). On the right is a marshy extension of Huacarpay lake. Here is some of the best birdwatching in the entire trek. Follow the main (or any secondary) path up the side of the valley, gaining the first ridge about 100 m beyond. Look south and see the dark walls of **Choquepuquio**, perhaps the most mysterious of the archaeological sites on the trek. The walls suggest two-storied houses, but also a redoubt, built to withstand siege and attack.

Choquepuquio was erected as a stronghold in insecure times. Its drama derives from it not being restored (as are most of the other sites in the park, a controversial topic, eg at Rumicolca). It is unkempt, there are thistles and brambles to deal with and, when seen up close, its walls appear even taller and more enigmatic than at first glance. From Choqepuquio follow any of the paths leading to the road which goes to Cusco. You will emerge directly opposite the Lucre turnoff where the hike began.

Southeast to Urcos

Andahuaylillas Continuing southeast towards Urcos you reach Andahuaylillas and the first of three fascinating 17th century churches. This is a simple structure, but it has been referred to as the Andean Sistine Chapel because of its beautiful frescoes, and internal architecture. Go in, wait for your eyes to adjust to the darkness, then turn to look at the two pictures either side of the splendid door. On the right is the path to heaven, which is narrow and thorny; on the left the way to hell, which is wide and littered with flowers. They are attributed to the artist Luis de Riaño.Above is the high choir, built in local wood, where there are two organs. Craning your neck further you will see the remarkable painted and carved ceiling. The main altar is gilded in 24-carat gold leaf and has symbols from both the Quechua and Christian religions, such as the sun and the lamb, respectively. Many of the canvases depict the lives of the church´s patron saints, St Peter and St Paul. Ask for Sr Eulogio; he is a good guide, but speaks Spanish only.

Outside, around the peaceful plaza, are massive trees apparently dripping with red seeds and hanging moss. These are Pisonay trees.

Sleeping E *La Casa del Sol*. Relaxing, clean and bright hostel close to the central plaza on Garcilaso. Well-decorated rooms set around a courtyard, this is excellent value. Owned by Dr Gladys Oblitas, the hostel funds her project to provide medical services to poor campesinos. While staying you can take a course or take part in workshops on natural and alternative medicine. She also has a practice in Cusco, at Procuradores 42 (T227264, medintegral@hotmail.com)

Transport Taxis go to Andahuaylillas, as does the ***Oropesa*** bus (from Av Huáscar in Cusco) via Tipón, Piquillacta and Rumicolca.

Huaro

The church is likely to be locked. For the giant key, look for Sr Pablo Ticuña at 2 de Mayo 367, a block away. He will show you around for US$0.85 per person (he only speaks Spanish)

Before the next major town of Urcos is the quiet village of Huaro (turn left off the main road to reach the appalling main plaza, dominated by a concrete lookout tower). The church on this plaza is stunning inside. Walking in takes your breath away. The walls are plastered with frescoes used to evangelize the illiterate. Grinning skeletons compete with dragons and devils ushering the living into the afterlife and punishing them thereafter. Although finished in 1802 by Tadeo Escalante, they are now mostly in a sad state of repair. Tour groups come here, but there is precious little money being spent on preservation. The first fresco on the right as you enter shows the torment of sinners in hell. A liar has his tongue torn out with pliers, a drunk has boiling alcohol poured down his throat through a funnel and others are impaled on a wheel. The torture is not confined to the masses. In a boiling cauldron, among the tortured, writhing, naked bodies are a priest, a cardinal and a bishop, identified by their hats.

Looking left of the door there is a priest giving absolution at the death of a girl in a poor house while below, a rich house plays host to a sumptuous banquet (with roasted guinea pig on the menu, of course). A woman here is choking and being led away by the skeleton of Death. The moral is clear. Right of the entrance, below another portrait of rich people having a feast, is the Tree of Life with good versus evil as Death wields an axe and Jesus sounds a bell.

To the right of this, on the left wall, is Judgement Day at its grimmest. Centre stage is a graveyard, the coffins of which are being yanked open by skeletons to drag the dead to either the underworldon the right (entered via the mouth of a dragon) or heaven (complete with Pearly Gates and musicians playing trumpets).

On the left are people being pulled from flames by angels. This is Purgatory and its inhabitants are those who have committed minor sins. Having paid their dues they will now be allowed into heaven. The democracy of the Catholic vision again allows these sinners to include cardinals and bishops.

To the right of this painting we see that Death is never far away. A huge skeleton containing the body of a woman (for we are all born of woman) has at its feet the paraphernalia of the rich, which cannot be taken into the next life. More skeletons stand behind people ignorant of their destiny. An angel sounds a trumpet from the top of a pillar at the moment of death. Meanwhile, the devil himself can be seen lurking under the bed of a person being given absolution. Again, look up at the wonderful ceiling.

Urcos

Beyond Huaro is Urcos. There is accommodation here, but basic to say the least. Best of a bad job is **G** *Hostal Señor de Qoillurrit´i* on the main road on the central plaza. Dormitory rooms are very basic but clean; there is also a private double of similar quality. Showers are cold in a block outside. **G** *Hostal Luvic*, also on the plaza, is identically priced, as is **G** *Hotel Laterraza*, which may look upmarket from the outside but should be avoided if possible. To eat, *Restaurante Pollería* on the main plaza is acceptable and cheap.

Urcos to Tinqui

A spectacular road from Urcos crosses the Eastern Cordillera to Puerto Maldonado in the jungle (see page 211). Some 47 km after passing the snow-line Hualla-Hualla pass, at 4,820 m, the super-hot thermal baths of Marcapata, 173 km from Urcos, provide a relaxing break (entry US$0.10). Some 82 km from Urcos, on the road to Puerto Maldonado, at the base of **Nevado Ausangate** (6,384 m), is the town of **Ocongate**, which has two hotels on the Plaza de Armas.

Tinqui
Colour map 2, grid B4

Beyond Ocongate is Tinqui, the starting point for hikes around Ausangate (6,372 m), the highest mountain in southeastern Per, in the Cordillera Vilcanota. On the flanks of the Nevado Ausangate is *Q'Olloriti*, where a church has been built close to the snout of a glacier. This place has become a place of pilgrimage (see page 111).

Sleeping **G** ***Hostal Tinqui Guide***, on the right-hand side as you enter the village, friendly, meals available, the owner can arrange guides and horses. **G** ***Ausangate***, very basic, trekking tours organized.

Transport Buses to Tinqui leave Cusco Mon-Sat at 1000 (6-7 hrs, US$3.50) from C Tomasatito Condemayta, near the Coliseo Cerrado.

Hiking around Ausangate

The hike around the mountain of Ausangate takes about five days. It is spectacular, but arduous, with three passes over 5,000 m, so you need to be acclimatized. Alternatively, a shorter and easier return trek can be made from Ausangate down the beautiful Pitumarca valley to the town of the same name and the Sacred valley. It is recommended to take a guide or *arriero*. *Arrieros* and muleteers have formed a union and as such they are much more organized than in recent years. Their prices have gone up, too. A chief *arriero* charges US$10 per day, US$12 per day for each mule and US$15 per day for a saddle horse. A chief *arriero* takes along one to two assistants (US$5 per day per assistant). *Arrieros* expect foodstuffs (noodles, sugar, rice, coca leaves), plus cigarettes, alcohol, and kerosene to be provided for a well-planned expedition. *Arrieros* and mules can be hired in Tinqui. A recommended *arriero* is Enrique Mandura, who also rents out equipment. Make sure you sign a contract with full details. Buy all food supplies in Cusco. Maps are available at the Instituto Geográfico Militar in Lima or South American Explorers (who can supply all the latest advice). Some tour companies in Cusco have details about the hike (for example *Luzma Tours*). The three Cayetano brothers in Cusco have been recommended as reliable sources of trekking and climbing information, for arranging trips and for being very safety-conscious, F227768.

Southeast from Urcos

Southeast from Urcos, the main road passes through **Cusipata**, with an Inca gate and wall. Here the ornate bands for the decoration of ponchos are woven. Close by is the Huari hilltop ruin of Llallanmarca.

Acomayo

Between Cusipata and Checacupe a road branches west up what soon becomes a dirt road. At the first fork, just before a beautiful mountain lake, turn right to travel past a small community and on to Acomayo, a pretty village which has a chapel with mural paintings of the 14 Incas. As mentioned above, this is best visited by four-wheel drive vehicle, although it is possible to travel by combi if you have more time. Giving locals a lift is both fun and helpful – they will make sure you take the right road. Alternatively, hire a vehicle with a driver. There are many places to camp wild by the lakes. Take warm clothing for night-time and plenty of water.

Sleeping Accommodation is available in ***Pensión Aguirre***.

Transport To get to Acomayo, take a Cusco-Sicuani bus or truck (US$1, 1½ hrs), then a truck or bus to Acomayo (three hours, same price). Alternatively, get off at Checacupe and take a truck on to Acomayo.

From Acomayo, you can walk to Huáscar, which takes one hour, and from there to Pajlia; a climb which leads through very impressive scenery. The canyons of the upper Apurímac are vast beyond imagination. Great cliffs drop thousands of metres into dizzying chasms and huge rocks balance menacingly overhead. The ruins of Huajra Pucará lie near Pajlia. They are small, but in an astonishing position.

South to Sicuani

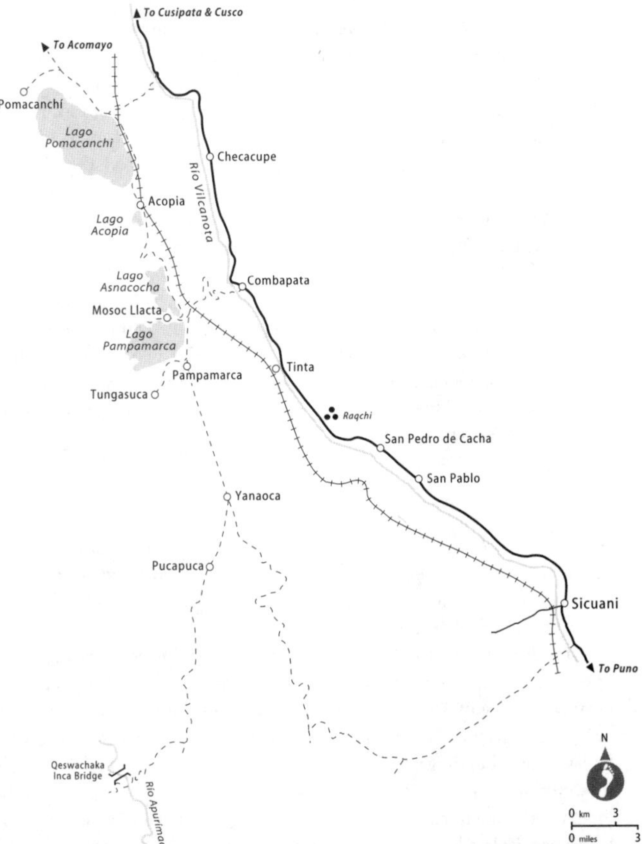

South & west of Cusco

Acomayo to the Inca bridge

From Acomayo, return down the same road, past the lake again until you reach the fork where you earlier turned right. Take a sharp right here to travel further along the lake. You will travel past three more beautiful lakes. If you become lost ask for Tungasuca via the *circuito de las quatro lagunas*. Stop awhile by the fourth. It is absolutely quiet here and a great place to recharge your soul. Set against the pale-green grass banks, serene waters reflect the red soil of the hills behind. The only sound is the occasional splash and hoot of a white-beaked Andean Coot. The air is thin, clear and crisp.

The road continues on to Yanaoca. From here it is possible to continue on to Sicuani, but a side trip to **Qeswachaka** and the **grass Inca bridge** 30km away is well worth the effort. Take a right just before you leave the village to join a road which, at times, is very rough. The way is marked with kilometre signs and you must turn right just after Km 22 where another road begins, marked with a Km 0. You will find steps down to the bridge shortly before Km 31, two bends from the bright orange road bridge.

The footbridge has been rebuilt every year for the past 400 years during a three-day festival. This starts on June 10 and is celebrated by the three communities who use the bridge. It is built entirely of *pajabrava* grass, woven and spliced to make six sturdy cables which are strung across the 15-m chasm. Look in the water at the far side and you will probably see the remains of the previous year´s effort; the work lasts five months, after which the fibres deteriorate and you should not attempt to cross.

The bridge can also be reached from Combapata on the main Cusco-Sicuani-Puno road. Combis and colectivos leave for the 30 km trip when full from the plaza for Yanaoca (US$0.50) where there are restaurants and basic accommodation. Then hitchhike either to Quehue (no accommodation), a 1½-hour walk from Qeswachaka, or to Qeswachaka itself, which is on the road to Livitaca. Be prepared for long waits on this road. On Wednesday and Saturday there are direct buses to Livitaca from Cusco with the *Warari* and *Olivares* companies which pass the site, returning on Monday and Thursday. There is good camping downstream, but take water.

Before Combapata is on the main road is **Checacupe** which has a fine church with good paintings and a handsome carved altar rail. **Tinta**, 23 km before Sicuani, has a church with brilliant gilded interior and an interesting choir vault. **G** *Casa Comunal*, offers dormitory accommodation, which is clean. Good food is served here. There are frequent buses and trucks to Cusco, or take the train from Cusco.

Raqchi

Colour map 2, grid B4

About 120 km southeast of Cusco in the province of Canchis, in a fertile tributary valley of the Vilcanota, is the colonial village of **San Pedro de Cacha**. Although unremarkable in itself, the village stands within one of the most important archaeological sites in Peru, Raqchi.

A few hundred metres beyond the village are the principal remains, the once great **Temple of Viracocha**, the pan-Andean god, creator of all living creatures. This is one of the only remaining examples of a two-storey building of Inca architecture. It was 90 m long and 15 m high and was probably the largest roofed building ever built by the Incas. Above walls of finely-dressed masonry 3-4 m high – stonework equal to that found in Cusco or Machu Picchu – rise the remains of another 5-6 m high wall of adobe brickwork of which only isolated sections remain. Similarly, of the 22 outer columns, which supported great sloping roofs, just one or two remain complete, the others being in various states of preservation. There are numerous other constructions, including *Acllahuasi* (houses of chosen women, spinners and weavers of ceremonial cloth), barracks, granaries, reservoirs, baths and fountains. The burial site includes round *chullpa* tombs of the sort found around Lake Titicaca. Much of it was damaged and demolished in search of treasure during or after the Spanish conquest. According to some accounts, the temple was built by Inca Viracocha in the late 14th century, but some chronicles attribute it to Pachacútec.

Archaeological research has shown that Raqchi was always a place associated with religious and ceremonial activity. This predates not only the Inca, but also the Canches (an ethnic group which flourished in the middle horizon of Tiahuanaco), who were conquered and incorporated into the Inca empire. Since Raqchi was the principal religious site of the Canches, it was natural that the Incas should dedicate their own temple on their allies' hallowed ground. Perhaps the most significant reason behind the choice of this as a sacred site is that Raqchi stands on the slopes of the only dormant volcano in the Cusco region, Kimsachata. The name in quechua means "three-cornered" or "triplets". Various myths of Viracocha's travels in the area tell of a hostile reception by local inhabitants resulting in their destruction by fire and brimstone invoked by Viracocha, others show him taming and overcoming a devastating eruption of Kimsachata.

On the volcano's slopes are pure water springs and sulphurous thermal springs, salt and rich clay deposits. These last provide the region's principal industry, pottery and ceramics (whence its other name, Raqchi, which in quechua is a large vessel or pot used in the preparation of chicha), as well as building materials such as tiles and particularly strong bricks.

■ *Entrance to the site is US$1.75. There is a basic shop at the site. The school next door greatly appreciates donations of books and materials.*

Local festivals

Raqchi is still a venue for ceremonial events. The *Wiracocha* festivities in San Pedro and neighbouring San Pablo start on 24 June. This date marks the dual Andean celebration of the ancient Inca festival of the sun (Inti Raymi) and the Christian feast day of San Juan Bautista, closely associated with water, streams and bathing, as well as being the patron saint of cattle and cattle breeders. It is the time of branding. On the eve of the fiesta, bonfires are lit across the Andes and fortunes are divined. Dancers come to Raqchi from all over Peru and through music and dance they illustrate everything from the ploughing of fields to bull fights. This leads into the feast of San Pedro and San Pablo on 29 June.

Sicuani

Phone code: 084
Colour map 2, grid B4
Altitude: 3,690 m

Sicuani, an important agricultural centre and an excellent place for items of llama and alpaca wool and skins. They are sold on the railway station and at the excellent Sunday morning market. The plaza is not as bad as the aberrations found in villages in the nearby mountains, but it is flanked along one entire side by a mirror-glass-fronted, purple-painted concrete monstrosity. On the other side are examples of what might have been much more appropriate olonial-style, balconied buildings. Around the plaza are several shops selling local hats.

The bus terminal is in the newer part of town, which is separated from the older part and the Plaza de Armas by a pedestrian walkway and bridge. At the ´new' end of the bridge, but also close to the centre of town, are several *hostales* advertising hot water and private bathrooms. *Banco de la Nación* has a branch on the plaza as does *Banco de Crédito*, but the one cash machine takes only local cards.

Sleeping **D** *Centro Vacacional* is the best in town but some way from the centre. Recommended. **E** ***Royal Inti***, Av Centenario 116, T352730, on the west side of the old pedestrian bridge across the river is modern, clean and friendly. **E** ***Hotel Obada***, Jr Tacna 104, T351214, has seen better days. There are large, clean rooms with hot showers. **E** ***Tairo***, Mejía 120, T351297. A modern hotel, but noisy. **E** ***Samariy***, Av Centenario 138 (next to *Royal Inti*), T352518. Good value rooms with bathroom. **F** ***Manzanal***, Av 28 de Julio 416. Basic and noisy with cold showers. **G** ***Hostal Obada***, 2 de Mayo, close to hotel of the same name. Basic dormitory accommodation with separate bathrooms. **G** ***Grau***, Jr Grau 324. Another basic place. **G** per person ***José's Hostal***, Av Arequipa 143, T351254. Rooms with bath, clean and good.

Eating and entertainment *Pizzería Ban Vino*, 2 de Mayo 129, 2nd floor, off the east side of the plaza, is good for an Italian meal, while Viracocha, on the west side of the plaza, left of the concrete monstrosity is also OK. On C Zevallos, the main drag down from the plaza, there are many *pollerías*. A good one is ***El Fogón*** (smart, painted pink, on the left heading down), which serves up chicken and chips for US$1.70. There are also several *picanterías* such as ***Mijuna Wasi***, Jr Tacna 146 (closed Sun), which prepares typical dishes such as *adobo* served with huge glasses of *chicha* in a delapidated but atmospheric courtyard. Recommended. On 2 de Mayo, running northeast from the plaza, there are several cafés which are good for snacks and breakfasts. ***Piano Bar***, just off the first block of 2 de Mayo, is the best nightspot in town.

Transport Sicuani lies 137 km from Cusco (bus, US$1.25) and 250 km from Puno. 38 km beyond the town is La Raya pass (4,321 m), the highest on this route, which marks the divide between Cusco Department and the altiplano which stretches Lake Titicaca.It is impossible to buy unleaded petrol in this town.

West of Cusco

Until fairly recently, this route was off limits to travellers because of terrorism and lawlessness, but order has been restored and safety more-or-less assured

West from Cusco is the road to the city of Ayacucho in the Central Highlands. Branching off this road at the town of Abancay (195 km from Cusco) is the principal overland route to Lima, via Nasca (of the famous Lines) and the coastal city of Pisco (from near where the famous booze of the same name comes). There are enough Inca sites on or near this road in the Department of Cusco, similarly to the south of the city, to remind us that the empire's influence spread to all four cardinal points. Add to this some magnificent scenery, especially in the canyon of the Apurímac river, and you have the makings of some fascinating excursions away from the centre. One, to the ruins of Choquequirao, is a tough but rewarding trip.

The Cusco-Machu Picchu train follows the road west from the city through the Anta canyon for 10 km, and then, at a sharp angle, the Urubamba canyon, and descends along the river valley, flanked by high cliffs and peaks. In the town of **Anta** felt trilby hats are on sale. There is lodging at **G** *Hostal Central*, Jirón Jaquijahuanca 714, a basic, friendly, place with motorbike parking; beware water shortages. The restaurant *Tres de Mayo* is very good and popular, with top service. The bus fare to Anta from Cusco is US$0.30.

Tarahuasi
Colour map 2, grid B2

Some 76 km from Cusco, beyond Anta, on the Abancay road, 2 km before Limatambo at the ruins of Tarahuasi, a few hundred metres from the road, is a very well-preserved Inca temple platform, with 28 tall niches, and a long stretch of fine polygonal masonry. The ruins are impressive, enhanced by the orange lichen which give the walls a beautiful honey colour. Near here the

Spanish *conquistadores* on their push towards the Inca capital of Cusco suffered what could have been a major setback. Having crossed the Río Apurímac, the expeditionary force under the command of Hernando de Soto encountered an Inca army at Vilcaconga. On the first day of the battle, de Soto's men were almost routed, although only five were killed, but in the night reinforcements led by Almagro arrived. The following morning the Incas were demoralised to see a larger force than the one they had defeated the day before and, after renewed fighting, left the field to the Spaniards.

There is accommodation in Limatambo at **G** *Hostal Rivera*, near the river, an old stone house built round a courtyard, clean, quiet and full of character. There is also a nice restaurant hidden from the road by trees.

One hundred kilometres from Cusco along the Abancay road is the exciting descent into the Apurímac canyon, near the former Inca suspension bridge that inspired Thornton Wilder's *The Bridge of San Luis Rey* (see **Further reading**, page 64). The bridge itself was made of rope and was where the royal Inca road crossed the river. When the *conquistadores* reached this point on the march to Cusco, they found the bridge destroyed. But luck was again on their side since, it being the dry season, the normally fierce Apurímac was low enough for the men and horses to ford. In colonial times the bridge was rebuilt several times, but it no longer exists. Thornton Wilder (1897-1975), whose novel won the 1928 Pulitzer prize, uses an episode in the bridge's history to meditate upon individual destiny. On 20 July 1714, five travellers are on the bridge when its ropes snap and it plummets into the river. A monk, Brother Juniper, witnesses their death and investigates the lives of each, trying to understand the role of divine providence in their demise. Three of the characters are fictional, but the other two are the son and teacher of La Perricholi, the most famous actress in Peru at the time and one-time mistress of the Viceroy Amat. For his efforts, and for his questioning of God's purpose, Juniper's book is declared heretical by the Inquisition and both book and author are burned at the stake.

Curahuasi & Saihuite

Also along the road to Abancay from Cusco, near Curahuasi (126 km from Cusco), famous for its anise herb, is the stone of **Saihuite**, carved with animals, houses, etc, which appears to be a relief map of an Indian village. Unfortunately, 'treasure hunters' have defaced the stone. There are other interesting carvings in the area around the Saihuite stone. Entry is US$1.45.

Sleeping and eating In Curahuasi **G** ***Hostal San Cristóbal***, clean, nice decor, pleasant courtyard, shared bath with cold shower (new bathroom block under construction). Camping is possible on the football pitch, but ask the police for permission. The best restaurant in town is ***La Amistad***, popular, with good food and moderate prices, but poor service.

Choquequirao

Colour map 2, grid B2

Choquequirao is another 'lost city of the Incas', built on a ridge spur almost 1,800 m above the Apurímac. Its Inca name is unknown, but research has shown that it was built during the reign of Inca Pachacútec. Although only 30% has been uncovered, it is reckoned to be a larger site than Machu Picchu, but with fewer buildings. The stonework is different from the classic Inca construction and masonry, simply because the preferred granite and andesite is not found in this region.

A number of high profile explorers and archaeologists, including Hiram Bingham, researched the site, but its importance has only recently been recognised. And now tourists are venturing in there, too. With new regulations being applied to cut congestion on the Inca Trail, Choquequirao is destined to replace the traditional hike as the serious trekker's alternative and Cusco tour companies are offering this adventure.

Peter Frost in *Exploring Cusco* describes it thus: "Its utterly spectacular location...reminds one of Machu Picchu itself. The buildings around its central plaza represent extremely fine ceremonial and high-status residential architecture. There is a chain of ritual baths, an enormous, curving bank of fine terraces, numerous intriguing outlier groups of buildings – a large group of buildings whose existence was hitherto unsuspected was discovered buried in forest on a ridge spur below the main site during the 1990s – and a vast area of irrigated terracing on a nearby mountain slope, evidently designed to feed the local population. In short, a huge investment of time and energy; another large, mysterious, remote ceremonial center that nobody in their right mind would build, but the Incas did."

There are three ways in to Choquequirao. None is a gentle stroll. The shortest way is from **Cachora**, a village on the south side of the Apurímac, reached by a side road from the Cusco-Abancay highway, shortly after Saihuite. It is four hours by bus from Cusco to the turn-off, then a three-hour descent from the road to Cachora (from 3,695 m to 2,875 m). Buses run from Abancay to Cachora, but there is none arriving after 1100. Accommodation (eg *Hospedaje Judith Catherine*, T320202, **G** per bed), guides (Celestino Peña is the official guide) and mules are available in Cachora. From the village you need a day to descend to the Río Apurímac on a newly-made trail. You can camp in the canyon by the suspension bridge across the river (take insect repellent). It then takes seven hours to climb up to Choquequirao. Allow 1-2 days at the site then return the way you came.

The second and third routes take a minimum of eight days and require thorough preparation. You can start at Huancacalle (see page 175) and cross the watershed of the Cordillera Vilcabamba between the Urubamba and Apurímac rivers. The pass of Choquetacarpo is 4,600 m high. You reach Choquequirao on the sixth day. Alternatively start the hike at Santa Teresa, between Machu Picchu and Chaullay and pick up the second route at the village of Yanama, one of the most remote in the area. Both routes pass the mines of La Victoria and both involve an incredible number of strenuous ascents and descents. In each case you end the trail at Cachora. En route you are rewarded with fabulous views of the Pumasillo massif, Salkantay, other snow peaks, and the deep canyons of the Río Blanco and the Apurímac. You will also see condors and meet very friendly people, but the highlight is Choquequirao itself. It is possible to start either of these long hikes at Cachora, continuing even from Choquequirao to Espíritu Pampa.

The Southern Jungle

The Southern Jungle

The immense Amazon Basin covers a staggering four million square kilometres, an area roughly equivalent to three quarters the size of the United States. But despite the fact that 60% of Peru is covered by this green carpet of jungle, less than 6% of its population lives there. This lack of integration with the rest of the country makes it difficult to get around easily but does mean that much of Peru's rainforest is still intact. The Peruvian jungles are home to a diversity of life unequalled anywhere on Earth, and it is this great diversity which makes the Amazon basin a paradise for nature lovers, be they scientists or simply curious amateurs.Overall, Peru's jungle lowlands contain some 10 million living species, including 2,000 species of fish and 300 mammals. They also contain over 10 % of the world's 8,600 bird species and, together with the adjacent Andean foothills, 4,000 butterfly species.

The southern part of Peru's Amazon jungle contains the **Manu National Biosphere Reserve** *(1,881,000 ha), the* **Tambopata Nature Reserve** *(254,358 ha) and the* **Bahuaja-Sonene National Park** *(1,091,416 ha); three great protected areas in the Department of Madre de Dios, which adjoins the eastern edge of the Department of Cusco and extends to the borders of Brazil and Bolivia.*

Things to do in the southern jungle

- Make sure you get to visit a *collpa* (macaw lick) to see the multitude of macaws and parrots getting their essential minerals.
- Take a trip on one of the many ox-bow lakes, where you may catch a glimpse of giant otters.
- Learn about the fiercesome fire ants, the even scarier bullet ant and sample some juicy jungle grub!
- Conduct the dawn chorus in the forest canopy and listen to the monkeys going about their business.
- Take time to appreciate that memorable first sight from the plane of the size and flatness of the forest as you leave the mountains behind.
- When the day is done, you've had your cold shower and eaten by the light of an oil lamp, go outside and marvel at the night sky with its shooting stars and the fireflies in the bushes . But be careful – it's a jungle out there.
- Take a bath in the river – if you dare – with the piranhas, electric eels, stingrays and watching caiman.

Ins and outs

Getting there The frontier town of Puerto Maldonado is the starting point for expeditions to Tambopata-Candamo and is only a 30-min flight from Cusco (see page 211). Cusco is also the starting point for trips to Manu (see 205).

Climate The climate is warm and humid, with a rainy season from Nov to Mar and a dry season from Apr to Oct. Cold fronts from the South Atlantic, called *friajes*, are characteristic of the dry season, when temperatures drop to 15-16°C during the day, and 13° at night. The best time to visit is in the dry season from May to the end of Nov, when there are fewer mosquitoes and the rivers are low, exposing the beaches. But trips can also be planned during the rainy season, especially for lodge-based trips. The dry season is also a good time to see birds nesting and to view the animals at close range, as they stay close to the rivers and are easily seen. A pair of binoculars is essential for wildlife viewing and insect repellent is a must.

Background

The forest of this lowland region is technically called Sub-tropical Moist Forest, which means that it receives less rainfall than tropical forest and is dominated by the floodplains of its meandering rivers. One of most striking features is the former river channels that have become isolated as ox-bow lakes (*cochas*). These are home to black caiman and giant otter and a host of other living organisms. Other rare species living in the forest are jaguar, puma, ocelot and tapir. There are also capybara, thirteen species of primate and many hundreds of bird species. If you include the cloud forests and highlands of the Manu Biosphere reserve, the bird count almost totals 1,000.

As well as containing some of the most important flora and fauna on Earth, however, the region also harbours gold-diggers, loggers and hunters. For years, logging, gold prospecting and the search for oil and gas have endangered the unique rainforest. Fortunately, though, the destructive effect of such groups has been limited by the various conservation groups working to protect it.This incredible biological diversity, however, brings with it an acute ecological fragility. Ecologists consider the Amazon rainforest as the lungs of the earth – the Amazon Basin produces 20% of the Earth's oxygen – and any fundamental change in its constitution, or indeed its disappearance, could have disastrous effects for our future on this planet.

The relative proximity to Cusco of Manu in particular has made it one of the prime nature watching destinations in South America. Despite its reputation, Manu is heavily protected, with visitor numbers limited and a large percentage of the park inaccessible to tourists. Nevertheless, there is no need to worry that this level of management is going to diminish your pleasure. There is more than enough in the way of birds, animals and plants to satisfy the most ardent wildlife enthusiast. Tambopata does have a town in the vicinity, Puerto Maldonado, and the area was under threat from exploitation and settlement. The suspension of oil exploration in 2000 led to a change of status for a large tract of this area, giving immediate protection to another of Peru's zones of record-breaking diversity.

Manu Biosphere Reserve

The Manu Biosphere Reserve covers an area of 1,881,000 ha (almost half the size of Switzerland) and is one of the largest conservation units on Earth, encompassing the complete drainage of the Manu river, with an altitudinal range from 200 to 4,100 m above sea-level. No other rainforest can compare with Manu for the diversity of life forms. The reserve is one of the great bird-watching spots of the world; a magical animal kingdom which offers the best chance of seeing giant otters, jaguars, ocelots and several of the 13 species of primates which abound in this pristine tropical wilderness. The more remote areas of the reserve are home to uncontacted indigenous tribes and many other indigenous groups with very little knowledge of the outside world.

Colour map 2, grid A3/4

Ins and outs

Getting there

By air There is an airstrip at **Boca Manu**, but no regular flights from Cusco. These are arranged the day before, if there are enough passengers. Contact ***Air Atlantic***, at Maruri 228, oficina 208, Cusco, T245440; ***Trans Andes*** in the Cusco airport T/F224638 and ***Manu Servicios*** in the Cusco airport T/F242104, or check with the tour operators in Cusco (see page 115).

For a detailed description of the overland route, see next page

By road Trucks leave every Mon, Wed and Fri from the Coliseo Cerrado in Cusco at about 1000 (be there by 0800) to **Pilcopata** and **Shintuya** (passing Atalaya). The journey takes at least 48 hrs and is rough and uncomfortable. They return the following day, but there is no service on Sun. There is also a bus service which leaves from the same place to **Pilcopata**, on Mon and Fri and returns on Tue and Sat. The journey takes 12 hrs in the dry season and costs US$8-10. From Pilcopata there are trucks to Atalaya (1 hr, US$8) and Shintuya (3 hrs, US$10). Trucks leave in the morning between 0600 and 0900. Make sure you go with a recommended truck driver. Only basic supplies are

Manu Biosphere Reserve

The Southern jungle

available after leaving Cusco, so take all your camping and food essentials, including insect repellent. Transport can be disrupted in the wet season because the road is in poor condition (tour companies have latest details). Tour companies usually use their own vehicles for the overland trip from Cusco to Manu.

Reserve information

The Biosphere Reserve comprises the **Manu National Park** (1,532,000 ha), where only government sponsored biologist and anthropologists may visit with permits from the Ministry of Agriculture in Lima, the **Manu Reserved Zone** (257,000 ha), which is set aside for applied scientific research and ecotourism, and the **Multiple Use Zone** (92,000 ha), which contains acculturated native groups and colonists, where the locals still employ their traditional way of life. Among the ethnic groups in the Multiple Use Zone are the Harakmbut, Machiguenga and Yine in the Amarakaeri Reserved Zone, on the east bank of the Alto Madre de Dios. They have set up their own ecotourism activities, which are entirely managed by indigenous people. Associated with Manu are other areas protected by conservation groups, or local people (for example the Blanquillo reserved zone) and some cloud forest parcels along the road. The **Nahua-Kugapakori Reserved Zone**, set aside for these two nomadic native groups, is the area between the headwaters of the Río Manu and headwaters of the Río Urubamba, to the north of the alto Madre de Dios

The Multiple Use Zone is accessible to anyone and several lodges exist in the area (see page 211). It is possible to visit these lodges under your own steam. The Reserved Zone of the Manu Biosphere Reserve is accessible by permit only. Entry is strictly controlled and visitors must visit the area under the auspices of an authorized operator with an authorized guide. Permits are limited and reservations should be made well in advance, though it is possible to book a place on a trip at the last minute in Cusco. In the Reserved Zone of the Manu Biosphere Reserve there are two lodges, the rustic *Casa Machiguenga* (see page 211) run by the Machiguenga communities of Tayakome and Yomibato with the help of a German NGO and the upmarket *Manu Lodge* (see page 211). In the Cocha Salvador area, several companies have tented safari camp infrastructures, some with shower and dining facilities, but all visitors sleep in tents. Some companies have installed walk-in tents with cots and bedding.

The road to Manu

The arduous trip over the Andes from Cusco to the end of the road at Shintuya takes about 16-18 hours by local truck (20-40 hours in the wet season). It is long and uncomfortable, but, throughout, the scenery is magnificent.

From Cusco you climb up to the Huancarani pass before **Paucartambo** (3½ hours), before dropping down to this picturesque mountain village in the Mapacho Valley (for details of accommodation etc in Paucartambo, see page 189). You can make detour to Tres Cruces, 44 km from Paucartambo, for a great view of the sunrise over the Amazon. The road then ascends to the Ajcanacu pass (cold at night), after which it goes down to the cloud forest and then the rainforest, reaching **Pilcopata** at 650 m (11 hours). One hour more and you are in Atalaya, which is the jumpoff point for river trips further into the Manu. On the way, you pass *Manu Cloudforest Lodge* and *Cock of the Rock Lodge* (see page 211).

Sleeping There are 3 basic *hostales* in Pilcopata: **F** per person ***Gallito de las Rocas*** is opposite the police checkpoint and is clean. The unnamed place of Sra Rubella is very basic, but friendly. **F *Albergue Eco Turístico Villa Carmen*** is new, but no details were available when going to press. A good restaurant is ***Las Palmeras***.

After Pilcopata, the route is hair-raising and breath-taking, passing through **Atalaya**, the first village on the Alto Madre de Dios river, which consists of a few houses. Basic accommodation can be found here. Even in the dry season this part of the road is appalling and trucks often get stuck. In Atalaya, meals are available at the family of Rosa and Klaus (very friendly people), where you can camp. Boats are available here to take you across the river to *Amazonia Lodge* (see page 211). The route continues to **Salvación**, where a Manu Park Office is situated. There are basic hostels and restaurants.

Shintuya

You can't arrange trips to the Reserved Zone from here; all arrangements must be made in Cusco

The end of the road is Shintuya, the starting point for river transport. It is a commercial and social centre, as wood from the jungle is transported from here to Cusco. There are a few basic restaurants and you can camp (beware of thieves). The priest will let you stay in the dormitory rooms at the mission. Supplies are expensive. There are two Shintuyas: one is the port and mission and the other is the native village. You can find a boat in the native village; ask for Diego Ruben Sonque or Miguel Visse.

Boca Colorado

From Shintuya infrequent cargo boats sail downriver to the gold mining centre of Boca Colorado on the Río Madre de Dios, via Boca Manu, and passing *Pantiacolla Lodge* and *Manu Wildlife Centre* (see page 211). The trip takes around nine hours, and costs US$15. Very basic accommodation can be found here, but it is not recommended for lone women travellers. To Boca Manu is three to four hours, US$12. From Colorado there are plenty of boats to **Laberinto** (six to seven hours, US$20). From here there are regular combis to **Puerto Maldonado** (see page 211), 1½ hours.

Boca Manu

Colour map 2, grid A4

Boca Manu is the connecting point between the rivers Alto Madre de Dios, Manu and Madre de Dios. It has a few houses, an air strip and some well-stocked shops. There is a comfortable lodge here, opposite the Boca Manu airstrip, run by Sr Carpio. It is also the entrance to the Manu Reserve and to go further you must be part of an organized group. The entrance fee to the Reserved Zone is 150 soles per person (about US$42-43) and is included in package tour prices. The Park ranger station is located in **Limonal**, 20 minutes by boat from Boca Manu. You need to show your permit here and camping is allowed here if you have a permit.

To the Reserved Zone

Upstream on the Río Manu you pass the *Manu Lodge* (see page 211), on the Cocha Juárez, 3-4 hours by boat. You can continue to Cocha Otorongo, 2 ½ hours and Cocha Salvador, 30 minutes, the biggest lake with plenty of wildlife where the *Casa Machiguenga Lodge* is located and several companies have safari camp concessions. From here it is two hours to **Pakitza**, the entrance to the National Park Zone. This is only for biologists with a special permit.

Between Boca Manu and Colorado is **Blanquillo**, a private reserve (10,000 ha). Bring a good tent with you and all food if you want to camp and do it yourself, or alternatively accommodation is available at the *Tambo Blanquillo* (full board or accommodation only). Wildlife is abundant, especially macaws and parrots at the macaw lick near *Manu Wildlife Centre* (see page 211). There are occasional boats to Blanquillo from Shintuya; US$10, 6-8 hours.

Birdwatching in Manu

This is the best site for the birder who craves the rare and the mysterious

Much of the Manu Biosphere Reserve is completely unexplored and the variety of birds is astounding: about 1,000 species, significantly more than the whole of Costa Rica and over one tenth of all the birds on earth. Although there are other places in the Manu area where you can see all the Manu bird specialities and an astonishing variety of other wildlife, the single best place for the visiting birder is the *Manu Wildlife Centre*.

A typical trip starts in Cusco and takes in the wetlands of Huacarpay Lakes (to the south of the city) where a variety of Andean waterfowl and marsh birds can be seen. Here, the endemic and beautiful bearded mountaineer hummingbird can be seen feeding on tree tobacco. Then the route proceeds to the cloud forest of the eastern slopes of the Andes. Driving slowly down the road through the cloud forest, every 500 m loss in elevation produces new birds. This is the home of the Andean cock-of-the-rock and a visit to one of their leks (they are common here) is one of the world's top ornithological experiences. These humid montane forests are home to a mind-boggling variety of multi-coloured birds and a mixed flock of tanagers, honeycreepers, and conebills turns any tree into a Christmas Tree! There are two species of quetzal here, too.

Levelling out onto the last forested foothills of the Andes, the upper tropical zone is then reached. This is a forest habitat that in many parts of South America has disappeared and been replaced by tea, coffee and coca plantations. In Manu, the forest is intact, and special birds such as Amazonian umbrellabird and blue-headed and military macaws can be found.

A good place to be based for upper tropical birding and an introduction to lowland Amazon species is the *Amazonia Lodge* (see next page), on the Río Alto Madre de Dios. From here on, transport is by river and the beaches are packed with nesting birds in the dry season. Large-billed terns scream at passing boats and Orinoco geese watch warily from the shore. Colonies of hundreds of sand-coloured nighthawks roost and nest on the hot sand.

As you leave the foothills behind and head into the untouched forests of the western Amazon, you are entering forest with the highest density of birdlife per square km on earth. Sometimes it seems as if there are fewer birds than in an English woodland; only strange calls betray their presence. Then a mixed flock comes through, containing maybe 70-plus species, or a brightly coloured group of, say, rock parakeets dashes out of a fruiting tree.

This forest has produced the highest day-list ever recorded anywhere on earth and it holds such little-seen gems as black-faced cotinga and rufous-fronted ant-thrush. Antbirds and ovenbirds creep in the foliage and give tantalizing glimpses until, eventually, they reveal themselves in a shaft of sunlight. Woodcreepers and woodpeckers climb tree-trunks and multicoloured tanagers move through the rainforest canopy. To get to this forest is difficult and not cheap, but the experience is well worth it.

The best place for lowland birding is the *Manu Wildlife Centre*, which is located close to a large macaw lick and to ox-bow lakes crammed with birds. This area has more forest types and micro-habitats than any other rainforest lodge in Peru, and it has recorded an amazing 560 species of birds and boasts a walk-up canopy tower where rainforest canopy species can be seen with ease.

A trip to Manu is one of the ultimate birding experiences and topping it off with a macaw lick is a great way to finish; hundreds of brightly coloured macaws and other parrots congregate to eat the clay essential to their digestion in one of the world's great wildlife spectacles.

Recommended reading *Birds of Colombia* by Steve Hilty, *South American Birds*, by John Dunning, *Birds of South America*, volumes 1 and 2, by Ridgeley and Tudor, and the recently-published *Birds of Ecuador* by Ridgeley and Greenfield give the best coverage of birds of Peru. Also *Neotropical Rainforest Mammals, A field guide*, by Louise H Emmons. *Tropical Nature*, by Adrian Forsyth and Ken Miyata, gives an explanation of the rainforest. *Manu National Park*, by Kim MacQuarrie and André and Cornelia Bartschi, is a large, expensive and excellent book, with beautiful photographs. *Madre de Dios Packet*, by South American Explorers, gives practical travel advice for the area. *The Ecology of Tropical Rainforests* (to be republished 2002), *Tambopata – A Bird Checklist*, *Tambopata – Mammal, Amphibian & Reptile Checklist* and *Reporte Tambopata* are all published by TReeS (see page 215 for address); they also produce CDs, tapes, *Jungle Sounds* and *Birds of Southeast Peru*.

Tours to Manu

A full list of the authorized travel agents who operate in Manu is given under Cusco, page 122

There are about 15 authorized agencies in Cusco offering tours to Manu. Prices vary considerably, from as little as US$600 per person for a six-day tour up to US$1,000-1,500 per person with the more experienced and reputable companies. The cheaper tours usually travel overland there and back, which takes at least three full days (in the dry season), meaning you'll spend much of your time on a bus or truck and will end up exhausted. Another important factor to consider is whether or not your boat has a canopy, as it can be very uncomfortable sitting in direct sunlight or rain for hours on end. Also the quality of guides varies a lot – you might want to meet your guide before deciding on a trip if you are in Cusco. Beware of pirate operators on the streets of Cusco who offer trips to the Reserved Zone of Manu and end up halfway through the trip changing the route 'due to emergencies', which, in reality means they have no permits to operate in the area. For a full list of all companies who are allowed access to the Reserved Zone, contact the Manu National Park office (address below). You can only enter the Reserved Zone with a recognized guide who is affiliated to an authorized tour company. Take finely-woven, long-sleeved and long-legged clothing and effective insect repellent. Note that for independent travellers, only the Multiple Use Zone is an option. Lodge reservations should be made at the relevant offices in Cusco as these lodges are often not set up to receive visitors without prior notice.

Eco-tour Manu, a non-profit making organization made up of tour operators, assures quality of service and actively supports conservation projects in the area. When you travel with an Eco-tour member you are ensuring that you support tropical rainforest conservation projects. Eco-tour Manu comprises *Manu Expeditions*, *Manu Nature Tours*, *Pantiacolla Tours*, *InkaNatura Travel*, *Aventuras Ecológicas Manu* and *Expedicones Vilca*. Contact any member company for information.

Useful addresses In Lima: ***Asociación Peruana para la Conservación de la Naturaleza*** (Apeco), Parque José Acosta 187, 2nd floor, Magdalena del Mar. ***Pronaturaleza***, Av de los Rosales 255, San Isidro, www.pronaturaleza.com.pe **In Cusco:** ***Asociación para la Conservación de la Selva Sur*** (ACSS), Ricaldo Palma J-1, Santa Mónica (same office as *Peru Verde*), T243408, F226392, acss@telser.com.pe A local NGO that can help with information and has free video shows about Manu National Park and Tambopata-Candamo Reserve. They are friendly and helpful and also have information on programmes and research in the jungle area of Madre de Dios. Further information can be obtained from the ***Manu National Park Office:*** Av Micaela Bastidas 310, Cusco, T240898, pqnmanu@cosapidata.mail.com.pe Casilla Postal 591. Open 0800-1400. They issue a permit for the Reserved Zone (see above under Boca Manu for the cost).

Lodges in Manu
For lodge prices, *see page 122*

Manu Cloud Forest Lodge, located at Unión at 1,800 m on the road from Paucartambo to Atalaya, owned by *Manu Nature Tours*, 6 rooms with 4 beds. ***Cock of the Rock Lodge***, on the same road at 1,500 m, next to a Cock of the Rock *lek*, double rooms with shared bath and 7 private cabins with en-suite bath, run by the ACSS group (see above). ***Amazonia Lodge***, on the Río Alto Madre de Dios just across the river from Atalaya, an old tea hacienda run by the Yabar family, famous for its bird diversity and fine hospitality, a great place to relax, contact Santiago in advance and he'll arrange a pick-up. In Cusco at Matará 334, T/F231370, amazonia1@correo.dnet.com.pe ***Pantiacolla Lodge***, 30 mins down-river from Shintuya. Owned by the Moscoso family. Book through *Pantiacolla Tours*. ***Manu Lodge***, situated on the Manu river, 3 hrs upriver from Boca Manu towards Cocha Salvador, run by *Manu Nature Tours* and only bookable as part of a full package deal with transport. ***Manu Wildlife Centre***, 2 hrs down the Río Madre de Dios from Boca Manu, near the Blanquillo macaw lick and also counts on a Tapir lick and walk-up canopy tower. Book through *Manu Expeditions* or *InkaNatura*. 22 double cabins, all with private bathroom and hot water. Also canopy towers for birdwatchinge Birdwatching above). ***Erika Lodge***, on the Alto Madre de Dios, 25 mins from Atalaya, is a biological station used by Pronaturaleza (see above), which now accepts a small number of visitors. It offers basic accommodation and is cheaper than the other, more luxurious lodges. Contact ***Aventuras Ecológicas Manu***, Plateros 356, Cusco; or Ernesto Yallico, Casilla 560, Cusco, T227765. ***Casa Machiguenga***, near Cocha Salvador, upriver from *Manu Lodge*. Machiguenga-style cabins run by local communities with NGO help. Contact Manu Expeditions or the Apeco NGO, T225595. ***Boca Manu Lodge*** (see above), run by long-standing Manu resident Juan de Dios Carpio.

Puerto Maldonado

Colour map 2, grid A6

Puerto Maldonado is the capital of the Department of Madre de Dios. Overlooking the confluence of the rivers Tambopata and Madre de Dios, it is a major logging and brazil-nut processing centre. It is also an important starting point for visiting the rainforest. Nothing much happens here, it's a hot, humid and sleepy place, disturbed only by the fleeting visit of tourists heading to or from the jungle lodges.

Ins and outs

Getting there
The vast majority of people fly

By air To/from **Lima**, daily with ***Tans*** at 1130 via Cusco. ***Aero Continente*** flies to **Cusco** Tue, Thu, Sat and Sun at 1030 (see under Cusco for fares). ***Aeroregional*** also have a daily flight to Lima via Cusco. ***Grupo Ocho*** sometimes flies to Cusco and to Iberia; the office is at the airport. A moto-taxi from town to the airport is US$1.50. A yellow fever vaccination is offered free at the airport on arrival, but check that a new needle is used.

By river To **Boca Manu and Shintuya**, via Colorado. Take a combi to Laberinto (see next page) and take a cargo boat from there to Colorado; several daily, US$12. You can get a daily cargo boat from there to Boca Manu and Shintuya, 9-10 hrs, US$15. From Shintuya trucks go to Pilcopata and Cusco (see above under Manu).

To **Puerto Heath** (Bolivian border), it can take several days to find a boat going all the way to the Bolivian border. Motorized dugout canoes go to Puerto Pardo on the Peruvian side, 5 hrs, US$4.50 per person (no hotels or shops); wait here for a canoe to Puerto Heath. It is fairly hard to get a boat from the border to Riberalta (a wait of up to 3 days is not uncommon), US$15-20. Alternatively, travel to the naval base at América, then fly.

The road from the cold of the high Andes to the steamy heat of the Amazon jungle can only be described as a challenge

By road From Cusco take a bus to Urcos; 1 hr, US$2.25 (see also page 193). Trucks leave from here for **Mazuko** around 1500-1600, arriving around 2400 the next day; 33 hrs, US$6.65. Catch a truck early in the morning from here for Puerto Maldonado, US$4.50, 13-14 hrs. It's a painfully slow journey on an appalling road. Trucks frequently get stuck or break down. The road passes through Ocongate and Marcapata, where there are hot thermal springs, before reaching **Quincemil**, 240 km from Urcos (15-20 hrs), a centre for alluvial gold-mining with many banks. Accommodation is available in **F** ***Hotel Toni***, friendly, clean, cold shower, good meals. Ask the food-carriers to take you to visit the miners washing for gold in the nearby rivers. Quincemil marks the half-way point and the start of the all-weather road. Gasoline is scarce in Quincemil because most road vehicles continue on 70 km to Mazuko, which is another mining centre, where they fill up with the cheaper gasoline of the jungle region.

The journey takes up to 50-55 hrs in total. The road is 99 km unpaved and the journey is very rough, but the changing scenery is magnificent and worth the hardship and discomfort. This road is impossible in the wet season. Make sure you have warm clothing for travelling through the Sierra. The trucks only stop four times each day, for meals and a short sleeping period for the driver. You should take a mosquito net, repellent, sunglasses, sunscreen, a plastic sheet, a blanket, food and water.

An alternative route from Cusco goes via Paucartambo, Pilcopata and Shintuya, and from there by boat to Puerto Maldonado (see above under Manu Biosphere Reserve).

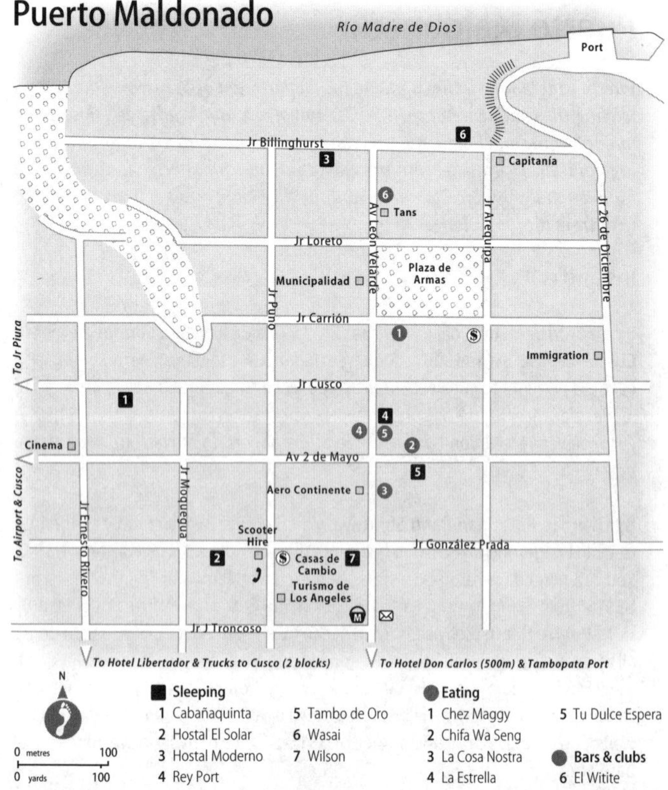

Getting around

Scooters and mopeds can de hired from ***Oconita***, on the corner of Puno and G Prada for US$1 per hr or US$10 per day. No deposit is required but your passport and driving licence need to be shown.

Trips from Puerto Maldonado

Lago Sandoval

There are 2 jungle lodges at the lake (see page 215)

The beautiful and tranquil lake is a one hour boat ride along the Río Madre de Dios, and then a 5-km walk into the jungle. It is possible to see giant river otters early in the morning and several species of monkeys, macaws and hoatzin. At weekends, especially on Sundays, the lake gets quite busy. Boats can be hired at the port for about US$20 a day – plus petrol – to go to Lago Sandoval, but don't pay the full cost in advance.

Upstream from Lago Sandoval, towards Puerto Maldonado, is the wreck of a boat that resembles the *Fitzcarrald*. The steamer lies a few metres from the Madre de Dios in the bed of a small stream. The German director, Werner Herzog, was inspired to make his famous film of the same name by the story of Fitzcarrald's attempt to haul a boat across the watershed from the Ucuyali to the Madre de Dios drainage basin (this happened in what is now the Manu National Park).

Other trips

For those interested in seeing a gold rush, a trip to the town of **Laberinto** is suggested. There is one hotel and several poor restaurants. Combis and trucks leave from Puerto Maldonado, 1½ hours, US$2.50, and returns in the afternoon daily. Boats leave from here to Manu (see previous page).

At Km 13 on the Cusco road is a pleasant recreational centre with a restaurant and natural pools where it's possible to swim. It gets busy at weekends. It's US$2 each way by *mototaxi* from town.

Trips can be made to **Lago Valencia**, 60 km away near the Bolivian border – four hours there, eight hours back. It is an ox-bow lake with lots of wildlife. Many excellent beaches and islands are located within an hour's boat ride. It is possible to stay overnight with local families.

Essentials

Sleeping

B *Wasai*, Billinghurst opposite the Capitanía, T572290, F571355, www.wasai.com (or Lima T/F01-436 8792). In a beautiful location overlooking the Madre de Dios river, with forest surrounding cabin-style rooms, which have a/c, TV and shower. There is a small pool with a waterfall and a good, if slightly expensive restaurant (local fish a speciality). Highly recommended. They can organize local tours and also have a lodge on the Tambopata river (see below).

C *Cabañaquinta*, Cusco 535, T571045, F571890. Rooms with bathroom and fan, very comfortable. The restaurant is good and there is a lovely garden. Airport transfer is arranged and the staff are friendly. Recommended. **C *Don Carlos***, Av León Velarde 1271, T571029, T/F571323. With a nice view over the Río Tambopata; rooms are air conditioned, with TV and phone, good. Restaurant.

D *Libertador*, Libertad 433, 10 mins from the centre, T573860. Comfortable lodging, with pool and garden. Good restaurant. Recommended. **D *Royal Inn***, Av 2 de Mayo 333, T571048. Modern and clean, the best of the mid-range hotels.

E *Hostal El Solar*, González Prada 445, T571571. Basic but clean, rooms have fan. **E** per person ***Hostal Iñapari***, 4 km from centre, 5 mins from the airport, T572575, F572155, joaquin@lullitec.com.pe Run by a Spanish couple, Isabel and Javier, the price includes breakfast and dinner, excellent food, very relaxing, friendly and clean. Recommended. **E *Rey Port***, Av León Velarde 457, T571177.

Room rate includes bath, clean, fan, good value, friendly. **E *Wilson***, Jr González Prada 355, T572838. Rooms with bath, clean, but basic.

F *Hostal Moderno*, Billinghurst 357, T571063. Brightly repainted, clean, quiet and friendly, the best of the cheaper hotels. **F *Tambo de Oro***, Av 2 de Mayo 277, T572057. Basic, but clean, water is available 24 hrs.

Eating The best restaurant in town is at the ***Hotel Wasai*** (see above). ***Chez Maggy***, on the plaza. Good pizzas served in a cosy atmosphere. This is a popular meeting place for travellers, conservationists and researchers. ***Chifa Wa Seng***, Av 2 de Mayo 353. Chinese food. ***La Estrella***, Av León Velarde 474. The smartest and best of the *pollos a la brasa* places. ***El Joselito***, Av León Velarde 328, and ***El Califa***, Piura 266 (recommended) often have bushmeat, mashed banana and palm hearts on the menu. There are several cafés for snacks and cakes, such as ***La Cosa Nostra***, Av León Velarde 515, and ***Tu Dulce Espera***, Av León Velarde 469.

Bars & nightclubs ***El Witite***, Av León Velarde 153. A popular and good disco which plays mostly latin music and charges US$1.50 after 2300, open only Fri and Sat. ***El Che***, on the plaza. A popular pub. There is a billiard hall at Puno 520.

Shopping Artesanía Shabuya, Plaza de Armas 279, T571856. The best shop in town for handicrafts.

Tour operators Turismo de los Angeles, Jr Puno 657, T571070. Run trips to Lago Sandoval and Lago Valencia. ***Transtours***, G Prada 341, T572606. Reputable guides are Hernán Llave Cortez and Willy Wither, who can be contacted on arrival at the airport, if available. Also Javier Salazar of *Hostal Iñapari* is a reputable guide who specializes in trips up the remote Río Las Piedras.

The ***Guides Association*** is at Fitzcarrald 341, T571413. The usual price for trips to Lago Sandoval is US$25 per person per day (minimum of 2 people), and US$35 per person per day for longer trips lasting 2-4 days (minimum of 4-6 people). All guides should have a Ministry of Tourism carnet for Lake Sandoval, which also verifies them as suitable guides for trips to other places and confirms their identity. Ask to see the carnet. Boat hire can be arranged through the Capitán del Puerto (Río Madre de Dios), T573003.

Directory **Airline offices** *Aero Continente*, Av León Velarde 506, T573702, F573704. ***Tans***, Av León Velarde 160. ***Aeroregional***, Av León Velarde 525. **Banks** *Banco de Crédito*, cash advances with Visa, no commission on TCs. ***Banco de la Nación***, cash on Mastercard, quite good rates for TCs. The best rates for cash are at the *casas de cambio* on Puno 6th block, eg *Cárdenas Hnos*, Puno 605. **Communications** **Serpost:** at Av León Velarde 6th block. **Telefónica:** on Puno 7th block. **Embassies and consulates** **Bolivian Consulate:** on the north side of the plaza. **Peruvian immigration:** is at 26 de Diciembre 356, 1 block from the plaza, get your exit stamp here.

Tambopata Region

Colour map 2, grid A6

In Puerto Maldonado you can arrange a tour into the Tambopata region, located between the rivers Madre de Dios, Tambopata and Heath. The area is an excellent alternative for those who do not have the time to visit Manu. It is a close rival in terms of seeing wildlife and boasts some superb ox-bow lakes. There are a number of lodges here which are excellent for lowland rainforest birding. Explorers' Inn is perhaps the most famous, but the Tambopata Research Centre and Posadas Amazonas Lodge are also good.

Ins and outs

The **Tambopata-Candamo Reserveed Zone** (TCRZ) comprises the Nature Reserve (254,358 ha) and Buffer zones (262,315 ha). The fee to enter the TCRZ is US$2 per person, if staying at a lodge, or US$20 per person if camping overnight. Some of the lodges mentioned below also offer guiding and research placements to biology and environmental science graduates. For more details send an SAE to **Tambopata Reserve Society (TreeS)**: UK – J Forrest, PO Box 33153, London NW3 4DR. USA – W Widdowson, PO Box 5668, Eureka, CA 95502.

The **Bahuaja-Sonene National Park** runs from the Río Heath, which forms the Bolivian border, across to the Río Tambopata, 50-80 km upstream from Puerto Maldonado. It was expanded to 1,091,416 ha in August 2000. The Park is closed to visitors though those visiting the *collpa* (see below) on the Tambopata or river rafting down the Tambopata will travel through it.

Essentials

Jungle Lodges

Most of the lodges in the Tambopata area use the term 'ecotourism', or something similar, in their publicity material, but it is applied pretty loosely. *Posada Amazonas'* collaboration with the local community is unique in the area, but fortunately no lodge offers trips where guests hunt for their meals and only one or two may offer an inappropriate visit to a local community. See **Responsible tourism**, on page 34, for points to note.

AL *Sandoval Lodge*, 1 km beyond *Mejía* (see below) on Lago Sandoval, usually accessed by canoe across the lake after a 3-km walk or rickshaw ride along the trail, can accommodate 50 people in 25 rooms, huge bar and dining area, electricity, hot water. There is a short system of trails nearby, guides are available in several languages. Book through *InkaNatura*, Manuel Bañon 461, San Isidro, Lima, T440 20222 8114, F422 9225, T944 4272 (Mob; Rodrigo Custodio), www.inkanatura.com (also with offices in Cusco and the USA: 6B Pinecrest CT, Columbia, SC 29204, T1-877-827 8350 (toll free), or T/F803-933 0058, Eliana Espejo eliana@inkanatura.com; and 14503 NW 146th, PO Box

Tambopata-Candamo Reserved Zone & Bahuaja-Sonene National Park

1065, Alachua, FL 33616, T 1-877-888 1770 (toll free), or T904-418 4390, F904-418 4391, Elizabeth Sanders, liz@inkanatura.com). They also have a small lodge on the Río Heath consisting of 6 cabins which can accommodate 12 people. Each cabin has a toilet and hot and cold shower. Bird and mammal sighting prospects in the area along the Heath on the fringes of the only tropical grassland in Peru are good (this is a remote western extension of the Pantanal, the vast wetland of central Brazil and northern Bolivia which becomes increasingly fragmented). **C *Casa de Hospedaje Mejía***, an attractive rustic, family-run lodge on Lago Sandoval, with 10 double rooms and basic facilities, canoes are available (to book T571428, or just turn up).

Casa de Hospedaje Buenaventura, is a new intiative set up by long-term colonists living along the Tambopata river, 50-75 km upriver from Puerto Maldonado, 5-6 hrs by *peque-peque*. Accommodation for up to 10 in basic, rustic facilities, provides an insight into local lifestyles, minimum of 2 nights, from US$20-35 per person, includes transport to/from Tambopata dock, all food, mosquito net and Spanish-speaking guide, check if the package includes a trip to a *collpa*, in which case you'll also need a tent. Contact in advance via buenaventura50@ hotmail.com There is usually a representative to meet incoming flights at Puerto Maldonado airport. ***Sachavaca Inn***, associated with the same scheme, has 2 bungalows for up to 20 people, located between *Explorer's Inn* and *Tambopata Jungle Lodge*. Visits are made to Lago Sachavacayoc. To book, T571883, F571297, Puerto Maldonado.

Cusco Amazónico Pueblo Lodge, 45 mins by boat down the Río Madre de Dios. Jungle tours available with multi-lingual guides, the lodge is surrounded by its own 10,000-ha private reserve, but most tours are to Lago Sandoval, US$160 per person for 3 days/2 nights package, plus US$25 for single room, 50 rustic bungalows with private bathrooms, friendly staff, very good food, multi-lingual guides. To book T/F422 6574, F422 4701, Lima; Pasaje J C Tello C-13, Urb Santa Monica, Cusco, T235314, amazonico@inkaterra.com ***Cuzco Tambo Lodge***, bungalows 15 km out on the northern bank of the Río Madre de Dios. 2, 3 and 4-day jungle programmes available, from US$90 per person in low season, tours visit Lago Sandoval. Book through Cusco-Maldonado Tour, Plateros 351 (T222332), Cusco.

Eco Amazonia Lodge, on the Madre de Dios, 1 hr down-river from Puerto Maldonado. Accommodation for up to 80 in basic bungalows and dormitories, good for birdwatching with viewing platforms and limited tree canopy access, US$150 for 3 days/2 nights. Book through their office in Cusco: Portal de Panes 109, oficina 6, T236159, F225068, ecolodge@qenqo-unsaac.edu.pe ***Explorers Inn***, book through Peruvian Safaris, Garcilaso de la Vega 1334, Casilla 10088, T313047 Lima, or Plateros 365, T235342 Cusco, safaris@amauta.rcp.net.pe The office in Puerto Maldonado is at Fitzcarrald 136, T/F572078. The lodge is located adjoining the original Tambopata Reserved Zone, which covered just 5,500 ha. It has a well-established trail system and more research has been undertaken here over the last 25 years than anywhere else in the region. It is 58 km from Puerto Maldonado and is a 3-hr ride up the Río Tambopata (2 hrs return, in the early morning, so take warm clothes and rain gear), one of the best places in Peru for seeing jungle birds (580 plus species have been recorded), butterflies (1,230 plus species), also giant river otters, but you probably need more than a 2-day tour to benefit fully from the location. The guides are biologists and naturalists from around the world who undertake research in return for acting as guides. They provide interesting wildlife-treks, including to the macaw lick (*collpa*). US$180 for 3 days/2 nights, US$165 in the low season.

Posada Amazonas Lodge, on the Tambopata river, 2½ hrs upriver from Puerto Maldonado. A unique collaboration between a tour agency the local native community of Infierno. 24 large and attractive rooms with bathroom, cold showers, visits to Lakes Cochacocha and Tres Chimbadas, with good birdwatching opportunities including the Tambopata *Collpa*. Prices start at US$190 for a 3 day/2 night package, or

US$522 for 5 days/4 nights including the *Tambopata Research Centre*, the company's older, more spartan lodge with 13 rooms, which is close to the macaw lick. Guests at the Tambopata Research Centre, whether staying there direct, or on a package from Posada Amazonas Lodge, are the only visitors to the macaw lick who do not have to camp. Book through ***Rainforest Expeditions***, Aramburú 166, of 4B, Miraflores, Lima 18, T421 8347 ext 102, F421 8183, M 816 5466, or Arequipa 401, Puerto Maldonado, T 571056, postmaster@rainforest.com.pe or through www.perunature.com

Tambopata Jungle Lodge, on the Río Tambopata, make reservations at Av Pardo 705, Cusco, T225701, F238911, postmast@patcusco.com.pe Trips usually go to Lake Condenado, some to Lake Sachavacayoc, and to the *Collpa de Chuncho*, guiding mainly in English and Spanish, usual package US$160 per person for 3 days/2 nights (US$145 in the low season), naturalists programme provided.

Wasai Lodge, on the Río Tambopata, 80 km (4 hrs) upriver from Puerto Maldonado, 2 hrs return, same owners as *Hotel Wasai* in town; lima@wasai.com This small lodge with 3 bungalows for 30 people has 15 km of trails around the lodge, guides in English and Spanish. They can arrange special tours for biologists, universities and schools, expeditions to the rainforest, cultural and adventure programmes based at either the lodge or the hotel. The *Collpa de Chuncho* is only 1 hr up river; 3 day trips US$160, 7 days US$500.

To Iberia and Iñapari

A very worthwhile one or two day excursion by motorcycle (see hire rates on page 213) is by boat across the Río Madre de Dios and follow the road towards **Iberia** and **Iñapari** on the border with Brazil. There is daily public transport, as well (see below), and the dirt road has been greatly improved to aid the logging industry, which is currently deforesting extensive areas to the west of the road. In the wet season the road may only be passable with difficulty, especially between Iberia and Iñapari. Along the road there remains no primary forest, only secondary growth and small farms (*chacras*). There are also picturesque *caseríos* (settlements) that serve as collecting and processing centres for the brazil nut. Approximately 70% of the inhabitants in the Madre de Dios are involved in the collection of this prized nut.

At **Planchón**, 40 km up the road, there is a hotel, **G**, which is clean, but has no mosquito nets, and two bar/restaurants. **Alegría** at Km 60 has a hotel/restaurant and Mavilla, at Km 80, a bar.

The hotel at **Alerta**, Km 115, is a room with four beds, **G**. The river is safe to swim in. If there is a boat here, it is the quickest route to Brasiléia (Brazil), apart from the plane. US$10-20 per person in a cargo canoe, or *peque-peque*, to Porvenir and then by road to Cobija (Bolivia), across the border from Brasiléia. At **San Lorenzo**, Km 145, is the *Bolpebra* bar, which serves cheap food and drink and is generally lively.

Iberia, Km 168, has two hotels, the best is **F** *Hostal Aquino*, basic, cold shower, rooms serviced daily. Just outside the town the local rubber tappers association has set up an interesting Reserve and Information Centre.

Iñapari, at the end of the road, Km 235, has two basic hotels and a restaurant, but **Assis Brasil** across the border is much more attractive and has a much nicer basic hotel (**F**) on the main plaza. In the dry season it is possible to walk across the Rio Acre to Assis, otherwise take the ferry.

There is a road from Assis Brasil into Brazil and connections to Bolivia. It can be cold travelling this road, so take a blanket or sleeping bag. There are no exchange facilities en route and poor exchange rates for Brazilian currency at Iñapari.

Crossing to Bolivia and Brazil

Exit stamps can be obtained in Iñapari. Check in advance that you do not need a consular visa for Brazil or Bolivia; they are not issued at the border

To Bolivia: take the boat to Puerto Heath (see above) and get a tourist visa at the Bolivian immigration office in Puerto Maldonado.

To Brazil: there is a daily bus at 0800 from the dock on the opposite side of the Madre de Dios from Puerto Maldonado to Iberia, 5 hrs, US$3. A few colectivos also make this run each day, 4 hrs, US$7. From Iberia to Iñapari there are occasional but regular colectivos, 2½ hrs, US$7. Alternatively take a flight to Iberia and continue by road. Get a tourist visa at the Brazilian immigration in Iñapari.

Lima

Lima

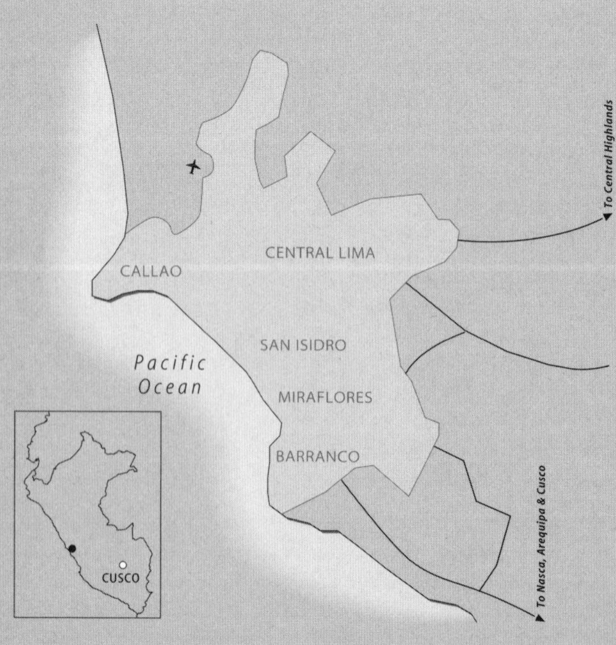

CENTRAL LIMA
CALLAO
SAN ISIDRO
Pacific Ocean
MIRAFLORES
BARRANCO
CUSCO
To Central Highlands
To Nasca, Arequipa & Cusco

The well-established cliché is to call Peru's capital a city of contradictions, but it's difficult to get beyond that description. Here you'll encounter grinding poverty and conspicuous wealth in abundance. The eight million inhabitants of this great, sprawling metropolis will defend it to the hilt and, in their next breath, tell you everything that's wrong with it. If the grim squalor of the poorer districts and constant begging of street children gets too much at least the visitor has the option of heading for Miraflores or San Isidro, whose chic shops, bars and restaurants would grace any major European city. Here, you can find almost every region of the country, in terms of food, handicrafts and museum exhibits. That said, it's rather a bizarre context to look for Inca gold or weavings from the high Sierra.

Lima is a big coastal city, over which a thick grey blanket of cloud descends in May and hangs around for the next seven months, seemingly perched on top of the many skyscrapers. Wait until the blanket is pulled aside in November to reveal bright blue skies and the visitor will see a very different place. This is beach weather for all Limeños, when weekends become a very crowded raucous mix of sun, sea, salsa and ceviche at the city's more popular coastal resorts.

Things to do in Lima

- Start the day in the city centre. If your hotel doesn't do breakfast, go to the **Café Carrara** at the Hostal Roma. You will then be close to the Plaza de Armas with its fine, enclosed wooden balconies, great Cathedral and the Government Palace.
- At lunchtime, you can feast royally on seafood or some other typical Peruvian dish. **El Segundo Muelle** in San Isidro is a good choice for ceviche.
- For the best overview of precolonial Peruvian history and art, visit the **Museo de la Nación**, housed in a spectacular modern building on Avenida Javier Prado Este, San Borja.
- **Las Brujas del Cachiche** in Miraflores will give you a first-class blow-out for dinner, with entertainment, too.
- You could do worse than spend all evening in Barranco. There are restaurants like **El Hornito**, where you can have pizza if you're full of local food, or **Manos Morenas**, which also has shows. The other bars, peñas and discotheques all within walking distance of each other, so you can try out as many as you choose.

Ins and outs

Getting there

Phone code: 01
Population: 8 mn
For information on all airport facilities and transport to and from the city, see page 31

By air All international flights land at Jorge Chávez Airport, some 16 km west of the centre of the city. It is a little further to Miraflores and Barranco. Transport is easy if a bit expensive. There are official taxis from inside the airport perimeter, or the cheaper option, which involves some effort after a long flight, of a taxi from outside the airport perimeter fence.

Several *hostales* and *pensiones* also provide transport to and from the airport. The tourist desk inside International Arrivals can help make hotel reservations. They often say that cheaper hotels are full or unsafe and, if you allow them to make a choice for you, it will probably be more expensive than you want (they may get commission). You will be bombarded as you leave the International gate by people touting for hotel business, representatives o0f travel agencies and taxi drivers. Be firm and don't let yourself be bullied. For places near the airport, see page 233.

By road If you arrive in Lima by bus, it is likely you'll pull into the main terminal at Jr Carlos Zavala, just south of the historical centre of Lima. It's recommended to take a taxi to your hotel even if it's close, as this area is not safe day or night. Most of the hotels are to the west.

Getting around

Downtown Lima is not really suitable for exploring on foot although the central hotels are fairly close to the many of the tourist sites

Bus The Lima public transportation system, at first glance very intimidating, is actually quite good. There are three different types of vehicles that will stop whenever flagged down: buses, *combis*, and *colectivos*. They can be distinguished by size; big and long, mid-size and mini-vans, respectively. The flat-rate fare for any of these three types of vehicle is US$0.35. On public holidays, Sun and from 2400 to 0500 every night, a small charge is added to the fare. Always try to pay with change to avoid hassles, delays and dirty looks from the *cobrador* (driver's assistant). Routes on any public transportation vehicle are posted on *windshields* with coloured stickers. Destinations written on the side of any vehicle should be ignored.

Buses between Lima centre and Miraflores: Av Arequipa runs 52 blocks between the downtown Lima area and Parque Kennedy in Miraflores. There is no shortage of public transport on this avenue; they have "Todo Arequipa" on the windscreen. When heading towards downtown from Miraflores the window sticker should say "Wilson/Tacna". To get to Parque Kennedy from downtown look on the windshield for "Larco/Schell/Miraflores", "Chorrillos/ Huaylas" or "Barranco/Ayacucho".

Vía Expresa: Lima's only urban freeway runs from Plaza Grau in the centre of town, to the northern tip of the district of Barranco. This six lane thoroughfare, locally known as *El Zanjón* (the Ditch), with a separate bus lane in the middle is by far the fastest way to cross the city. In order from Plaza Grau the 8 stops are: 1) Av México; 2) Av Canadá; 3) Av Javier Prado; 4) Corpac; 5) Av Aramburu; 6) Av Angamos; 7) Av Ricardo Palma, for Parque Kennedy; 8) Av Benavides. Buses downtown for the *Vía Expresa* can be caught on Av Tacna, Av Wilson (also called Garcilaso de la Vega), Av Bolivia and Av Alfonso Ugarte. These buses when full, are of great interest to highly skilled pickpockets who sometimes work in groups. If you're standing in the aisle be extra careful.

Taxi Colectivos: regular private automobiles charging US$0.50 make this a faster, more comfortable option than municipal public transportation. There are 3 routes: 1) between Av Arequipa and Av Tacna which runs from Miraflores to the centre of Lima; 2) between Plaza San Martín and Callao; 3) between the *Vía Expresa* and the district of Chorrillos. Look for the coloured sticker posted on the windshield. These cars will stop at any time to pick people up. When full (usually 5 or 6 passengers) they will only stop for someone getting off, then the process begins again to fill the empty space.

Taxis: meters are not used, therefore the fare should be agreed upon before you get in. Tips are not expected. The Daewoo is the taxi of choice. They are quick, clean and invariably yellow, but most importantly, they have seatbelts that work. Whatever the size or make, yellow taxis are usually the safest since they have a number, the driver's name and radio contact. A large number of taxis are white, but as driving a taxi in Lima (or for that matter, anywhere in Peru) simply requires a windshield sticker saying "Taxi", they come in all colours and sizes.

The following are taxi fares for some of the more common routes, give or take a sol. From downtown Lima to: Parque Kennedy (Miraflores), US$2. Gold Museum, US$2.30. Museo de la Nación, US$1.70. South American Explorers, US$1.15. Archaeology Museum, US$1.40. Immigration, US$1.15. From Miraflores (Parque Kennedy) to: Gold Museum, US$1.70. Museo de la Nación, US$1.40. South American Explorers, US$1.70. Archaeology Museum, US$2.30. Immigration, US$2. Official taxi companies, registered with the Municipality of Lima are without a doubt the safest option but cost much more than just picking one up in the street. Hourly rates possible: Taxi Real, T470 6263. Taxi Seguro, T275 2020. Moli Taxi, T479 0030. Taxi América, T265 1960. Taxi Tata, T274 5151.

Tourist information

Highly recommended is Siduith Ferrer Herrera, CEO of ***Fertur Peru***. Her agency not only offers up to date, correct tourist information on a national level, but also great prices on national and international flights, discounts for those with ISIC and Youth cards and South American Explorers members (of which she is one). Other services include flight reconfirmations, hotel reservations and transfers to and from the airport or bus stations. For those needing any or all of the services listed above, contact Fertur Peru: Jr Junín 211 (main office) at the Plaza de Armas, T427 1958, T/F428 3247, fertur@terra.com.pe. Open 0900-1900. Fertur also has a satellite at *Hostal España*, Jr Azangaro 105, T427 9196.

South American Explorers Av República de Portugal 146, district of Breña (block 13 of Av Alfonso Ugarte between Avs Bolivia and España). T/F425 0142, www.samexplo.org SAE is a non-profit educational organization which functions as a travel resource centre for South America and is widely recognized as the best place to get the most up-to-date information regarding everything from travel advisories to volunteer opportunities. Hours are Mon-Fri 0930-1700 and Sat 0930-1300. A yearly membership is currently

US$50 per person and US$75 per couple. Services include access to member-written trip reports, a full map room for reference, an extensive library in English and a book exchange. Members are welcome to use the SAE's PO Box for receiving post and can store luggage as well as valuables in their very secure deposit space. SAE sells official maps from the Instituto Geografico Nacional, SAE-produced trekking maps, used equipment and a large variety of Peruvian crafts. Note that all imported merchandise sold at SAE is reserved for members only, no exceptions. At least once a month, they host presentations on various topics ranging from jungle trips to freedom of the press. SAE also offers a discount in membership fees to researchers, archaeologists and scientists in exchange for information and/or presentations. If you're looking to study Spanish in Peru, hoping to travel down the Amazon or in search of a quality Inca Trail tour company, they have the information you'll need to make it happen. South American Explorers, apart from the services mentioned above, is simply a great place to step out of the hustle and bustle of Lima and delight in the serenity of a cup of tea, a magazine and good conversation with a fellow traveller.

Climate Only 12° south of the equator, you would expect a tropical climate, but Lima has 2 distinct seasons. The winter is from May to Nov, when a damp *garúa* (sea mist) hangs over

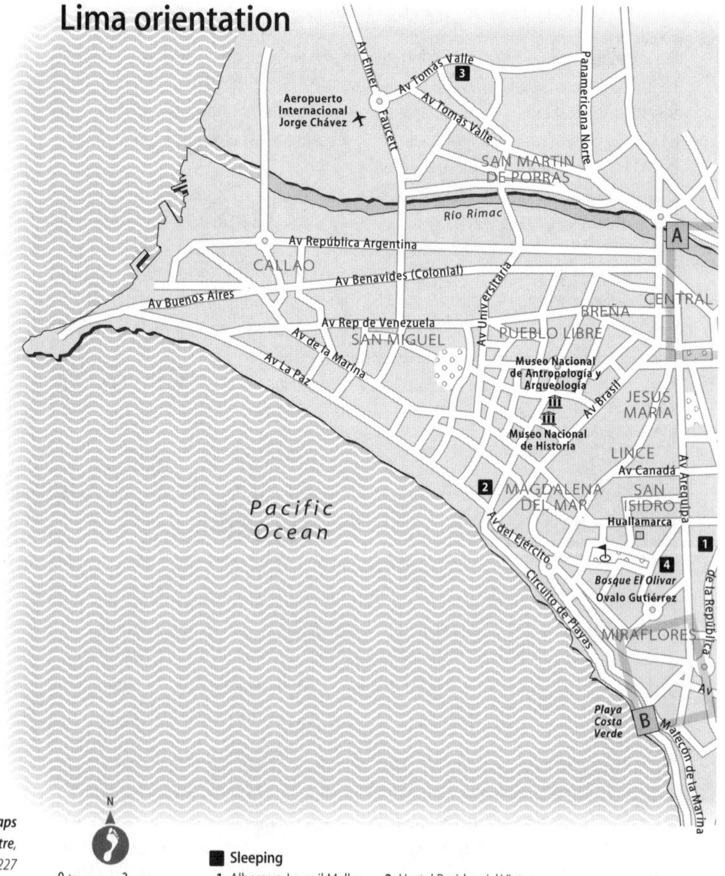

Related maps
A Lima centre,
page 227
B Miraflores,
page 231

Sleeping
1 Albergue Juvenil Malka
2 Hostal Mami Panchita
3 Hostal Residencial Victor
4 Sonesta Posadas del Inca

the city, making everything look greyer than it is already. It is damp and cold, 8° to 15°C. The sun breaks through around Nov and temperatures rise as high as 30°C. Note that the temperature in the coastal suburbs is lower than the centre because of the sea's influence. You should protect yourself against the sun's rays when visiting the beaches around Lima, or elsewhere in Peru.

Sights

Central Lima

One block south of the Río Rímac lies the **Plaza de Armas**, which has been declared a World Heritage site by Unesco. The plaza used to be the city's most popular meeting point and main market. In the centre of the plaza is a bronze fountain dating from 1650. The **Palacio de Gobierno** (Government Palace), on the north side of the Plaza, stands on the site of the original palace built by Pizarro. The changing of the guard is at 1200. In order to take a tour of the Palace you must register at the office of public relations at Parque Pizarro, next to the Palace, a few days in advance. There is no charge.

The Cathedral stands on the site of two previous buildings. The first, finished in 1555, was partly paid for by Francisca Pizarro on the condition that her father, the *Conquistador*, was buried there. A larger church, however, was soon required to complement the city's status as an Archbishopric. In 1625, the three naves of the main building were completed while work continued on the towers and main door. The new building was reduced to rubble in the earthquake of 1746 and the existing church, completed in 1755, is a reconstruction on the lines of the original. The interior is immediately impressive, with its massive columns and high nave. Also of note are the splendidly carved stalls (mid-17th century), the silver-covered altars surrounded by fine woodwork, mosaic-covered walls bearing the coats of arms of Lima and Pizarro and an allegory of Pizarro's commanders, the 'Thirteen Men of Isla del Gallo'. The assumed remains of Francisco Pizarro lie in a small chapel, the first on the right of the entrance, in a glass coffin, though later research indicates that they reside in the crypt.

There is a **Museo de Arte Religioso** in the cathedral, with free guided tours (English available, give tip), ask to see the picture restoration room. ■ *The cathedral is open to visitors Mon-Sat 1000-1430. All-inclusive entrance ticket is US$1.50. A recommended guide for the Cathedral is Patricia Cerrillo, T542 4019, English/German/French. Also Julio Torres, T475 6044.*

Next to the cathedral is the **Archbishop's Palace**, rebuilt in 1924, with a superb wooden balcony. On the opposite side of the Plaza is the **Municipalidad de Lima**, just behind which is **Pasaje Ribera el Viejo**, is a pleasant place to hang out with several good cafés with huge terraces.

Santo Domingo church and monastery is on the first block of Jirón Camaná (from the Plaza de Armas, walk one block northwest, past the Post Office). Built in 1549, the church is still as originally planned with a nave and two aisles covered by a vaulted ceiling, though the present ceiling dates from the 17th century. The cloister is one of the most attractive in the city and dates from 1603. The second cloister is much less elaborate. A chapel, dedicated to San Martín de Porres, one of Peru's most revered saints, leads off from a side corridor. Between the two cloisters is the Chapter House (1730), which was once the premises of the Universidad de San Marcos. Beneath the sacristy are the tombs of San Martín de Porres and Santa Rosa de Lima (first saint of the Americas and patron saint of Lima). ■ *Open 0900-1300, 1500-1800 Mon-Sat; Sun and holidays, mornings only. Entrance US$0.75. Basílica de La Veracruz is open lunchtimes. The main hall has some interesting relics. T427 6793.*

San Francisco church and monastery stand on the first block of Jirón Lampa, corner of Ancash, northeast of the Plaza de Armas. The baroque church, which was finished in 1674, was one of the few edifices to withstand the 1746 earthquake. There is a valuable collection of paintings by the Spanish artist, Francisco de Zuburán (1598-1664), which depict the apostles and various saints. The monastery is famous for the Sevillian tilework and panelled ceiling in the cloisters (1620). The Catacombs under the church and part of the monastery are well worth seeing. This is where an estimated 25,000 Limeños were buried before the main cemetery was opened in 1808. ■ *Open daily 0930-1745. Entrance US$1.75, US$0.50 children, guided tours only. T4271381.*

On Plaza Bolívar, near the corner of Avenida Abancay, is the **Museo del Tribunal de la Santa Inquisición**. The Court of Inquisition was first held here in 1584, after being moved from its first home opposite the church of La Merced. From 1829 until 1938 the building was used by the Senate. In the basement there is an accurate recreation *in situ* of the gruesome tortures. The whole tour is fascinating, if a little morbid. A description in English is available at the desk. ■ *Mon-Sun 0900-1700. Entrance free. Students offer to show you round for a tip; good explanations in English.*

San Pedro church and monastery is on the third block of Jirón Ucayali. The church, finished by Jesuits in 1638, has an unadorned façade, different from any other in the city. In one of the massive towers hangs a five tonne bell called *La Abuelita* (the grandmother), first rung in 1590, which sounded the Declaration of Independence in 1821. The contrast between the sober exterior and sumptuous interior couldn't be more striking. The altars are marvellous, in particular the high altar, attributed to the skilled craftsman, Matías Maestro. The church also boasts Moorish-style balconies and rich, gilded wood carvings in the choir and vestry, all tiled throughout. The most important paintings in the church are hung near the main entrance. In the monastery, the sacristy is a beautiful example of 17th century architecture. Also of note are La Capilla de Nuestra Señora de la O and the penitentiary. Several Viceroys are buried below. ■ *Open Mon-Sat 0800-1200, 1700-2000.*

At Jirón Ucayali 363, is the **Palacio Torre Tagle**, the city's best surviving specimen of secular colonial architecture. It was built in 1735 for Don José Bernardo de Tagle y Bracho, to whom King Philip V gave the title of First Marquis of Torre Tagle. The house remained in the family until it was acquired by the government in 1918. Today, it is still used by the Foreign Ministry, but visitors are allowed to enter courtyards to inspect the fine, Moorish-influenced wood-carving in the balconies, wrought iron work, and a 16th-century coach complete with commode. From the Palacio, turn right, then left to return to the Plaza de Armas. ■ *During working hours, Mon-Fri, visitors may enter the patio only.*

The newer parts of the city are based on **Plaza San Martín**, south of Jirón de la Unión, with a statue of San Martín in the centre. The plaza has been restored and is now a nice place to sit and relax.

La Merced church and monastery are in Plazuela de la Merced, Unión y Huancavelica. The first mass in Lima was said here on the site of the first church to be built. At independence the Virgin of La Merced was made a Marshal of the Peruvian army. The restored colonial façade is a fine example of Baroque architecture. Inside are some magnificent altars and the tilework on some of the walls is noteworthy. A door from the right of the nave leads into the Monastery where you can see some 18th century religious paintings in the sacristy. The cloister dates from 1546. ■ *Open 0800-1200, 1600-2000 every day and its monastery 0800-1200 and 1500-1730 daily. T427 8199.*

North of the Río Rimac, is the **Convento de los Descalzos**, founded in 1592. It contains over 300 paintings of the Cusco, Quito and Lima schools which line the four main cloisters and two ornate chapels. The chapel of El Carmen was constructed in 1730 and is notable for its baroque gold leaf altar. A small chapel dedicated to Nuestra Señora de la Rosa Mística has some fine Cusqueña paintings. The museum shows the life of the Franciscan friars during colonial and early republican periods. The cellar, infirmary, pharmacy and a typical cell have been restored.

■ *Open daily 1000-1300 and 1500-1800 except Tue. Entrance is US$1, by guided tour only, 45 mins in Spanish, but worth it. T481-0441. This can be a dangerous area to wander around alone, so take care.*

Outside the centre

Museo de la Nación

At Javier Prado Este 2465, in San Borja, is the anthropological and archaeological museum for the exhibition and study of the art and history of the aboriginal races of Peru. There are good explanations in Spanish on Peruvian history, with ceramics, textiles and displays of many ruins in Peru. It is arranged so that you can follow the development of Peruvian precolonial history through to the time of the Incas. There are displays of the tomb of the Señor de Sipán, artefacts from Batán Grande near Chiclayo (Sicán culture), reconstructions of the friezes found at Huaca La Luna and Huaca El Brujo, near Trujillo, and of Sechín and other sites. Temporary exhibitions are held in the basement, where there is also an Instituto de Cultura bookshop. ■ *Open Tue-Sun 1000-1700. Entrance US$1.75, 50% discount with ISIC card. From Av Garcilaso de la Vega in downtown Lima take a combi with a window sticker that says "Javier Prado/Aviacion". Get off at the 21st block of Javier Prado at Av Aviacion. The museum is caddy-corner. From Miraflores take a bus down Av Arequipa to Av Javier Prado (27th block), then take a bus with a window sticker saying "Tdo Javier Prado" or "Aviación." A taxi from downtown Lima or from the centre of Miraflores costs US$1.50. The museum has a cafetería. T476 9875.*

Museo Nacional de Antropología, Arqueología e Historia

On Plaza Bolívar in Pueblo Libre (not to be confused with Plaza Bolívar in the centre), are displays of ceramics of the Chimú, Nasca, Mochica and Pachacámac cultures, various Inca curiosities and works of art, and interesting textiles. The museum houses the Raimondi Stela and the Tello obelisk from Chavín, and a reconstruction of one of the galleries at Chavín. It also has a model of Machu Picchu. ■ *Open Tue-Sat 0915-1700, Sun and holidays 1000-1700. Entrance US$3. Photo permit US$5. Guides are available. Take any public transportation* *vehicle on Av Brasil with a window sticker saying "Tdo Brasil." Get off at the 21st block called Av Vivanco. Walk about 5 blocks down Vivanco. The museum will be on your left. Taxi from downtown Lima US$1.50; from Miraflores US$2. T463 5070.*

Next door is the **Museo Nacional de Historia** is in a mansion built by Viceroy Pezuela and occupied by San Martín (1821-1822) and Bolívar (1823-1826). Take the same buses to get there (see above). The exhibits comprise colonial and early republican paintings, manuscripts, portraits, uniforms, etc. The paintings are mainly of historical episodes.

Museo de Oro del Perú y Armas del Mundo

Museo de Oro (Gold Museum) is the private collection of Miguel Mujica Gallo, on the 18th block of Prolongación Avenida Primavera (Alonzo Molina 1110), in Monterrico. The underground museum contains items which have been exhibited in the world's leading museums. The collection includes precolumbian gold, silver and bronze, ceramics, mummies, etc. Allow plenty of time to appreciate it fully as it is positively full to bursting with artefacts. While the exhibits are excellent, explanations in the display cases are limited and the layout inspires mixed reactions. The catalogue costs US$15 and the complete book US$80. On the ground floor is a remarkable arms and uniforms collection with an impressive exhibition from Spanish colonial times to the present (including regalia of General Pinochet of Chile). On the first floor is an enormous collection of Peruvian textiles. In the garden are high quality, expensive craft shops. ■ *Open daily (including Sun and holidays) 1130-1900. Entrance US$5.75, children US$2. No photography allowed. From downtown, take a bus or microbus to the 47th block of Av Arequipa (Av Angamos). Get off, cross Av Angamos and take a colectivo with a window sticker saying "U de Lima". Tell the cobrador (driver's assistant) you want to get off at the Museo de Oro. From Miraflores walk or take public transport to 47th block of Av Arequipa at Av Angamos and take a bus up Angamos with sticker that says "U de Lima" and say you want to get off at the Museo de Oro. T345 1291.*

Museo de Arte

The Museo de Arte in the Palacio de la Exposición, at 9 de Diciembre (Paseo Colón) 125, was built in 1868 in Parque de la Exposición. There are more than 7,000 exhibits, giving a chronological history of Peruvian cultures and art from the Paracas civilization up to today. It includes excellent examples of 17th and 18th century Cusco paintings, a beautiful display of carved furniture, heavy silver and jewelled stirrups and also precolumbian pottery. ■ *Open Tue-Sun 1000-1700. Entrance US$2.30. The* Filmoteca *(movie club) is on the premises and shows films just about every night. See the local paper for details, or look in the museum itself. Free guide, signs in English. T423 4732.*

San Isidro & Miraflores

There are many good hotels and restaurants in San Isidro and Miraflores (see Sleeping and Eating sections)

The district of San Isidro combines some upscale residential areas, many of Lima's fanciest hotels and important commercial zones with a huge golf course smack in the middle. About 15 km south of the centre is Miraflores, which, apart from being a nice residential part of Lima, is also home to a busy mercantile district full of fashionable shops, cafés, discotheques, fine restaurants and five star hotels (see pages 230 and 233).

At the end of Avenida Larco and running along the Malecón de la Reserva is the renovated **Parque Salazar** and the very modern shopping centre called Centro Comercial Larcomar. Here you will find expensive shops, fancy cafés and discos and a wide range of restaurants, all with a beautiful ocean view. The 12-screen cinema is one of the best in Lima and even has a 'cine-bar' in the twelfth theatre. Don't forget to check out the Cosmic Bowling Alley with its black lights and fluorescent balls.

South of Miraflores is **Barranco**, a quiet, sleepy suburb which comes alive at night when the city's young flock here to party at weekends. Squeezed together into a few streets are dozens of good bars and restaurants (see pages 233 and 235).

Essentials

More visitors stay in the Miraflores area than in the centre, as it is generally cleaner and safer, but more expensive. Backpackers prefer the cheaper *hostales* in the centre, which has more theft problems and is more chaotic, but which, with care and attention to your belongings, is OK.

Sleeping

In Miraflores
■ *on maps*

The top of the range in Lima is the **LL** ***Miraflores Park Plaza***, Av Malecón de la Reserva 1035, T242 3000, F242 3393, Mirapph@ibm.net The price (over US$300 a night) includes tax, a beautiful ocean view from luxurious rooms. Service and facilities are excellent.

AL ***Antigua Miraflores***, Av Grau 350 at C Francia, T241 6116, F241 6115, www.peru-hotels-inns.com A beautiful, small and elegant hotel in a quiet but central location. The 35 rooms are tastefully furnished and decorated. There is a gym, cable TV, good restaurant and the service is very good. **AL** ***Sonesta Posadas del Inca***, Alcanfores 329, Miraflores, T241 7688, F447 1164, www.sonesta.com.pe A member of this recommended chain of hotels, with restaurant and cable TV.

A ***Hostal La Castellana***, Grimaldo del Solar 222, T444 3530, F446 8030. Price includes tax; there is a 10% discount for South American Explorers (SAE) members. This pleasant hotel is good value and safe. It has a nice garden, restaurant, laundry, and English is spoken. **A** ***Hostal Torreblanca***, Av José Pardo 1453, near the seafront, T447 0142, F447 3363, torreble@ett.com.pe The price includes breakfast. The rooms are cosy and this is a quiet, safe, friendly place with laundry, restaurant and bar. They can help with travel arrangements. **A** ***Sipán***, Paseo de la República 6171, T447 0884, F445 5298. Breakfast and tax are included in price. A very pleasant hotel in a residential area. Rooms are with bath, cable TV, fridge and security box. There is internet access for guests.

B ***Hostal Bellavista de Miraflores***, Jr Bellavista 215, T445 7834, F444 2938. Price includes tax. A quiet, pleasant hotel in an excellent location. **B** ***Villa Molina***, C Teruel 341, T440 4018, F222 5623, sbeleunde@electrodata.com.pe Breakfast and tax are included in the price. The hotel is in a beautiful house, which is quiet and friendly.

C ***Hospedaje Atahualpa***, Atahualpa 646c, T447 6601. Rooms are cheaper without bath, but breakfast is included; long-stay rates available. There is parking, hot water, cooking and laundry facilities, luggage can be stored and they have a taxi service. **C** ***Pensión Yolanda***, Domingo Elias 230, T445 7565. A family house where the owner speaks English. Clean, quiet and safe; reservations are required.

F per person ***Albergue Turístico Juvenil Internacional***, Av Casimiro Ulloa 328, San Antonio between San Isidro and Miraflores, T446 5488, F444 8187. A youth hostel, situated in a nice villa, with dormitory accommodation (double private rooms are available at **C**). There is a basic cafeteria, minimal cooking and laundry facilities (extra is charged for using the kitchen) and travel information. The swimming pool is often empty. It's clean and safe. **F** per person ***Friend's House***, Jr Manco Cápac 368, near Larcomar shopping centre, T446 6248. Very popular with backpackers, this place is among the cheapest in Miraflores. It has hot water, cable TV and use of the kitchen at no extra cost.

In San Isidro

LL ***Sonesta El Olivar***, Pancho Fierro 194, T221 2120, F221-2141, www.el-olivar.com.pe/www.sonesta.com Top luxury hotel with restaurant, pool and full business facilities.

Part of the same chain is **L** ***Sonesta Posadas Del Inca***, Av Libertadores 490, T222 4777, F422 4345, www.posadas.com.pe/www.sonesta.com **AL** ***Garden Hotel***, Rivera Navarrete 450, T442 1771, F222 7175, reservas@gardenhotel.com.pe Price includes tax and breakfast. A good hotel with large beds and showers. There is a small restaurant and travel agency.

F ***Albergue Juvenil Malka***, Los Lirios 165 (near 4th block of Av Javier Prado Este), T442 0162, T/F222 5589, hostelmalka@terra.com.pe A youth hostel with 20% discount ISIC card holders. Accommodation is dormitory style, 4-8 beds per room. English is spoken, cable TV, laundry, kitchen, and a nice café.

In Barranco

D ***Hostal Los Girasoles***, Av Sáenz Peña 210, opposite Mutual FAP, T477 2843, losgirasoles@hotmail.com Very good. **F** per person ***Mochileros Hostal***, Av Pedro de Osma 135, 1 block from main plaza, T477 4506, www.rcp.net.pe/backpacker A beautiful house, very clean, with a friendly English-speaking owner. Rooms are shared. Gays are welcome. There is a good pub on the premises, which are a stone's throw from Barranco nightlife.

Miraflores

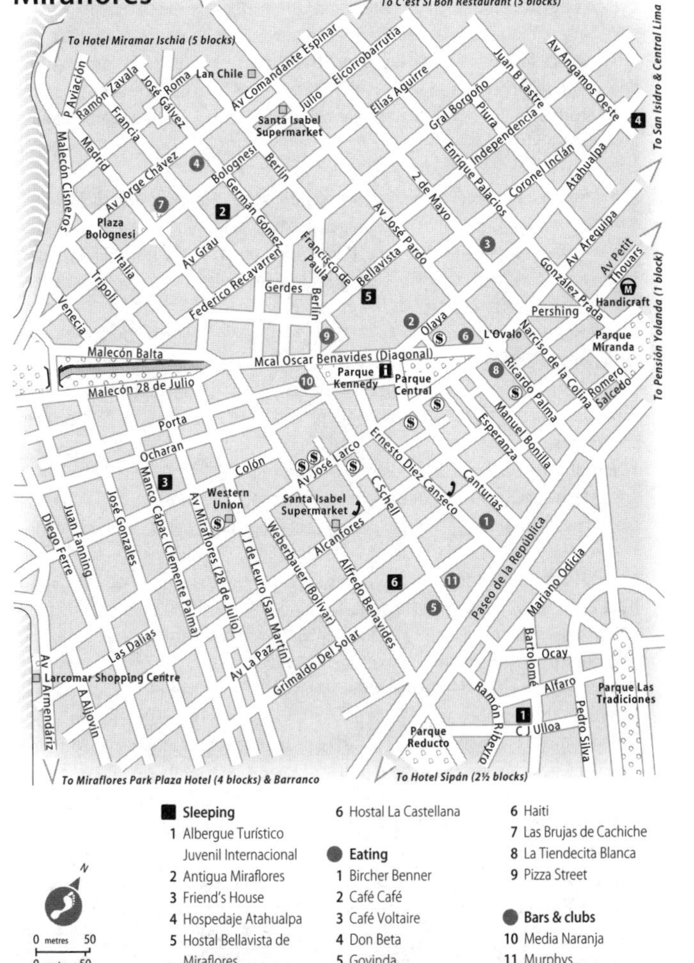

Sleeping
1 Albergue Turístico Juvenil Internacional
2 Antigua Miraflores
3 Friend's House
4 Hospedaje Atahualpa
5 Hostal Bellavista de Miraflores
6 Hostal La Castellana

Eating
1 Bircher Benner
2 Café Café
3 Café Voltaire
4 Don Beta
5 Govinda
6 Haiti
7 Las Brujas de Cachiche
8 La Tiendecita Blanca
9 Pizza Street

Bars & clubs
10 Media Naranja
11 Murphys

In Santa Beatriz **B** *Hostal La Posada del Parque*, Parque Hernán Velarde 60, near 2nd block of Av Petit Thouars, T433 2412, F332 6927, www.incacountry.com.pe Breakfast is US$3 extra. Run by Sra Mónica Moreno and her husband Leo who both speak good English, this charmingly refurbished old house is in a safe area. It has excellent bathrooms andis very good value. Airport transfer is available 24 hrs for US$14 for up to 3 passengers. **C** ***Renacimiento***, Parque Hernán Velarde 51, T433 2806, hostalrenacimiento@hotmail.com **D** without bath, price includes taxes. A colonial building close to national stadium. There is a snack bar for breakfast and lunch in a vegetarian restaurant. This quiet hotel has parking and is clean and helpful.

In Pueblo Libre **E** *Guest House Marfil*, Parque Ayacucho 126, at the 3rd block of Bolívar, T463 3161, F261 1206, cosycoyllor@yahoo.com Breakfast is included in the price. A family atmosphere, clean and friendly, English is spoken here. There are kitchen facilities and a laundry free of charge, also internet service. Spanish classes can be arranged.

In San Miguel **C** *Hostal Mami Panchita*, Av Federico Callese 198, T263 7203, F263 0749, raymi_travels@perusat.net.pe Price includes breakfast and a welcome drink. Dutch-Peruvian owned, English, French, Dutch, Spanish and German spoken. The comfortable rooms have bath with hot water and no TV. There is a nice living room and bar and a patio. Email service for guests, book exchange. The owners have their own *Raymi* Travel agency (good service). It's 15 mins from airport, 15 mins from Miraflores, 20 mins from the historical centre. There are several chicken places and *chifas* nearby around Mercado Magdalena.

In Central Lima The most luxurious hotel in the historical centre is **L-AL** *Maury*, Jr Ucayali 201, T428 8188/8174, F426 1273, hotmaury@amauta.rcp.net.pe It's fancy, secure, very clean and breakfast is included in the price. **B** *El Balcón Dorado*, Jr Ucayali 199, T427 6028, balcondorado@terra.com.pe Price includes tax, service and continental breakfast. This centrally-located hotel is very friendly, with a café.

C ***Hostal Roma***, Jr Ica 326, T/F427 7572, resroma@terra.com.pe or dantereyes@hotmail.com Price is for rooms with bathroom, **D** without bath, hot water all day. A safe to leave luggage, it's basic but clean and often full. There is motorcycle parking. *Roma Tours* is helpful for trips, reservations and flight confirmations, Dante Reyes speaks English.

E ***Hostal de las Artes***, Jr Chota 1460 near SAE, T433 0031/332 1868 (office), artes@terra.com.pe http://arteswelcome.tripod.com Price includes bath, but there are rooms at **F** without bath (no singles with bath), and **G** per person in the dormitory. This hotel in a nice colonial building is Dutch owned, English spoken. It's clean and friendly (and gay-friendly) with a safe luggage store. There is usually hot water and it has a book exchange. **E** ***Hostal Iquique***, Jr Iquique 758, Breña, round the corner from SAE (discount for members), T423 3699, F433 4724, http://barrioperu.terra.com.pe/hiquique Price is for a room with bathroom; **F** without bath. It's clean but noisy and draughty. You can use the kitchen, the water is warm and there are storage facilities. Rooms on the top floor at the back are best. Friendly staff. **E** ***Plaza Francia Inn***, Jr Rufino Torrico 1117, near 9th block of Av Garcilaso de la Vega (aka Wilson), T330 6080, franciasquareinn@yahoo.com Or **F** in the dormitory. Discounts are offered to ISIC cardholders, SAE members and readers of this Handbook. A new *hostal* with the same owner as the *Posada del Parque*. It's very clean and cosy with hot water 24 hrs and a safety box in each room for each bed. Airport pick up for up to 4 people costs US$12.

F ***Europa***, Jr Ancash 376, T427 3351, opposite San Francisco church. Good, clean rooms with shared bathrooms, excellent hot showers. There is also dormitory accommodation for **G** per person: great value, friendly, popular with backpackers. Keep valuables secure. **F** per person ***Familia Rodríguez***, Av Nicolás de Piérola 730, 2nd floor,

T423 6465, jotajot@terra.com.pe Price includes breakfast, also has dormitory accommodation with only one bathroom (same price). Clean, secure, friendly and popular, but some rooms are noisy. Luggage can be stored. Transport to the airport costs US$10 per person for 2 people, US$4 per person for 3 or more, good information. **F** ***Pensión Ibarra***, Av Tacna 359, 14th-16th floor, T/F427 8603 (no sign). Breakfast is US$2 extra, discounts offered for longer stay, full board available (good small café next door). Guests can use the kitchen, the balcony has views of the city. A clean, friendly place with hot water. The owner is very helpful owner. **F** ***Hostal España***, Jr Azángaro 105, T427 9196, T/F428 5546, feertur@terra.com.pe Price rises to **E** with private bath (3 rooms), and falls to **G** per person in a dormitory. Shared bathrooms, hot showers possible either very early or very late. A fine old building, run by a French-speaking Peruvian painter and his Spanish wife, English spoken, friendly. There is internet service, motorcycle parking, a luggage store (free), laundry service, a roof garden and a good café. It's very popular, but don't leave valuables in rooms.

G per person ***Hospedaje Huaynapicchu***, Jr Pedro Ruiz 703 y Pasaje Echenique 1108, Breña, access from 11th block of Av Brazil, T431 2565, F447 9247, huaynapicc@business.com.pe Price includes breakfast. Bathrooms are shared, hot water all day, very clean. A welcoming family, English is spoken., There is internet access, laundry service and it's secure.

Near the airport

B ***Hostal Residencial Victor***, Manuel Mattos 325, Urb San Amadeo de Garagay, Lima 31, T567 5107/5083, F568 9570, hostalvictor@terra.com.pe 5 mins from the airport by taxi, or phone in advance to be collected by the hotel. American breakfast is included, evening meals can be ordered from local pizza or chicken places; there is also a *chifa* nearby. Large, clean, comfortable rooms with bath and hot water and cable TV. Very helpful staff and theowner, Victor Melgar, has a travel agency.

Eating

In Miraflores

● *on maps*

Expensive ***Rosa Náutica***, T447 0057, built on old British-style pier (Espigón No 4), in Lima Bay. Delightful opulence with the finest fish cuisine; experience the atmosphere by buying an expensive beer in the bar at sunset, open 1230-0200 daily. ***Astrid y Gaston***, C Cantuarias 175, T444 1496. Excellent local and international cuisine, one of the best in the city. ***Las Brujas de Cachiche***, Av Bolognesi 460, T447 1883/446 6536. An old mansion converted into bars and dining rooms, beautifully decorated, serving traditional food (menu in Spanish and English) including the best Lomo Saltado in town. They have live *criollo* music. ***Café Voltaire***, Av Dos de Mayo 220, T447 4807. International cuisine with the emphasis on French dishes, all beautifully-cooked and served in a pleasant ambience with good service. ***El Pantagruel***, C Cantuarias 151, T242 8465. Serves typical dishes of the Sierra.

Mid-range ***Bohemia***, Av Santa Cruz 805, on the Ovalo Gutiérrez, T446 5240. A large menu of international food with great salads and sandwiches. Also at Av El Polo 706, 2nd floor, T435 9924 and at Pasaje Nicolás de Rivera 142, opposite the main post office near the Plaza de Armas, Lima centre, T427 5537. ***Café de Paris***, C Diez Canseco 180, T242 2469. A pleasant restaurant offering delicious soups, crepes etc, they also do a set 3-course meal for US$10, and serve good coffee. ***Dalmacia***, C San Fernando 401, T445 7917. A Spanish-owned, casual gourmet restaurant, which is excellent. ***Don Beta***, José Gálvez 667, T446 9465. Open 0800-2200 daily, a good place for seafood. ***Torero Sí Señor***, Av Angamos Oeste 598, T446 5150. Serves Spanish food in a fun, loud setting.

Cheap ***Big Apple Bagels***, Av Espinar 520 and Larcomar shopping centre, T441 4224 for delivery. The only bagels in Lima, they are surprisingly good. ***Dino's Pizza***, Av Comandante Espinar 374, T242 0606. For great pizza at a good price, they also have a delivery service. ***Pardo's Chicken***, Av Benavides 730, T446 4790. Chicken and chips, very good and popular (with branches throughout Lima). ***Ricota***, Pasaje Tarata 248, T445 2947. A charming café on a pedestrian walkway, it has a huge menu, big portions and is friendly. For cakes and sweets, ***C'est si bon***, Av Comandante Espinar 663, T446 9310. Excellent cakes by the slice or whole, the best in Lima. There are various small restaurants which are good for a cheap set meal along C Los Pinos with Av Schell, at the bottom of Parque Kennedy. C San Ramón, more commonly known as **Pizza Street** (across from Parque Kennedy), is a pedestrian walkway lined with restaurants specializing in Italian food. Very popular and open all night at weekends.

Vegetarian *Bircher Benner*, Diez Canseco 487 y Grimaldo del Solar. Closed Sun, has a natural food store inside, slow service, good cheap *menú*. ***Govinda***, Shell 634. Also sells natural products, good. ***Madre Natura***, C Chiclayo 815, T445 2522. Great natural foods shop. ***El Paraíso***, C Alcanfores 416, 2 blocks from Av Benavides. Natural foods/snacks, fruit salads and juices.

Cafés ***Haiti***, Av Diagonal 160, Parque Kennedy. Open almost round the clock daily, great for people watching. ***La Tiendecita Blanca***, Av Larco 111 on Parque Kennedy, T445 9797. One of Miraflores' oldest, expensive, good people-watching, very good cakes, European-style food and delicatessen. ***Café Café***, Martin Olaya 250, near the Parque Kennedy roundabout. Very popular, good atmosphere, over 100 different blends of coffee, good salads and sandwiches, very popular with 'well-to-do' Limeños. Also at Alvarez Calderón 198, San Isidro. ***Café de la Paz***, middle of Parque Kennedy, T445 0940. Good outdoor café right on the park, expensive. ***Café D'Oro***, Av Larco 763. Nice place for a sandwich or coffee.

In San Isidro

Expensive *Antica Pizzería*, Av Dos de Mayo 728, T222 8437. A very popular, Italian-owned restaurant with great ambience and excellent food. ***Le Bistrot de mes Fils***, Av Conquistadores 510, T422 6308. This cosy French bistrot serves great food. ***Valentino***, C Manuel Bañon 215, T441 6174. One of Lima's best international restaurants.

Mid-range *Segundo Muelle*, Av Conquistadores 490, T421 1206, and Av Canaval y Moreyra (aka Corpac) 605, T224 3007. Excellent ceviche, younger crowd. Highly recommended.

Cheap *Delicass*, C Miguel Dasso 131, T221 3309/3247. This great deli has imported meats and cheeses. It's open late, but the service is slow. ***Pits & Gloton***, 5th block of Av Espinar. These two back-to-back restaurants are very popular with the late, late-night crowds coming from bars and discotheques, chicken, sandwiches, etc, open 24 hrs.

In Barranco

La Costa Verde, on Barranquito beach, T247 1244. Excellent fish and wine, expensive but recommended as the best by Limeños. It's open 1200-2400 daily, and has a Sun buffet. ***Festín***, Av Grau 323, T477 3022. This place has a huge menu of typical and international food. ***El Hornito***, Av Grau 209, on corner of the main plaza, T477 2465. Serves pizza and creole food. ***Manos Morenas***, Av Pedro de Osma 409, T467 0421. Open 1230-1630, 1900-2300, for creole cuisine with shows on some evenings (there is cover charge for the shows).

In Central Lima

L'Eau Vive, Ucayali 370, T427 5612, across from the Torre Tagle Palace. Restaurant run by nuns, open Mon-Sat, 1230-1500 and 1930-2130. They offer A fixed-price lunch menu, Peruvian-style in the interior dining room, or à la carte in either of the dining rooms that open onto the patio. Excellent, profits go to the poor, Ave Maria is sung nightly at 2100. ***Heydi***, Puno 367. Good for cheap seafood, open daily 1100-2000, popular. ***El Damero de Pizarro***, Jr de la Unión 543, T427 2209. Serves typical Peruvian food with huge helpings, popular with locals, loud music. ***Café Carrara***, Jr Ica 330, attached to *Hostal Roma*, is open daily until 2300. It has multiple breakfast combinations, pancakes and sandwiches. Good food in a nice ambience. ***Cordano***, Jr Ancash 202, T427

0181. This typical old Lima restaurant/watering hole has slow service and is a bit grimy, but is full of character. Definitely worth the time it takes to drink a few beers. On Sat and Sun, 1100-1700, traditional dishes from all over Peru are served in Plaza Italia, plenty of seating, music, well-organized. Highly recommended. ***La Choza Náutica***, Jr Breña 102, close to SAE behind Plaza Bolognesi. For good *ceviche* and friendly service.

There are many highly recommended *chifas* in the district of Barrios Altos, which is east of the historical centre and next to the Central Market. For example, ***Wa Lok***, Jr Paruro 864, T427 2656, whose owner, Liliana Com, speaks fluent English and is very friendly. Also ***Salon Capon***, Jr Paruro 819, ***Chun Koc Sen***, Jr Paruro 886, T427 5281, ***Fung Yen***, Jr Ucayali 744, T427 6567, and ***Chifa Capon***, Ucayali 774.

Vegetarian *Natur*, Moquegua 132, 1 block from Jr de la Unión, T427 8281. The owner, Humberto Valdivia, is also president of the South American Explorers' board of directors, the casual conversation, as well as his restaurant is highly recommended. ***Centro de Medicina Natural***, Jr Chota 1462, next door to *Hostal de las Artes*. Very good.

Entertainment

Bars & nightclubs

Lima has an excellent nightlife, with many places to choose from, all with different styles and themes. Often there is a cover charge ranging from US$3-10 per person.

In Miraflores *Barra Brava*, Av Grau 192, T241 5840. Lot's of fun, sports bar(ish). ***Media Naranja***, C Schell 130, at the bottom of Parque Kennedy. Brasilian bar with typical drinks and food. ***Murphys***, C Schell 627. Great Irish pub, "a must". ***Pub Dionysos***, Av Dos de Mayo 385, T447 7958. Nice pub with Greek décor. ***Roca's*** *Pub*, C Bellavista 241, T242 8655. Cosy pub with late-night live shows.***Ministry***, Altos de D'Onofrio, opposite Parque Kennedy, T938 9231. Good music, performances and demonstrations of dance, exhibitions, tattooing, entry US$3. ***Santa Sede***, Av 28 de Julio 441. Very popular, great music, fun crowd. ***Satchmo***, Av La Paz 538, T442 8425. Live jazz, creole and blues shows. ***Tequila Rocks***, C Diez Canseco 146, ½ block from Parque Kennedy. Good music, very popular.

Barranco is the capital of Lima nightlife

In Barranco Pasaje Sánchez Carrión, right off the main plaza, is the heart of it all. Watering holes and discos line both sides of this pedestrian walkway. Av Grau, just across the street from the plaza, is also lined with bars. ***Sargento Pimienta***, Bolognesi 755. Live music, always a favourite with Limeños. ***Juanitos***, Av Grau, opposite the park. Barranco's oldest bar, and perfect to start the evening. ***El Ekeko***, Av Grau 266. ***La Estación***, Av Pedro de Osma 112. Live music, older crowd. ***La Posada del Mirador***, near the *Puente de los Suspiros* (Bridge of Sighs). Beautiful view of the ocean, but you pay for the privilege. ***Kitsch Bar***, Bolognesi 743. The name says it all, decorated with flock wallpaper, dolls, religious icons, after midnight it becomes unbearably packed. ***El Caserio***, Pasaje Sánchez Carrion 110. Great for dancing. Recommended. ***La Noche***, Bolognesi 307, at Pasaje Sánchez Carrión. A Lima institution. ***Bar Quispe***, Plaza Raimondi, 1 block from Bolognesi. Photos of old Lima, large jar on the bar from which you can help yourself ot peach brandy, wide range of music, popular at weekends. ***El Grill de Costa Verde***, part of the *Costa Verde* restaurant on Barranco beach. Young crowd, packed at weekends. ***Dirty Nelly's***, Av Pedro de Osma 135. Good crack Irish pub. Many of the bars in this area turn into discos as the evening goes on. ***Noctambul***, Av Grau. Once Lima's most popular disco, large and modern. ***Decimo Planeta***, Bolognesi 198. ***My Place***, C Domeyer 122. ***Las Terrazas***, Av Grau 290.

In Central Lima *Queirolo Bar*, Jr Camaná 900 at Jr Quilca. Excellent for local colour. ***Estadio Futbol Sports Bar***, Av Nicolás de Piérola 926 on the Plaza San Martín, T428 8866. Beautiful bar with a discotheque on the bottom floor, international football theme, good international and creole food. ***El Rincón Cervecero***, Jr de la Unión (Belén) 1045. German pub without the beer, fun. ***Piano Bar Munich***, Jr de la Unión 1044 (basement). Small and fun.

Cinemas There are many good cinemas throughout the city. Most films are in English with subtitles and cost US$2 in the centre and around US$4-5 in Miraflores. Cinemas in the centre tend to have poor sound quality. The best cinema chains in the city are ***Cinemark, Cineplanet*** and ***UVK Multicines***, Among the best of the other movie theatres are: **In Miraflores**: ***Cine Romeo y Julieta***, Pasaje Porta 115, at the bottom of Parque Kennedy, T447 5476. ***Multicine Starvision El Pacífico***, on the Ovalo by Parque Kennedy, T445 6990.

Tue is half price at most cinemas for shows throughout the day and night

Peñas ***Las Brisas de Titicaca***, Pasaje Walkuski 168, at the 1st block of Av Brasil near Plaza Bolognesi, T332 1881. A Lima institution. ***Sachun***, Av Del Ejército 657, Miraflores, T441 0123/4465. Great shows on weekdays as well. ***De Cajón***, C Merino 2nd block, near 6th block of Av Del Ejército, Miraflores. Good *música negra*.

Festivals On **18 Jan** is the anniversary of the *founding of Lima*. **Semana Santa**, or Holy Week, is a colourful spectacle with processions. **28-29 Jul** is *Independence*, with music and fireworks in the Plaza de Armas on the evening before. **Oct** is the month of *Our Lord of the Miracles* with impressive processions (see *El Comercio* for dates and routes). On **3 Nov** is *San Martín de Porres*.

Shopping

Parque Kennedy, the main park of Miraflores, hosts a daily crafts market from 1700-2300. **Artesanía Carabaya**, Jr Carabaya 319 at the Plaza de Armas. There are crafts markets on **Av Petit Thouars** in Miraflores near Parque Kennedy. Av Petit Thouars runs parallel to Av Arequipa. Its 54 blocks end at Av Ricardo Palma, a few blocks from Parque Kennedy. At the 51st block you'll find an unnamed crafts market area with a large courtyard and lots of small flags. This is the largest crafts arcade in Miraflores. From here to Calle Ricardo Palma the street is lined with crafts markets. One of the newer ones has a small café. All are open 7 days a week until late(ish). On C García Naranjo, La Victoria, just off Av Grau in the centre of town is **Polvos Azules**, the official black market of Lima. The normal connotations of a 'black market' do not apply here as this establishment is an accepted part of Lima society, condoned by the government and frequented by people of all economic backgrounds. It's good for cameras, hiking boots, music and an extensive selection of walkmans. This is not a safe area, so be alert and put your money in your front pockets.

Lima has 3 supermarket chains: *Santa Isabel*, *E Wong* and *Metro*. They all are well stocked and carry a decent supply of imported goods (Marmite, Tesco products etc.). The *Santa Isabel* on Av Benavides y Av Alcanfores in Miraflores is open 24 hrs. *Jockey Plaza*, Av Javier Prado Este, Surco, is a shopping, restaurant and cinema complex.

Transport

Air For all information on international flight arrivals and departures, see page 31. For all information on domestic flights, see page 39. To enquire about arrivals or departures, T575 1712 (international), or T574 5529 (domestic). For airport facilities and transport to and from Lima airport, see page 31.

Buses Although Lima is home to a seemingly never-ending list of bus companies, only a small percentage are actually recommended. Companies that offer service between Cusco and Lima, and their fares, are listed on page 125. Confirm that the bus leaves from same place that the ticket was purchased.

One company that is recommended for service to all parts of Peru is ***Cruz del Sur***: Jr Quilca 531, Lima centre, T424 1005. This terminal has routes to many destinations in Peru with *Ideal* ('ee-de-al') service, meaning quite comfortable buses and periodic stops for food and bathroom breaks, a cheap option with a quality company. Its terminal for *Ideal* buses to Cusco is at Av Paseo de la República 801, across the expressway from the National Stadium, T433 6765/332 4000/4330231. They also go to: Ica, Pisco, Arequipa, Juliaca, Puno and northern destinations. The other terminal is at Av Javier Prado Este 1109, San Isidro, T225 6163/6164. This terminal offers the *Imperial* service (luxury buses), more expensive and direct, with no chance of passengers in the aisle, and *Cruzero* service (super luxury buses).

Directory

Banks

Interbank, Jr de la Union 600, Lima Centre (main branch). Open Mon-Fri 0900-1800. Also Av Pardo 413, Av Larco 690 and in Larcomar, Miraflores, Av Grau 300, Barranco, Av Pezet 1405 and Av Pardo y Aliaga 634, San Isidro, and supermarkets *Wong* and *Metro*. Accepts and sells American Express TCs only, ATM for Amex and Visa/Plus (at Av Larco branch). ***Banco de Crédito***, Jr Lampa 499, Lima Centre (main branch), Av Pardo 425 and Av Larco at Pasaje Tarata, Miraflores, Av Pardo y Aliaga at Av Camino Real, San Isidro.). Open Mon-Fri 0900-1800, Sat 0930-1230. Accepts and sells American Express TCs only, accepts Visa card and brances have Visa ATM. ***Banco Santander Central Hispano (BSCH)***, Av Pardo 482 and Av Larco 479, Miraflores, Av Augusto Tamayo 120, San Isidro (main branch). Open Mon-Fri 0900-1800, Sat 0930-1230. TCs (Visa and Citicorp). Unicard ATM for Visa/Plus and Mastercard/Cirrus systems. ***Banco de Comercio***, Av Pardo 272 and Av Larco 265, Miraflores, Jr Lampa 560, Lima Centre (main branch). Open Mon-Fri 0900-1800, Sat 0930-1200. Changes and sells American Express TCs only, Unicard ATM accepts Visa/Plus and Mastercard/Cirrus systems. ***Banco Financiero***, Av Ricardo Palma 278, near Parque Kennedy (main branch). Open Mon-Fri 0900-1800, Sat 0930-1230. TCs (American Express), Unicard ATM for Visa/Plus and Mastercard/Cirrus systems. ***Banco Latino***, Av Larco 337, Miraflores, Av Paseo de la República 3505, San Isidro (main branch). Open Mon-Fri 0830-2000, Sat 0900-1300. TCs (Mastercard, American Express), sells Amex and Mastercard cheques, ATM for Mastercard and Cirrus system at Av Larco branch and Av Alfonso Ugarte 1206 (2 blocks from South American Explorers). ***Banco Continental***, corner of Av Larco and Av Benavides and corner of Av Larco and Pasaje Tarata, Miraflores, Jr Cusco 286, Lima Centre near Plaza San Martín. Open Mon-Fri 0900-1800, Sat 0930-1230. TCs (American Express). ***Banco Wiese Sudameris***, Av Diagonal 176 on Parque Kennedy, Av José Pardo 697, Miraflores, Av Alfonso Ugarte 1292, Breña (near South American Explorers), Miguel Dasso 286, San Isidro. Open Mon-Fri 0915-1800, Sat 0930-1230. TCs (American Express only), Unicard ATM for Visa/Plus and Mastercard/Cirrus systems. ***Citibank***, in all *Blockbuster* stores, and at Av 28 de Julio 886, Av Benavides 23rd block and Av Emilio Cavenecia 175, Miraflores, Av Las Flores 205 and branch in Centro Comercial Camino Real, Av Camino Real 348, San Isidro. *Blockbuster* branches open Sat and Sun 1000-1900. Changes and sells Citicorp cheques.

Exchange houses and street changers There are many ***casas de cambio*** on and around Jr Ocoña off the Plaza San Martín. On the corner of Ocoña and Jr Camaná you'll no doubt see the large concentration of ***cambistas*** (street changers) with huge wads of dollars and soles in one hand and a calculator on the other. They should be avoided. Changing money on the street should only be done with official street changers wearing an identity card with a photo. Keep in mind that this card doesn't *automatically* mean that they are legitimate but most likely you won't have a problem. Around Parque Kennedy and down Av Larco in Miraflores are dozens of official *cambistas* with ID photo cards attached to their usually blue, sometimes green vest. There are also those who are independent and are dressed in street clothes, but it's safer to do business with an official money changer. A repeatedly recommended *casa de cambio* is

LAC Dolar, Jr Camaná 779, 1 block from Plaza San Martín, 2nd floor, T428 8127, T/F427 3906, also at Av La Paz 211, Miraflores, T242 4069/4085. Open Mon-Sat 0900-1900, Sun and holidays 0900-1400, good rates, very helpful, safe, fast, reliable, 2% commission on cash and TCs (Amex, Citicorp, Thomas Cook, Visa), will come to your hotel if you're in a group. Another recommended *casa de cambio* is ***Virgen P Socorro***, Jr Ocoña 184, T428 7748. Open daily 0830-2000, safe, reliable and friendly.

American Express Office Av Belén 1040 in the Lima Tours office, near Plaza San Martín. Official hours are Mon-Fri 0900-1700, Sat 0900-1300, but there is always someone there in case of emergencies. Services are as follows: replaces lost or stolen American Express cheques of any currency in the world. Can purchase Amex cheques with Amex card only. Also at Av Pardo y Aliaga 698, San Isidro, T222 2525, F222 5700.

Car hire

Most rental companies have an office at the airport, where you can arrange everything and pick up and leave the car

Alamo Rent A Car, Av Benavides 1180, Miraflores, T444 4122, F241 7431. ***Dollar Rent A Car***, C Diez Canseco 236 no 201, Miraflores, T445 2239, C Cantuarias 341, Miraflores, T444 4920, Airport T575 1719. ***Budget Car Rental***, Av La Paz 522, Miraflores, T442 8703, Av Canaval y Moreyra, San Isidro, T442 8706. ***Hertz Rent A Car***, C Aristides Aljovin 472, Miraflores, T444 4441. ***Inka's Rent a Car***, Cantuarias 160, Miraflores, T445 5716/447 2129, F447 2583, airport T/F575 1390, www.peruhot.com/inkas ***National Car Rental***, Av España 449, Lima centre, T433 3750, C Los Eucaliptos 555, San Isidro, T222 1010, Airport T575 1111. ***Paz Rent A Car***, Av Diez Canseco 319, Miraflores, T446 4395, F242 4306.

Communications

Internet Lima is completely inundated with internet cafés, so you will have absolutely no problem finding one regardless of where you are. An hour will cost you approximately S/5 (US$1.50).

Post Office The central post office is on Jr Camaná 195 in the centre of Lima near the Plaza de Armas. Hours are Mon-Fri 0730-1900 and Sat 0730-1600. Poste Restante is in the same building but is considered unreliable. In Miraflores the main post office is on Av Petit Thouars 5201 in Miraflores (same hours). There are many more small branches scattered around Lima, but they are less reliable. For express service, there are a few companies to choose from: ***DHL***, Los Castaños 225, San Isidro, T215-7500. ***UPS***, Av del Ejército 2107, San Isidro, T264 0105. ***Federal Express***, Av Jorge Chávez 475, T242 2280, Miraflores, C José Olaya 260, Miraflores. ***EMS***, next to central post office in downtown Lima, T533 2020.

Telephone There are many ***Telefónica del Perú*** offices all over Lima. Most allow collect calls but some don't. All offer fax service (sending and receiving). There are payphones all over the city. Some accept coins, some only phone cards and some honour both. Phone cards can often be purchased in the street near these booths. Some ***Telefónica del Perú*** offices are: Pasaje Tarata 280, Miraflores (near Av Alcanfores); Av Bolivia 347, Lima Centre (at Jr Chota near South American Explorers); C Porta 139, Miraflores (near the bottom of Parque Kennedy).

Useful addresses

Tourist Police, address is given on page 73. They are friendly and very helpful, English spoken. **Immigration**: Av España 700 y Jr Huaraz, Breña (2 blocks from SAE), open 0830-1500, but they only allow people to enter until 1330. See page 22 for procedures on visa extensions. Provides new entry stamps if passport is lost or stolen. The ***Peruvian Touring and Automobile Club***: Av César Vallejo 699 (Casilla 2219), Lince, T221 2432. Offers help to tourists and particularly to members of the leading motoring associations. Good maps available of whole country; regional routes and the South American sections of the Pan-American Highway available (US$3.50).

Background

Background

History

Inca Dynasty

The origins of the Inca Dynasty are shrouded in mythology. The best known story reported by the Spanish chroniclers talks about Manco Cápac and his sister rising out of Lake Titicaca, created by the Sun as divine founders of a chosen race. This was in approximately AD 1200. Over the next 300 years the small tribe grew to supremacy as leaders of the largest empire ever known in the Americas, the four territories of Tawantinsuyo, united by Cusco as the umbilicus of the Universe. The four quarters of Tawantinsuyo, all radiating out from Cusco, were:
1 Chinchaysuyo, north and northwest; 2 Cuntisuyo, south and west; 3 Collasuyo, south and east; 4 Antisuyo, east.

At its peak, just before the Spanish Conquest, the Inca Empire stretched from the Río Maule in central Chile, north to the present Ecuador-Colombia border, containing most of Ecuador, Peru, western Bolivia, northern Chile and northwest Argentina. The area was roughly equivalent to France, Belgium, Holland, Luxembourg, Italy and Switzerland combined (980,000 sq km).

The Incas, under their first ruler, Manco Cápac, migrated north to the fertile Cusco region, settling between the rivers Saphi and Tullumayo (marked today by the two Cusco streets which still bear their names). Here they established Cusco as their capital. They were initially a small group of *ayllus*, or family-based clans, devoted to agriculture. They began their expansion gradually, by forging links over a long period with other ethnic groups in the area in order to acquire more land for cultivation. Successive generations of rulers were fully occupied with overcoming local rivals, such as the Colla and Lupaca to the south, and the Chanca to the northwest. The Incas had had a long-running dispute with the Chanca, a powerful people based around Ayacucho, whose lands adjoined theirs. The Inca oral histories recorded by the Spanish recount that, towards the end of the reign of Viracocha, the Chanca finally felt strong enough to launch an all-out attack on Cusco itself and that the people of Cusco emerged victorious under the command of a young general called Cusi Yupanqui, who would later take the name Inca Pachacútec, which in Quechua means "Earth changer". The hero was subsequently crowned as the new ruler.

From the start of Pachacútec's own reign in 1438, barely 100 years before the arrival of the Spanish, imperial expansion grew in earnest, the defeat of the Chanca being the trigger. With the help of his son and heir, Túpac, territory was conquered from the Titicaca basin south into Chile, and all the north and central coast down to the Lurin Valley. The Incas also subjugated the Chimú, the highly sophisticated rival empire who had re-occupied the abandoned Moche capital at Chan Chán, in the north, near present-day Trujillo. Typical of the Inca method of government, some of the Chimú skills were assimilated into their own political and administrative system, and some Chimú nobles were even given positions in Cusco.

Perhaps the pivotal event in Inca history came in 1527 with the death of the ruler, Huayna Cápac. Civil war broke out in the confusion over his rightful successor. One of his legitimate sons, Huáscar, ruled the southern part of the empire from Cusco. Atahualpa, Huáscar's half-brother, governed Quito, the capital of Chinchaysuyo. In 1532, soon after Atahualpa had won the civil war, **Francisco Pizarro** arrived in Tumbes with 179 *conquistadores*, many on horseback. Atahualpa's army was marching south, probably for the first time, when he clashed with Pizarro at Cajamarca, in the northeastern Peruvian Andes.

The children of the sun

Like any agrarian society, the Incas were avid sky watchers, but their knowledge of astronomy was naturally limited to what could be of practical use to them with regard to their farming activities. In common with other cultures throughout the world, they realised that the seasons on which their subsistence depended were governed by the apparent movement of the sun, who they called Inti, *and placed at the head of their pantheon of gods. As the Inca Garcilaso de la Vega explains in his Royal Commentaries (1609), the Incas gave the name* huata *to the sun's annual movement, which in Quechua can mean either "year", or "to attach". They believed that the sun had been created by the supreme creator god Viracocha, who caused it to rise from an island on Lake Titicaca now known as Isla del Sol, and that the moon goddess, the sun's sister, called Mama Killa, rose from the nearby island of Coatí (known today as the Island of the Moon). Lake Titicaca is central to the creation legends of the Incas, having also been the birthplace of the first two Incas (also brother and sister) and the scene of a great flood sent, it is said, by Viracocha, to punish mankind for having disobeyed his teachings. Colourful as they may seem, such myths were also central to the political structure of the Inca State, in that they established the Inca's divine right to rule, as a direct descendant of the sun god Inti and, therefore, his representative on earth.*

Any agrarian society learns over time when to sow and harvest its crops by observing the cycle of nature around it. But in a planned, centralized economy governed by a self-proclaimed elite, the seasons of the year must be anticipated and, if it is to remain in power, that elite must be seen to monopolise the knowledge required for such predictions. The Incas, therefore, recruited the high priests, or tarpuntaes, *who made astronomical observations from the empire's many temples dedicated to the sun, from the ranks of their own nobility, who were essentially the Inca's extended family. These priests observed solar and lunar eclipses, which were variously interpreted as the sexual union of the two astral bodies or, more calamitously, manifestations of their anger with their chosen people, a warning of the imminent death of a public figure, or indications that they themselves were under attack.*

These astronomer-priests divided the year into twelve lunar months, which they themselves realised fell short of the solar year. They corrected this discrepancy by carefully following the course of the sun using cylindrical stone columns erected on the hills around the city of Cusco and measuring their shadows to calculate the solstices, placing their new year at the time of the summer solstice and their greatest celebration, Inti Raymi, during the winter solstice (June in the modern calendar). The equinoxes were calculated using a single stone pillar placed in the centre of each temple dedicated to the sun. At noon, when the stone barely cast a shadow, Inti was said to be sitting "with all his light on the column". As the Incas extended their empire towards present-day Ecuador, they realised that at the new temples they established, the further north they went, the more the shadow cast by the stones they erected was reduced. Quito's temple, therefore, just 22 km south of the ecuator, where the sun casts no shadow at midday, was held to be the favourite resting place oflnti, thereby rivalling the importance of the oldest and most venerated shrine in the empire at Qoricancha, in Cusco.

This was one of the biggest cities in the Inca Empire and was where the Incas and Spanish had their first showdown. Here Pizarro ambushed and captured Atahualpa and slaughtered his guards. Despite their huge numerical inferiority, the heavily-armed Spaniards took advantage of an already divided Inca Empire to launch their audacious attack. The Incas attempted to save their leader by collecting the outrageous ransom demanded by Pizarro for Atahualpa's release. This proved futile as the Spanish, fearing a mobilisation of Inca troops, executed the Inca leader once the treasure had been collected. There was no army coming to Atahualpa's rescue. Pizarro and his fellow *conquistador*, Diego de Almagro, had reacted hastily to a false rumour and their fatal decision was criticized at the time, including by Emperor Charles V. Pushing on to Cusco, Pizarro was at first hailed as the executioner of a traitor: Atahualpa had ordered the death of Huáscar in 1533, while himself a captive of Pizarro, and his victorious generals were bringing the defeated Huáscar to see his half-brother. Panic followed when the *conquistadores* set about sacking the Inca capital and they fought off with difficulty an attempt by Manco Inca to recapture Cusco in 1536.

Inca society

The people we call the Incas were a small aristocracy numbering only a few thousand, centred in the highland city of Cusco. They rose gradually as a small regional dynasty, similar to others in the Andes of that period, starting around 1200 AD. Then, suddenly, in the mid-1400s, they began to expand explosively under Pachacútec, a sort of Andean Alexander the Great, and later his son, Túpac. Less than100 years later, they fell before the rapacious warriors of Spain. The Incas were not the first dynasty in Andean history to dominate their neighbours, but they did it more thoroughly and went further than anyone before them.

Empire building

Enough remains today of their astounding highways, cities and agricultural terracing for people to marvel and wonder how they accomplished so much in so short a time. They seem to have been amazingly energetic, industrious and efficient – and the reports of their Spanish conquerors confirm this hypothesis.

They must also have had the willing cooperation of most of their subject peoples, most of the time. In fact, the Incas were master diplomats and alliance-builders first, and military conquerors only second, if the first method of expansion failed. The Inca skill at generating wealth by means of highly efficient agriculture and distribution brought them enormous prestige and enabled them to 'out-gift' neighbouring chiefs in huge royal feasts involving ritual outpourings of generosity, often in the form of vast gifts of textiles, exotic products from distant regions, and perhaps wives to add blood ties to the alliance. The 'out-gifted' chief was required by the Andean laws of reciprocity to provide something in return, and this would usually be his loyalty, as well as a levy of manpower from his own chiefdom.

Thus, with each new alliance the Incas wielded greater labour forces and their mighty public works programmes surged ahead. These were administered through an institution known as *mit'a*, a form of taxation through labour. The state provided the materials, such as wool and cotton for making textiles, and the communities provided skills and labour.

Mit'a contingents worked royal mines, royal plantations for producing coca leaves, royal quarries and so on. The system strove to be equitable, and workers in such hardship posts as high altitude mines and lowland coca plantations were given correspondingly shorter terms of service.

Organization

Huge administrative centres were built in different parts of the empire, where people and supplies were gathered. Articles such as textiles and pottery were produced there in large workshops. Work in these places was carried out in a festive manner, with plentiful food, drink and music. Here was Andean reciprocity at work: the subject supplied his labour, and the ruler was expected to provide generously while he did so.

Aside from *mit'a* contributions there were also royal lands claimed by the Inca as his portion in every conquered province, and worked for his benefit by the local population. Thus, the contribution of each citizen to the state was quite large, but

All roads lead to Cusco

There was a time when roads of colossal dimensions and magnificent construction crossed the difficult Andean terrain, thousands and thousands of kilometres in the most amazing network ever seen in antiquity. Through the building and management of this complex system, the Inca empire achieved both its expansion and its consolidation.

Cusco, navel of the world and capital of the powerful Tawantinsuyo, was where these roads began and ended. From the city's civic arena, Huacaypata (today's Plaza de Armas), the four trunk roads set out to each of the four (tahua) quarters (suyus) into which the empire was divided: Chinchaysuyo to the northwest as far as Quito and the borders of Colombia; Collasuyu to the south, incorporating the altiplano as far as Argentina and Chile; Cuntisuyu to the west, bound by the Pacific Ocean; and Antisuyu to the east and the Amazon lowlands.

The obvious limits presented by the sea and the jungle made the roads to north and south into a great axis which eventually came to be known as ***Capaq Ñan*** *– "Royal, or Principal Road", in Quechua – which exceeded in grandeur not only the other roads, but also their utilitarian concept. They became the Incas' symbol of power over men and over the sacred forces of nature. So marvellous were these roads that the Spaniards who saw them at the height of their glory said that there was nothing comparable in all Christendom and that, for example, a young girl from court could run their length barefoot as they were even swept clean. Amazement was not the sole preserve of the Europeans, as an early chronicle reveals. A settler who lived a long way from the capital reached the road in his district and said, "At last, I have seen Cusco."*

Imperial life revolved around these roads. Via them the produce of the coastal valleys and Amazonia were collected in tribute, to be exchanged prudently with those of the Sierra, or to be stored for times of shortage. Whole

apparently, the imperial economy was productive enough to sustain this.

Another institution was the practice of moving populations around wholesale, inserting loyal groups into restive areas, and removing recalcitrant populations to loyal areas. These movements of *mitmakuna*, as they were called, were also used to introduce skilled farmers and engineers into areas where productivity needed to be raised.

Communications The huge empire was held together by an extensive and highly efficient highway system. There were an estimated 30,000 km of major highway, most of it neatly paved and drained, stringing together the major Inca sites. Two parallel highways ran north to south, along the coastal desert strip and the mountains, and dozens of east-west roads crossing from the coast to the Amazon fringes. These roadways took the most direct routes, with wide stone stairways zig-zagging up the steepest mountain slopes and rope suspension bridges crossing the many narrow gorges of the Andes.

Every 12 km or so there was a *tambo*, or way station, where goods could be stored and travellers lodged. The *tambos* were also control points, where the Inca state's accountants tallied movements of goods and people. Even more numerous than *tambos*, were the huts of the *chasquis*, or relay runners, who continually sped royal and military messages along these highways.

The Inca state kept records and transmitted information in various ways. Accounting and statistical records were kept on skeins of knotted strings known as *quipus* (see box). Numbers employed the decimal system, and colours indicated the categories being recorded. An entire class of people, known as *quipucamayocs*, existed whose job was to create and interpret these. Neither the Incas nor their *communities were moved along these roads, to keep rebellion in check or to take the skills they possessed to another corner of the empire. These people had been conquered by armies thousands strong who advanced, unstoppable, along the roads, their supplies guaranteed at the* tambos *(storehouses) that were placed at regular intervals. News and royal decrees travelled with all haste, delivered by the famous* chasquis, *a race of men dedicated exclusively to running in relay along the roads.*

While the roadbuilding did not happen all at once, the speed with which Pachacútec and his successors transformed the Andean world was incredible. In scarcely a century the most important civilization of the southern hemisphere had been created, only to be destroyed as the Spaniards capitalized on the fratricidal war between Huáscar and Atahualpa. What happened to the roads after that parallels what happened to the civilization itself. The hold which Cusco had over its territory evaporated and everything took on a new focus: the ports and the sea, on the other side of which was Spain. For a while the Spaniards used the very same roads which had been used to feed this immense body, only to leave it weakened and lifeless. Then, the large populations which the roads connected were exiled to live in reductions in the valleys where they could be controlled more easily and the roads, now running from one ghost town to the next, faded into oblivion.

The Incas, however, built for eternity. Many sections of the great network can be found today, not only in good condition but still in use, like the Inca Trail to Machu Picchu. Many sections are lost under vegetation, time or mere lack of interest. Happily, all this is changing. Today Inca roads have been considered of national importance and there is a hope that work will begin on their conservation, especially the Capaq Ñan, which possesses singular architectural characteristics and universal value.

Andean predecessors had a system of writing as we understand it, but there may have been a system of encoding language into *quipus*.

Archaeologists are studying this problem today. History and other forms of knowledge were transmitted via songs and poetry. Music and dancing, full of encoded information which could be read by the educated elite, were part of every major ceremony and public event information was also carried in textiles, which had for millennia been the most vital expression of Andean culture.

Textiles

Clothing carried insignia of status, ethnic origin, age and so on. Special garments were made and worn for various rites of passage. It has been calculated that, after agriculture, no activity was more important to Inca civilization than weaving. Vast stores of textiles were maintained to sustain the Inca system of ritual giving. Armies and *mit'a* workers were partly paid in textiles. The finest materials were reserved for the nobility, and the Inca emperor himself displayed his status by changing into new clothes every day and having the previous day's burned.

Most weaving was done by women and the Incas kept large numbers of 'chosen women' in female-only houses all over the empire. Among their duties was to supply textiles to the elite and the many deities, to whom the weavings were frequently given as burned offerings. These women had other duties, such as making *chicha* – the Inca corn beer which was consumed and sacrificed in vast quantities on ceremonial occasions. They also became wives and concubines to the Inca elite and loyal nobes. And some may have served as priestesses of the moon, in parallel to the male priesthood of the sun.

Quipus: holding the strings of empire

Despite their extraordinary advances in the fields of government, agriculture, architecture, astronomy and engineering, it is generally agreed that the Incas never developed a written language. But given the phenomenal degree to which the Inca State was centrally planned and governed, it should come as no surprise to learn that they did employ a complex mnemonic device for the keeping of state records.

The quipu consisted of a series of strings with knots tied in them. Those quipus found so far by archaeologists vary in length from just a few centimetres to more than a metre. By varying the colour of the strings, and the position and type of knot, the Incas were able to record vast amounts of information related to the affairs of the empire in a series of censuses of its entire population of more than ten million.

The quipucamayocs, *an hereditary group trained in the art of compiling and deciphering the quipus, were charged with keeping a complete demographic record, from births and deaths to age groups, the number of men-under-arms, marriages, and the material wealth of the empire, which comprised great storehouses like those discovered by the Spanish when they reached Cusco in 1533. These huge rectangular sheds contained everything that was grown or manufactured in an empire where private ownership was almost unknown, including grain, cloth, military equipment, coca, metal, shoes and items of clothing. All of this vast treasure, which the gold-hungry Spanish completely ignored, would have been precisely documented using quipus.*

The Inca social system of ayllus, *or clans, was based on groups of multiples of ten, and its arithmetical system was therefore also decimal. Apparently the concept of zero was understood but had no symbol; on those quipus deciphered by researchers it is represented by the absence of a knot. The data recorded on a quipu was calculated using an abacus, or* yupana, *which was fashioned from a rectangular tablet divided into smaller rectangular blocks, upon which grains of quinoa and corn of different colours were used to add, subtract, multiply and divide complex sums. The Spanish chronicler José de Acosta (1590) was astonished by the dexterity and exactitude of the Incas'* yupanacamayocs, *who he claimed never made a mistake and were much faster and more accurate than the Spanish accountants who used pen and paper.*

While most scholars maintain that quipus were only used to record numbers, some others assert that they were also utilised to record other kinds of information, and that they were therefore effectively written records, or books. Recent research has suggested that the Incas employed a decimal alphabet in which consonants were represented by numbers and vowels were omitted, enabling them to communicate, and conserve, abstract concepts like poetry and storytelling on both their quipus and in the geometric designs of their weavings. If such theories can be proved, they would make the Incas the inventors of written language in South America, and the quipucamayocs their court historians and Peru's first chroniclers.

Religious worship The Incas have always been portrayed as sun-worshippers, but it now seems that they were just as much mountain-worshippers. Recent research has shown that Machu Picchu was at least partly dedicated to the worship of the surrounding mountains, and Inca sacrificial victims have been excavated on frozen Andean peaks at 6,700 m. In fact, until technical climbing was invented, the Incas held the world altitude record for humans.

Human sacrifice was not common, but every other kind was, and ritual attended every event in the Inca calendar. The main temple of Cusco was dedicated to the numerous deities: the Sun, the Moon, Venus, the Pleiades, the Rainbow, Thunder and Lightning, and the countless religious icons of subject peoples which had been brought to Cusco, partly in homage, partly as hostage. Here, worship was continuous and the fabulous opulence included gold cladding on the walls, and a famous garden filled with life-size objects of gold and silver. Despite this pantheism, the Incas acknowledged an overall Creator God, whom they called Viracocha. A special temple was dedicated to him, at Raqchi, about 100 km southeast of Cusco. Part of it still stands today.

Military forces

The conquering Spaniards noted with admiration the Inca storehouse system, still well-stocked when they found it, despite several years of civil war among the Incas. Besides textiles, military equipment, and ritual objects, they found huge quantities of food. Like most Inca endeavours, the food stores served a multiple purpose: to supply feasts, to provide during lean times, to feed travelling work parties, and to supply armies on the march.

Inca armies were able to travel light and move fast because of this system. Every major Inca settlement also incorporated great halls where large numbers of people could be accommodated, or feasts and gatherings held, and large squares or esplanades for public assemblies.

Inca technology is usually deemed inferior to that of contemporary Europe. Their military technology certainly was. They had not invented iron-smelting and basically fought with clubs, palmwood spears, slings, wooden shields, cotton armour and straw-stuffed helmets. They did not even make much use of the bow and arrow, a weapon they were well aware of. Military tactics, too, were primitive. The disciplined formations of the Inca armies quickly dissolved into melees of unbridled individualism once battle was joined.

This, presumably, was because warfare constituted a theatre of manly prowess, but was not the main priority of Inca life. Its form was ritualistic. Battles were suspended by both sides for religious observance. Negotiation, combined with displays of superior Inca strength, usually achieved victory, and total annihilation of the enemy was not on the agenda.

Architecture

Other technologies, however, were superior in every way to their 16th century counterparts: textiles; settlement planning; and agriculture in particular with its sophisticated irrigation and soil conservation systems, ecological sensitivity, specialized crop strains and high productivity under the harshest conditions.

Unlike modern cities, Inca towns, or *llaqtas*, were not designed to house large, economically active populations. Inca society was essentially agrarian and, among the common people, almost everyone worked and lived on the land. The towns and cities that the Incas did build were meant to serve as residential areas for the state's administrative and religious elite. Throughout Tawantinsuyo, the *llaqtas* were divided into two zones, along blood lines, between the two principal *ayllus*, of Hanan and Urin. The streets were laid out in a simple grid pattern, with the whole forming a trapezoid. The trapezoid was the fundamental basis of Inca architecture, from niches and doorways to buildings and entire towns, and has been called the Inca version of the arch.

The Incas fell short of their Andean predecessors in the better-known arts of ancient America – ceramics, textiles and metalwork – but it could be argued that their supreme efforts were made in architecture, stoneworking, landscaping, roadbuilding, and the harmonious combination of these elements. These are the outstanding survivals of Inca civilization, which still remain to fascinate the visitor: the huge, exotically close-fit blocks of stone, cut in graceful, almost sensual curves; the astoundingly craggy and inaccessible sites encircled by great sweeps of Andean scenery; the rhythmic layers of farm terracing that provided land and food to this still-enigmatic people. The finest examples of Inca architecture can be seen in the city of Cusco and throughout the Sacred Valley.

Ruling elite The ruling elite lived privileged lives in their capital at Cusco. They reserved for themselves and privileged insiders certain luxuries, such as the chewing of coca, the wearing of fine vicuña wool, and the practice of polygamy. But they were an austere people, too. Everyone had work to do, and the nobility were constantly being posted to state business throughout the empire. Young nobles were expected to learn martial skills, besides being able to read the *quipus*, speak both Quechua and the southern language of Aymara, and know the epic poems.

The Inca elite belonged to royal clans known as *panacas*, which each had the unusual feature of being united around veneration of the mummy of their founding ancestor – a previous Inca emperor, unless they happened to belong to the *panaca* founded by the Inca emperor who was alive at the time. Each new emperor built his own palace in Cusco and amassed his own wealth rather than inheriting it from his forebears, which perhaps helps to account for the urge to unlimited expansion.

This urge ultimately led the Incas to overreach themselves. Techniques of diplomacy and incorporation no longer worked as they journeyed farther from the homeland and met ever-increasing resistance from people less familiar with their ways. During the reign of Huayna Cápac, the last emperor before the Spanish invasion, the Incas had to establish a northern capital at Quito in order to cope with permanent war on their northern frontier. Following Huayna Cápac's death came a devastating civil war between Cusco and Quito, and immediately thereafter came the Spanish invasion. Tawantisuyo, the empire of the four quarters, collapsed with dizzying suddenness.

Conquest and after

Peruvian history after the arrival of the Spaniards was not just a matter of *conquistadores* versus Incas. The vast majority of the huge empire remained unaware of the conquest for many years. The Chimú and the Chachapoyas cultures of northern Peru were powerful enemies of the Incas. The Chimú developed a highly sophisticated culture and a powerful empire stretching for 560 km along the coast from Paramonga south to Casma. Their history was well-recorded by the Spanish chroniclers and continued through the conquest possibly up to about 1600. The Kuelap/Chachapoyas people were not so much an empire as a loose-knit 'confederation of ethnic groups with no recognized capital' (Morgan Davis *Chachapoyas: The Cloud People*, Ontario, 1988). But the culture did develop into an advanced society with great skill in roads and monument building. Their fortress at Kuelap, in the northeast, where the Andes meet the Amazon, was known as the most impregnable in Tawantinsuyo. It remained intact against Inca attack and Manco Inca even tried, unsuccessfully, to gain refuge here against the Spaniards.

In 1535, wishing to secure his communications with Spain, Pizarro founded Lima, near the ocean, as his capital. The same year Diego de Almagro set out to conquer Chile. Unsuccessful, he returned to Peru, quarrelled with Pizarro, and in 1538 fought a pitched battle with Pizarro's men at the Salt Pits, near Cusco. He was defeated and put to death. Pizarro, who had not been at the battle, was assassinated in his palace in Lima by Almagro's son three years later.

For the next 27 years each succeeding representative of the Kingdom of Spain sought to subdue the Inca successor state of Vilcabamba, north of Cusco, and to unify the fierce Spanish factions. Francisco de Toledo (appointed 1568) solved both problems during his 14 years in office: Vilcabamba was crushed in 1572 and the last reigning Inca, Túpac Amaru, put to death.

For the next 200 years the Viceroys closely followed Toledo's system, if not his methods. The Major Government – the Viceroy, the *Audiencia* (High Court), and *corregidores* (administrators) – ruled through the Minor Government – Indian chiefs put in charge of large groups of natives – a rough approximation to the original Inca system.

Towards independence

The Indians rose in 1780, under the leadership of an Inca noble who called himself Túpac Amaru II. He and many of his lieutenants were captured and put to death under torture at Cusco. Another Indian leader in revolt suffered the same fate in 1814, but this last flare-up had the sympathy of many of the locally-born Spanish, who resented their status, inferior to the Spaniards born in Spain, the refusal to give them any but the lowest offices, the high taxation imposed by the home government, and the severe restrictions upon trade with any country but Spain.

Help came to them from the outside world. José de San Martín's Argentine troops, convoyed from Chile under the protection of Lord Cochrane's squadron, landed in southern Peru on 7 September, 1820. San Martín proclaimed Peruvian independence at Lima on 28 July, 1821, though most of the country was still in the hands of the Viceroy, José de La Serna. Bolívar, who had already freed Venezuela and Colombia, sent Antonio José de Sucre to Ecuador where, on 24 May, 1822, he gained a victory over La Serna at Pichincha.

San Martín, after a meeting with Bolívar at Guayaquil, left for Argentina and a self-imposed exile in France, while Bolívar and Sucre completed the conquest of Peru by defeating La Serna at the battle of Junín (6 August, 1824) and the decisive battle of Ayacucho (9 December, 1824). For over a year there was a last stand in the Real Felipe fortress at Callao by the Spanish troops under General Rodil before they capitulated on 22 January, 1826. Bolívar was invited to stay in Peru, but left for Colombia in 1826.

Modern Peru

Political developments

19th century

Independence from Spanish rule meant that power passed into the hands of the Creole elite with no immediate alternation of the colonial social system. The *contribución de indíginas*, the colonial tribute collected from the native peoples was not abolished until 1854, the same year as the ending of slavery. For much of the period since independence Peruvian political life has been dominated by these traditional elites. Political parties have been slow to develop and the roots of much of the political conflict and instability which have marked the country's history lie in personal ambitions and in regional and other rivalries within the elite.

The early years after independence were particularly chaotic as rival caudillos (political bosses) who had fought in the independence wars vied with each other for power. The increased wealth brought about by the guano boom led to greater stability, though political corruption became a serious problem under the presidency of **José Rufino Echenique** (1851-1854) who paid out large sums of the guano revenues as compensation to upper class families for their (alleged) losses in the Wars of Independence. Defeat by Chile in the War of the Pacific discredited civilian politicians even further and led to a period of military rule in the 1880s.

Early 20th century

Even though the voting system was changed in 1898, this did little to change the dominance of the elite. Voting was not secret so landowners herded their workers to the polls and watched to make sure they voted correctly. Yet voters were also lured by promises as well as threats. One of the more unusual presidents was **Guillermo Billinghurst** (1912-1914) who campaigned on the promise of a larger loaf of bread for five cents, thus gaining the nickname of "Big Bread Billinghurst". As president he proposed a publically-funded housing programme, supported the introduction of an eight hour day and was eventually overthrown by the military who, along with the elite, were alarmed at his growing popularity among the urban population.

The 1920s was dominated by **Augusto Leguía**. After winning the 1919 elections Leguía claimed that Congress was plotting to prevent him from becoming president and induced the military to help him close Congress. Backed by the armed forces, Leguía introduced a new constitution which gave him greater powers and enabled him to be re-elected in 1924 and 1929. Claiming his goal was to prevent the rise of communism, he proposed to build a partnership between business and labour. A large programme of public works, particularly involving building roads, bridges and railways, was begun, the work being carried out by poor rural men who were forced into unpaid building work. The Leguía regime dealt harshly with critics: opposition newspapers were closed and opposition leaders arrested and deported. His overthrow in 1930 ended what Peruvians call the "Oncenio" or 11 year period.

The 1920s also saw the emergence of a political thinker who would have great influence in the future, not only in Peru but elsewhere in Latin America. **Juan Carlos Mariátegui**, a socialist writer and journalist, argued that the solution to Peru's problems lay in the reintegration of the Indians through land reform and the breaking up of the great landed estates.

Another influential thinker of this period was **Víctor Raúl Haya de la Torre**, a student exiled by Leguía in 1924. He returned after the latter's fall to create the **Alianza Popular Revolucionaria Americana** (APRA), a political party which called for state control of the economy, nationalization of key industries and protection of the middle classes, which, Haya de la Torre argued, were threatened by foreign economic interests.

In 1932 APRA seized control of Trujillo; when the army arrived to deal with the rising, the rebels murdered about 50 hostages, including 10 army officers. In reprisal the army murdered about 1,000 local residents suspected of sympathizing with APRA. APRA eventually became the largest and easily the best-organized political party in Peru, but the distrust of the military and the upper class for Haya de la Torre ensured that he never became president.

A turning point in Peruvian history occurred in 1948 with the seizure of power by **General Manuel Odría**, backed by the coastal elite. Odría outlawed APRA and went on to win the 1950 election in which he was the only candidate. He pursued policies of encouraging export earnings and also tried to build up working class support by public works projects in Lima. Faced with a decline in export earnings and the fall in world market prices after 1953, plus increasing unemployment, Odría was forced to stand down in 1956.

In 1962 Haya de la Torre was at last permitted to run for the presidency. But although he won the largest percentage of votes he was prevented from taking office by the armed forces who seized power and organized fresh elections for 1963. In these the military obtained the desired result: Haya de la Torre came second to **Fernando Belaúnde Terry**. Belaúnde attempted to introduce reforms, particularly in the landholding structure of the sierra; when these reforms were weakened by landowner opposition in Congress, peasant groups began invading landholdings in protest.

At the same time, under the influence of the Cuban revolution, guerrilla groups began operating in the sierra. Military action to deal with this led to the deaths of an estimated 8,000 people. Meanwhile Belaúnde's attempts to solve a long-running dispute with the International Petroleum Company (a subsidiary of Standard Oil) resulted in him being attacked for selling out to the unpopular oil company and contributed to the armed forces' decision to seize power in 1968.

The 1968 coup

This was a major landmark in Peruvian history. Led by **General Juan Velasco Alvarado**, the Junta had no intention of handing power back to the civilians. A manifesto issued on the day of the coup attacked the 'unjust social and economic order' and argued for its replacement by a new economic system 'neither capitalist nor communist'. Partly as a result of their experiences in dealing with the guerrilla movement, the coup leaders concluded that agrarian reform was a priority.

Wide-ranging land reform was launched in 1969, during which large estates were taken over and reorganized into cooperatives. By the mid-1970s, 75% of productive land was under cooperative management. The government also attempted to improve the lives of shanty-town dwellers around Lima, as well as attempting to increase the influence of workers in industrial companies. At the same time attempts were made to reduce the influence of foreign companies with the nationalization of several transnationals.

Understandably, opposition to the Velasco government came from the business and landholding elite. The government's crack-down on expressions of dissent, the seizure of newspapers and taking over of TV and radio stations all offended sections of the urban middle class. Trade unions and peasant movements found that, although they agreed with many of the regime's policies, it refused to listen and expected their passive and unqualified support. As world sugar and copper prices dropped, inflation rose and strikes increased. Velasco's problems were further increased by opposition within the armed forces and by his own ill-health. In August 1975 he was replaced by **General Francisco Morales Bermúdez**, a more conservative officer, who dismantled some of Velasco's policies and led the way to a restoration of civilian rule.

Belaúnde returned to power in 1980 by winning the first elections after military rule. His government was badly affected by the 1982 debt crisis and the 1981-1983 world recession, and inflation reached over 100% a year in 1983-1984. His term was also marked by the growth of the Maoist guerrilla movement **Sendero Luminoso** (Shining Path) and the smaller **Túpac Amaru** (MRTA).

Initially conceived in the University of Ayacucho, Shining Path gained most support for its goal of overthrowing the whole system of Lima-based government from highland Indians and migrants to urban shanty towns. The activities of Sendero Luminoso and another guerrilla group, Túpac Amaru (MRTA), frequently disrupted transport and electricity supplies, although their strategies had to be reconsidered after the arrest of both their leaders in 1992. Víctor Polay of MRTA was arrested in June and Abimael Guzmán of Sendero Luminoso was captured in September and sentenced to life imprisonment. Although Sendero did not capitulate, many of its members took advantage of the Law of Repentance, which guaranteed lighter sentences in return for surrender, and freedom in exchange for valuable information. Meanwhile, Túpac Amaru was thought to have ceased operations (see below).

In 1985 APRA, in opposition for over 50 years, finally came to power. With Haya de la Torre dead, the APRA candidate **Alan García Pérez** won the elections and was allowed to take office by the armed forces. García attempted to implement an ambitious economic programme intended to solve many of Peru's deep-seated economic and social problems. He cut taxes, reduced interest rates, froze prices and devalued the currency. However, the economic boom which this produced in 1986-1987 stored up problems as increased incomes were spent on imports. Moreover, the government's refusal to pay more than 10% of its foreign debt meant that it was unable to borrow. In 1988 inflation hit 3,000% and unemployment soared. By the time his term of office ended in 1990 Peru was bankrupt and García and APRA were discredited.

Peru under Fujimori

In presidential elections held over two rounds in 1990, **Alberto Fujimori** of the Cambio 90 movement defeated the novelist **Mario Vargas Llosa**, who belonged to the Fredemo (Democratic Front) coalition. Fujimori, without an established political network behind him, failed to win a majority in either the senate or the lower house. Lack of congressional support was one of the reasons behind the dissolution of congress and the suspension of the constitution on 5 April 1992.

President Fujimori declared that he needed a freer hand to introduce market reforms and combat terrorism and drug trafficking, at the same time as rooting out corruption. Initial massive popular support, although not matched internationally, did not evaporate. In elections to a new, 80-member Democratic Constituent Congress (CCD) in November 1992, Fujimori's Cambio 90/Nueva Mayoría coalition won a majority of seats. A new constitution drawn up by the CCD was approved by a narrow majority of the electorate in October 1993. Among the new articles were the immediate re-election of the president (previously prohibited for one presidential term), the death penalty for terrorist leaders, the establishment of a single-chamber congress, the reduction of the role of the state, the designation of Peru as a market economy and the favouring of foreign investment. As expected, Fujimori stood for re-election on 9 April 1995 and the opposition chose as an independent to stand against him former UN General Secretary, Javier Pérez de Cuéllar. Fujimori was re-elected by a resounding margin, winning about 65% of the votes cast. The coalition that supported him also won a majority in Congress.

The government's success in most economic areas did not appear to accelerate the distribution of foreign funds for social projects. Rising unemployment and the austerity imposed by economic policy continued to cause hardship for many, despite the government's stated aim of alleviating poverty.

Dramatic events on 17 December 1996 thrust several of these issues into sharper focus: 14 Túpac Amaru guerrillas infiltrated a reception at the Japanese Embassy in Lima, taking 490 hostages. Among the rebel's demands were the release of their imprisoned colleagues, better treatment for prisoners and new measures to raise living standards. Most of the hostages were released and negotiations were pursued during a stalemate that lasted until 22 April 1997. The president took sole responsibility for the successful, but risky assault which freed all the hostages (one died of heart failure) and killed all the terrorists.

The popularity that Fujimori garnered from not yielding to Túpac Amaru deflected attention from his plans to stand for a third term following his unpopular manipulation of the law to persuade Congress that the new constitution did not apply to his first period in office. By 1998, opposition to Fujimori standing again had gained a substantial following, but not enough to dissuade the president or his supporters. Until the last month of campaigning for the 2000 presidential elections, Fujimori had a clear lead over his two main rivals, ex-mayor of Lima Alberto Andrade and former social security chief Luis Castaneda. Meanwhile, the popularity of a fourth candidate, Alejandro Toledo, a former World bank official of humble origins, surged to such an extent that he and Fujimori were neck-and neck in the first poll. Toledo, a pro-marketeer given to left-wing rhetoric, and his supporters claimed that Fujimori's slim majority was the result of fraud, a view echoed in the pressure put on the president, by the US government among others, to allow a second ballot.

The run-off election, on 28 May 2000, was also contentious since foreign observers, including the Organization of American States, said the electoral system was unprepared and flawed, proposing a postponement. The authorities refused to delay. Toledo boycotted the election and Fujimori was returned unopposed, but with scant approval. Having won, he proposed "to strengthen democracy".

This pledge proved to be utterly worthless following the airing of a secretly-shot video on 14 September 2000 of Fujimori's close aide and head of the National Intelligence Service (SIN), Vladimiro Montesinos, handing US$15,000 to a congressman, Alberto Kouri, to persuade him to switch allegiances to Fujimori's coalition. Fujimori's demise was swift. His initial reaction was to close down SIN and announce new elections, eventually set for 8 April 2001, at which he would not stand.

Montesinos was declared a wanted man and fled to Panama, where he was denied asylum. He returned to Peru in October, prompting First Vice-president Francisco Tudela to resign in protest over Montesinos' continuing influence. Fujimori personally led the search parties to find his former ally and Peruvians watched in amazement as this game of cat-and-mouse was played out on their TV screens.

While Montesinos himself successfully evaded capture, investigators began to uncover the extent of his empire, which held hundreds of senior figures in its web. His activities encompassed extortion, money-laundering, bribery, intimidation, probably arms and drugs dealing and possibly links with the CIA and death squads. Swiss bank accounts in his name were found to contain about US$70 million, while other millions were discovered in accounts in the Cayman Islands and elsewhere.

Meanwhile, Fujimori, apparently in pursuit of his presidential duties, made various overseas trips, including to Japan. Here, on 20 November, he sent Congress an email announcing his resignation. Congress rejected this, firing him instead on charges of being "morally unfit" to govern. An interim president, Valentín Paniagua, was sworn in, with ex-UN Secretary General Javier Pérez de Cuéllar as Prime Minister, and the government set about uncovering the depth of corruption associated with Montesinos and Fujimori. Further doubt was cast over the entire Fujimori period by suggestions that he may not have been born in Peru, as claimed, but in Japan. If he was indeed Japanese by birth as well as ancestry, he should never have been entitled to stand for the highest office in Peru.

In the run-up to the 2001 elections, the front-runner was Alejandro Toledo, but with far from a clear majority. As the campaign progressed, ex-President Alan García, recently returned from exile, emerged as Toledo's main rival. The first vote was close enough for a run-off to be held on 3 June 2001. This was won by Toledo with 52% of the vote, compared with 48% for García. Toledo pledged to heal the wounds that had opened in Peru since his first electoral battle with the disgraced Fujimori.

Society

The most remarkable thing about Peru, population 25.7 million in 2000, is its people. For most Peruvians life is a daily struggle to survive in the face of seemingly insurmountable problems. But most people do get by, through a combination of ingenuity, determination and sheer hard work. Many hold down two jobs to make ends meet, others work full time and study at night school and those without work invent their own jobs.

Peru may not be the poorest country in South America, but recent estimates put the number of poor at 49% of the population, while almost a fifth of people live in extreme poverty. Over a third of homes have no electricity or running water and a third of children suffer from chronic malnutrition.

Health

There have been major improvements in health care in recent years, but almost a third of the population have no access to public health services. The infant mortality rate is high – 37 deaths per 1,000 births – and the figure rises steeply in some rural areas where one in ten infants die within a year of birth.

Though health services are free, people still have to pay for prescribed medicines, which are very expensive, and so rarely finish a course of treatment. Lack of health education and limited primary health care also means that many women die in childbirth. Abortion is illegal in Peru, but those with cash can always find a private doctor. Those without the means to pay for a doctor run the risk of death or infection from botched abortions.

Education Education is free and compulsory for both sexes between six and 14. There are public and private secondary schools and private elementary schools. There are 32 state and private universities, and two Catholic universities. But resources are extremely limited and teachers earn a pittance. Poorer schoolchildren don't have money to buy pencils and notebooks and textbooks are few and far between in state schools. Furthermore, many children have to work instead of attending school; a quarter of those who start primary school don't finish. This is also due to the fact that classes are taught in Spanish and those whose native tongue is Quechua, Aymara or one of the Amazonian languages find it difficult and give up.

Migration The structure of Peruvian society, especially in the coastal cities, has been radically altered by internal migration. This movement began most significantly in the 1950s and 1960s as people from the Highlands sought urban jobs in place of work on the land. It was a time of great upheaval as the old system of labour on large estates was threatened by the peasant majority's growing awareness of the imbalances between the wealthy cities and impoverished sierra. The process culminated in the agrarian reforms of the government of General Juan Velasco (1968-75). Highland-to-city migration was given renewed impetus during the war between the state and Sendero Luminoso in the 1980s. Many communities which were depopulated in that decade are now beginning to come alive again.

Culture

People

Peru has a substantial indigenous population, only smaller as a percentage of the total than Bolivia and Guatemala of the Latin American republics. The literacy rate of the indigenous population is the lowest of any comparable group in South America and their diet is 50% below acceptable levels. The highland Indians bore the brunt of the conflict between Sendero Luminoso guerrillas and the security forces, which caused thousands of deaths and mass migration from the countryside to provincial cities or to Lima. Many indigenous groups are also under threat from colonization, development and road-building projects. Long after the end of Spanish rule, discrimination, dispossession and exploitation is still a fact of life for many native Peruvians.

Quechua According to Inca legend, the Quechuas were a small group who originally lived near Lake Titicaca. They later moved to Cusco, from where they expanded to create the Inca Empire. Their language and culture soon spread from Quito in the north through present-day Ecuador, Peru and Bolivia to northern Chile.

Predominantly an agricultural society, growing potatoes and corn as their basic diet, they are largely outside the money economy. Today, there remain two enduring legacies of Inca rule; their magnificent architecture and their unwritten language, Quechua, which has given its name to the descendants of their subjects. About two million Indians speak no Spanish, their main tongue being Quechua, but there are many more descendants of the Quechua who now speak only Spanish. Though recognized as an official language, little effort is made to promote Quechua nationally. It is only the remoteness of many Quechua speakers which has preserved it in rural areas. This isolation has also helped preserve many of their ancient traditions and beliefs. See also Festivals, on page 262.

Aymara High up in the Andes, in the southern part of Peru, lies a wide, barren and hostile plateau, the *altiplano*. Prior to Inca rule Tiahuanaco on Lake Titicaca was a highly-organized centre for one the greatest cultures South America has ever witnessed: the Aymara people. Today, the shores of this lake and the plains that surround it remain the homeland of the Aymara. The majority live in Bolivia, the rest are scattered on the southwestern side of Peru and northern Chile. The climate is so harsh on the *altiplano* that, though they are extremely hard-working, their lives are very poor. They speak their own unwritten language, Aymara.

Amazonian peoples

Before the arrival of the Europeans, an estimated six million people inhabited the Amazon basin, comprising more than 2,000 tribes or ethnic-linguistic groups who managed to adapt to their surroundings through the domestication of a great variety of animals and plants, and to benefit from the numerous nutritional, curative, narcotic and hallucinogenic properties of thousands of wild plants.

It's not easy to determine the precise origin of these aboriginal people. What is known, however, is that since the beginning of colonial times this population slowly but constantly decreased, mainly because of the effect of western diseases such as influenza and measles. This demographic decline reached dramatic levels during the rubber boom of the late 19th and early 20th centuries, as a result of forced labour and slavery.

Today, at the basin level, the population is calculated at no more than two million inhabitants making up 400 ethnic groups, of which approximately 200-250,000 live in the Peruvian jungle. Within the basin it is possible to distinguish at least three large conglomerates of aboriginal societies: the inhabitants of the *varzea*, or seasonally flooded lands alongside the large rivers (such as the Omagua, Cocama and Shipibo people); the people in the interfluvial zones or firm lands (such as the Amahuaca, Cashibo and Yaminahua) and those living in the Andean foothills (such as the Amuesha, Ashaninka and Matsigenka).

The Amazonian natives began to be decimated in the 16th century, and so were the first endangered species of the jungle. These communities still face threats to their traditional lifestyles, notably from timber companies, gold miners and multinational oil giants. There appears to be little effective control of deforestation and the intrusion of colonists who have taken over native lands to establish small farms. And though oil companies have reached compensation agreements with local communities, previous oil exploration has contaminated many jungle rivers, as well as exposing natives to risk from diseases against which they have no immunity.

Criollos & mestizos

The first immigrants were the Spaniards who followed Pizarro's expeditionary force. Their effect, demographically, politically and culturally, has been enormous. They intermarried with the indigenous population and the children of mixed parentage were called *mestizos*. The Peruvian-born children of Spanish parents were known as *criollos*, though this word is now used to describe people who live on the coast, regardless of their ancestory, and coastal culture in general.

Afro-Peruvians

Peru's black community is based on the coast, mainly in Chincha, south of Lima, and also in some working-class districts of the capital. Their forefathers were originally imported into Peru in the 16th century as slaves to work on the sugar and cotton plantations on the coast. Though small – between two and 5% of the total population – the black community has had a major influence on Peruvian culture, particularly in music and dancing and cuisine.

Asian immigrants

There are two main Asian communities in Peru, the Japanese and Chinese. Large numbers of poor Chinese labourers were brought to Peru in the mid-19th century to work in virtual slavery on the guano reserves on the Pacific coast and to build the railroads in the central Andes. The culinary influence of the Chinese can be seen in the many *chifas* found throughout the country.

The Ancient Leaf

Coca flourishes in the subtropical valleys of the eastern Andes, as well as in the Sierra Nevada de Santa Marta in Colombia, and for millenia it has been central to the daily life and religious rituals of many of the indigenous cultures of South America. The coca plant (Erythroxylum coca) is an evergreen shrub found in warm, fertile valleys. Its leaves are oval and between three and five cm long, and resemble laurel or bay leaves. Chewed with lime, which acts as a catalyst, the leaf releases a mild dose of cocaine alkaloid, numbing the senses, dulling both hunger and pain and even providing some vitamins otherwise absent in the starch-heavy diet of the highland Indian.

Under the Incas, the use of coca was restricted to ceremonies involving the nobility and priesthood and after the conquest the Spanish promoted the use of the leaf among the half-starved slaves of the mines of Huancavelica and Potosí. It wasn't until 1862 that an Austrian chemist refined the leaf to produce pure cocaine, which was subsequently marketed as a cure for opium addiction, a local anaesthetic, a tonic and (as Coca Cola) a headache remedy. In the 1970s, with the drug's growth in popularity in the United States and Europe, cocaine became big business, funding entire guerrilla movements and creating multi-billion dollar fortunes for men like Colombia's Pablo Escobar.

The word coca comes from the Aymara word q'oka, which means "food for travellers and workers". There is some controversy regarding the plant's precise origin. Some ethnobiologists estimate that coca has been cultivated in the Andes for at least 4,000 years and in Ecuador archaeological discoveries from the Valdivia Period (1500 BC) seem to provide early evidence of the use of coca: ceramic figurines have been found representing men whose most outstanding features are the bulges in the cheeks characteristic of the coca chewer. Whatever its true origin, the traditional consumption of coca remains an important symbol of ethnic identity for the indigenous peoples of the South American highlands.

Under the Incas, coca was revered as a gift from the gods and its production and distribution were strictly controlled by the

The Japanese community, now numbering some 100,000, established itself in the first half of the 20th century. The normally reclusive community gained prominence when Alberto Fujimori, one of its members, became the first president of Japanese descent outside Japan anywhere in the world. During Fujimori's presidency, many other Japanese Peruvians took prominent positions in business, central and local government. Despite the nickname 'chino', which is applied to anyone of Oriental origin, the Japanese and Japan are respected for their industriousness and honesty (well, most of them, anyway).

Europeans Like most of Latin America, Peru received many emigrés from Europe seeking land and opportunities in the late 19th century. The country's wealth and political power remains concentrated in the hands of this small and exclusive class of whites, which also consists of the descendants of the first Spanish families. There still exists a deep divide between people of European descent and the old colonial snobbery persists.

Religion

The Inca religion (described on page 246) was displaced by Roman Catholicism from the 16th century onwards, the conversion of the inhabitants of the 'New World' to Christianity being one of the stated aims of the Spanish *state. It was used in religious rites and burials and for divination, and it was only with the Spanish conquest and the fall of the Inca empire that the sacred leaf was commercialized and its use became more widespread.After the conquest, the role of coca in indigenous religious practices and divination provoked the catholic extirpators of idolatry to ban its use. Diego de Robles began the Western-led demonization of coca which continues to this day when he declared that it was "a plant that the devil invented for the total destruction of the natives", and it was condemned outright at the first ecclesiastical council of Lima in 1551.*

However, it did not take the Spanish very long to recognize the enormous business potential of coca and they began to encourage its consumption. As the Uruguayan historian Eduardo Galeano writes: "In the mines of Potosí in the 16th century as much was spent on European clothing for the oppressors as on coca for the oppressed. In Cusco, four hundred Spanish merchants made their living from trafficking coca, one hundred thousand baskets, containing a million kilos of coca leaves, entered the silver mines of Potosí annually. The Church extracted taxes from the traffic. Inca Garcilaso de la Vega tells us, in his "Royal Commentaries", that the greater part of the income of the bishop, canons and other church ministers came from the tithe on coca...With the few coins that they received for their work, the Indians bought coca leaves...chewing the leaves they could stand better... the inhuman tasks imposed upon them".

Today, despite the distortion of its social function caused by both its years of misuse as an instrument of colonial manipulation and, more recently, its mass production and refinement into cocaine, coca continues to play an important role in the lives of Peru's indigenous highlanders. Exchanged, given or shared, the act of chewing coca is, intrinsically, a form of social bonding, and this innocuous little leaf can stave off the hunger and fatigue of a working day, relieve the effects of altitude as well as a score of other ailments, help to divine the future, or appease Mother Earth in ceremonies as old as the cultures that have guarded them so jealously through the centuries.

conquistadores. Today, official statistics state that 92.5% of the population declares itself Catholic.

One of the first exponents of Liberation Theology, under which the Conference of Latin American Bishops in 1968 committed themselves to the 'option for the poor', was Gustavo Gutiérrez, from Huánuco. This doctrine caused much consternation to orthodox Catholics, particularly those members of the Latin American church who had traditionally aligned themselves with the oligarchy. Gutiérrez, however, traced the church's duty to the voiceless and the marginalized back to Fray Bartolomé de las Casas.

The Catholic Church faced a further challenge to its authority when President Fujimori won the battle over family planning and the need to slow down the rate of population growth. Its greatest threat, however, comes from the proliferation of evangelical Protestant groups throughout the country. Some 5.5% of the population now declare themselves Protestant and one million or more people belong to some 27 different non-Catholic denominations.

Although the vast majority of the population ostensibly belongs to the Roman Catholic religion, in reality religious life for many Peruvians is a mix of Catholic beliefs imported from Europe and indigenous traditions based on animism, the worship of deities from the natural world such as mountains, animals and plants. Some of these ancient indigenous traditions and beliefs are described throughout this section.

Arts and crafts

Peru is exceptionally rich in handicrafts. Its geographic division into four distinct regions – coast, mountains, valleys and Amazon basin – coupled with cultural differences, has resulted in numerous variations in technique and design. Each province, even each community, has developed its own style of weaving or carving.

The Incas inherited 3,000 years of skills and traditions: gold, metal and precious stonework from the Chimú; feather textiles from the Nasca; and the elaborate textiles of the Paracas. All of these played important roles in political, social and religious ceremonies. Though much of this artistic heritage was destroyed by the Spanish conquest, the traditions adapted and evolved in numerous ways, absorbing new methods, concepts and materials from Europe while maintaining ancient techniques and symbols.

Textiles & costumes Woven cloth was the most highly-prized possession and sought after trading commodity in the Andes in precolumbian times. It is, therefore, not surprising that ancient weaving traditions have survived. **The Incas** inherited this rich weaving tradition. They forced the Aymaras to work in *mitas* or textile workshops. The ruins of some enormous *mitas* can be seen at the temple of Raqchi, south of Cusco (see page 196). Inca textiles are of high quality and very different from coastal textiles, being warp-faced, closely woven and without embroidery. The largest quantities of the finest textiles were made specifically to be burned as ritual offerings – a tradition which still survives. The Spanish, too, exploited this wealth and skill by using the *mitas* and exporting the cloth to Europe.

Prior to Inca rule Aymara men wore a tunic (*llahua*) and a mantle (*llacata*) and carried a bag for coca leaves (*huallquepo*). The women wore a wrapped dress (*urku*) and mantle (*iscayo*) and a belt (*huaka*); their coca bag was called an *istalla*. The *urku* was fastened at shoulder level with a pair of metal *tupu*, the traditional Andean dress-pins.

The Inca men had tunics (*unkus*) and a bag for coca leaves called a *ch'uspa*. The women wore a blouse (*huguna*), skirts (*aksu*) and belts (*chumpis*), and carried foodstuffs in large, rectangular cloths called *lliclIas*, which were fastened at the chest with a single pin or a smaller clasp called a *ttipqui*. Women of the Sacred Valley now wear a layered, gathered skirt called a *pollera* and a *montera*, a large, round, red Spanish type of hat. Textiles continue to play an important part in society. They are still used specifically for ritual ceremonies and some even held to possess magical powers.

Textile materials & techniques The Andean people used mainly alpaca or llama wool. The former can be spun into fine, shining yarn when woven and has a lustre similar to that of silk, though sheep's wool came to be widely used following the Spanish conquest.

A commonly used technique is the drop spindle. A stick is weighted with a wooden wheel and the raw material is fed through one hand. A sudden twist and drop in the spindle spins the yarn. This very sensitive art can be seen practised by women while herding animals in the fields. Spinning wheels were introduced by Europeans and are now prevalent owing to increased demand. Pre-Columbian looms were often portable and those in use today are generally similar. A woman will herd her animals while making a piece of costume, perhaps on a backstrap loom, or waist loom, so-called because the weaver controls the tension on one side with her waist with the other side tied to an upright or tree. The pre-Columbian looms are usually used for personal costume while the treadle loom is used by men for more commercial pieces.

The skills of **dyeing** were still practised virtually unchanged even after the arrival of the Spanish. Nowadays, the word *makhnu* refers to any natural dye, but originally

The family that weaves together...

Nowadays, and presumably for at least the last 200-300 hundred years, the women weave most of the men's garments and the men weave the women's, or at least a very important part of them: the men weave the women's skirts. It works like this: the women weave the fine warp-faced pieces like Lliclias *(mantas), ponchos,* Chumpis *(belts),* Ch'uspas*, and similar items. But the plainer elements, men's pantaloons, women's skirts, the colourful wide* Golones *(the decorative edging attached to them), are woven by men on large treadle looms, imported from Europe soon after the conquest. The men also weave the thick blankets, but on heavier versions of the traditional backstrap loom (or waist loom). The men are also the knitters and crochet makers. There are a few elements of Andean garb that are not woven at all, the most important being the* Chullo *(the classic wool cap with the earl flaps), but there are also Chullos for children of either sex and, in some areas like Pitumarca, for young girls until puberty. All of these are knitted, the preferred alternative to the standard knitting needles being the spokes of bicycle wheels.*

was the name for cochineal, an insect which lives on the leaves of the nopal cactus. These dyes were used widely by precolumbian weavers. Today, the biggest centre of production in South America is the valleys around Ayacucho. Vegetable dyes are also used, made from the leaves, fruit and seeds of shrubs and flowers and from lichen, tree bark and roots.

Pottery

Inca ceramic decoration consists mainly of small-scale geometric and usually symmetrical designs. One distinctive form of vessel which continues to be made and used is the *arybola*. This pot is designed to carry liquid, especially chicha, and is secured with a rope on the bearer's back. It is believed that *arybolas* were used mainly by the governing Inca élite and became important status symbols. Today, Inca-style is very popular in Cusco and Pisac.

With the Spanish invasion many indigenous communities lost their artistic traditions, others remained relatively untouched, while others still combined Hispanic and indigenous traditions and techniques. The Spanish brought three innovations: the potter's wheel, which gave greater speed and uniformity; knowledge of the enclosed kiln; and the technique of lead glazes. The enclosed kiln made temperature regulation easier and allowed higher temperatures to be maintained, producing stronger pieces. Today, many communities continue to apply pre-Hispanic techniques, while others use more modern processes.

Jewellery & metalwork

Some of the earliest goldwork originates from the Chavín culture – eg the *Tumi* knife found in Lambayeque. These first appeared in the Moche culture, when they were associated with human sacrifice. Five centuries later, the Incas used *Tumis* for surgical operations such as trepanning skulls. Today, they are a common motif.

The Incas associated gold with the Sun. However, very few examples remain as the Spanish melted down their amassed gold and silver objects. They then went on to send millions of Indians to their deaths in gold and silver mines.

During the colonial period gold and silver pieces were made to decorate the altars of churches and houses of the élite. Metalworkers came from Spain and Italy to develop the industry. The Spanish preferred silver and strongly influenced the evolution of silverwork during the colonial period. A style known as Andean baroque developed around Cusco embracing both indigenous and European elements. Silver bowls in this style – *cochas* – are still used in Andean ceremonies.

Woodcarving Wood is one of the most commonly used materials. Carved ceremonial objects include drums, carved sticks with healing properties, masks and the Incas' *keros* – wooden vessels for drinking chicha. *Keros* come in all shapes and sizes and were traditionally decorated with scenes of war, local dances, or harvesting coca leaves. The Chancay, who lived along the coast between 100 BC and AD 1200, used *keros* carved with sea birds and fish. Today, they are used in some Andean ceremonies, especially during *Fiesta del Cruz*, the Andean May festival.

Glass mirrors were introduced by the Spanish, although the Chimú and Lambayeque cultures used obsidian and silver plates, and Inca *chasquis* (messengers) used reflective stones to communicate between hilltop forts. Transporting mirrors was costly, therefore they were produced in Lima and Quito. Cusco and Cajamarca then became centres of production. In Cusco the frames were carved, covered in gold leaf and decorated with tiny pieces of cut mirror. Cajamarca artisans, meanwhile, incorporated painted glass into the frames.

Gourd-carving Gourd-carving, or *máte burilado*, as it is known, is one of Peru's most popular and traditional handicrafts. It is thought even to predate pottery – engraved gourds found on the coast have been dated to some 3,500 years ago. During the Inca empire gourd-carving became a valued art form and workshops were set up and supported by the state. Gourds were used in rituals and ceremonies and to make *poporos* – containers for the lime used while chewing coca leaves.

Music and dance

The music of Peru can be described as the very heartbeat of the country. Peruvians see music as something in which to participate, and not as a spectacle. Just about everyone, it seems, can play a musical instrument or sing. Just as music is the heartbeat of the country, so dance conveys the rich and ancient heritage that typifies much of the national spirit. Peruvians are tireless dancers and dancing is the most popular form of entertainment. Unsuspecting travellers should note that once they make that first wavering step there will be no respite until they collapse from exhaustion.

Each region has its own distinctive music and dance that reflects its particular lifestyle, its mood and its physical surroundings. The music of the sierra, for example, is played in a minor key and tends to be sad and mournful, while the music of the lowlands is more up-tempo and generally happier. Peruvian music divides at a very basic level into that of the highlands ('Andina') and that of the coast ('Criolla').

Highlands When people talk of Peruvian music they are almost certainly referring to the music of the Quechua- and Aymara-speaking Indians of the highlands which provides the most distinctive Peruvian sound. The highlands themselves can be very roughly subdivided into some half dozen major musical regions, of which perhaps the most characteristic are Ancash and the north, the Mantaro Valley, Cusco, Puno and the Altiplano, Ayacucho and Parinacochas.

Urban and other styles Owing to the overwhelming migration of peasants into the barrios of Lima, most types of Andean music and dance can be seen in the capital, notably on Sundays at the so-called 'Coliseos', which exist for that purpose. This flood of migration to the cities has also meant that the distinct styles of regional and ethnic groups have become blurred. One example is **Chicha music**, which comes from the *pueblos jóvenes*, and was once the favourite dance music of Peru's urban working class. Chicha is a hybrid of Huayno music and the Colombian Cumbia rhythm – a meeting of the highlands and the tropical coast.

The latest music sensation is **Tecno-cumbia**, which originated in the jungle region with groups such as Rossy War, from Puerto Maldonado, and Euforia, from Iquitos. It is a vibrant dance music which has gained much greater popularity across Peruvian society than chicha music ever managed. There are now also many exponents on the coast such as Agua Marina and Armonía 10. Many of the songs comment on political issues and Fujimori used to join Rossy War on stage.

Música Criolla, the music from the coast, could not be more different from that of the Sierra. Here the roots are Spanish and African. The immensely popular **Valsesito** is a syncopated waltz that would certainly be looked at askance in Vienna and the **Polca** has also undergone an attractive sea change.

Reigning over all, though, is the **Marinera**, Peru's national dance, a splendidly rhythmic and graceful courting encounter and a close cousin of Chile's and Bolivia's Cueca and the Argentine Zamba, all of them descended from the Zamacueca. The Marinera has its 'Limeña' and 'Norteña' versions and a more syncopated relative, the Tondero, found in the northern coastal regions, is said to have been influenced by slaves brought from Madagascar.

All these dances are accompanied by guitars and frequently the *cajón*, a resonant wooden box on which the player sits, pounding it with his hands. Some of the great names of 'Música Criolla' are the singer/composers Chabuca Granda and Alicia Maguiña, the female singer Jesús Vásquez and the groups Los Morochucos and Hermanos Zañartu.

Afro-Peruvian Also on the coast is the music of the small but influential black community, the 'Música Negroide' or 'Afro-Peruano', which had virtually died out when it was resuscitated in the 1950s, but has since gone from strength to strength, thanks to Nicomedes and Victoria Santa Cruz who have been largely responsible for popularizing this black music and making it an essential ingredient in contemporary Peruvian popular music. It has all the qualities to be found in black music from the Caribbean – a powerful, charismatic beat, rhythmic and lively dancing, and strong percussion provided by the *cajón* and the *quijada de burro*, a donkey's jaw with the teeth loosened. Its greatest star is the Afro-Peruvian diva Susana Baca. Her incredible, passionate voice inspired Talking Head's David Byrne to explore this genre further and release a compilation album in 1995, thus bringing Afro-Peruvian music to the attention of the world. Another notable exponent is the excellent Perú Negro, one of the best music and dance groups in Latin America.

Musical instruments Before the arrival of the Spanish in Latin America, the only instruments were wind and percussion. Although it is a popular misconception that Andean music is based on the panpipes, guitar and *charango*, anyone who travels through the Andes will realize that these instruments only represent a small aspect of Andean music. The highland instrumentation varies from region to region, although the harp and violin are ubiquitous. In the Mantaro area the harp is backed by brass and wind instruments, notably the clarinet. In Cusco it is the *charango* and *quena* and on the Altiplano the *sicu* panpipes.

The *Quena* is a flute, usually made of reed, characterized by not having a mouthpiece to blow through. As with all Andean instruments, there is a family of *quenas* varying in length from around 15 cm to 50 cm. The *sicu* is the Aymara name for the *zampoña*, or panpipes. It is the most important prehispanic Andean instrument, formed by several reed tubes of different sizes held together by knotted string. Virtually the only instrument of European origin is the *Charango*. When stringed instruments were first introduced by the Spanish, the indigenous people liked them but wanted something that was their own and so the *charango* was born. Originally, they were made of clay, condor skeletons and armadillo or tortoise shells.

Dances The highlands are immensely rich in terms of music and dance, with over 200 dances recorded. Every village has its fiestas and every fiesta has its communal and religious dances. *Comparsas* are organized groups of dancers who perform for spectators dances following a set pattern of movements to a particular musical accompaniment, wearing a specific costume. These dances have a long tradition, having mostly originated from certain contexts and circumstances and some of them still parody the ex-Spanish colonial masters.

Many dances for couples and/or groups are danced spontaneously at fiestas throughout Peru. These include indigenous dances which have originated in a specific region and ballroom dances that reflect the Spanish influence. One of the most popular of the indigenous dances is the **Huayno**, which originated on the Altiplano but is now danced throughout the country. It involves numerous couples, who whirl around or advance down the street, arm-in-arm, in a 'Pandilla'. During fiestas, and especially after a few drinks, this can develop into a kind of uncontrolled frenzy.

Festivals

Fiestas (festivals) are a fundamental part of life for most Peruvians, taking place up and down the length and breadth of the country and with such frequency that it would be hard to miss one, even during the briefest of stays. This is fortunate, because arriving in any town or village during these inevitably frenetic celebrations is one of the great Peruvian experiences.

While Peru's festivals can't rival those of Brazil for fame or colour, the quantity of alcohol consumed and the partying run them pretty close. What this means is that, at some point, you will fall over, through inebriation or exhaustion, or both. After several days of this, you will awake with a hangover the size of the Amazon rainforest and probably have no recollection of what you did with your backpack.

It is only when they don their extravagant costumes and masks and drink, eat and dance to excess that the Peruvian Indians show their true character. The rest of the time they hide behind a metaphorical mask of stony indifference as a form of protection against the alien reality in which they are forced to live. When they consume alcohol and coca and start dancing, the pride in their origins resurfaces. The incessant drinking and dancing allows them to forget the reality of poverty, unemployment and oppression and reaffirms their will to live as well as their unity with the world around them.

The object of the fiesta is a practical one, such as the success of the coming harvest or the fertility of animals. Thus the constant eating, drinking and dancing serves the purpose of giving thanks for the sun and rain that makes things grow and for the fertility of the soil and livestock, gifts from Pachamama, or Mother Earth, the most sacred of all gods. So, when you see a Peruvian spill a little *chicha* (maize beer) every time they refill, it's not because they're sloppy but because they're offering a *ch'alla* (sacrifice) to Pachamama.

Literature

The fact that the Incas had no written texts in the conventional European sense and that the Spaniards were keen to suppress their conquest's culture means that there is little evidence today of what poetry and theatre was performed in pre-conquest times. It is known that the Incas had two types of poet, the *amautas*, historians, poets and teachers who composed works that celebrated the ruling class' gods, heroes and events, and *haravecs*, who expressed popular sentiments. Written Quechua even today is far less common than works in the oral tradition. Although Spanish culture has had some influence on Quechua, the native stories, lyrics and fables retain their own identity. Not until the 19th century did Peruvian writers begin seriously to incorporate indigenous ideas into their art, but their audience was limited. Nevertheless, the influence of Quechua on Peruvian literature in Spanish continues to grow.

Colonial Period

In 16th-century Lima, headquarters of the Viceroyalty of Peru, the Spanish officials concentrated their efforts on the religious education of the new territories and literary output was limited to mainly histories and letters.

Chroniclers such as **Pedro Cieza de León** (*Crónica del Perú*, published from 1553) and **Agustín de Zárate** (*Historia del descubrimiento y conquista del Perú*, 1555) were written from the point of view that Spanish domination was right. Their most renowned successors, though, took a different stance. **Inca Garcilaso de la Vega** was a mestizo, whose *Comentarios reales que tratan del origen de los Incas* (1609) were at pains to justify the achievements, religion and culture of the Inca Empire. He also commented on Spanish society in the colony. A later work, *Historia general del Perú* (1617) went further in condemning Viceroy Toledo's suppression of Inca culture. Through his work, written in Spain, many aspects of Inca society, plus poems and prayers have survived.

Writing at about the same time as Inca Garcilaso was **Felipe Guaman Poma de Ayala**, whose *El primer nueva corónica y buen gobierno* (1613-15) is possibly one of the most reproduced of Latin American texts (eg on T-shirts, CDs, posters and carrier bags). Guaman Poma was a minor provincial Inca chief whose writings and illustrations, addressed to King Felipe III of Spain, offer a view of a stable pre-conquest Andean society (not uniquely Inca), in contrast with the unsympathetic colonial society that usurped it.

In the years up to Independence, the growth of an intellectual elite in Lima spawned more poetry than anything else. As criollo discontent grew, satire increased both in poetry and in the sketches which accompanied dramas imported from Spain. The poet **Mariano Melgar** (1791-1815), who wrote in a variety of styles, died in an uprising against the Spanish but played an important part in the Peruvian struggle from freedom from the colonial imagination.

After Independence

After Independence, Peruvian writers imitated Spanish *costumbrismo*, sketches of characters and life-styles from the new Republic. The first author to transcend this fashion was **Ricardo Palma** (1833-1919), whose inspiration, the *tradición*, fused *costumbrismo* and Peru's rich oral traditions. Palma's hugely popular *Tradiciones peruanas* is a collection of pieces which celebrate the people, history and customs of Peru through sayings, small incidents in mainly colonial history and gentle irony.

Much soul-searching was to follow Peru's defeat in the War of the Pacific. **Manuel González Prada** (1844-1918), for instance, wrote essays fiercely critical of the state of the nation: *Páginas libres* (1894), *Horas de lucha* (1908). **José Carlos Mariátegui**, the foremost Peruvian political thinker of the early 20th century, said that González Prada represented the first lucid instant of Peruvian consciousness.

20th century

Mariátegui himself (1895-1930), after a visit to Europe in 1919, considered deeply the question of Peruvian identity, writing about politics, economics, literature and the Indian question from a Marxist perspective (see *Siete ensayos de interpretación de la realidad peruana*, 1928). Other writers had continued this theme. **Clorinda Matto de Turner** (1854-1909), with *Aves sin nido* (1889), was the forerunner by several years of the 'indigenist' genre in Peru and the most popular of those who took up González Prada's cause. Other prose writers continued in this vein at the beginning of the 20th century, but it was **Ciro Alegría** (1909-67) who gave major, fictional impetus to the racial question. Of his first three novels, *La serpiente de oro* (1935), *Los perros hambrientos* (1938) and *El mundo es ancho y ajeno* (1941), the latter is his most famous.

Contemporary with Alegría was **José María Arguedas** (1911-1969), whose novels, stories and politics were also deeply-rooted in the ethnic question. Arguedas, though not Indian, had a largely Quechua upbringing and tried to reconcile this with the hispanic world in which he worked. This inner conflict was one of the main causes of his suicide. His books include *Agua* (short stories – 1935), *Yawar fiesta* (1941), *Los ríos profundos* (1958) and *Todas las sangres* (1964).

In the 1950s and 1960s, there was a move away from the predominantly rural and indigenist to an urban setting. At the forefront were, among others, **Mario Vargas Llosa**, **Julio Ramón Ribeyro**, **Enrique Congrains Martín**, **Oswaldo Reynoso**, **Luis Loayza**, **Sebastián Salazar Bondy** and **Carlos E Zavaleta**. They explored all aspects of the city, including the influx of people from the Sierra. These writers incorporated new narrative techniques in the urban novel, which presented a world where popular culture and speech were rich sources of literary material, despite the difficulty in transcribing them.

Alfredo Bryce Echenique (born 1939) has enjoyed much popularity following the success of *Un mundo para Julius* (1970), a satire on the upper and middle classes of Lima. Other contemporary writers of note are **Sergio Bambarén**, whose 1995 debut novel, *The Dolphin – story of a dreamer,* was written in English and became a bestseller when published in Spanish, and **Jaime Bayly**, who is also a journalist and TV presenter. His novels include *Fue ayer y no me acuerdo, Los últimos días de la prensa* and *La noche es virgen*. Without doubt, the most important poet in Peru, if not Latin America, in the first half of the 20th century, was **César Vallejo**, born in 1892 in Santiago de Chuco (Libertad). In 1928 he was a founder of the Peruvian Socialist Party, then he joined the Communist Party in 1931 in Madrid. From 1936 to his death in Paris in 1938 he opposed the fascist takeover in Spain. His first volume was *Los heraldos negros* in which the dominating theme of all his work, a sense of confusion and inadequacy in the face of the unpredictability of life, first surfaces. *Trilce* (1922), his second work, is unlike anything before it in the Spanish language. *Poemas humanos* and *España, aparta de mí este cáliz* (written as a result of Vallejo's experiences in the Spanish Civil War) were both published posthumously, in 1939.

Painting

The Catholic Church was the main patron of the arts during the colonial period. The innumerable churches and monasteries that sprang up in the newly-conquered territories created a demand for paintings and sculptures, met initially by imports from Europe of both works of art and of skilled craftsmen, and later by home-grown products. An essential requirement for the inauguration of any new church was an image for the altar and many churches in Lima preserve fine examples of sculptures imported from Seville during the 16th and 17th centuries. But sculptures were expensive and difficult to import, and as part of their policy of relative frugality the Franciscan monks tended to favour paintings. The Jesuits, too, tended to commission paintings and several major works by Sevillian artists can be seen in Lima's churches.

Painters and sculptors soon made their way to Peru in search of lucrative commissions including several Italians who arrived during the later 16th century. The Jesuit **Bernardo Bitti** (1548-1610), for example, trained in Rome before working in Lima, Cusco, Juli and Arequipa. European imports, however, could not keep up with demand and local workshops of creole, mestizo and Indian craftsmen flourished from the latter part of the 16th century. As the Viceregal capital and the point of arrival into Peru, the art of Lima was always strongly influenced by European, especially Spanish models, but the old Inca capital of Cusco became the centre of a regional school of painting which developed its own characteristics.A series of paintings of the 1660s, now hanging in the Museo de Arte Religioso in Cusco, commemorate the colourful Corpus Christi procession of statues of the local patron saints through the streets of Cusco. These paintings document the appearance of the city and local populace, including Spanish and Inca nobility, priests and laity, rich and poor, Spaniard, Indian, African and mestizo. Many of the statues represented in this series are still venerated in the local parish churches. They are periodically painted and dressed in new robes, but underneath are the original sculptures, executed by native craftsmen. Some are of carved wood while others use the pre-conquest technique of maguey cactus covered in sized cloth.

One of the most successful native painters was **Diego Quispe Tito** (1611-1681) who claimed descent from the Inca nobility and whose large canvases, often based on Flemish engravings, demonstrate the wide range of European sources that were available to Andean artists in the 17th century. But the **Cusco School** is best known for the anonymous devotional works where the painted contours of the figures are overlaid with flat patterns in gold, creating highly decorative images with an underlying tension between the two- and three-dimensional aspects of the work. The taste for richly-decorated surfaces can also be seen in the 17th and 18th century frescoed interiors of many Andean churches, as in Chinchero, Andahuaylillas and Huaro, and in the ornate carving on altarpieces and pulpits throughout Peru.

Land and environment

Geography

Peru is the third largest South American country, the size of France, Spain and the United Kingdom combined, and presents formidable difficulties to human habitation. Virtually all of the 2,250 km of its Pacific coast is desert. From the narrow coastal shelf the Andes rise steeply to a high plateau dominated by massive ranges of snow-capped peaks and gouged with deep canyons. The heavily forested and deeply ravined Andean slopes are more gradual to the east. Further east, towards Brazil and Colombia, begin the vast jungles of the Amazon basin.

Highlands

The Highlands, or *la sierra*, extend inland from the coastal strip some 250 km in the north, increasing to 400 km in the south. The average altitude is about 3,000 m and 50% of Peruvians live there. Essentially it is a plateau dissected by dramatic canyons and dominated by some of the most spectacular mountain ranges in the world.

In spite of these ups and downs which cause great communications difficulties, the presence of water and a more temperate climate on the plateau has attracted people throughout the ages. Present day important population centres in the Highlands include Cajamarca in the north, Huancayo in central Peru and Cusco in the south, all at around 3,000 m. Above this, at around 4,000 m, is the 'high steppe' or *puna*, with constant winds and wide day/night temperature fluctuations. Nevertheless, fruit and potatoes (which originally came from the *puna* of Peru and Bolivia) are grown at this altitude and the meagre grasslands are home to the ubiquitous llama.

Eastern Andes and Amazon basin Almost half of Peru is on the eastern side of the Andes and about 90% of the country's drainage is into the Amazon system. It is an area of heavy rainfall with cloudforest above 3,500 m and tropical rainforest lower down. There is little savanna, or natural grasslands, characteristic of other parts of the Amazon basin.

There is some dispute on the Amazon's source. Officially, the mighty river begins as the Marañón, whose longest tributary rises just east of the Cordillera Huayhuash. However, the longest journey for the proverbial raindrop, some 6,400 km, probably starts in southern Peru, where the headwaters of the Apurímac (Ucayali) flow from the snows on the northern side of the Nevado Mismi, near Cailloma.

With much more rainfall on the eastern side of the Andes, rivers are turbulent and erosion dramatic. Although vertical drops are not as great – there is a whole continent to cross to the Atlantic – valleys are deep, ridges narrow and jagged and there is forest below 3,000 m. At 1,500 m the Amazon jungle begins and water is the only means of surface transport available, apart from three roads which reach Borja (on the Marañón), Yurimaguas (on the Huallaga) and Pucallpa (on the Ucayali), all at about 300 m above the Atlantic which is still 4,000 km or so downstream. The vastness of the Amazon lowlands becomes apparent and it is here that Peru bulges 650 km northeast past Iquitos to the point where it meets Colombia and Brazil at Leticia. Oil and gas have recently been found in the Amazon, and new finds are made every year, which means that new pipelines and roads will eventually link more places to the Pacific coast.

Climate In the highlands, April to October is the dry season. It is hot and dry during the day, around 20°-25°C, and cold and dry at night, often below freezing. From November to April is the wet season, when it is dry and clear most mornings, with some rainfall in the afternoon. There is a small temperature drop (18°C) and not much difference at night (15°C). In the Amazonian lowlands April-October is the dry season, with temperatures up to 35°C. In the jungle areas of the south, a cold front can pass through at night. November-April is the wet season. It is humid and hot, with heavy rainfall at any time.

Wildlife and vegetation

Peru is a country of great biological diversity. It contains 84 of the 104 recognized life zones and is one of the eight "mega-diverse countries" on earth. The fauna and flora are to a large extent determined by the influence of the Andes, the longest uninterrupted mountain chain in the world, and the mighty Amazon river, which has by far the largest volume of any river in the world.

Andes From the desert rise the steep Andean slopes. In the deeply incised valleys Andean fox and deer may occasionally be spotted. Herds of llamas and alpacas graze the steep hillsides. Mountain caracara and Andean lapwing are frequently observed soaring, and there is always the possibility of spotting flocks of mitred parrots or even the biggest species of hummingbird in the world (*Patagonia gigas*).

The Andean zone has many lakes and rivers and countless swamps. Exclusive to this area short-winged grebe and the torrent duck which feeds in the fast flowing rivers, and giant and horned coots. Chilean flamingo frequent the shallow soda lakes.

The *puna*, a habitat characterized by tussock grass and pockets of stunted alpine flowers, gives way to relict elfin forest and tangled bamboo thicket in this inhospitable windswept and frost-prone region. Occasionally the dissected remains of a *Puya* plant can be found; the result of the nocturnal foraging of the rare spectacled bear. There are quite a number of endemic species of rodent including the viscacha, and it is the last stronghold of the chinchilla. Here also pumas roam preying on the herbivores which frequent these mountain – pudu, Andean deer or guemal and the mountain tapir.

Tropical Andes

The elfin forest gradually grades into mist enshrouded cloud forest at about 3,500 m. In the tropical zones of the Andes, the humidity in the cloud forests stimulates the growth of a vast variety of plants particularly mosses and lichens. The cloud forests are found in a narrow strip that runs along the eastern slopes of the spine of the Andes. It is these dense, often impenetrable, forests clothing the steep slopes that are important in protecting the headwaters of all the streams and rivers that cascade from the Andes to form the mighty Amazon as it begins its long journey to the sea.

This is a verdant world of dripping epiphytic mosses, lichens, ferns and orchids which grow in profusion despite the plummeting overnight temperatures. The high humidity resulting from the 2 m of rain that can fall in a year is responsible for the maintenance of the forest and it accumulates in puddles and leaks from the ground in a constant trickle that combines to form a myriad of icy, crystal-clear tumbling streams that cascade over precipitous waterfalls.

In secluded areas flame-red Andean cock-of-the-rock give their spectacular display to females in the early morning mists. Woolly monkeys are also occasionally sighted as they descend the wooded slopes. Mixed flocks of colourful tanagers are commonly encountered, and the golden-headed quetzal and Amazon umbrella bird are occasionally seen.

Amazon basin

At about 1,500 m there is a gradual transition to the vast lowland forests of the Amazon basin, which are warmer and more equable than the cloud forests clothing the mountains above. The daily temperature varies little during the year with a high of 23-32°C falling slightly to 20-26°C overnight. This lowland region receives some 2 m of rainfall per year most of it falling from November to April. The rest of the year is sufficiently dry, at least in the lowland areas to inhibit the growth of epiphytes and orchids which are so characteristic of the highland areas. For a week or two in the rainy season the rivers flood the forest. The zone immediately surrounding this seasonally flooded forest is referred to as *terre firme* forest.

The vast river basin of the Amazon is home to an immense variety of species. The environment has largely dictated the lifestyle. Life in or around rivers, lakes, swamps and forest depend on the ability to swim and climb and amphibious and tree-dwelling animals are common. Once the entire Amazon basin was a great inland sea and the river still contains mammals more typical of the coast, eg manatees and dolphins.

Here in the relatively constant climatic conditions animal and plant life has evolved to an amazing diversity over the millennia. It has been estimated that 3.9 square km of forest can harbour some 1,200 vascular plants, 600 species of tree, and 120 woody plants. Here, in these relatively flat lands, a soaring canopy some 50 m overhead is the power-house of the forest. It is a habitat choked with strangling vines and philodendrons among which mixed troupes of squirrel monkeys and brown capuchins forage. In the high canopy small groups of spider monkeys perform their lazy aerial acrobatics, whilst lower down, cling to epiphyte-clad trunks and branches, groups of saddle-backed and emperor tamarins forage for blossom, fruit and the occasional insect prey.

The most accessible part of the jungle is on or near the many great meandering rivers. At each bend of the river the forest is undermined by the currents during the seasonal floods at the rate of some 10-20 m per year leaving a sheer mud and clay bank, whilst on the opposite bend new land is laid down in the form of broad beaches of fine sand and silt.

A succession of vegetation can be seen. The fast growing willow-like *Tessaria* first stabilizes the ground enabling the tall stands of caña brava *Gynerium* to become established. Within these dense almost impenetrable stands the seeds of rainforest trees germinate and over a few years thrust their way towards the light. The fastest growing is a species of *Cercropia* which forms a canopy 15-18 m over the caña but even this is relatively short-lived. The gap in the canopy is quickly filled by other species. Two types of mahogany outgrow the other trees forming a closed canopy at 40 m with a lush understory of shade tolerant *Heliconia* and ginger. Eventually even the long-lived trees die off to be replaced by others providing a forest of great diversity.

Jungle wildlife The meandering course of the river provides many excellent opportunities to see herds of russet-brown capybara – a sheep-sized rodent – peccaries and brocket deer. Of considerable ecological interest are the presence of ox-bow lakes, or *cochas*, since these provide an abundance of wildlife which can easily be seen around the lake margins.

The best way to see the wildlife, however, is to get above the canopy. Ridges provide elevated view points from which you can enjoy excellent views over the forest. From here, it is possible to look across the lowland flood plain to the very foothills of the Andes, possibly some 200 km away. Flocks of parrots and macaws can be seen flying between fruiting trees and noisy troupes of squirrel monkeys and brown capuchins come very close.

The lowland rainforest of Peru is particularly famous for its primates and giant otters. Giant otters were once widespread in Amazonia but came close to extinction in the 1960s owing to persecution by the fur trade. The giant otter population in Peru has since recovered and is now estimated to be at least several hundred. Jaguar and other predators are also much in evidence. Although rarely seen their paw marks are commonly found along the forest trails. Rare bird species are also much in evidence, including fasciated tiger-heron and primitive hoatzins.

The (very) early-morning is the best time to see peccaries, brocket deer and tapir at mineral licks (*collpa*). Macaw and parrot licks are found along the banks of the river. Here at dawn a dazzling display arrives and clambers around in the branches overhanging the clay-lick. At its peak there may be 600 birds of up to six species (including red and green macaws, and blue-headed parrots) clamouring to begin their descent to the riverbank where they jostle for access to the mineral rich clay. A necessary addition to their diet which may also neutralize the toxins present in the leaf and seed diet. Rare game birds such as razor billed curassows and piping guans may also be seen.

A list of over 600 bird species has been compiled. Particularly noteworthy species are the black-faced cotinga, crested eagle, and the spectacular Harpy eagle, perhaps the world's most impressive raptor, easily capable of taking an adult monkey from the canopy. Mixed species flocks are commonly observed containing from 25 to over 100 birds of perhaps more than 30 species including blue dacnis, blue-tailed emerald, bananaquit, thick-billed euphoria and the paradise tanager. Each species occupies a slightly different niche, and since there are few individuals of each species in the flock, competition is avoided. Mixed flocks foraging in the canopy are often led by a white-winged shrike, whereas flocks foraging in the understorey are often led by the bluish-slate antshrike. (For more information on the birds of Peru, see page 49.)

10 Footnotes

Footnotes

Spanish words and phrases

No amount of dictionaries, phrase books or word lists will provide the same enjoyment as being able to communicate directly with the people of the country you are visiting. Learning Spanish is a useful part of the preparation for a trip to the Peru and you are encouraged to make an effort to grasp the basics before you go. As you travel you will pick up more of the language and the more you know, the more you will benefit from your stay. The following secion is designed to be a simple point of departure.

Whether you have been taught the 'Castillian' pronounciation (all *z*'s, and *c*'s followed by *i* or *e*, are pronounced as the *th* in *think*) or the 'American' pronounciation (they are pronounced as *s*), you will encounter little difficulty in understanding either: Spanish pronunciation varies geographically much less than English. There are, of course, regional accents and usages; but the basic language is essentially the same everywhere.

General pronunciation

The stress in a Spanish word conforms to one of three rules: **1** if the word ends in a vowel, or in **n** or **s**, the accent falls on the penultimate syllable *(ventana, ventanas)*; **2** if the word ends in a consonant other than **n** or **s**, the accent falls on the last syllable *(hablar)*; **3** if the word is to be stressed on a syllable contrary to either of the above rules, the acute accent on the relevant vowel indicates where the stress is to be placed *(pantalón, metáfora)*. Note that adverbs such as *cuando*,'when', take an accent when used interrogatlvely; *¿cuándo?*, 'when?'

Vowels

a not quite as short as in English 'cat'
e as in English 'pay', but shorter in a syllable ending in a consonant
i as in English 'seek'
o as in English 'shop', but more like 'pope' when the vowel ends a syllable
u as in English'food', after 'q' and in 'gue', 'gui' **u** is unpronounced; in 'güe' and 'güi' it is pronounced
y when a vowel, pronounced like 'I'; when a semiconsonant or consonant, it is pronounced like English 'yes'
ai, ay as in English 'ride'
el, ey as in English 'they'
oi, oy as in English 'toy'

Consonants

Unless listed below consonants can be pronounced in Spanish as they are in English.

b, v their sound is interchangeable and is a cross between the English **b** and **v**, except at the beginning of a word or after **m** or **n** when it is like English **b**
c like English **k**, except before **e** or **i** when it is the **s** in English 'sip'
g before **e** and **i** it is the same as **j**
h when on its own, never pronounced
j as the **ch** in the Scottish 'loch'
ll as the **g** in English 'beige'; sometimes as the 'lli' in 'million'
ñ as the 'ni' in English 'onion'
rr trilled much more strongly than in English

x	depending on its location, pronounced as in English 'fox', or 'sip', or like 'gs'
z	as the **s** in English 'sip'

Pronouns

In the Americas, the plural, familar pronoun *vosotros* (with the verb endings - *áis*, - *éis*), though much used in Spain, is never heard. Two or more people, including small children, are always addressed as *Ustedes* (*Uds*).

Inappropriate use of the familiar forms (*tú*, *vos*) can sound imperious, condescending, infantile, or imply a presumption of intimacy that could annoy officials, one's elders, or, if coming from a man, women.

To avoid cultural complications if your Spanish is limited, stick to the polite forms: *Usted* (*Ud*) in the singular, *Ustedes* in the plural, and you will never give offense.

Remember also that a person who address you as *tú*, does not necessarily expect to be *tuteada* (so addressed) in return.

You should, however, violate this rule when dealing with a small child, who might be intimidated by *Usted*: he/she is, after all, normally so addressed only in admonitions such as *'¡No, Señor, Ud no tomará un helado antes del aimuerzo!'* 'No, Sir, you will not have ice cream before lunch!'

General hints

Note that in Peru, a common response to *¡Gracias!* is often *¡A sus ordenes!* ('Yours to command!') rather than the '*¡De nada!*' ('Tis nought!') taught in school.

Travellers whose names include *b*'s and *v*'s should learn to distinguish between them when spelling aloud as *be larga* and *ve corta* or *uve*. (Children often say *ve de vaca* and *be de burro* to distinguish between the two letters, pronounced interchangeably, either as *b* or *v*, in Spanish.)

Greetings, courtesies

excuse me/I beg your pardon	*permiso*
Go away!	*¡Váyase!*
good afternoon/evening/night	*buenas tardes/noches*
good morning	*buenos días*
goodbye	*adiós/chao*
hello	*hola*
How are you?	*¿cómo está?/¿cómo estás?*
I do not understand	*no entiendo*
leave me alone	*déjame en paz/no me moleste*
no	*no*
please	*por favor*
pleased to meet you	*mucho gusto/encantado/encantada*
see you later	*hasta luego*
thank you (very much)	*(muchas) gracias*
What is your name?	*¿Cómo se llama?*
yes	*sí*
I speak ...	*Hablo ...*
I speak Spanish	*Hablo español*
I don't speak Spanish	*No hablo español*
Do you speak English?	*¿Habla usted inglés?*
We speak German	*Hablamos alemán*
They speak French	*Hablan francés*
Please speak slowly	*hable despacio por favor*
I am very sorry	*lo siento mucho/disculpe*
I'm fine	*muy bien gracias*

I'm called_ *me llamo_*
What do you want? *¿Qué quiere?*
I want *quiero*
I don't want it *No lo quiero*
long distance phone call *la llamada a larga distancia*
good *bueno*
bad *malo*

Nationalities and languages

American *Americano/a*
Australian *Australiano/a*
Austrian *Austriaco/a*
British *Británico/a*
Canadian *Canadiense*
Danish *Danés/Danesa*
Dutch *Holandés/Holandesa*
English *Inglés/Inglesa*
French *Francés/Francesa*
German *Alemán/Alemana*
Irish *Irlandés/Irlandesa*
Italian *Italiano/a*
Mexican *Mexicano/a*
New Zealand *Neozelandés/Neozelandesa*
Norwegian *Noruego/a*
Portuguese *Portugués/Portuguesa*
Scottish *Escocés/Escocesa*
Spanish *Español/a*
Swedish *Sueco/a*
Swiss *Suizo/a*
Welsh *Galés/Galesa*

Basic questions

Have you got a room for two people?
¿Tiene habitación para dos personas?
How do I get to_? *¿Cómo llegar a_?*
How much does it cost? *¿ Cuánto cuesta?*
How much is it? *¿Cuánto es?*
When does the bus leave?
¿A qué hora sale el bus?
-arrive? *-llega-*
When? *¿Cuándo?*
Where is_? *¿Dónde está_?*
Where is the nearest petrol station?
¿Dónde está el grifo más cerca?
Why? *¿Por qué?*

Basics

bank *el banco*
bathroom/toilet *el baño*
bill *la factura/la cuenta*
cash *el efectivo*
cheap *barato*
church/cathedral *La iglesia/catedral*
exchange house *la casa de cambio*
exchange rate *la tasa de cambio*
expensive *caro*
market *el mercado*
notes/coins *los billetes/las monedas*
police (policeman) *la policia (el policia)*
post office *el correo*
supermarket *el supermercado*
telephone office *el centro de llamadas*
ticket office *la boletería/la taquilla*
travellers' cheques *los travelers/los cheques de viajero*

Getting around

aeroplane/airplane *el avión*
airport *el aeropuerto*
bus station *la terminal (terrestre)*
bus stop *la parada*
bus *el bus/el autobus etc*
minibus *el combi*
motorcycle taxi *el mototaxi*
bus route *el corredor*
first/second class *primera/segunda clase*
on the left/right *a la izquierdo/derecha*
second street on the left
la segunda calle a la izquierda
ticket *el boleto*
to walk *caminar*
Where can I buy tickets?
¿Dónde se puede comprar boletos?
Where can I park?
¿Dónde se puede parquear?

Orientation and motoring

arrival *la llegada*
avenue *la avenida*
block *la cuadra*
border *la frontera*
car used for public transport on a fixed route *colectivo*
corner *la esquina*
customs *la aduana*
departure *la salida*
east *el este, el oriente*
empty *vacío*
full *lleno*
highway, main road *carretera*
immigration *la inmigración*
insurance *el seguro*
the insured *el asegurado/la asegurada*
to insure yourself against *asegurarse contra*
luggage *el equipaje*
motorway, dual carriageway *autopista/carretera*
north *el norte*
oil *el aceite*
passport *el pasaporte*
petrol/gasoline *la gasolina*
puncture *el pinchazo*
south *el sur*
street *la calle*
that way *por allí/por allá*
this way *por aquí/por acá*
tourist card *la tarjeta de turista*
tyre *la llanta*
unleaded *sin plomo*
visa *el visado*
waiting room *la sala de espera*
west *el oeste/el poniente*

Accommodation

air conditioning *el aire acondicionado*
all-inclusive *todo incluído*
blankets *las mantas*
clean/dirty towels *las toallas limpias/sucias*
dining room *el comedor*
double bed *la cama matrimonial*
guest house *la casa de huéspedes*
hot/cold water *agua caliente/fría*
hotel *el hotel*
Is service included? *¿Está incluído el servicio?*
Is tax included? *¿Están incluidos los impuestos?*
noisy *ruidoso*
pillows *las almohadas*
power cut *apagón/corte*
restaurant *el restaurante*
room *el cuarto/la habitación*
sheets *las sábanas*
shower *la ducha*
single/double *sencillo/doble*
soap *el jabón*
to make up/clean *limpiar*
toilet *el sanitario*
toilet paper *el papel higiénico*
with private bathroom *con baño privado*
with two beds *con dos camas*

Health

aspirin *la aspirina*
blood *la sangre*
chemist/pharmacy *la farmacia*
condoms *los preservativos*
contact lenses *las lentes de contacto*
contraceptive (pill) *el anticonceptivo (la píldora anticonceptiva)*
diarrhoea *la diarrea*
doctor *el médico*
fever/sweat *la fiebre/el sudor*
(for) pain *(para) dolor*
head *la cabeza*
period/towels *la regla/las toallas*
stomach *el estómago*

Time

At one o'clock *a la una*
At half past two/two thirty *a las dos y media*
At a quarter to three *a cuarto para las tres or a las tres menos quince*
It's one o'clock *es la una*
It's seven o'clock *son las siete*
It's twenty past six/six twenty *son las seis y veinte*
It's five to nine *son cinco para las nueve/son las nueve menos cinco*
In ten minutes *en diez minutos*
five hours *cinco horas*
Does it take long? *¿Tarda mucho?*
We will be back at ... *Regresamos a las ...*
What time is it? *¿Qué hora es?*

Monday *lunes*
Tuesday *martes*
Wednesday *miércoles*
Thursday *jueves*
Friday *viernes*
Saturday *sábado*
Sunday *domingo*
January *enero*
February *febrero*
March *marzo*
April *abril*
May *mayo*
June *junio*
July *julio*
August *agosto*
September *septiembre*
October *octubre*
November *noviembre*
December *diciembre*

Numbers

one *uno/una*
two *dos*
three *tres*
four *cuatro*
five *cinco*
six *seis*
seven *siete*
eight *ocho*
nine *nueve*
ten *diez*
eleven *once*
twelve *doce*
thirteen *trece*
fourteen *catorce*
fifteen *quince*
sixteen *dieciséis*
seventeen *diecisiete*
eighteen *dieciocho*
nineteen *diecinueve*
twenty *veinte*
twenty one, two *veintiuno, veintidos etc*
thirty *treinta*
forty *cuarenta*
fifty *cincuenta*
sixty *sesenta*
seventy *setenta*
eighty *ochenta*
ninety *noventa*
hundred *cien or ciento*
thousand *mil*

Family

aunt *la tía*
brother *el hermano*
cousin *la/el prima/o*
daughter *la hija*
family *la familia*
father *el padre*
fiance/fiancee *el novio/la novia*
friend *el amigo/la amiga*
grandfather *el abuelo*
grandmother *la abuela*
husband *el esposo/marido*
married *casado/a*
mother *la madre*
single/unmarried *soltero/a*
sister *la hermana*
son *el hijo*
uncle *el tío*
wife *la esposa*

Key verbs

To go *ir*
I go *voy*
you go (familiar singular) *vas*
he, she, it goes, you (unfamiliar singular) go *va*
we go *vamos*
they, you (plural) go *van*
To have (possess) *tener*
I have *tengo*
You have *tienes*
He she, it have, you have *tiene*
We have *tenemos*
They, you have *tienen*
(Also used as 'To be', as in 'I am hungry' *tengo hambre*)
(NB *Haber* also means 'to have', but is used with other verbs, as in 'he has gone' *ha ido*)
I have gone *he ido*
You have said *has dicho*
He, she, it has, you have done *ha hecho*
We have eaten *hemos comido*
They, you have arrived *han llegado*
Hay means 'there is' and is used in questions such as *¿Hay cuartos?* 'Are there any rooms?'; perhaps more common is *No hay* meaning 'there isn't any'

To be (in a permanent state) *ser*
I am (a teacher) *soy (profesor)*
You are *Eres*
He, she, it is, you are *es*
We are *somos*
They, you are *son*

To be (positional or temporary state) *estar*
I am (in London) *estoy (en Londres)*
You are *estás*
He, she, it is, you are (happy) *está (contenta)*
We are *estámos*
They, you are *están*

To do/make *Hacer*
I do *hago*
You do *haces*
He, she, it does, you do *hace*
We do *hacemos*
They, you do *hacen*

The above section was compiled on the basis of glossaries by André de Mendonça and David Gilmour of South American experience, London, and the LatinAmerican Travel Advisor, No 9, March 1996

Food

avocado *la palta*
baked *al horno*
bakery *la panadería*
beans *los frijoles/las habichuelas*
beef *la carne de res*
beef steak or pork fillet *el bistec*
boiled rice *el arroz blanco*
bread *el pan*
breakfast *el desayuno*
butter *la mantequilla*
cassava, yucca *la yuca*
casserole *la cazuela*
chewing gum *el chicle*
chicken *el pollo*
chilli pepper or green pepper *el ají*
clear soup, stock *el caldo*
cooked *cocido*
dining room *el comedor*
egg *el huevo*
fish *el pescado*
fork *el tenedor*
fried *frito*
fritters *las frituras*
garlic *el ajo*
goat *el chivo*
grapefruit *el pomelo*
grill *la parrilla*
grilled/griddled *a la plancha*
guava *la guayaba*
ham *el jamón*
hamburger *la hamburgueso*
hot, spicy *picante*
ice cream *el helado*
jam *la mermelada*
knife *el cuchillo*
lime *el limón*
lobster *la langosta*
lunch *el almuerzo*
margarine, fat *la manteca*
meal, supper, dinner *la comida*
meat *la carne*
minced meat *el picadillo*
mixed salad *la ensalada mixta*
onion *la cebolla*
orange *la naranja*
pepper *el pimiento*
plantain, green banana *el plátano*
pasty, turnover *la empanada/el pastelito*
pork *el cerdo*
potato *la papa*
prawns *los camarones*
raw *crudo*
restaurant *el restaurante*
roast *el asado*
salad *la ensalada*
salt *el sal*
sandwich *el bocadillo*
sauce *la salsa*
Sausage *la longaniza*
scrambled eggs *los huevos revueltos*
seafood *los mariscos*
small sandwich, filled roll *el bocadito*
soup *la sopa*
spoon *la cuchara*
squash *la calabaza*
squid *los calamares*
supper *la cena*
sweet *dulce*
sweet potato *la batata*
to eat *comer*
toasted *tostado*
turkey *el pavo*
vegetables *los legumbres/vegetales*
without meat *sin carne*
yam *el camote*

Drink

beer *la cerveza*
boiled *hervido*
bottled *en botella*
camomile tea *la manzanilla*
canned *en lata*
cocktail *el coctel*
coconut milk *la leche de coco*
coffee *el café*
coffee, small, strong *el cafecito*
coffee, white *el café con leche*
cold *frío*
condensed milk *la leche condensada*
cup *la taza*
drink *la bebida*
drunk *borracho*
fruit milk shake *el batido*
glass *el vaso*
glass of liqueur *la copa de licor*
hot *caliente*
ice *el hielo*
juice *el jugo*
lemonade *la limonada*
milk *la leche*
mint *la menta*
orange juice *el jugo de naranja*
pineapple milkshake *el batido de piña con leche*
rough rum, firewater *el aguardiente*
rum *el ron*
soft drink *el refresco*
soft fizzy drink *la gaseosa/cola*
sugar *el azúcar*
tea *el té*
to drink *beber/tomar*
water *el agua*
water, carbonated *el agua mineral con gas*
water, still mineral *el agua mineral natural/sin gas*
wine, red *el vino tinto*
wine, white *el vino blanco*

Glossary

Food has always played an important role in Peruvian culture. The country's range of climates has also made this South American nation internationally recognized for its diverse cuisine.

Savoury dishes

Ají (hot pepper)
Ají is found in many varieties and is used to add `spice' to everything from soup to fish to vegetable dishes. It is a staple in Peruvian kitchens from the coast to the most remote jungle villages. These peppers can be extremely spicy, so the inexperienced palate should proceed with caution!

Papa (potato)
The potato is as Peruvian as the Inca himself. There are more than 2,000 varieties of tubers although only a fraction are edible. *The International Potato Institute* is located on the outskirts of metropolitan Lima so those with a potato fetish might wish to visit. The *papa amarilla* (yellow potato) is by far the best-tasting of the lot.

Causa
A casserole served cold with a base of yellow potato and mixed with hot peppers, onion, avocado, with either chicken, crab or meat. A fantastic starter.

Estofado
A mild chicken stew, with lots of potatoes and other vegetables, served with rice.

Lomo saltado
Strips of sirloin sautéed with tomato, onion, *ají amarillo* (a spicy orange pepper) and french fried potatoes served with rice.

Papa Ocopa
A typical dish from the Arequipa region. A spicy peanut sauce served over cold potatoes with a slice of hard boiled egg.

Papa a la Huancaína
A dish which originated in the central department of Huancayo. This creamy cheese sauce served over cold potatoes is a common starter for set menus everywhere.

Papa Rellena (stuffed potato)
First baked then fried, the potato is stuffed with meat, onions, olives, boiled egg and raisins. *Camote* (yams) can be substituted for potatoes.

Choclo (corn)
Another staple in the Peruvian diet. The large kernels are great with the fresh cheese produced all over the country.

Maíz morado (purple corn)
This type of corn is not edible for humans. It's boiled and the liquid is used to make *chicha*, a sweet and very traditional Peruvian refreshment.

Chicha de Jora
A strong fermented beverage mostly found in mountain communities. The people who make it use their saliva to aid in the fermenting process.

Granos (grains)
Kiwicha and Quinoa are very high sources of protein and staples of the Inca diet. Quinoa is wonderful in soups and Kiwicha is a common breakfast food for children throughout the country.

Arroz (rice)
Another major staple in Peruvian cooking.

Anticuchos (beef heart kebabs)
Beef heart barbecued and served with cold potato and a wonderful assortment of spicy sauces. A must for all meat lovers.

Cuy (guinea pig)
Prepared in a variety of ways, from stewed to fried.

Cau Cau
Tripe and potatoes.

Rocoto relleno (stuffed hot peppers)
Stuffed with meat and potatoes, then baked.

Pachamanca
Typical mountain cuisine, so popular it's now prepared everywhere. Beef, pork and chicken mixed with a variety of vegetables, and cooked together over heated stones in a hole in the ground.

Seco de cabrito
A favorite dish from the north coast. Roasted goat marinated with fermented *chicha*, served with beans and rice.

Ají de Gallina
A rich mix of creamed, spicy chicken over rice and boiled potatoes.

Arroz con pato (duck with rice)
A dish originally from the north coast but found everywhere.

Ceviche
The national dish of Peru. Raw fish or seafood marinated in a mixture of lime juice, red onions and hot peppers usually served with a thick slice of boiled yam (*camote*) and corn. With a coastline of more than 1,800 km, the fruits of the sea are almost limitless. Sea bass, flounder, salmon, red snapper, sole and many varieties of shellfish are all in abundance. Keep in mind that *ceviche* is a dish served for lunch. Most *cevicherías* (*ceviche* restaurants) close around 1600.

Postres (desserts)

Arroz con leche
Rice pudding.

Manjar blanco
A caramel sweet made from boiled milk and sugar.

Picarones
Deep-fried donut batter bathed in a honey sauce.

Suspiro a la limeña
Manjar blanco with baked egg-white.

Turrón
This popular sweet, shortbread covered in molasses or honey, is sold everywhere during the October celebration of *Señor de los Milagros* (Lord of Miracles) in Lima.

Fruta (fruit)

There's a great selection of fruit in Peru. Aside from common fruits such as mandarins, oranges, peaches and bananas, there are exotic tropical fruits to choose from.

Chirimoya
Custard apple. In Quechua means "the sweet of the gods".

Lúcuma
Eggfruit.

Maracuyá
Passionfruit, often served as a juice.

Tuna
Prickly pear.

Bebidas (drinks)

The national beers are *Cristal*, *Cusqueña*, *Bremen* and *Pilsen*. There are also some dark beers.

Although not known as great wine producing country, there are a couple of good quality wines to choose from. *Blanco en Blanco* is a surprisingly pleasant white wine from the Tacama winery which also makes a great red wine called *Reserva Especial.*

Pisco, a strong brandy made from white grapes is produced in the departments of Ica, Moquegua and Tacna. Pisco Sour, the national drink is made with lime juice, egg white, sugar and a dash of cinnamon.

Index

Maps

Shorts

Advertisers

Colour section
Milla Turismo, Peru
Sonesta Posadas Del Inca, Peru

Will you help us?

We try as hard as we can to make each Footprint Handbook as up-to-date and accurate as possible but, of course, things always change. Many people email or write to us – with corrections, new information, or simply comments. If you want to let us know about your experiences and adventures – be they good, bad or ugly – then don't delay; we're dying to hear from you. And please try to include all the relevant details and juicy bits. Your help will be greatly appreciated, especially by other travellers. In return we will send you details about our special guidebook offer.

email Footprint at:
cus1_online@footprintbooks.com

or write to:

Elizabeth Taylor
Footprint Handbooks
6 Riverside Court
Lower Bristol Road
Bath
BA2 3DZ
UK

Sales & distribution

Footprint Handbooks
6 Riverside Court
Lower Bristol Road
Bath BA2 3DZ England
T 01225 469141
F 01225 469461
discover
@footprintbooks.com

Australia
Peribo Pty
58 Beaumont Road
Mt Kuring-Gai
NSW 2080
T 02 9457 0011
F 02 9457 0022

Austria
Freytag-Berndt Artaria
Kohlmarkt 9
A-1010 Wien
T 01533 2094
F 01533 8685

Freytag-Berndt
Sporgasse 29
A-8010 Graz
T 0316 818230
F 3016 818230-30

Belgium
Craenen BVBA
Mechelsesteenweg 633
B-3020 Herent
T 016 23 90 90
F 016 23 97 11

Waterstones
The English Bookshop
Blvd Adolphe Max 71-75
B-1000 Brussels
T 02 219 5034

Canada
Ulysses Travel Publications
4176 rue Saint-Denis
Montréal
Québec H2W 2M5
T 514 843 9882
F 514 843 9448

Europe
Bill Bailey
16 Devon Square
Newton Abbott
Devon TQ12 2HR. UK
T 01626 331079
F 01626 331080

Denmark
Nordisk Korthandel
Studiestraede 26-30 B
DK-1455 Copenhagen K
T 3338 2638
F 3338 2648

Scanvik Books
Esplanaden 8B
DK-1263 Copenhagen K
T 3312 7766
F 3391 2882

Finland
Akateeminen Kirjakauppa
Keskuskatu 1
FIN-00100 Helsinki
T 09 121 4151
F 09 121 4441

Suomalainen Kirjakauppa
Koivuvaarankuja 2
01640 Vantaa 64
F 09 852751

France
FNAC – major branches

L'Astrolabe
46 rue de Provence
F-75009 Paris 9e
T 01 42 85 42 95
F 01 45 75 92 51

VILO Diffusion
25 rue Ginoux
F-75015 Paris
T 01 45 77 08 05
F 01 45 79 97 15

Germany
GeoCenter ILH
Schockenriedstrasse 44
D-70565 Stuttgart
T 0711 781 94610
F 0711 781 94654

Brettschneider
Feldkirchnerstrasse 2
D-85551 Heimstetten
T 089 990 20330
F 089 990 20331

Geobuch
Rosental 6
D-80331 München
T 089 265030
F 089 263713

Gleumes
Hohenstaufenring 47-51
D-50674 Köln
T 0221 215650

Globetrotter Ausrustungen
Wiesendamm 1
D-22305 Hamburg
T040 679 66190
F 040 679 66183

Dr Götze
Bleichenbrücke 9
D-2000 Hamburg 1
T 040 3031 1009-0

Hugendubel Buchhandlung
Nymphenburgerstrasse 25
D-80335 München
T 089 238 9412
F 089 550 1853

Kiepert Buchhandlung
Hardenbergstrasse 4-5
D-10623 Berlin 12
T 030 311 880
F 030 311 88120

Greece
GC Eleftheroudakis
17 Panepistemiou
Athens 105 64
T 01 331 4180-83
F 01 323 9821

India
India Book Distributors
1007/1008 Arcadia
195 Nariman Point
Mumbai 400 021
T 91 22 282 5220
F 91 22 287 2531

Israel
Eco Trips
8 Tverya Street
Tel Aviv 63144
T 03 528 4113
F 03 528 8269

For a fuller list, see www.footprintbooks.com

Italy
Librimport
Via Biondelli 9
I-20141 Milano
T 02 8950 1422
F 02 8950 2811

Libreria del Viaggiatore
Via dell Pelegrino 78
I-00186 Roma
T/F 06 688 01048

Netherlands
Nilsson & Lamm bv
Postbus 195
Pampuslaan 212
N-1380 AD Weesp
T 0294 494949
F 0294 494455

Waterstones
Kalverstraat 152
1012 XE Amsterdam
T 020 638 3821

New Zealand
Auckland Map Centre
Dymocks

Norway
Schibsteds Forlag A/S
Akersgata 32 - 5th Floor
Postboks 1178 Sentrum
N-0107 Oslo
T 22 86 30 00
F 22 42 54 92

Tanum
Karl Johansgate 37-41
PO Box 1177 Sentrum
N-0107 Oslo 1
T 22 41 11 00
F 22 33 32 75

Olaf Norlis
Universitetsgt 24
N-1062 Oslo
T 22 00 43 00

Pakistan
Pak-American Commercial
Hamid Chambers
Zaib-un Nisa Street
Saddar, PO Box 7359
Karachi
T 21 566 0418
F 21 568 3611

South Africa
Faradawn CC
PO Box 1903
Saxonwold 2132
T 011 885 1787
F 011 885 1829

South America
Humphrys Roberts
Associates
Caixa Postal 801-0
Ag. Jardim da Gloria
06700-970 Cotia SP
Brazil
T 011 492 4496
F 011 492 6896

Southeast Asia
APA Publications
38 Joo Koon Road
Singapore 628990
T 865 1600
F 861 6438

In Hong Kong, Malaysia, Singapore and Thailand: MPH, Kinokuniya, Times

Spain
Altaïr
C/Balmes 69
08007 Barcelona
T 933 233062
F 934 512559

Altaïr
Gaztambide 31
28015 Madrid
T 0915 435300
F 0915 443498

Libros de Viaje
C/Serrano no 41
28001 Madrid
T 01 91 577 9899
F 01 91 577 5756

Il Corte Inglés – major branches

Sweden
Hedengrens Bokhandel
PO Box 5509
S-11485 Stockholm
T 08 611 5132

Kart Centrum
Vasagatan 16
S-11120 Stockholm
T 08 411 1697

Kartforlaget
Skolgangen 10
S-80183 Gavle
T 026 633000
F 026 124204

Lantmateriet Kartbutiken
Kungsgatan 74
S-11122 Stockholm
T 08 202 303
F 08 202 711

Switzerland
Office du Livre OLF
ZI3, Corminboeuf
CH-1701 Fribourg
T 026 467 5111
F 026 467 5666

Schweizer Buchzentrum
Postfach
CH-4601 Olten
T 062 209 2525
F 062 209 2627

Travel Bookshop
Rindermarkt 20
Postfach 216
CH-8001 Zürich
T 01 252 3883
F 01 252 3832

Tanzania
A Novel Idea
The Slipway
PO Box 76513
Dar es Salaam
T/F 051 601088

USA
Publishers Group West
1700 Fourth Street
Berkeley
CA 94710
T 510 528 1444
F 510 528 9555

Barnes & Noble, Borders, specialist travel bookstores

Footprint travel list

Footprint publish travel guides to over 120 countries worldwide. Each guide is packed with practical, concise and colourful information for everybody from first-time travellers to travel aficionados . The list is growing fast and current titles are noted below. For further information check out the website **www.footprintbooks.com**

Andalucía Handbook
Argentina Handbook
Bali & the Eastern Isles Hbk
Bangkok & the Beaches Hbk
Barcelona Handbook
Bolivia Handbook
Brazil Handbook
Cambodia Handbook
Caribbean Islands Handbook
Central America & Mexico Hbk
Chile Handbook
Colombia Handbook
Costa Rica Handbook
Cuba Handbook
Cusco & the Sacred Valley Hbk
Dominican Republic Handbook
Dublin Handbook
East Africa Handbook
Ecuador & Galápagos Handbook
Edinburgh Handbook
Egypt Handbook
Goa Handbook
Guatemala Handbook
India Handbook
Indian Himalaya Handbook
Indonesia Handbook
Ireland Handbook
Israel Handbook
Jordan Handbook
Laos Handbook
Libya Handbook
London Handbook
Malaysia Handbook
Marrakech & the High Atlas Hbk
Myanmar Handbook
Mexico Handbook
Morocco Handbook
Namibia Handbook
Nepal Handbook
New Zealand Handbook
Nicaragua Handbook
Pakistan Handbook
Peru Handbook
Rajasthan & Gujarat Handbook
Rio de Janeiro Handbook
Scotland Handbook
Scotland Highlands & Islands Hbk
Singapore Handbook
South Africa Handbook
South American Handbook
South India Handbook
Sri Lanka Handbook
Sumatra Handbook
Syria & Lebanon Handbook
Thailand Handbook
Tibet Handbook
Tunisia Handbook
Turkey Handbook
Venezuela Handbook
Vietnam Handbook

Also available from Footprint
Traveller's Handbook
Traveller's Healthbook

Available at all good bookshops

Map 1 Urubamba & Vilcanota Valleys

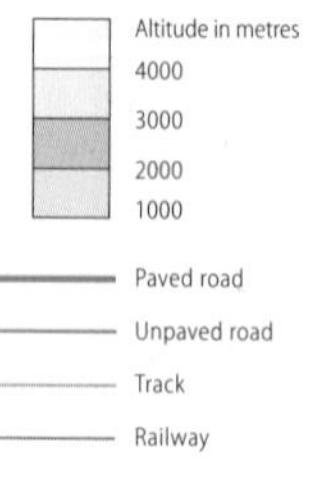

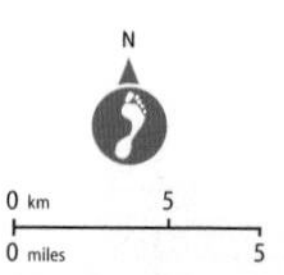

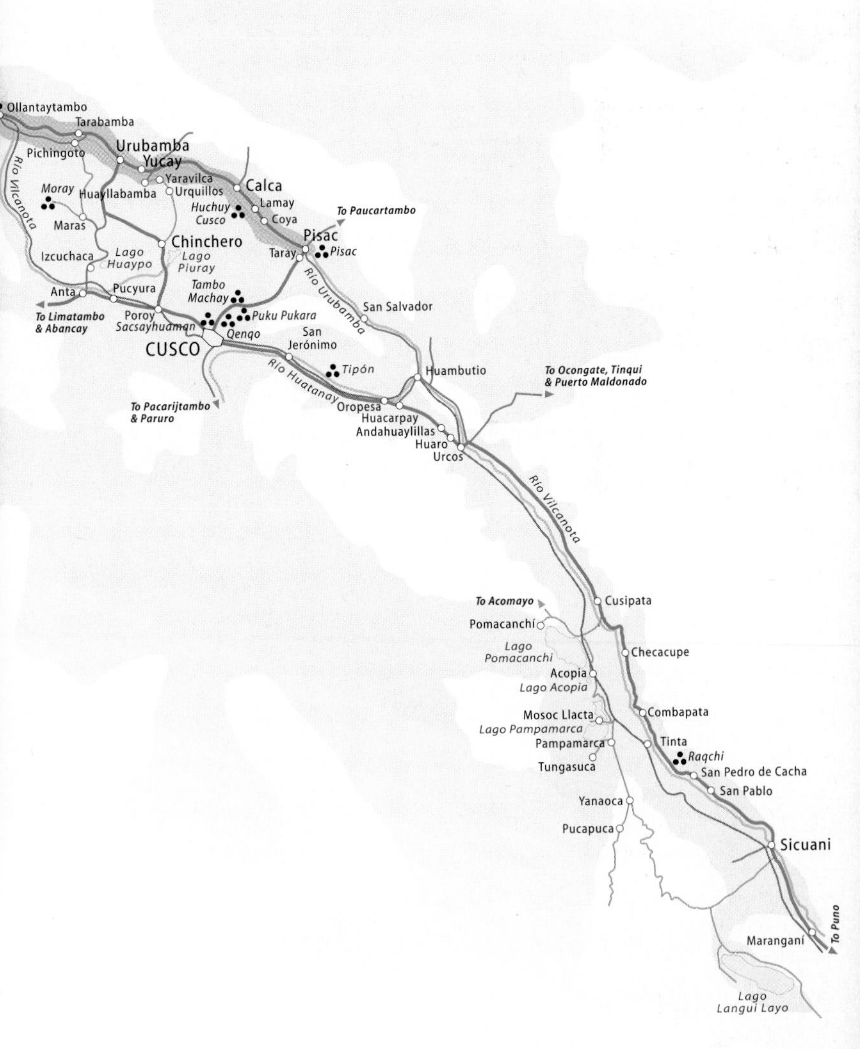
Ollantaytambo
Tarabamba
Pichingoto
Urubamba
Yucay
Yaravilca
Urquillos
Calca
Lamay
Coya
Huchuy Cusco
Moray
Huayllabamba
Maras
Río Vilcanota
To Paucartambo
Pisac
Pisac
Taray
Chinchero
Lago Piuray
Izcuchaca
Lago Huaypo
Anta
Pucyura
Tambo Machay
Puku Pukara
To Limatambo & Abancay
Poroy
Sacsayhuaman
Qenqo
CUSCO
Río Urubamba
San Salvador
San Jerónimo
Tipón
Río Huatanay
Huambutio
To Ocongate, Tinqui & Puerto Maldonado
To Pacarijtambo & Paruro
Oropesa
Huacarpay
Andahuaylillas
Huaro
Urcos
Río Vilcanota
To Acomayo
Cusipata
Pomacanchí
Lago Pomacanchi
Checacupe
Acopia
Lago Acopia
Combapata
Mosoc Llacta
Lago Pampamarca
Pampamarca
Tinta
Raqchi
Tungasuca
San Pedro de Cacha
San Pablo
Yanaoca
Pucapuca
Sicuani
To Puno
Maranganí
Lago Langui Layo

Map 2 Cusco region

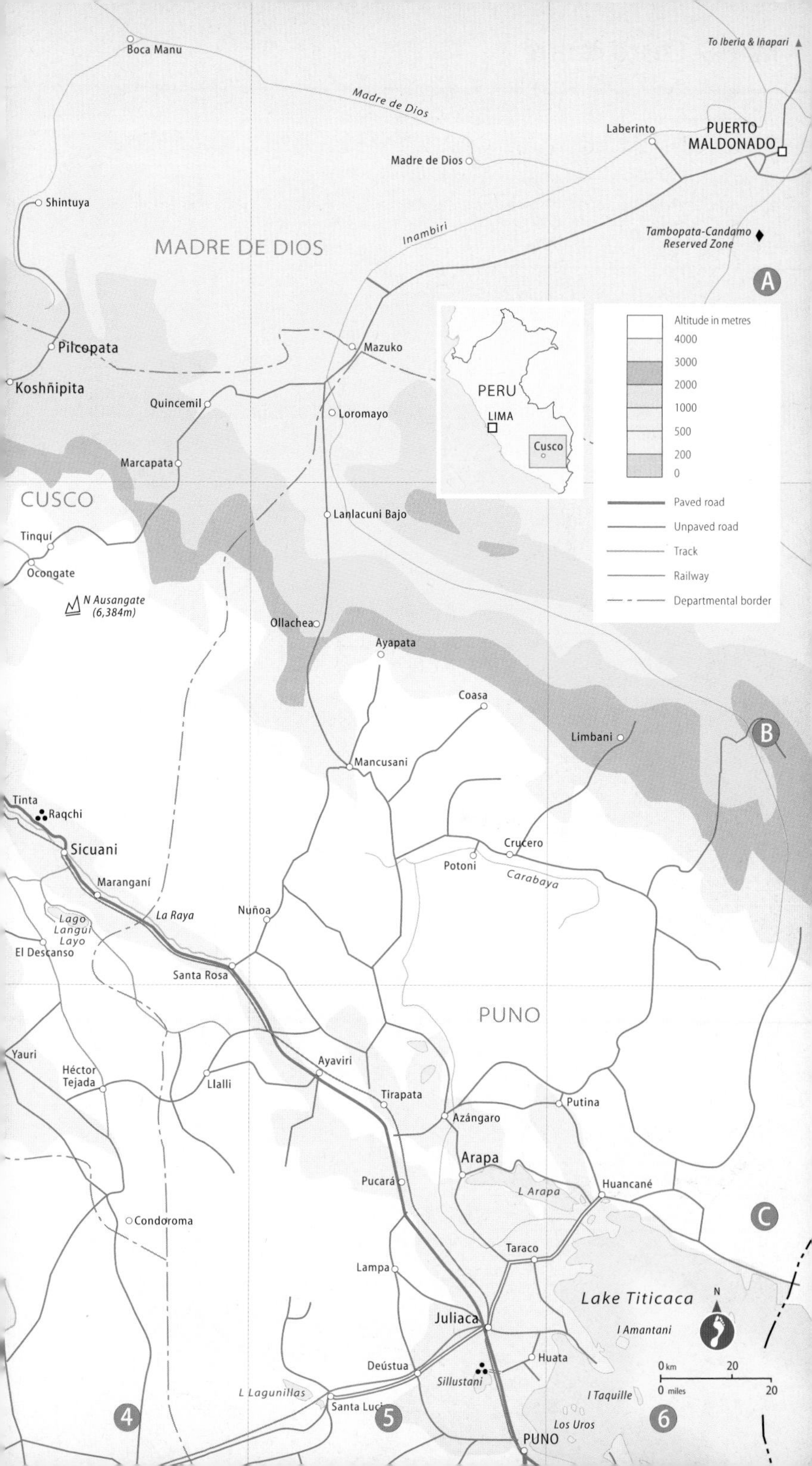

To Iberia & Iñapari
Boca Manu
Madre de Dios
Laberinto
PUERTO MALDONADO
Madre de Dios
Shintuya
Inambiri
Tambopata-Candamo Reserved Zone
MADRE DE DIOS
A
Pilcopata
Mazuko
Koshñipita
Quincemil
Loromayo
PERU
LIMA
Cusco
Marcapata
CUSCO
Lanlacuni Bajo
Tinquí
Ocongate
N Ausangate (6,384m)
Ollachea
Ayapata
Coasa
Limbani
B
Mancusani
Tinta
Raqchi
Sicuani
Crucero
Potoni
Carabaya
Maranganí
La Raya
Nuñoa
Lago Langui Layo
El Descanso
Santa Rosa
PUNO
Yauri
Héctor Tejada
Llalli
Ayaviri
Tirapata
Azángaro
Putina
Arapa
Pucará
L Arapa
Huancané
C
Condoroma
Taraco
Lampa
Lake Titicaca
N
Juliaca
I Amantani
Huata
Deústua
Sillustani
L Lagunillas
Santa Lucia
I Taquille
Los Uros
PUNO
4
5
6
Altitude in metres
4000
3000
2000
1000
500
200
0
Paved road
Unpaved road
Track
Railway
Departmental border
0 km 20
0 miles 20

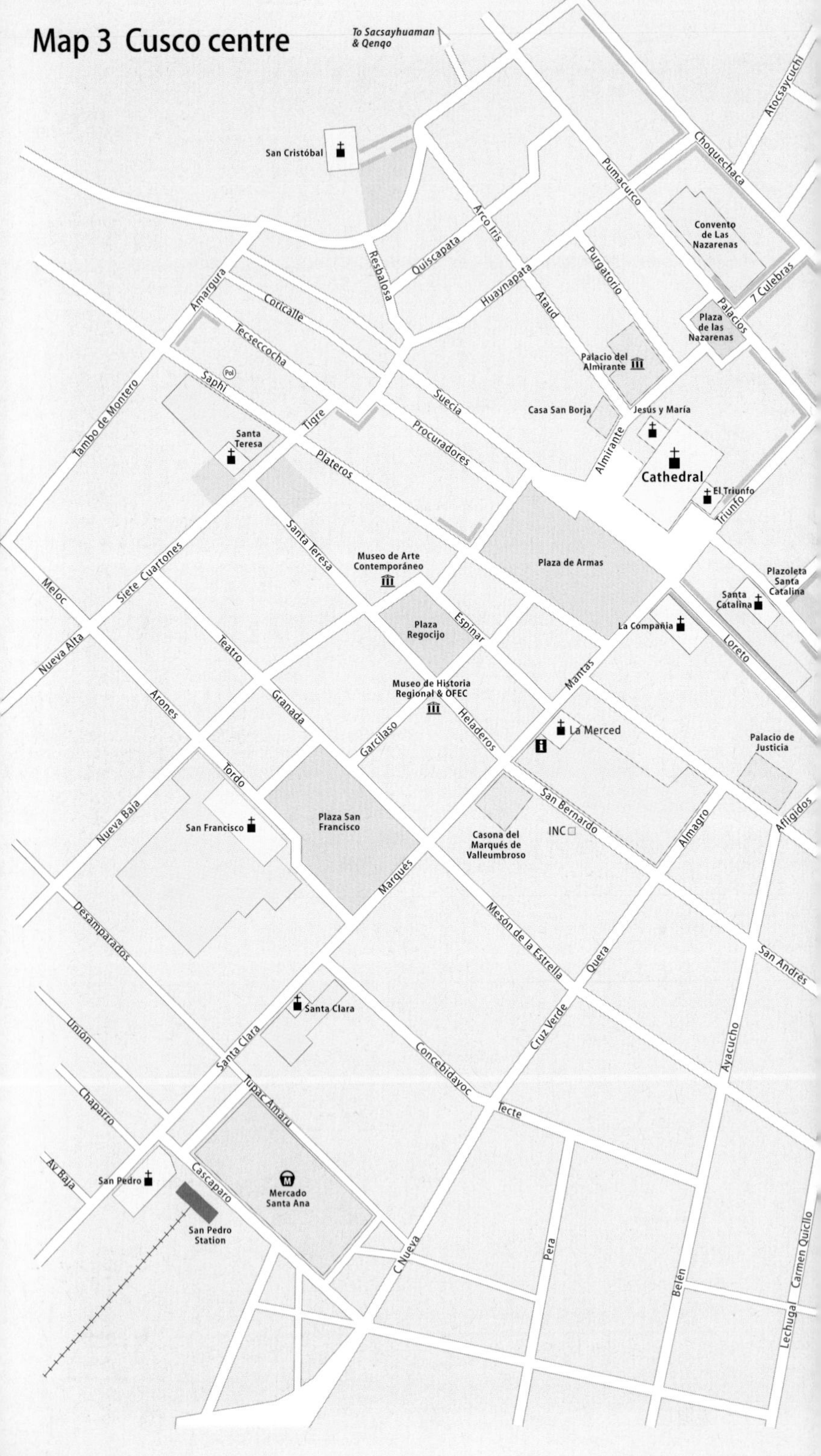

Map 3 Cusco centre
To Sacsayhuaman & Qenqo
San Cristóbal
Atocsaycuchi
Choquechaca
Pumacurco
Convento de Las Nazarenas
Arco Iris
Quiscapata
Resbalosa
Purgatorio
Huaynapata
Ataud
7 Culebras
Palacios
Plaza de las Nazarenas
Amargura
Coricalle
Tecseccocha
Palacio del Almirante
Saphi
Pol
Tambo de Montero
Suecia
Casa San Borja
Jesús y María
Tigre
Santa Teresa
Procuradores
Almirante
Cathedral
Plateros
El Triunfo
Triunfo
Santa Teresa
Museo de Arte Contemporáneo
Plaza de Armas
Plazoleta Santa Catalina
Siete Cuartones
Santa Catalina
Meloc
Espinar
Plaza Regocijo
La Compañía
Nueva Alta
Teatro
Loreto
Mantas
Museo de Historia Regional & OFEC
Arones
Granada
Heladeros
La Merced
Palacio de Justicia
Garcilaso
Tordo
San Bernardo
Plaza San Francisco
Nueva Baja
San Francisco
INC
Casona del Marqués de Valleumbroso
Almagro
Afligidos
Marqués
Desamparados
Mesón de la Estrella
Quera
San Andrés
Santa Clara
Cruz Verde
Unión
Santa Clara
Ayacucho
Concebidayoc
Tupac Amaru
Chaparro
Tecte
Av Baja
San Pedro
Cascaparo
Mercado Santa Ana
San Pedro Station
C. Nueva
Pera
Belén
Carmen Quicllo
Lechuga

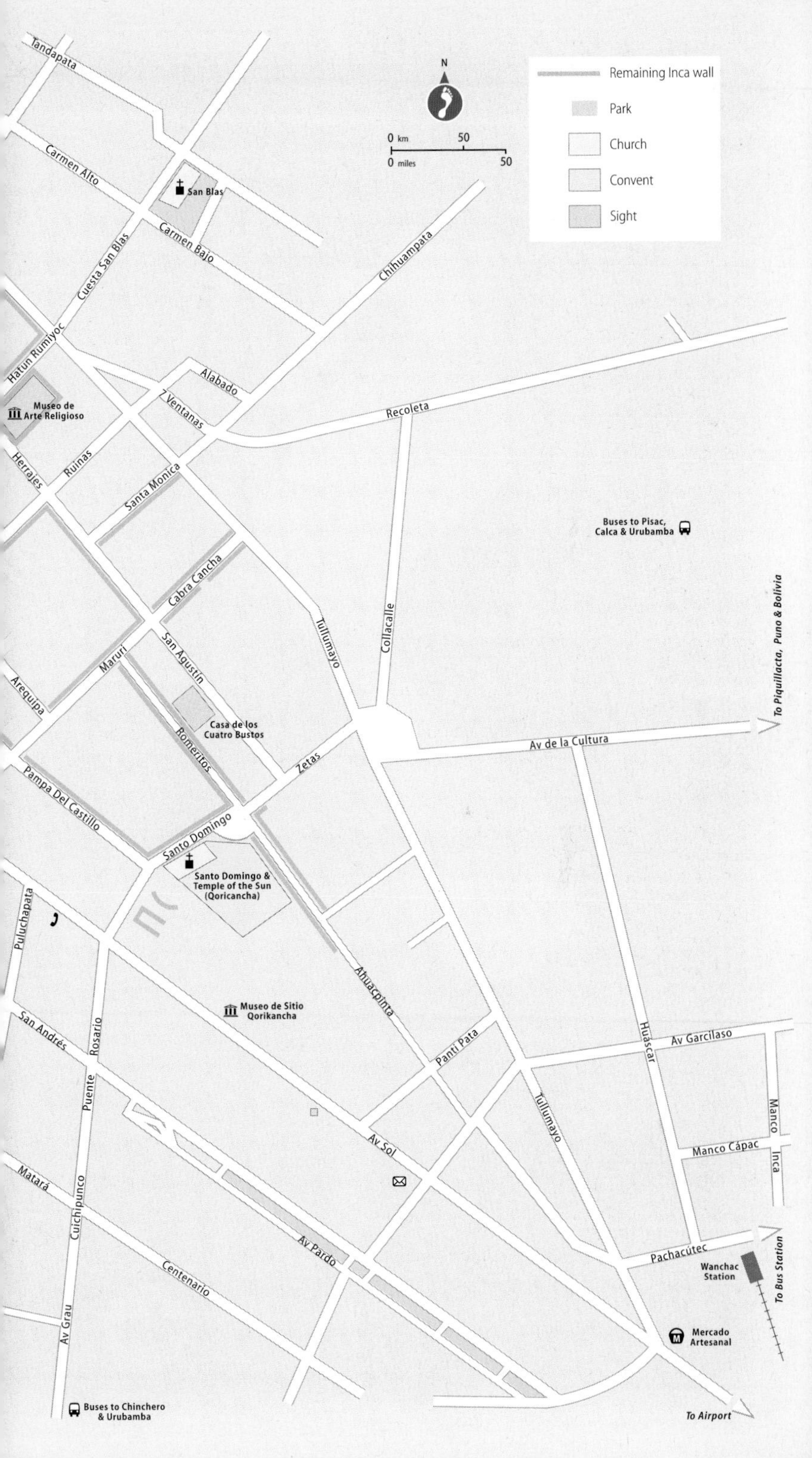

Remaining Inca wall
Park
Church
Convent
Sight
N
0 km 50
0 miles 50
Tandapata
Carmen Alto
San Blas
Carmen Bajo
Cuesta San Blas
Chihuampata
Hatun Rumiyoc
Museo de Arte Religioso
Alabado
7 Ventanas
Recoleta
Herrajes
Ruinas
Santa Monica
Buses to Pisac, Calca & Urubamba
Cabra Cancha
To Piquillacta, Puno & Bolivia
Tullumayo
Collacalle
San Agustín
Maruri
Arequipa
Casa de los Cuatro Bustos
Romeritos
Zetas
Av de la Cultura
Pampa Del Castillo
Santo Domingo
Santo Domingo & Temple of the Sun (Qoricancha)
Puluchapata
Ahuacpinta
Museo de Sitio Qorikancha
San Andrés
Rosario
Panti Pata
Av Garcilaso
Huáscar
Tullumayo
Puente
Manco
Manco Cápac
Inca
Av Sol
Matará
Cuichipunco
Av Pardo
Pachacútec
Wanchac Station
To Bus Station
Centenario
Mercado Artesanal
Av Grau
Buses to Chinchero & Urubamba
To Airport